Unicorn Executions

AND OTHER CRAZY STUFF MY KIDS MAKE ME DRAW

Unicorn Executions

and Other Crazy Stuff My Kids Make Me Draw

Steve Breen

Skyhorse Publishing

Skyhorse Publishing books may be purchased in bulk at special discounts for sales promotion, corporate gifts, fund-raising, or educational purposes. Special editions can also be created to specifications. For details, contact the Special Sales Department, Skyhorse Publishing, 307 West 36th Street, 11th Floor, New York, NY 10018 or info@ skyhorsepublishing.com.

Skyhorse® and Skyhorse Publishing® are registered trademarks of Skyhorse Publishing, Inc.®, a Delaware corporation.

www.skyhorsepublishing.com

10 9 8 7 6 5 4 3 2 1

Library of Congress Cataloging-in-Publication Data is available on file.

ISBN: 978-1-62914-173-2

Printed in China

CONTENTS

FOREWORD

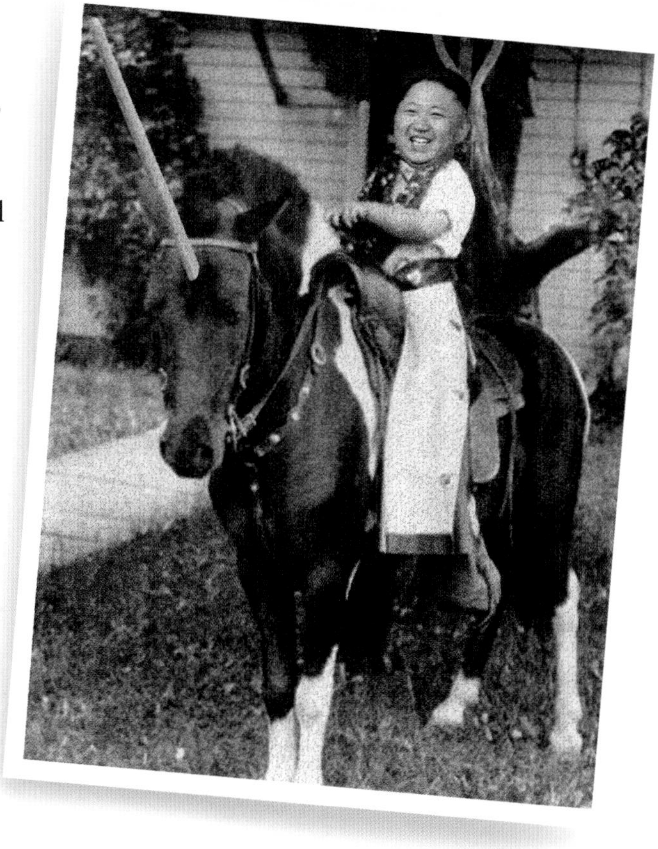

When I was approached about writing a foreword to this delightful collection of renderings, I didn't hesitate. After all, unicorns and executions are two of my favorite things! You see, for my ninth birthday, my dear father gave me a pet unicorn he told me his hunters had captured in the enchanted hill country. I named my new friend Sunshine From Heaven. The poor animal died after three weeks, but the days I spent riding him through the palace, trampling servants, are some of my finest childhood memories. My science tutor tried to tell me that unicorns didn't exist. He said that Sunshine From Heaven was just a lobotomized pony with a broomstick screwed into its head. He was executed, naturally. Anyway, I was provided with many cages of kidnapped Japanese movie stars for my amusement, but life was never the same without my beloved Sunshine.

But I digress. I was fascinated with the etchings presented in this book because I could relate to much of the subject matter. For instance, I would play with my father's flamethrower when I was a toddler just like the child depicted on page 102. We'd totally cackle when the nannies caught fire! Good times.

And like the image on page 119, I too use Siberian tigers to train our Olympic track team. The hydrochloric acid pool long jump is a new concept, but I may implement it soon. And how I would make South Korea tremble with fear if my scientists could develop a magnificent army of thunder bunnies! Yes, reader, this volume is a treasure. I pride myself on my support of the arts and I would be happy to hang lithographs of these masterpieces in some of our drab government buildings. These drawings are the perfect blend of terror and whimsy . . . just like the People's Republic of North Korea. Enjoy!

Well, I have to run. Rodman's here and we're going clubbing. Look out, Pyongyang!

Peace out, yo.
Kim Jong Un
Kim Jong Un

INTRODUCTION

There's a weird kid in every class who sits in the back row sketching strange pictures in the margins of his textbooks. That was me. Dragons eating teachers, students barfing up cockroaches, the principal as a zombie mutant . . . that kind of stuff. A big part of it was that I loved to draw, but a bigger part was that I wanted the attention. I loved it when my classmates would gather around my desk to look at what I was doing, laugh, and say "Cooooool."

Today, I'm an editorial cartoonist with kids of my own, and I'm still in need of attention. I love the occasional emails and Facebook comments I get from readers saying how much they liked this or that cartoon. (What artist doesn't enjoy positive feedback?) But I found that getting my three sons excited about the things I drew for a living proved to be a trick.

Me: "I did a good cartoon today at work."
Kid: "What'd you draw?"
Me: "Uncle Sam and the chairman of the Federal Reserve in a rowboat, which I labeled 'economy' and a big wave is coming labeled . . ."
Kid: "That's nice. What's for dinner?"

Cartoons about health care reform and Egyptian politics elicit similar reactions from my lads—can you blame 'em? So I learned that a good way to interest my kids was to draw—you guessed it—dragons and mutant zombies. I now sit at my drafting table and take requests, and that's gotten them even more interested in what I draw, of course. There's almost a magic in watching these collaborations take shape and come to life on paper. And not only is it a great way to bond with my kids, I have a blast creating these things. I feel like I'm that twelve-year-old back at St. Simon and Jude elementary school hunched over my desk, scribbling with a pencil, grinning like an idiot. There are no editors to please, no readers to offend, no deadlines to meet, no political messages to deliver, and no punch lines to polish. It's just drawing for the sheer fun of it.

I should note here that even though I'm a cartoonist, most of the images in this book are not cartoons. Some are. But the vast majority would best be described simply as drawings. Cartoons are hard to create (good ones, anyway). They need to have a message and/or deliver a gag. A drawing, on the other hand, is just that . . . a picture of anything you want. A drawing of a

fig. 1a
Drawing

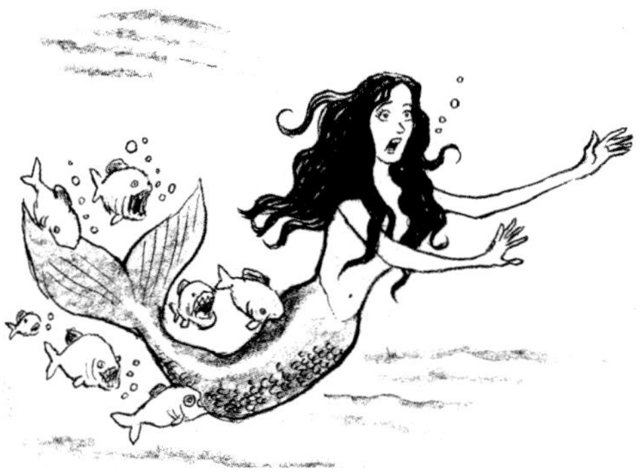

fig. 1b
Cartoon

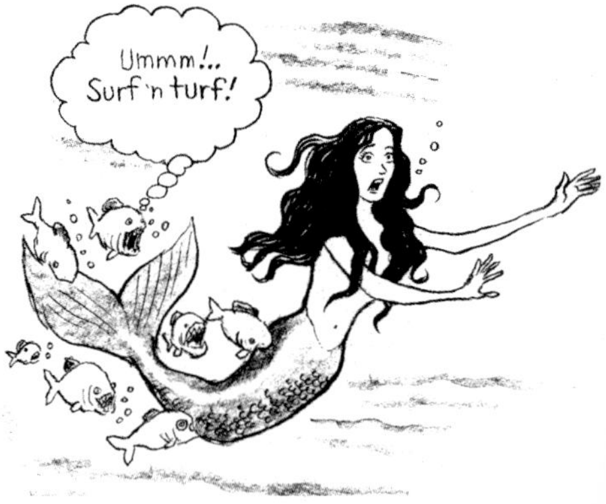
Ummm!.. Surf 'n turf!

piranha eating a mermaid is all it needs to be. But if you tell people it's a cartoon, there's an expectation of some humor or a point . . . usually in the form of a thought bubble or a caption. That's more work, and for the sake of my small audience, unnecessary.

People ask me what my wife thinks of all of this. The short answer is that she doesn't get it. The more diplomatic answer is that she thinks these drawings are sick and kind of a waste of energy . . . but she appreciates the time my boys and I spend together. She's a great mom, supportive wife, and a good sport, but for the record, has yet to make a sketch request. And for those of you who think I'm warping the brains of my progeny with such macabre and gory pieces of art, I say . . . you're probably right. But in defense of our parenting, I should tell you that my wife and I set certain limits on the subject matter. For instance, no guns being fired, no excessive human blood, no kids or women getting hurt, and no moral ambiguity (i.e. in the end, good should triumph over evil). I think "Santa Claus Blowing Up a Nazi with a Bazooka" fits within these parameters. It doesn't need a caption or a punch line. It's just Santa blowing up a Nazi with a bazooka. Yes, it's kind of pointless and juvenile. But admit it . . . as you looked at the drawing, you said to yourself "Coooooool."

Enjoy,
Steve Breen

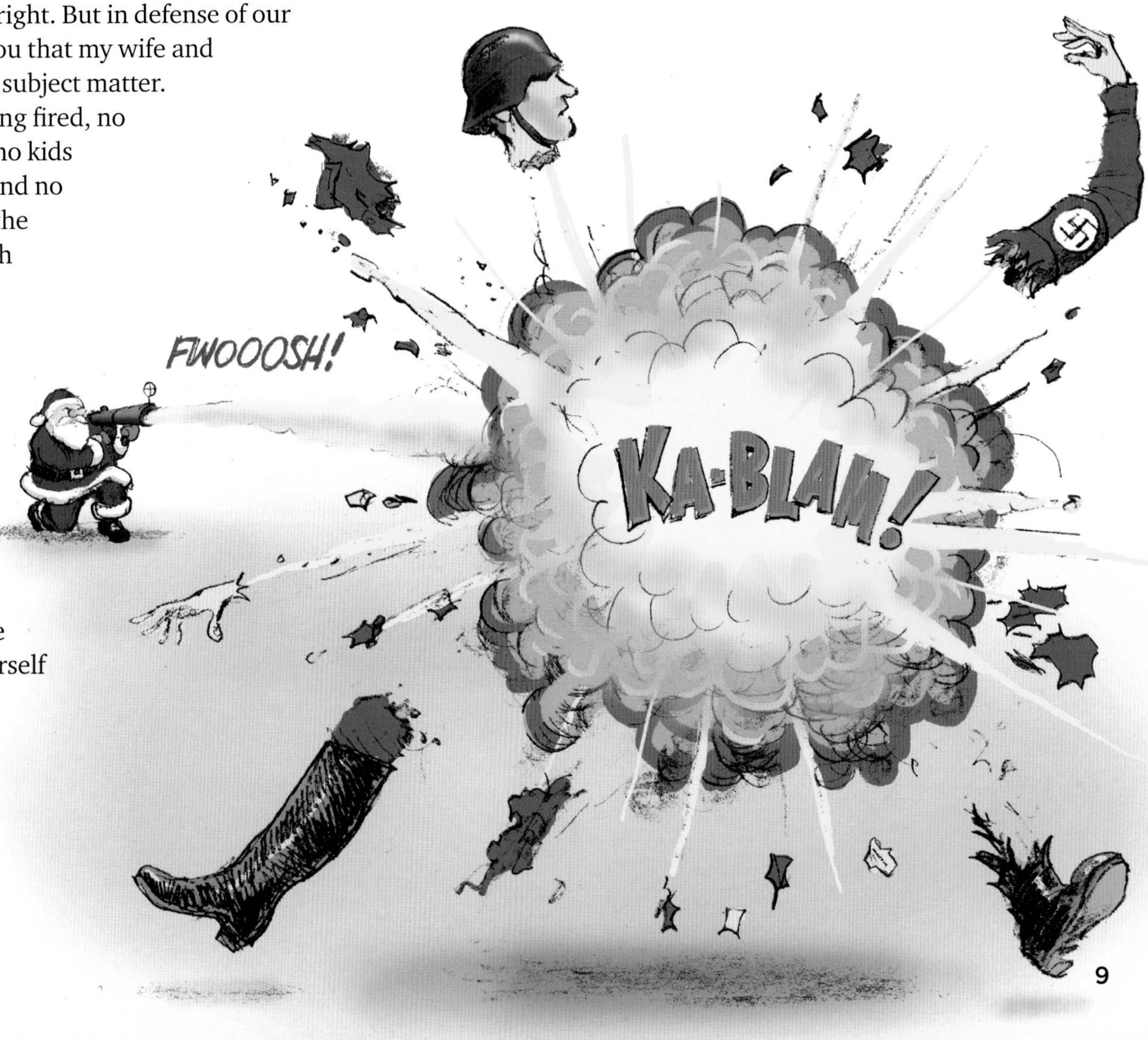
FWOOOSH!
KA-BLAM!

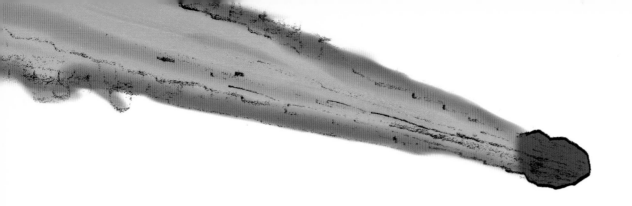

DINOSAURS

Who isn't just a little bit fascinated by dinosaurs? They come in all kinds of shapes and sizes, but let's face it . . . the most interesting are ones that could eat a human like a fun-sized Snickers bar. I wish my boys were the kind of studious chaps who had all the species memorized, but they basically just know the raptors and tyrannosaurs. I can't tell you how many of these carnivorous reptiles I've drawn for them over the years, but if you put all the sketches in a heap, it would be bigger than a pile of alamosaurus poop. Here are a few of our faves . . .

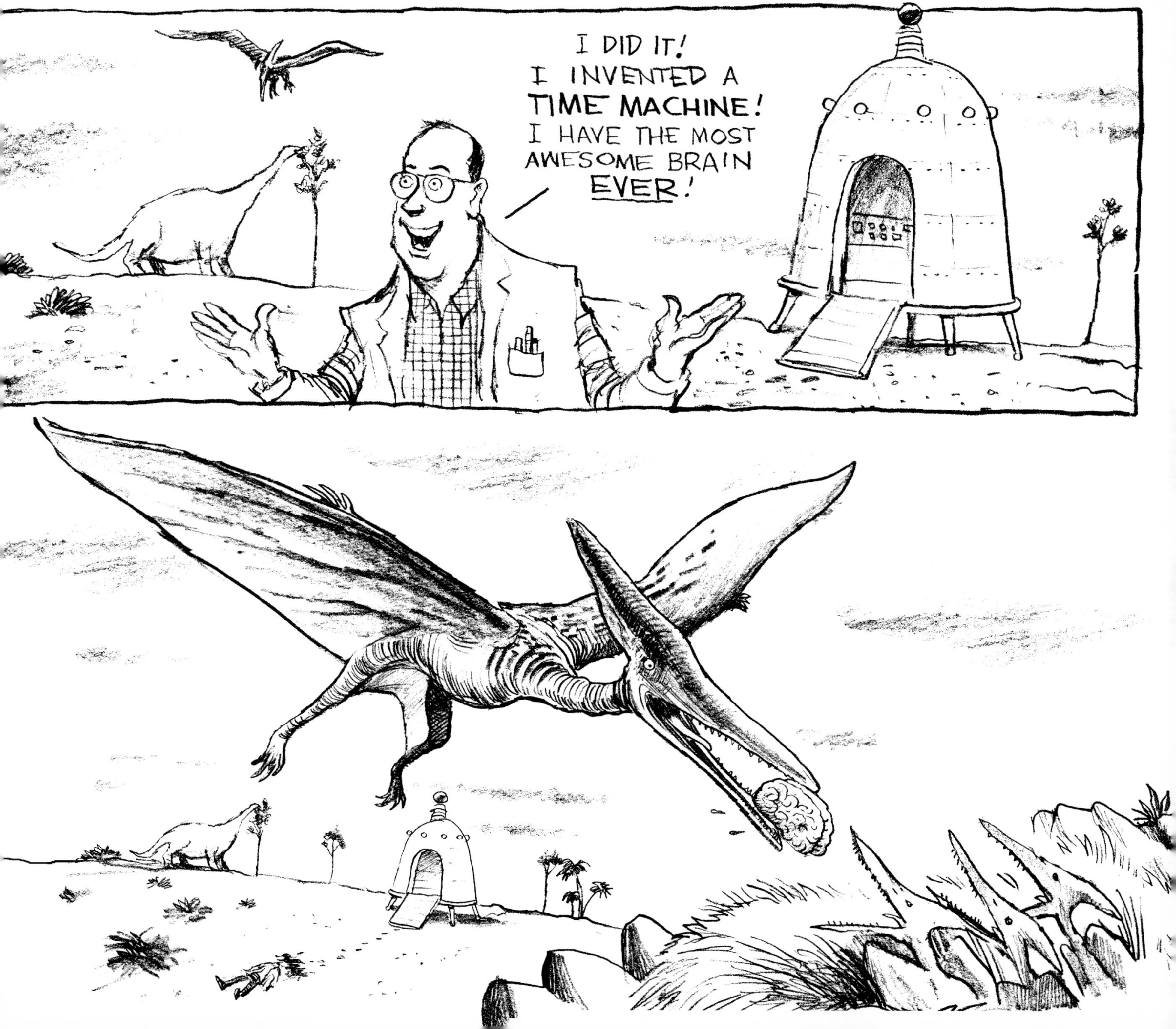
I DID IT! I INVENTED A TIME MACHINE! I HAVE THE MOST AWESOME BRAIN EVER!

IF HUMANS HAD T. REX PROPORTIONS:

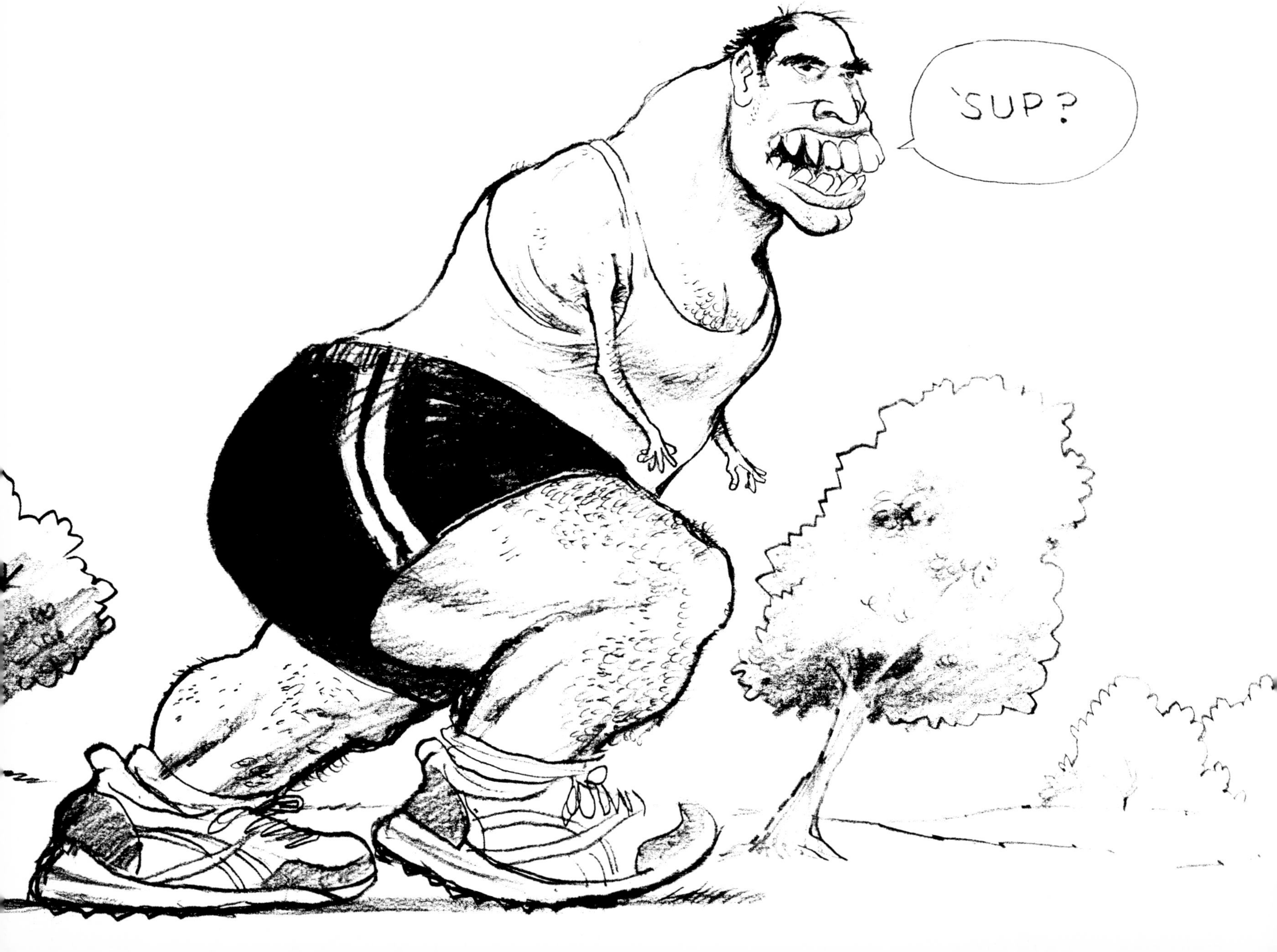
'SUP?

My kids asked me to draw someone being eaten by a T. Rex . . .

I suggested Donald Trump.

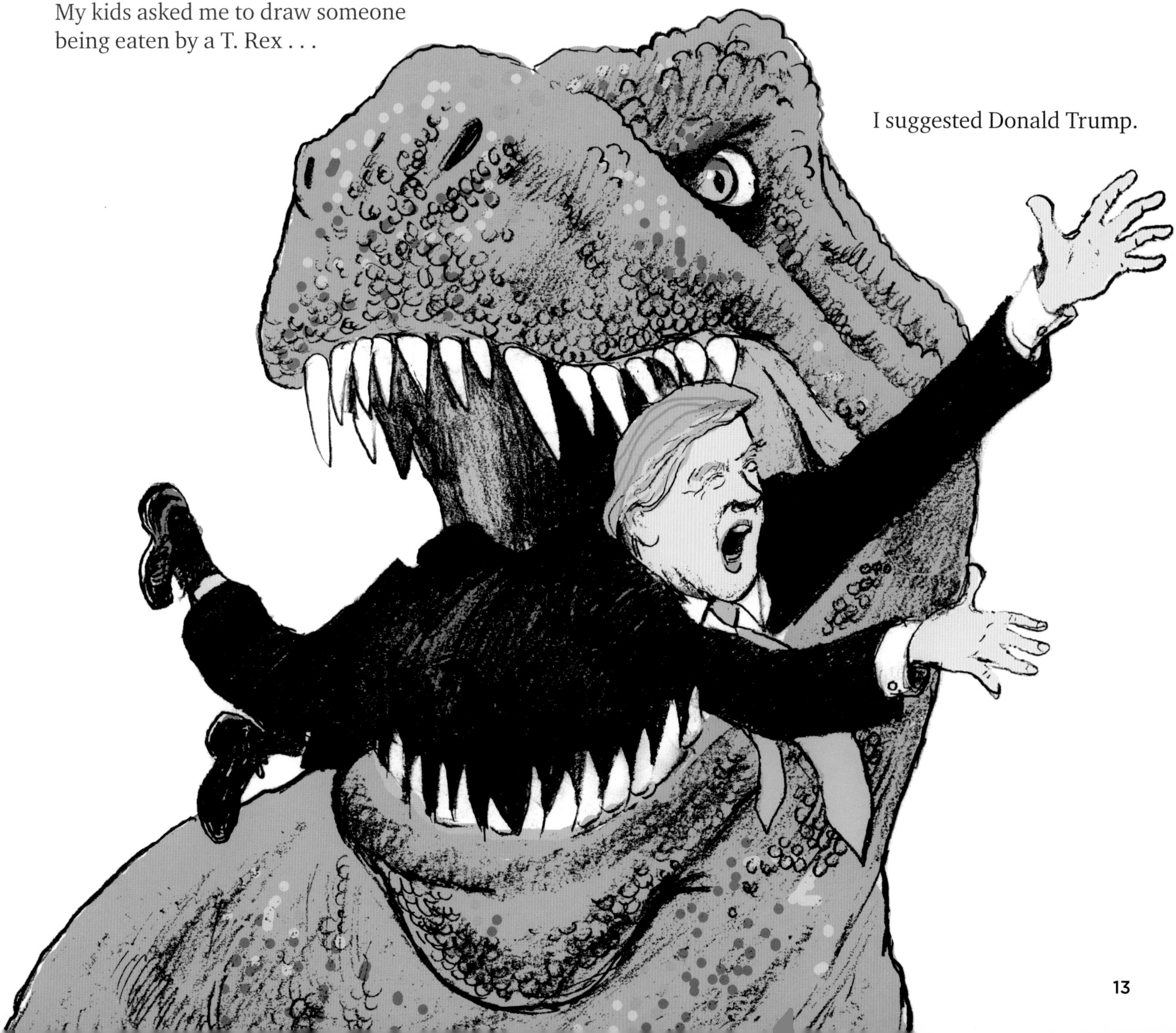

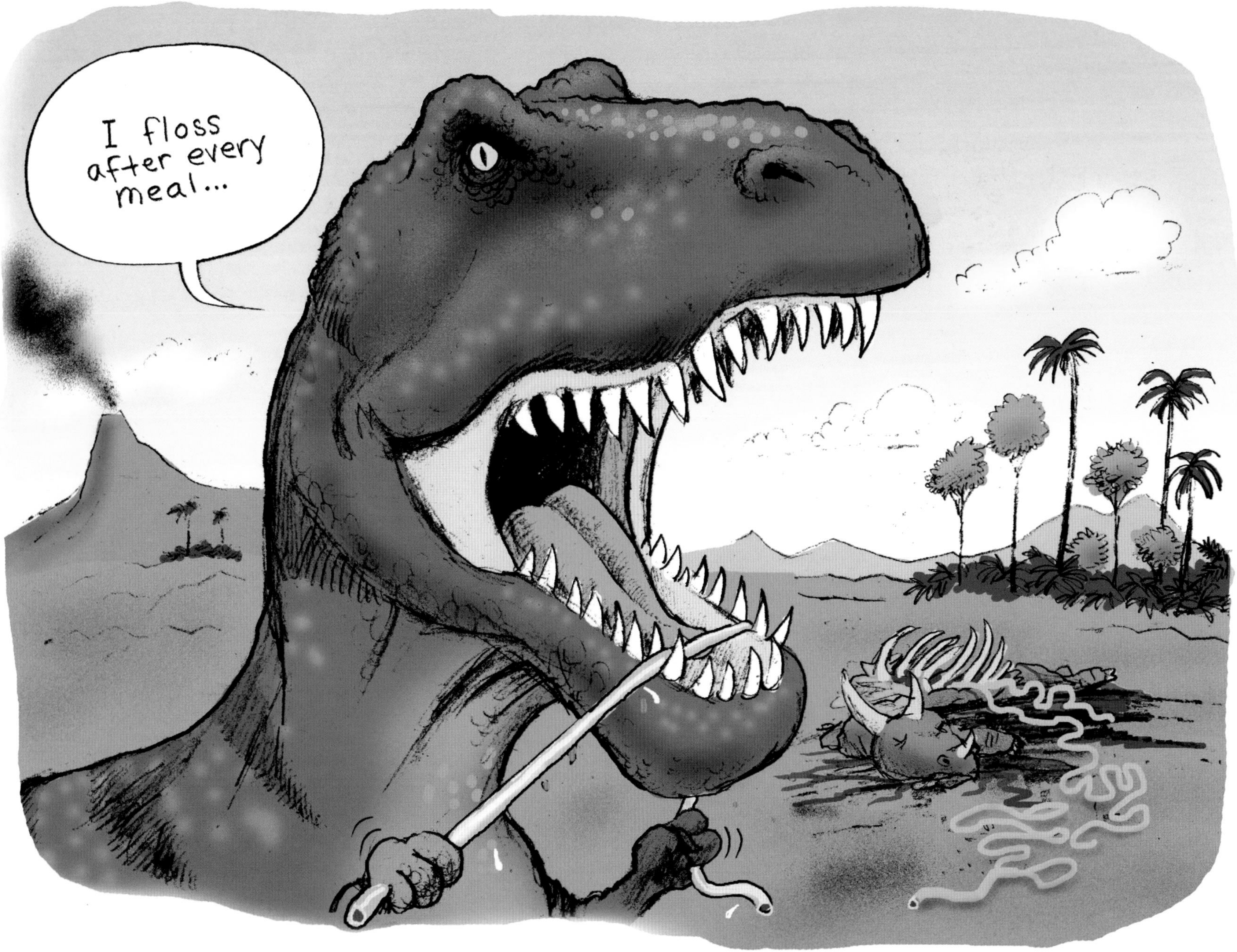
I floss after every meal...

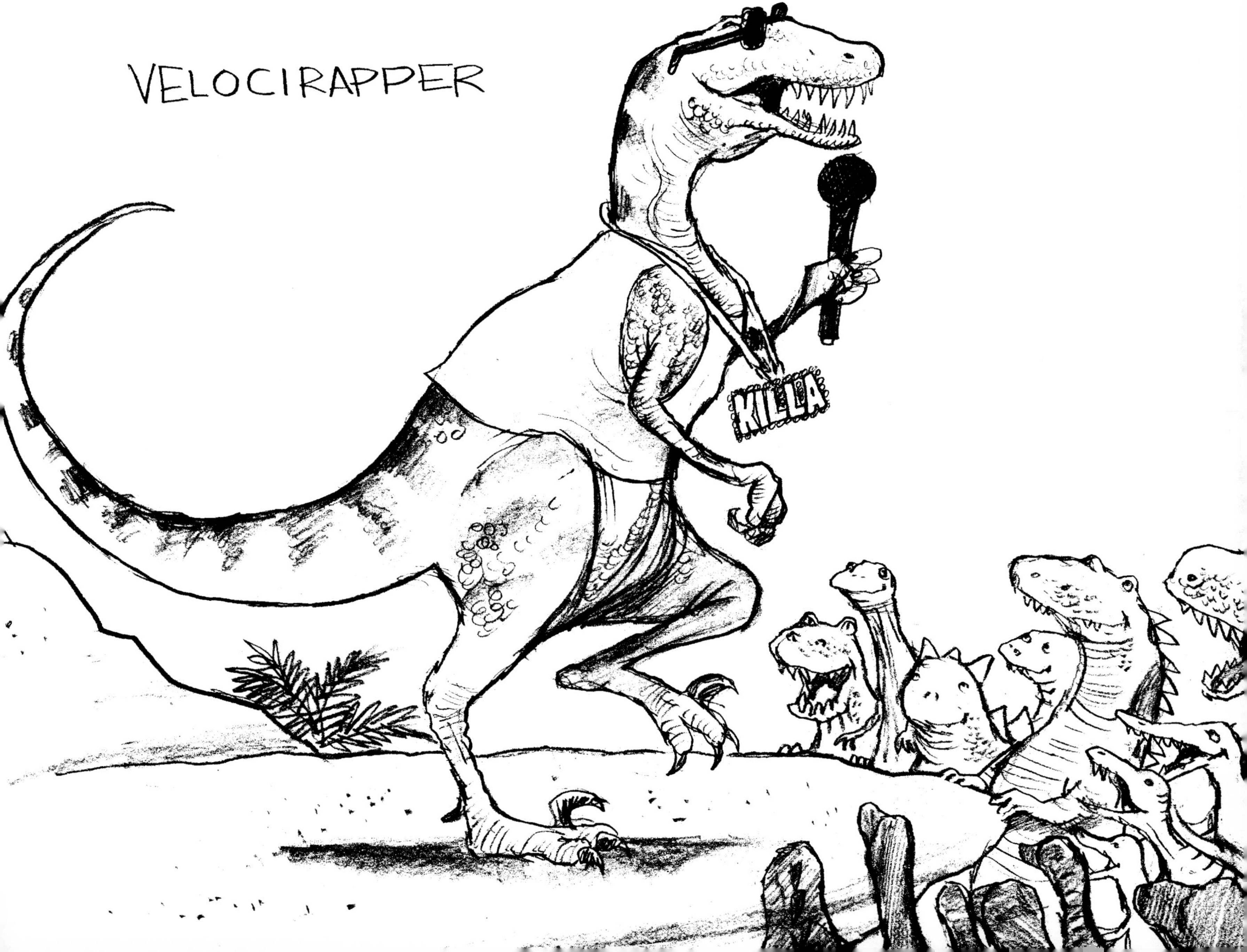
VELOCIRAPPER
KILLA

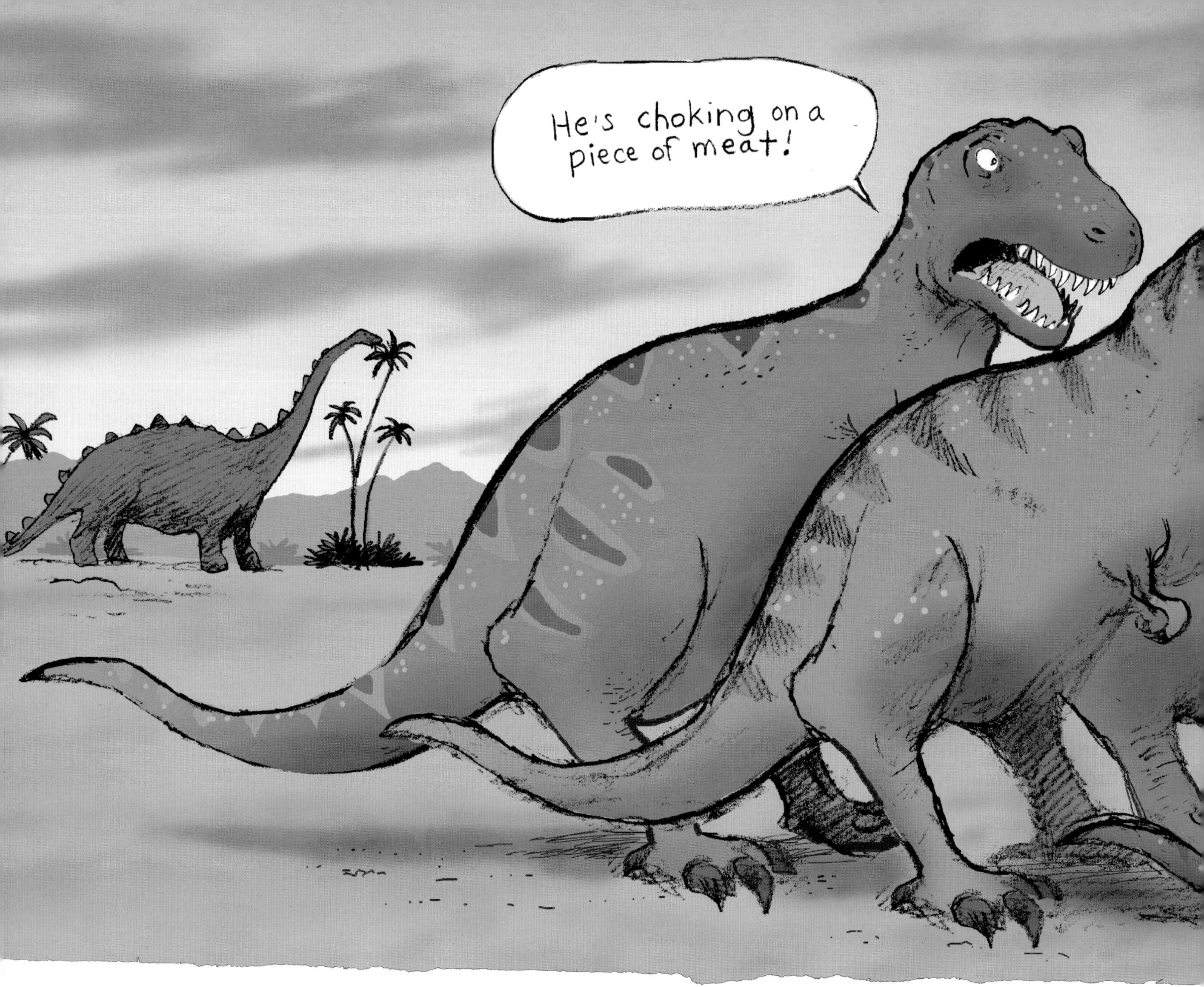
He's choking on a piece of meat!

I think I was channeling Gary Larson with this one.

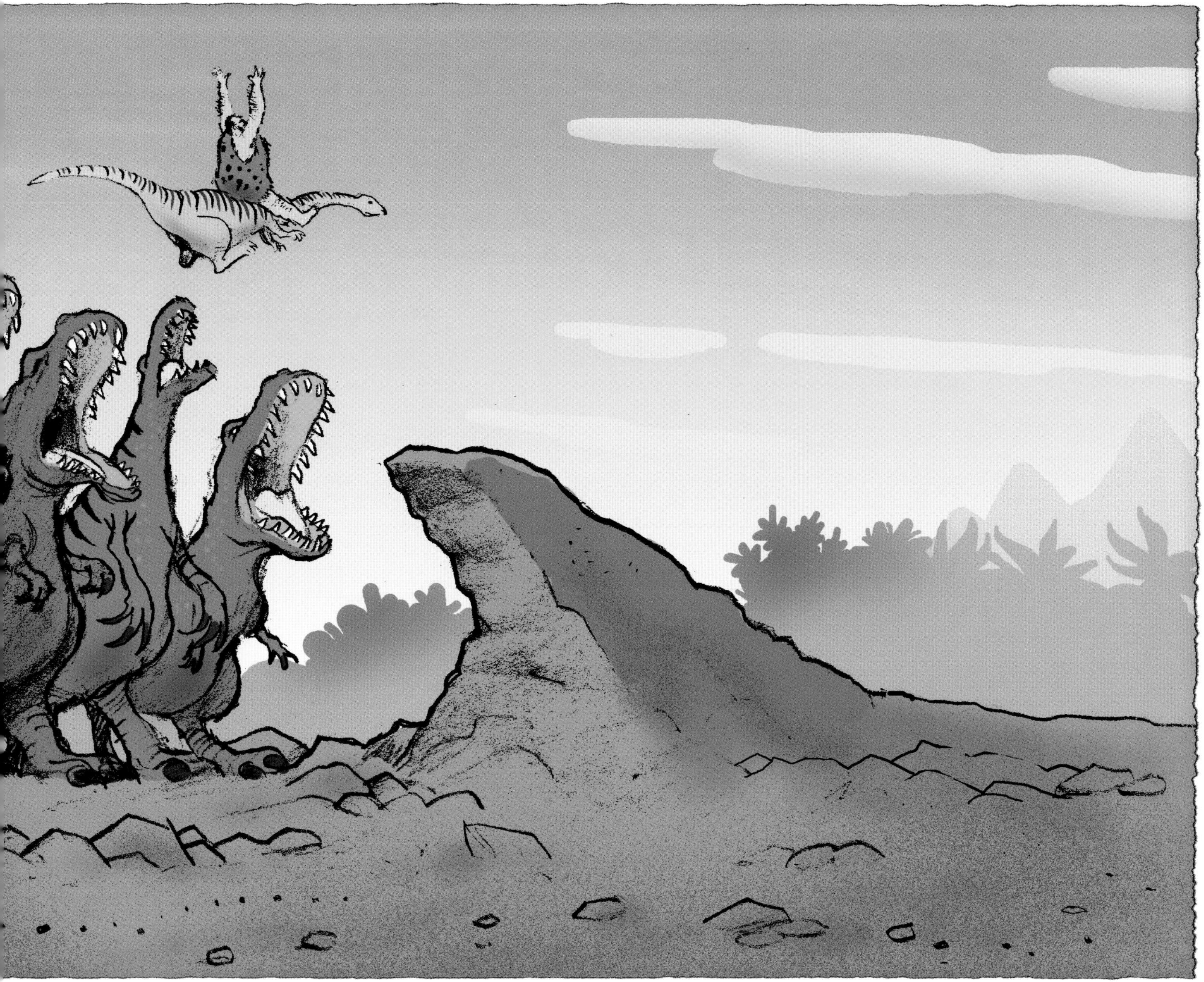

I was quick to point out that facts should never get in the way of a cool drawing.

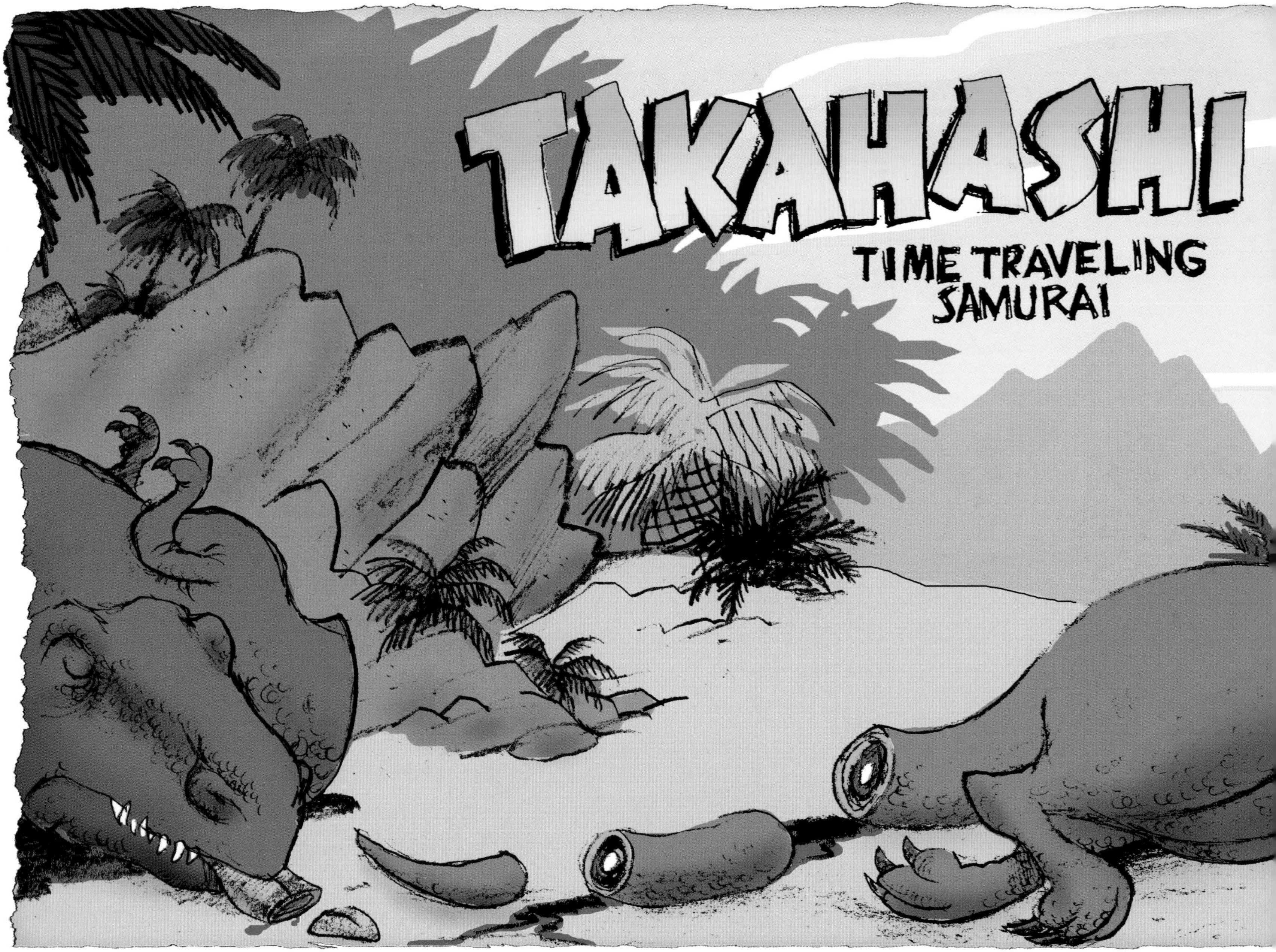
TAKAHASHI
TIME TRAVELING
SAMURAI

We want to see this movie!

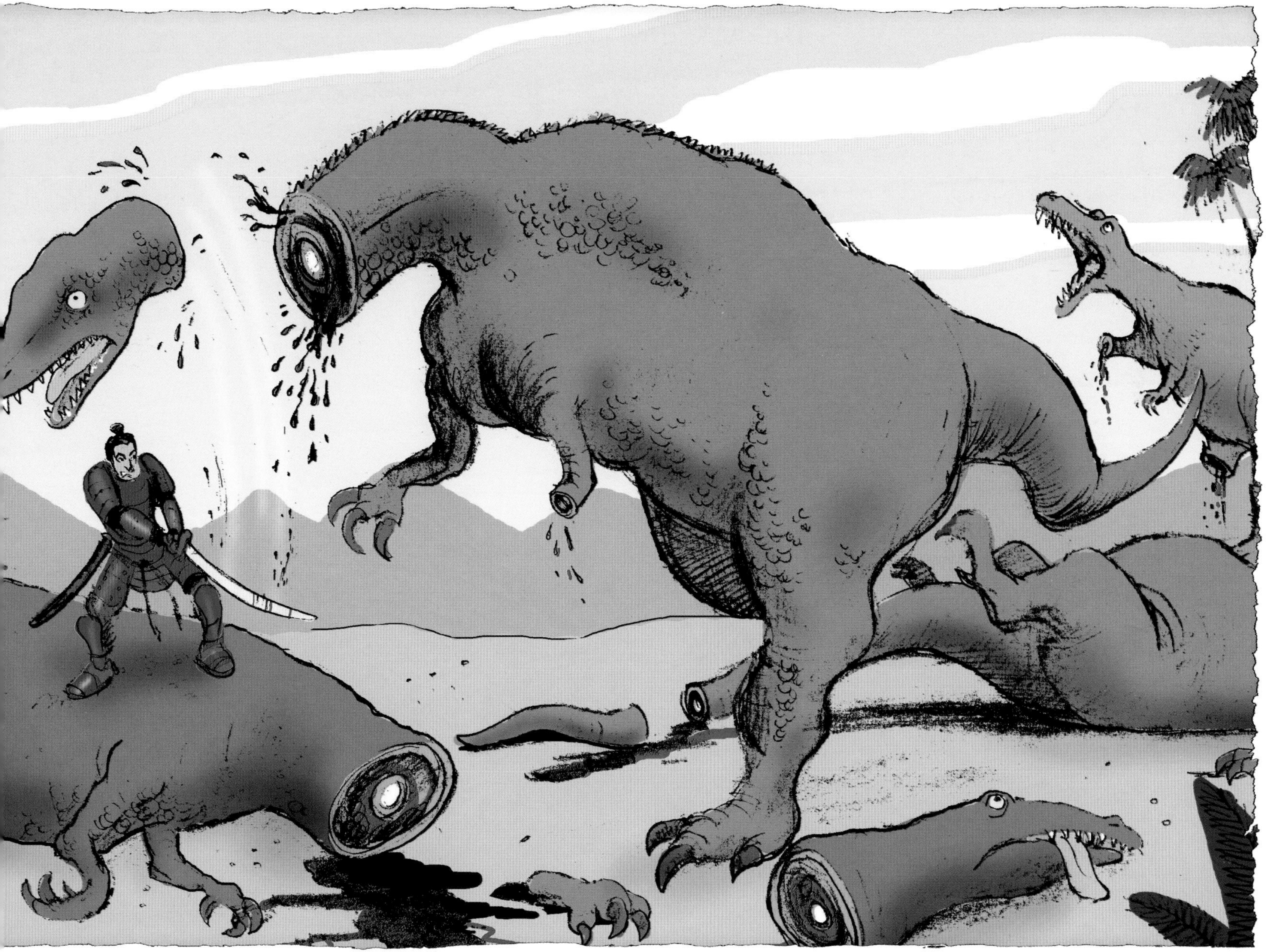

What's more terrifying than a velociraptor?

A velociraptor with a flamethrower-jetpack . . .

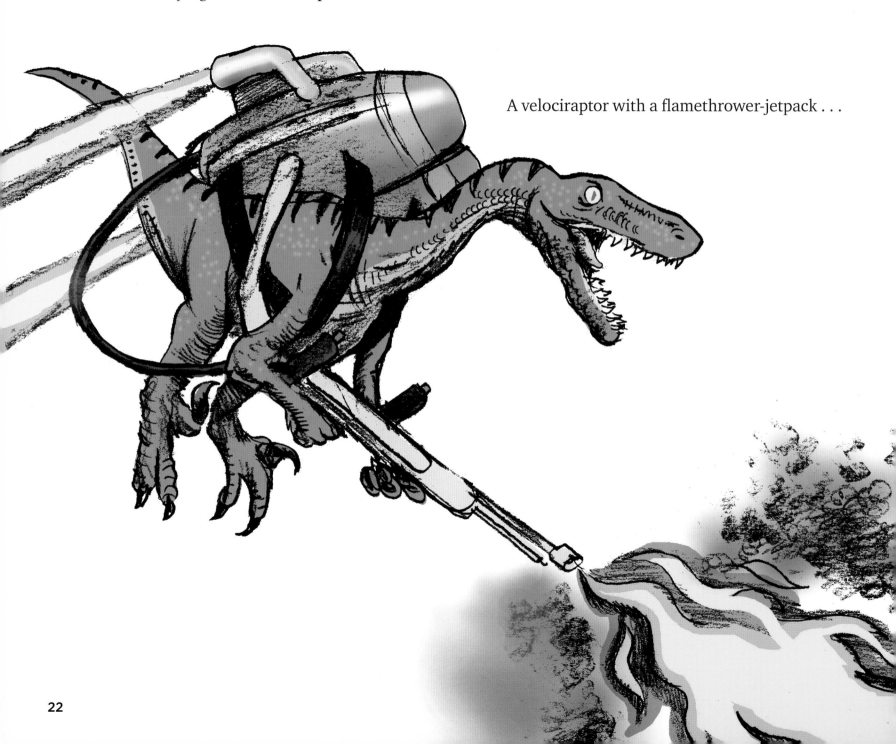

SHARKS

Just like dinosaurs, sharks are awesome because they can eat you. And there's an additional cool factor because they're not extinct or made-up monsters, they're real . . . and they could be *swimming right under your boogie board*. *Jaws* is one of my all-time favorite movies, but I think I showed it to my kids when they were too young (read barely out of diapers). It probably traumatized them a bit but it also taught them a little about nature: things with rows of serrated teeth are to be avoided. Hours of watching "Shark Week" on the Discovery Channel every summer only fuels their fear and feeds their imagination.

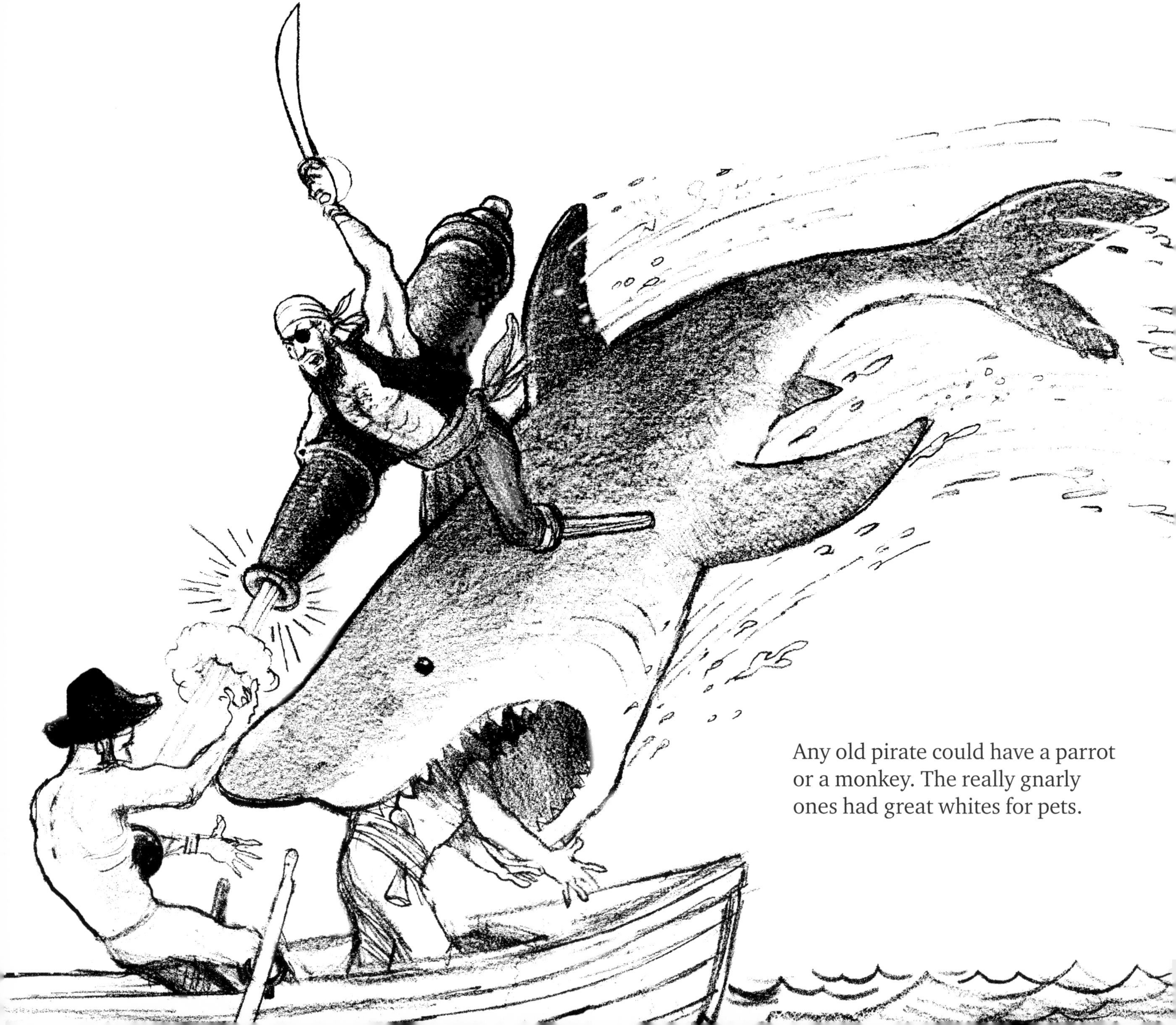

Any old pirate could have a parrot or a monkey. The really gnarly ones had great whites for pets.

RIDING A WAVE LIKE THIS IS HARD...

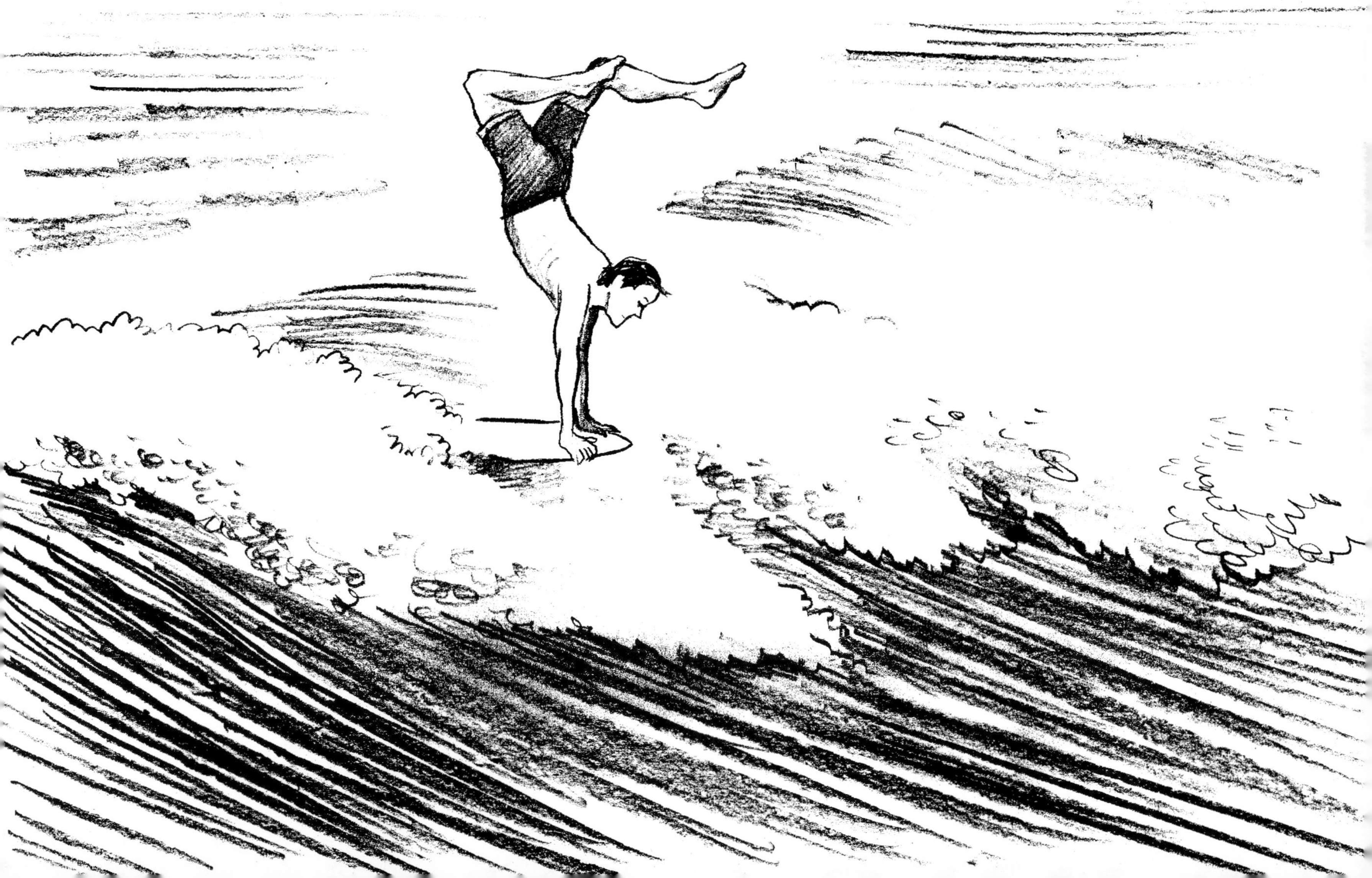

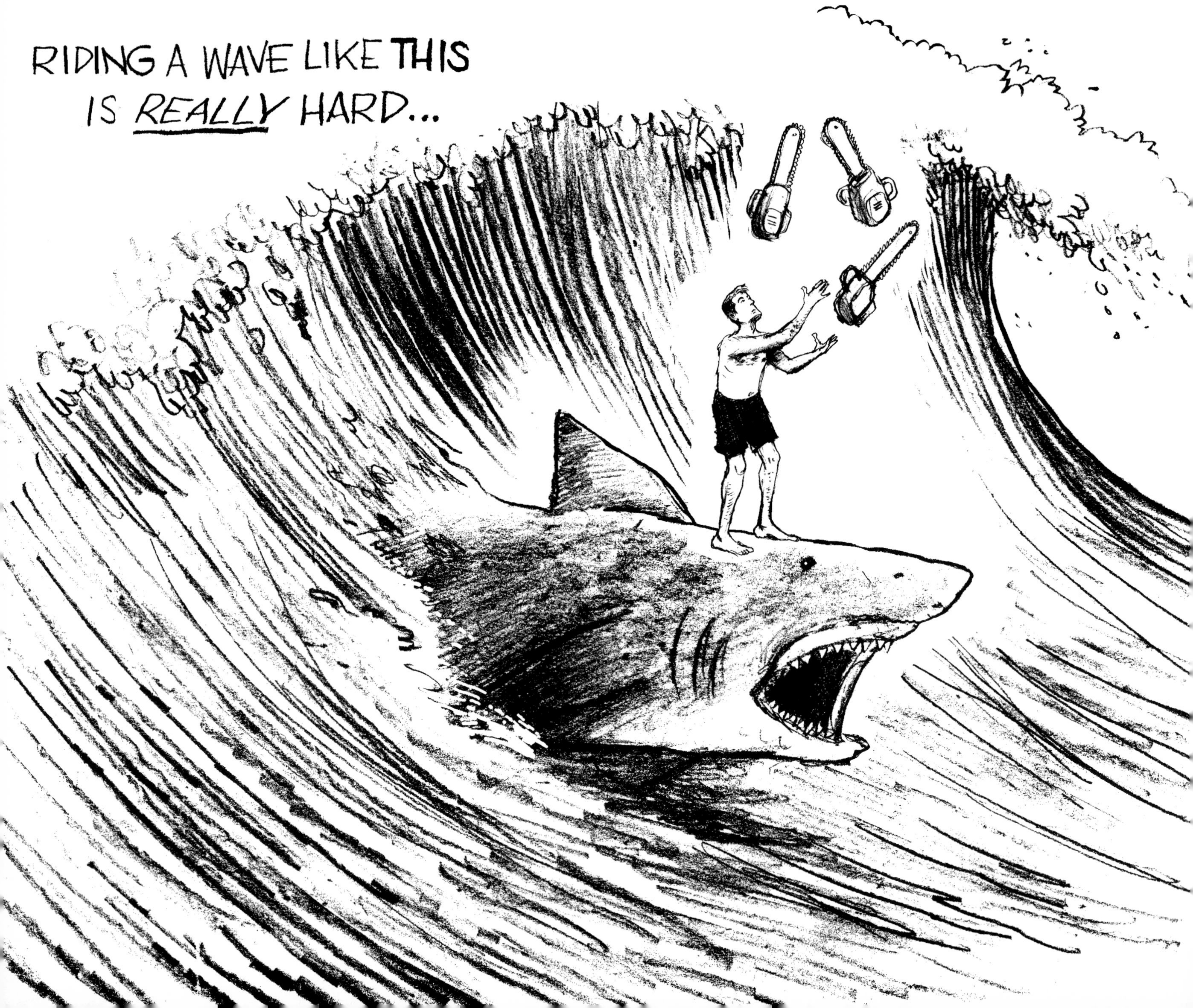
RIDING A WAVE LIKE THIS IS REALLY HARD...

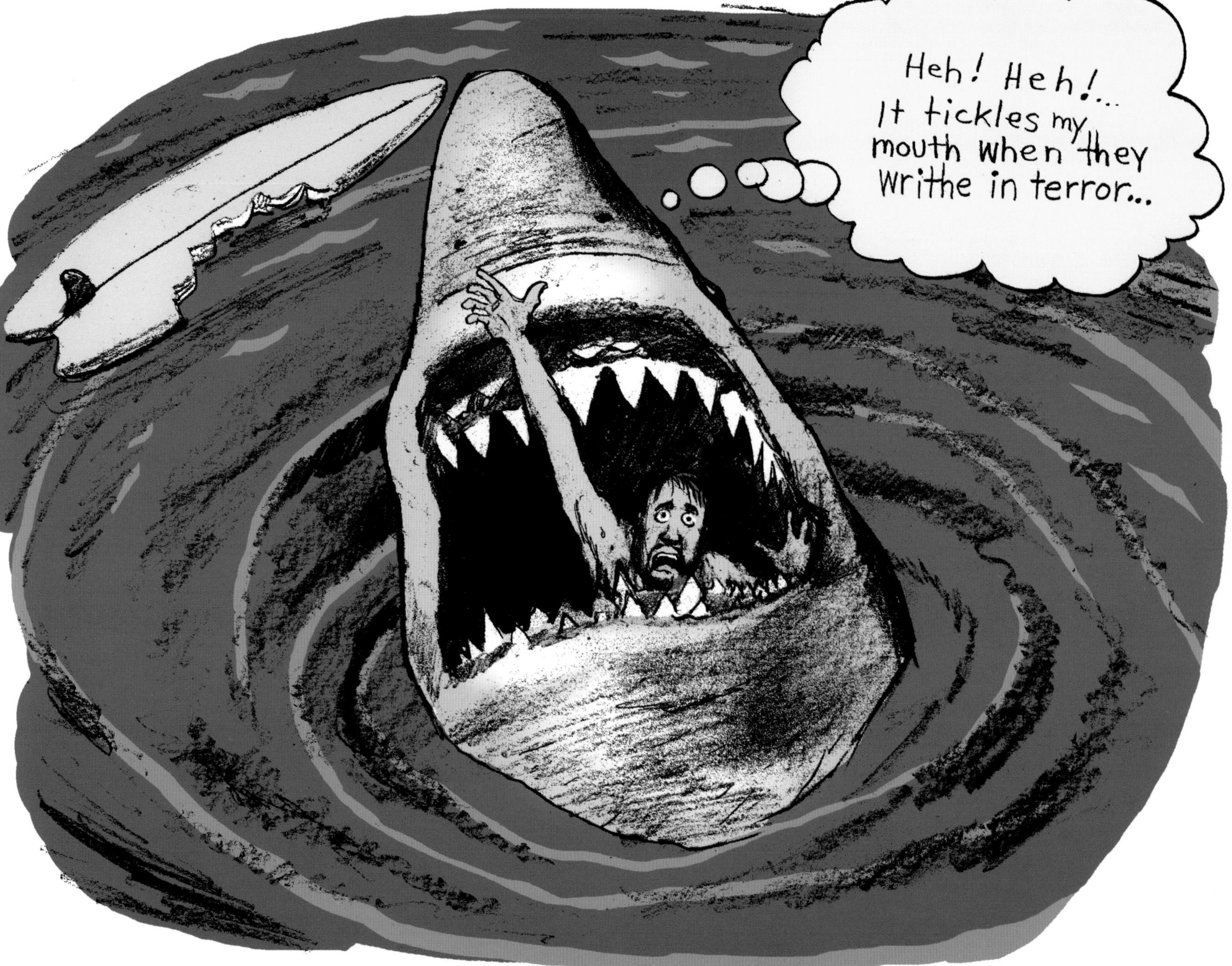
Heh! Heh!... It tickles my mouth when they writhe in terror...

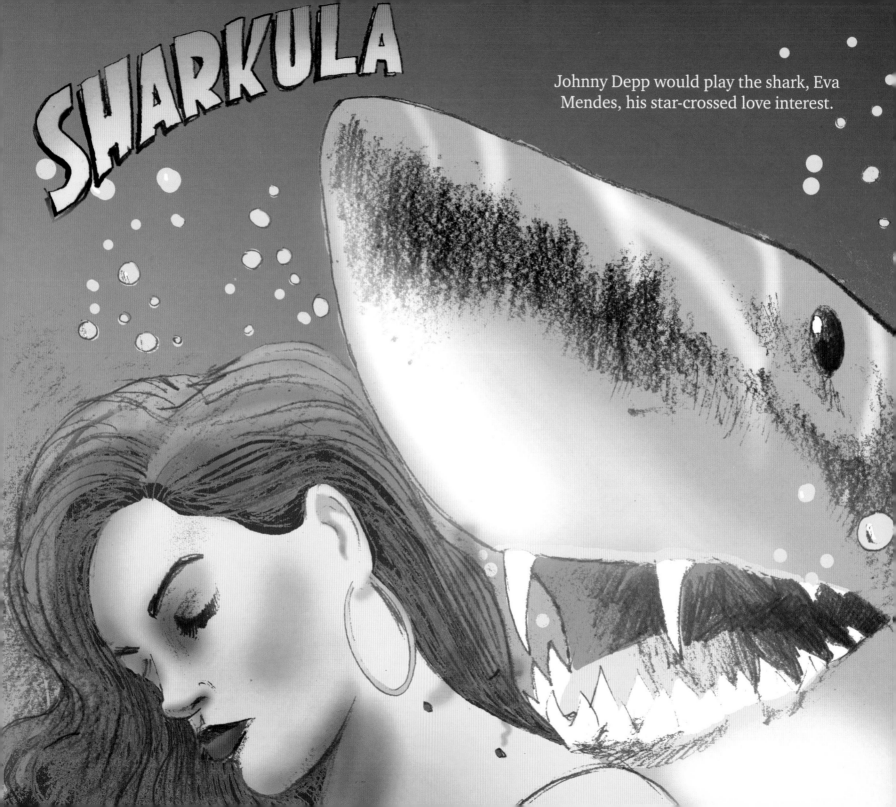

SHARKULA

Johnny Depp would play the shark, Eva Mendes, his star-crossed love interest.

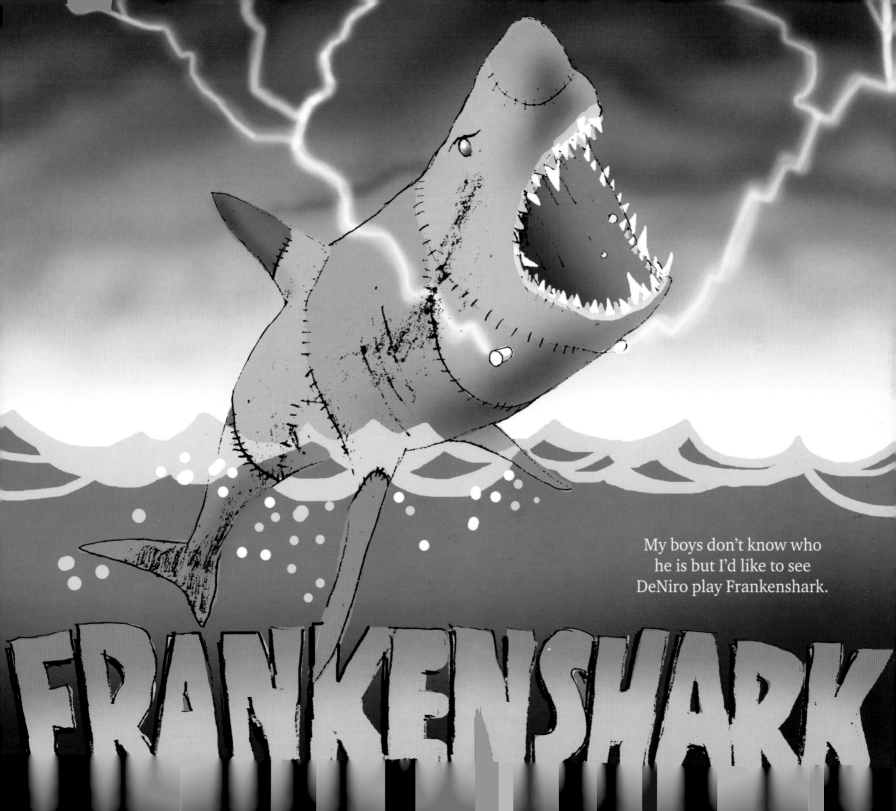

My boys don't know who
he is but I'd like to see
DeNiro play Frankenshark.

FRANKENSHARK

EXTREME MAKO-VER

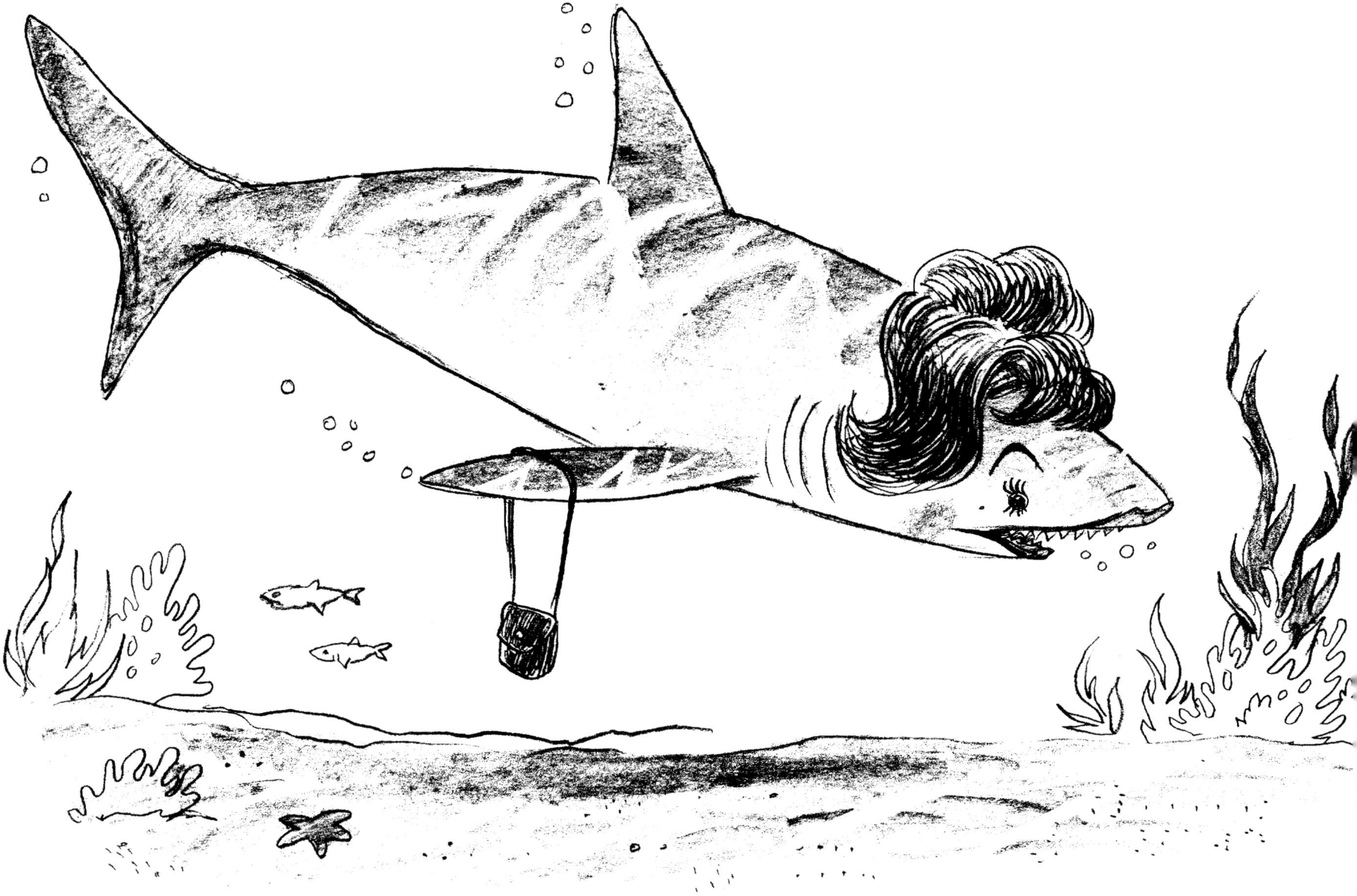

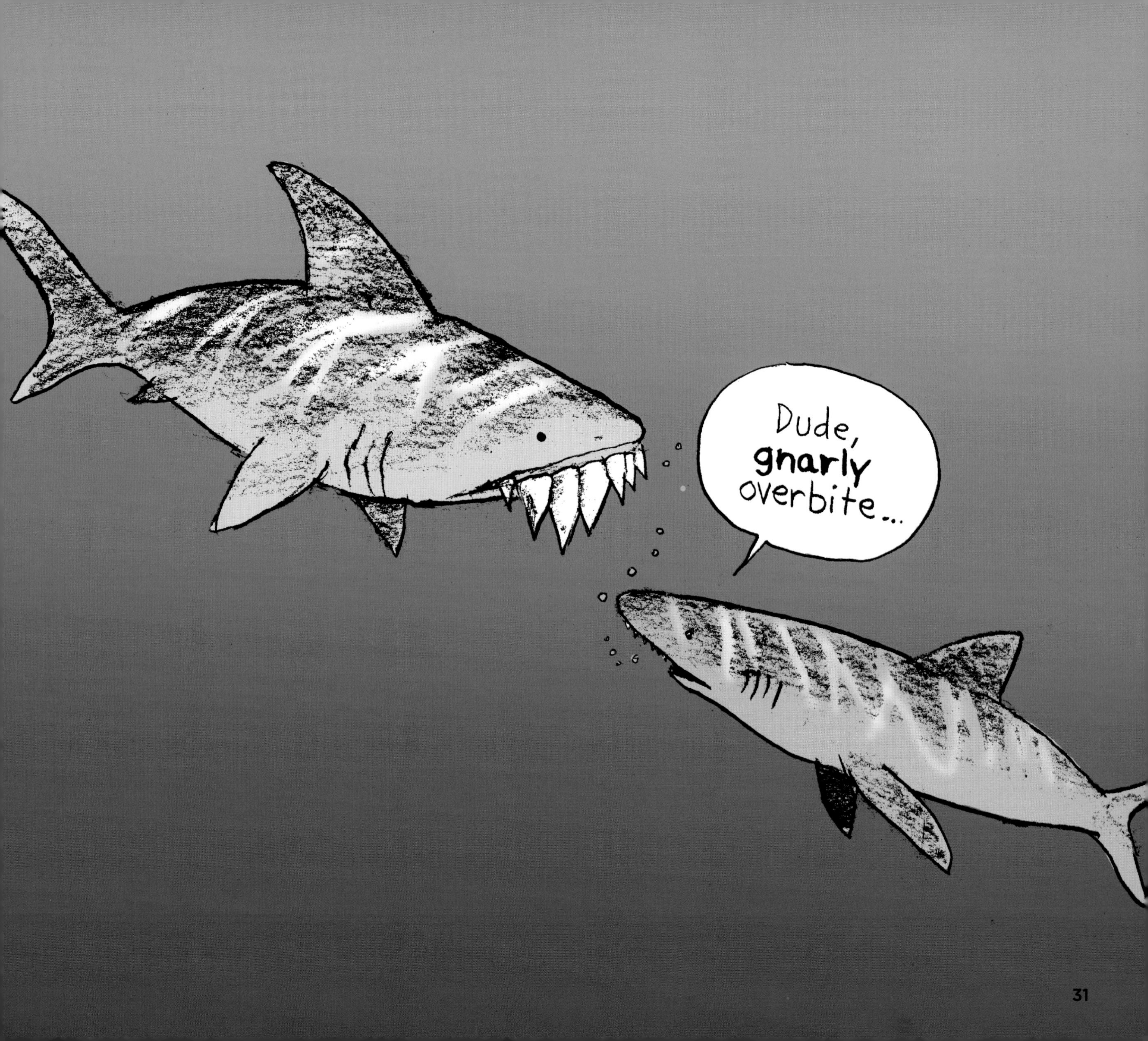
Dude, **gnarly** overbite...

GIANT SQUID VS. GREAT WHITE

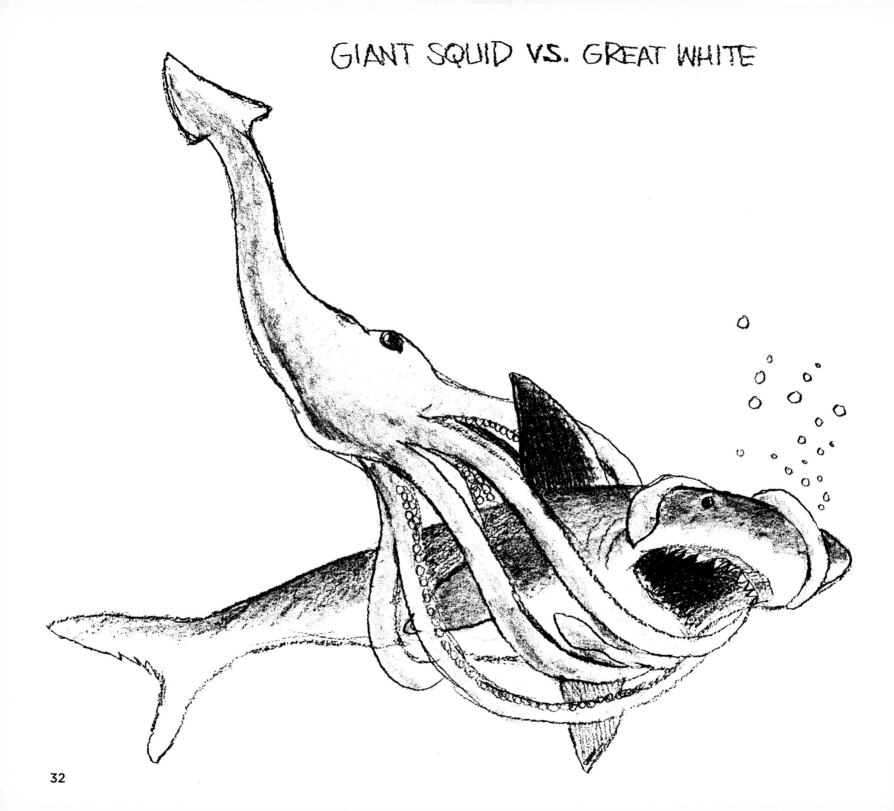

SPERM WHALE VS. GIANT SQUID

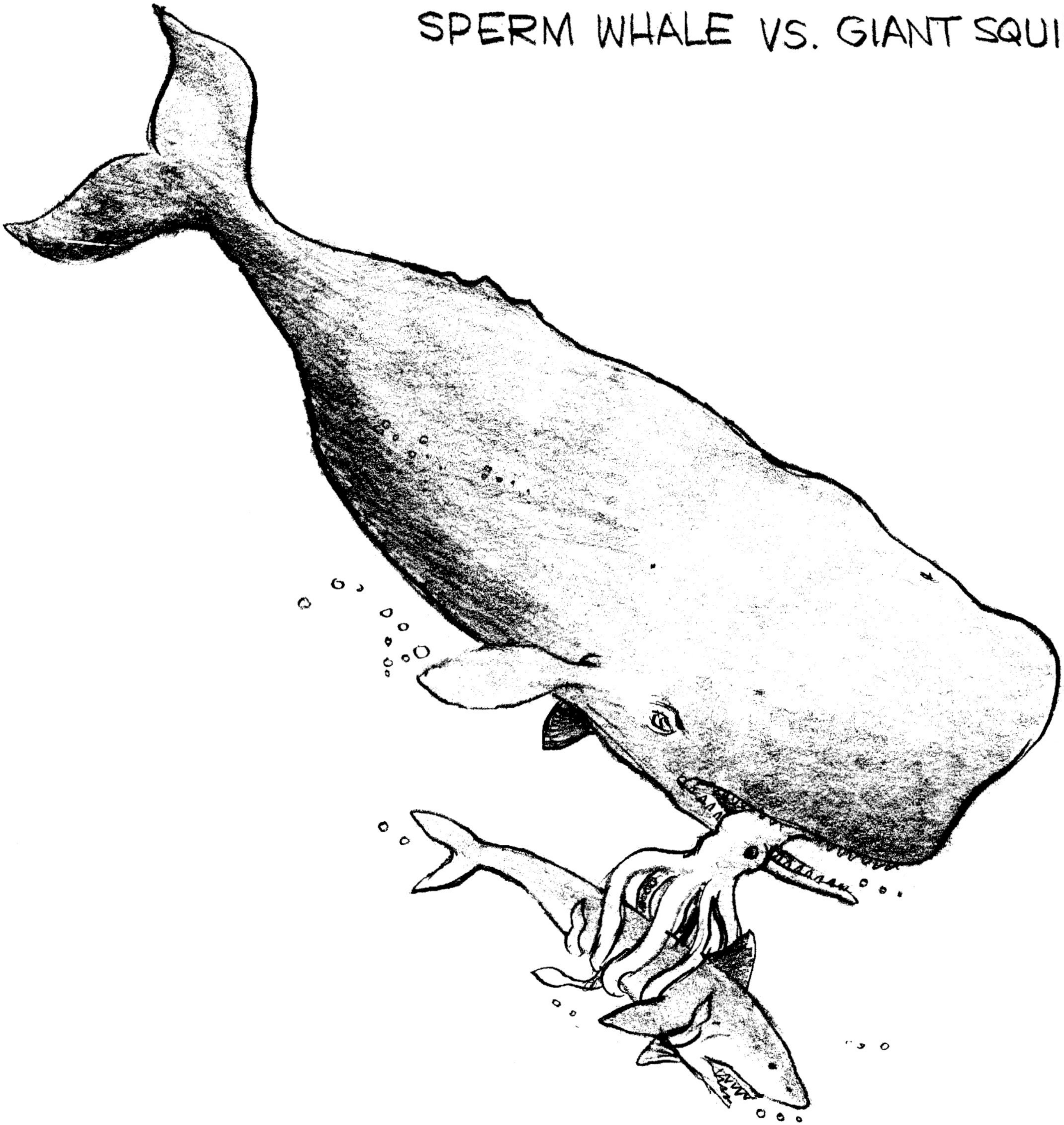

MEGALADON VS. SPERM WHALE

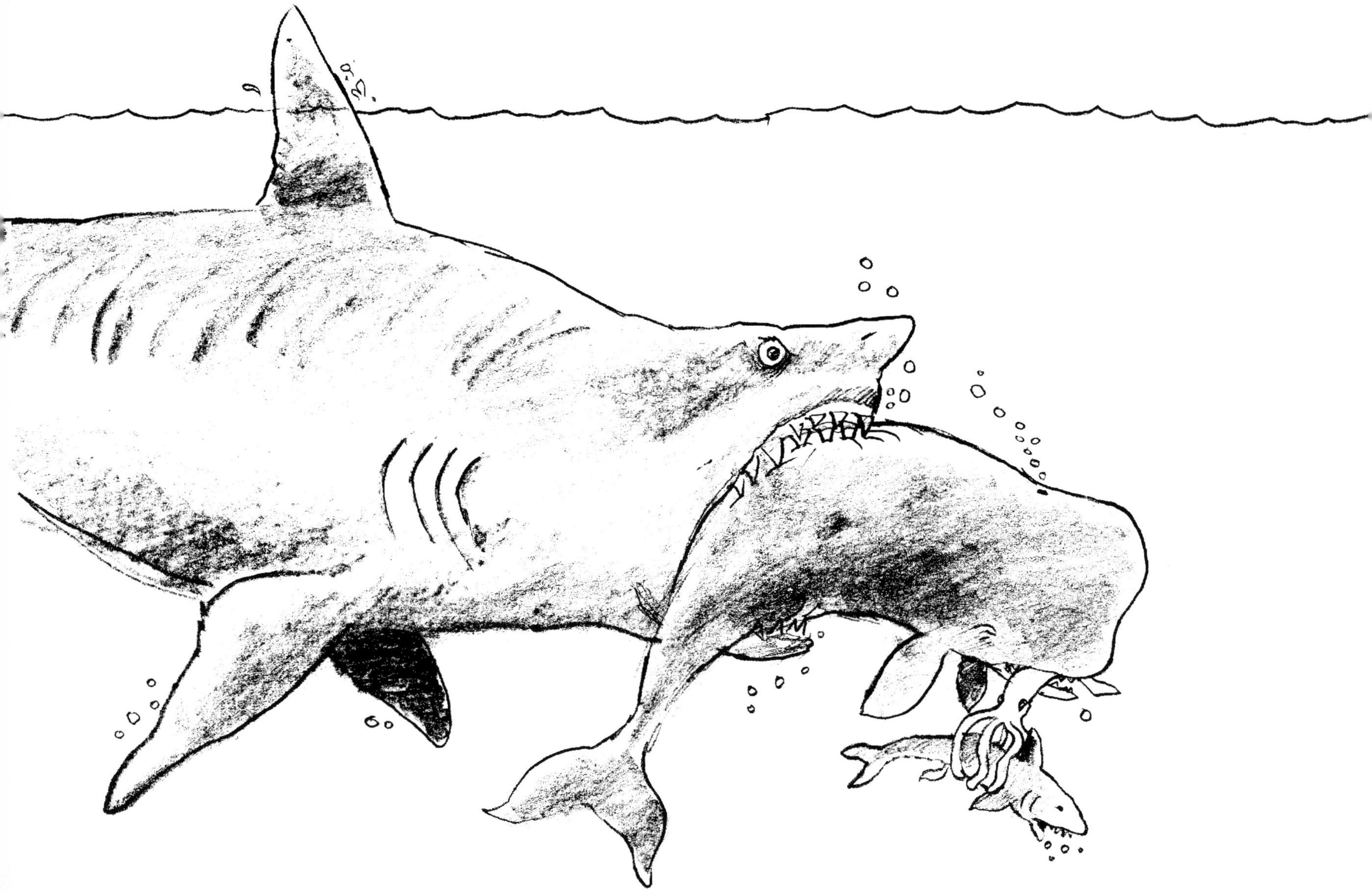

MEGALADACTYL VS. MEGALADON

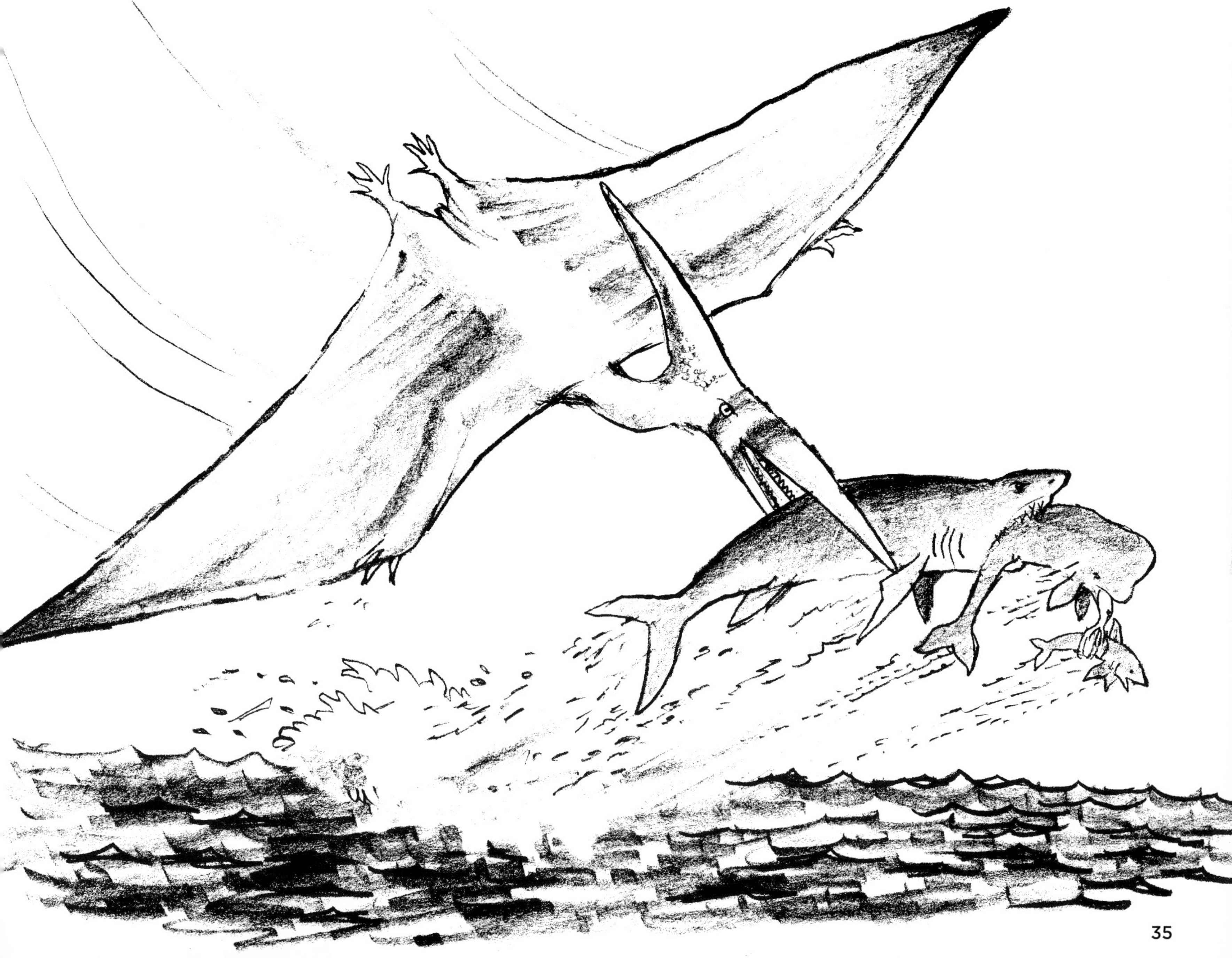

CRUISE MISSLE VS. MEGALADACTYL

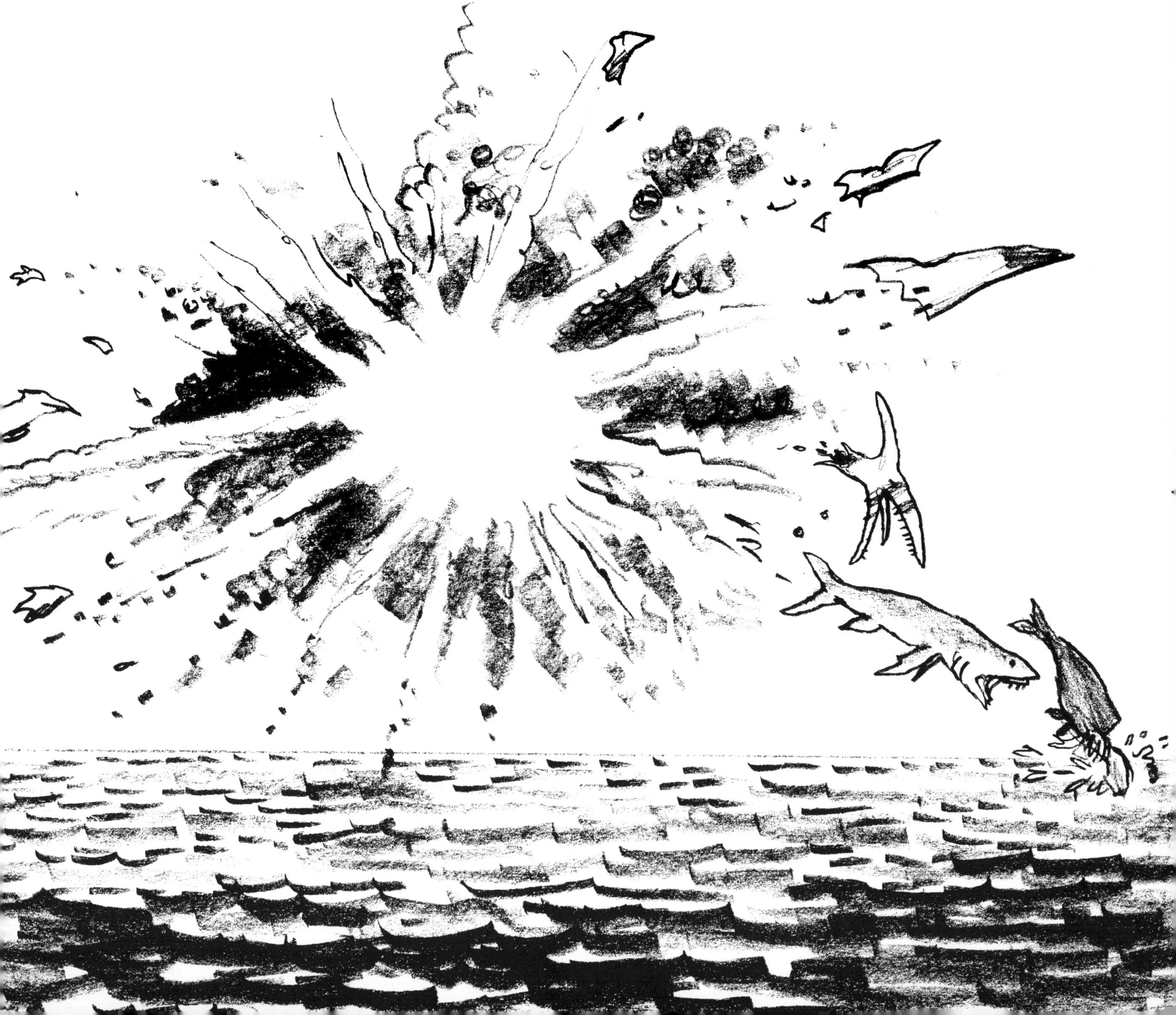

ZOMBIES

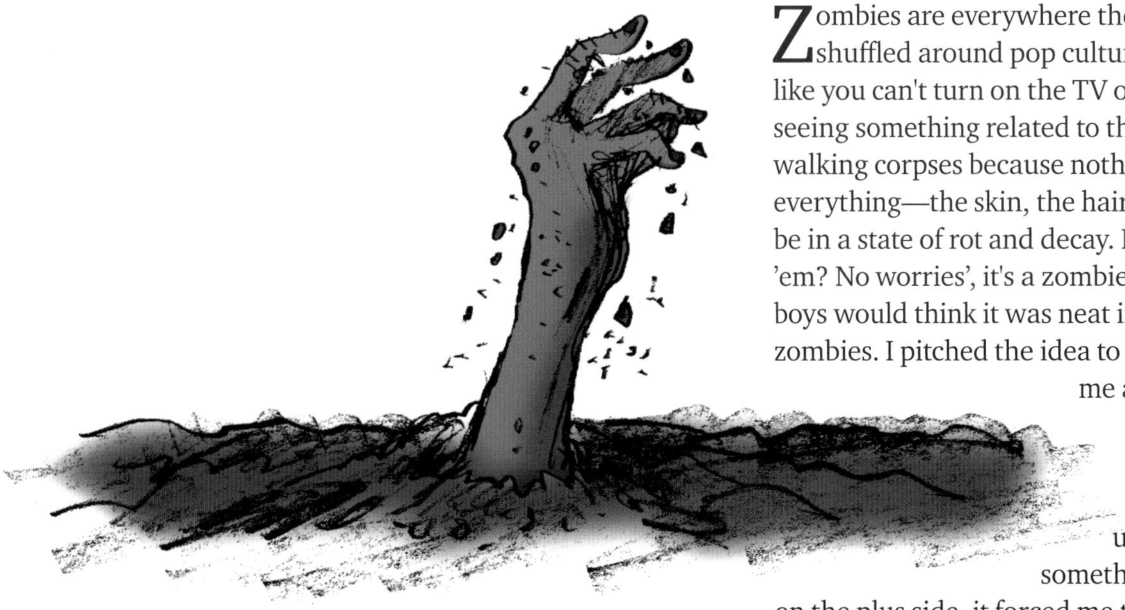

Zombies are everywhere these days. I realize they've shuffled around pop culture for a while, but now it seems like you can't turn on the TV or open a magazine without seeing something related to the undead. I love drawing walking corpses because nothing has to be perfect . . . everything—the skin, the hair, the clothes—are supposed to be in a state of rot and decay. Forgot to put an ear on one of 'em? No worries', it's a zombie! A few years ago, I thought my boys would think it was neat if I did a kids' picture book on zombies. I pitched the idea to a publisher and they offered me a contract. The problem was my manuscript was way too gory for two- to four-year-old readers (go figure). We ultimately had to do a book on something completely different, but on the plus side, it forced me to come up with a bunch of great ways to kill the walking dead. My boys are actually kind of hoping for WWZ so we can employ these methods one day.

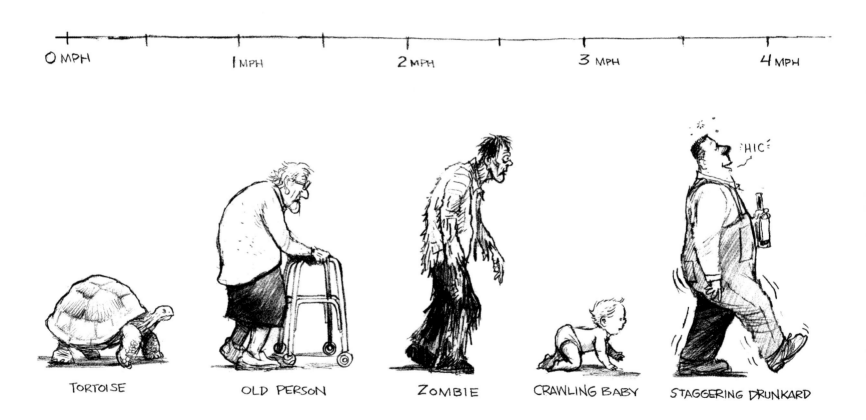

0 MPH   1 MPH   2 MPH   3 MPH   4 MPH

TORTOISE   OLD PERSON   ZOMBIE   CRAWLING BABY   STAGGERING DRUNKARD

Your classic, slow-moving, dim-witted zombies are,
of course, the easiest ones to kill . . .

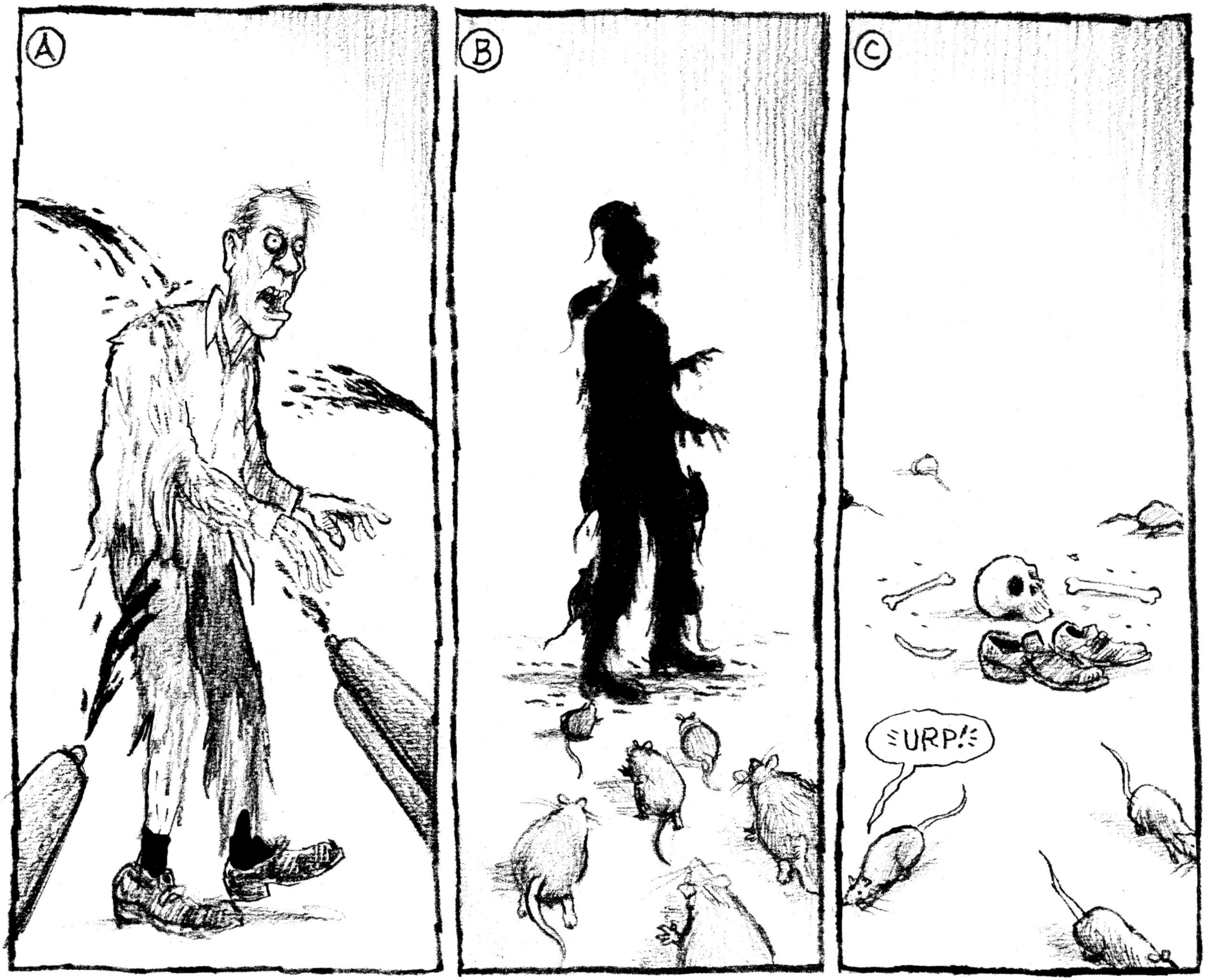
A
B
C
URP!

One of the most fun ways to dispatch a zombie is to load up some Super Soakers with steak sauce and let 'em have it. Wait an hour or so and the rats will do the rest.

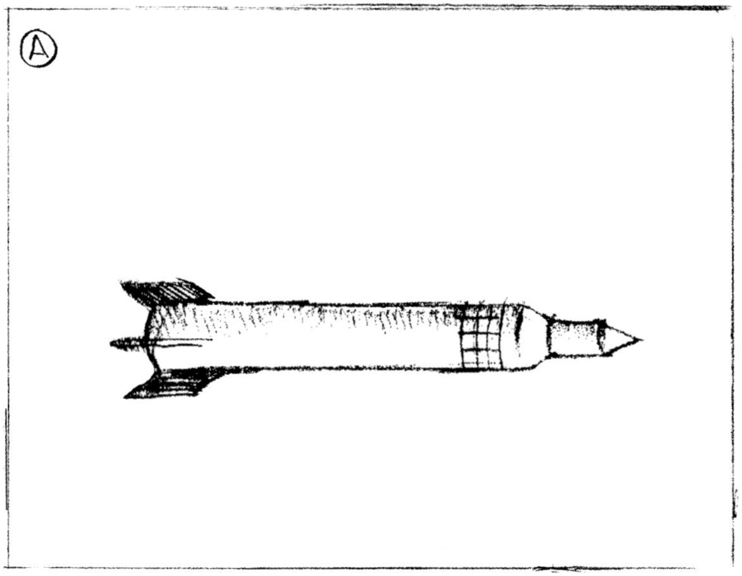
A

Get your hands on a
nuclear device.

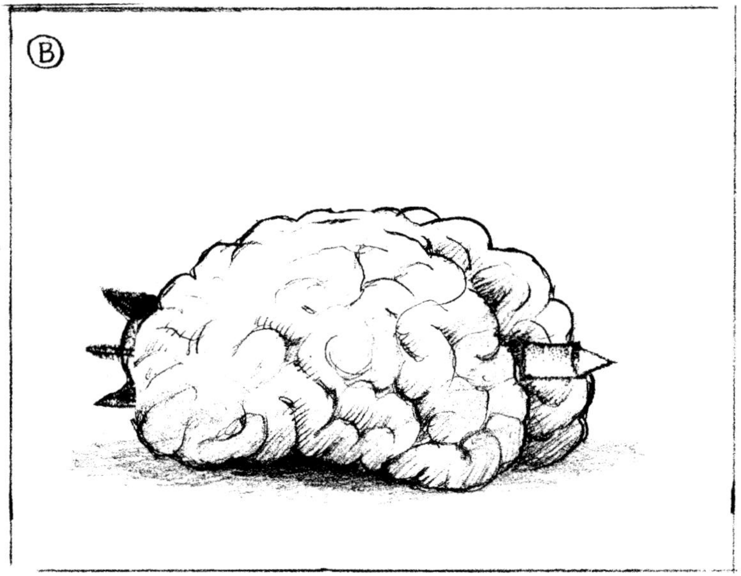
B

Sculpt a giant brain around
it using soft cheese.

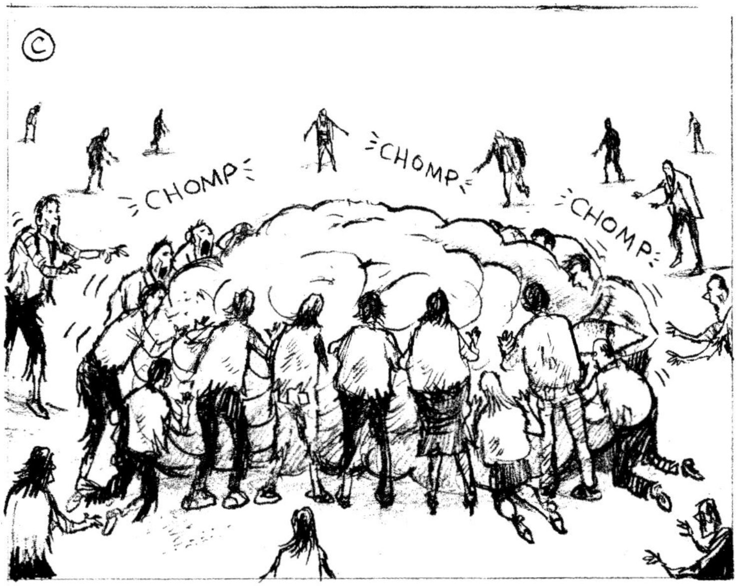
C
CHOMP
CHOMP
CHOMP

Wait for lots of zombies to come
and eat the giant brain.

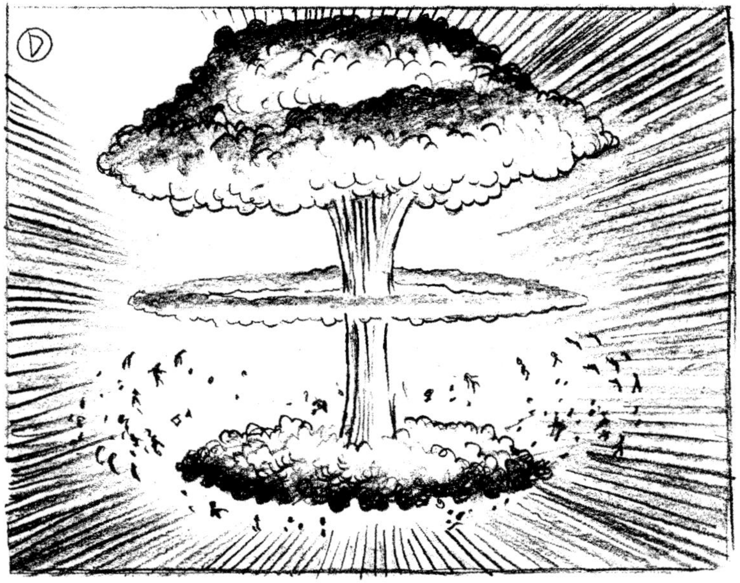
D

Detonate!

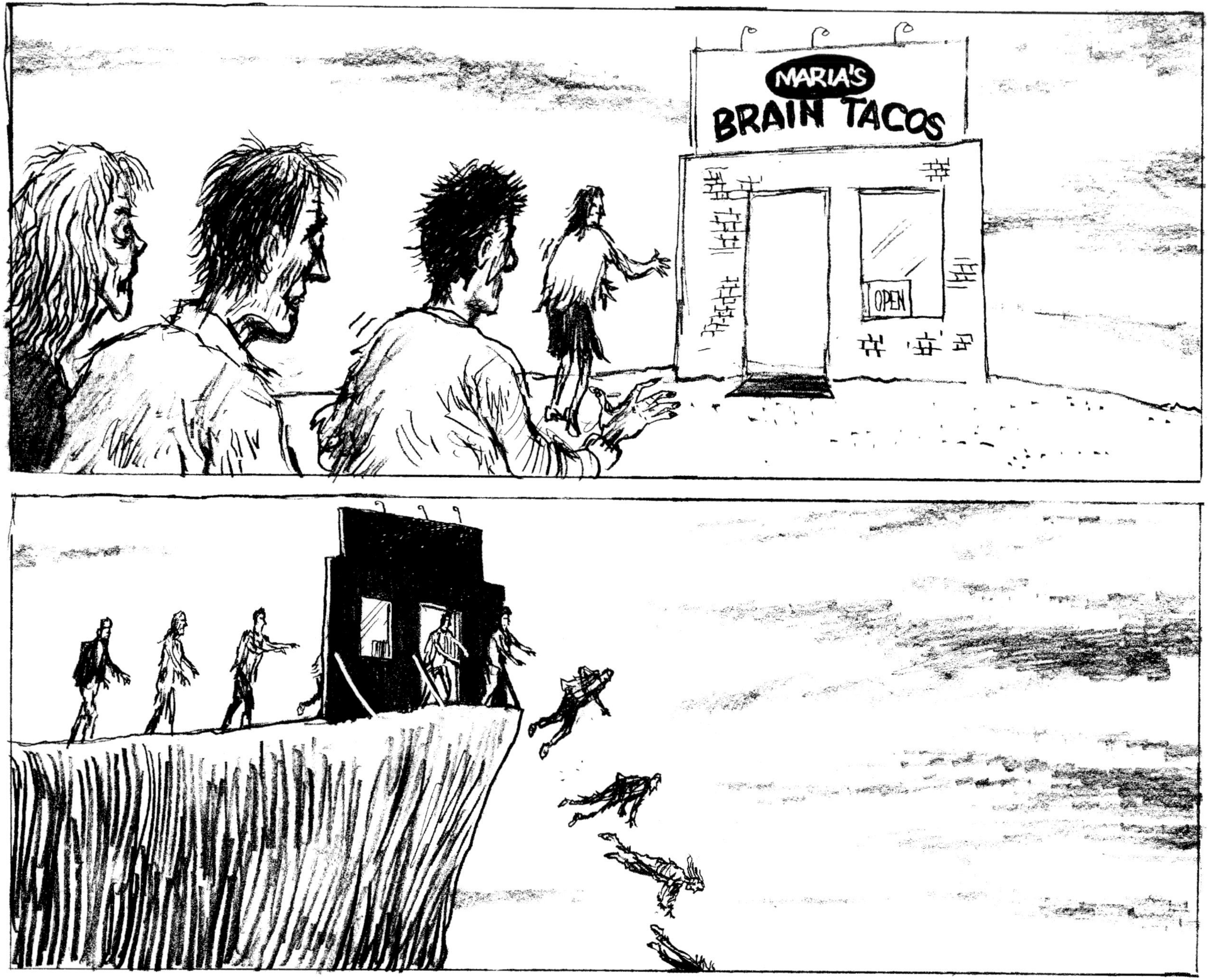
MARIA'S
BRAIN TACOS
OPEN

Using brains as bait is almost too easy . . .

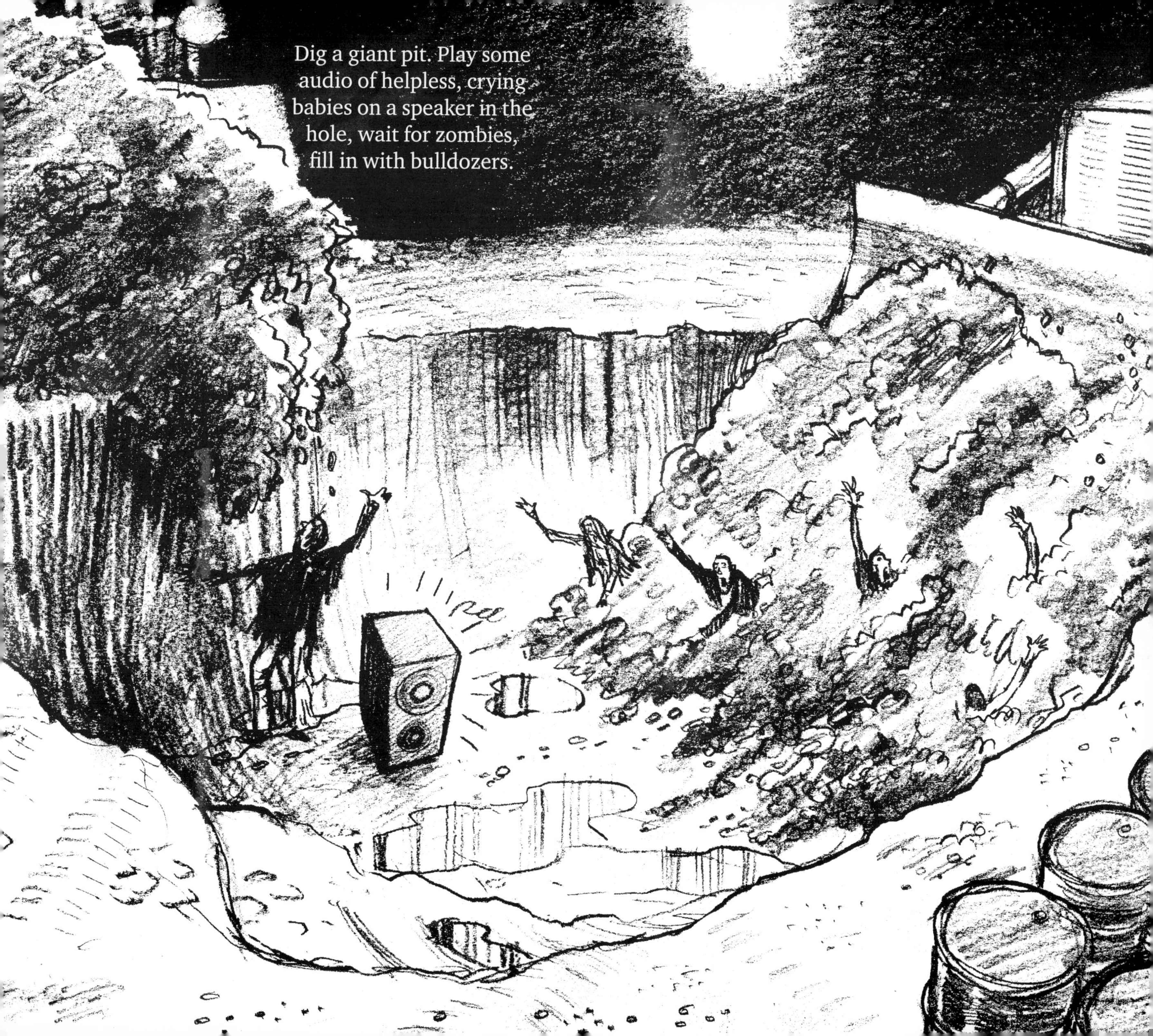
Dig a giant pit. Play some audio of helpless, crying babies on a speaker in the hole, wait for zombies, fill in with bulldozers.

Drop thousands of Chargers caps over zombie-infested parts of downtown Oakland.

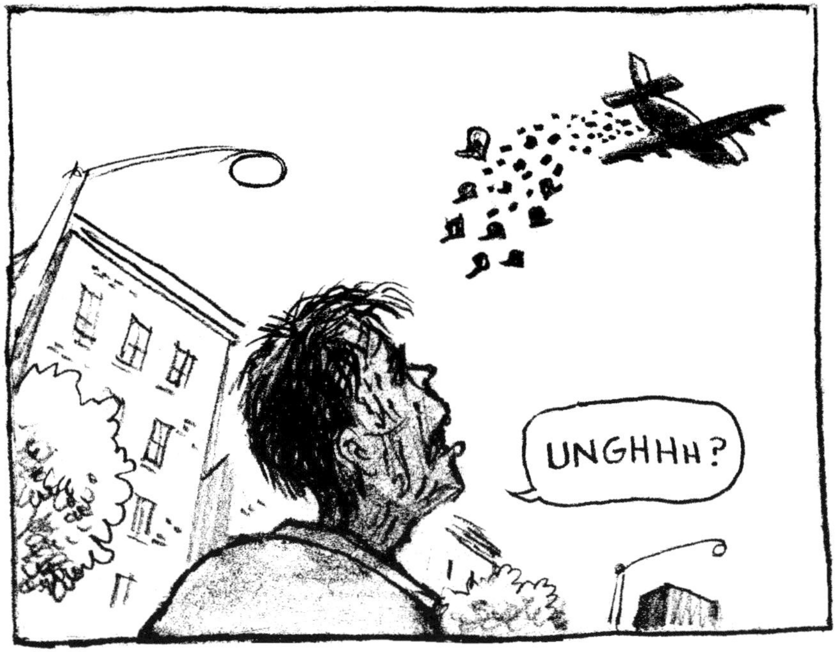
UNGHHH?

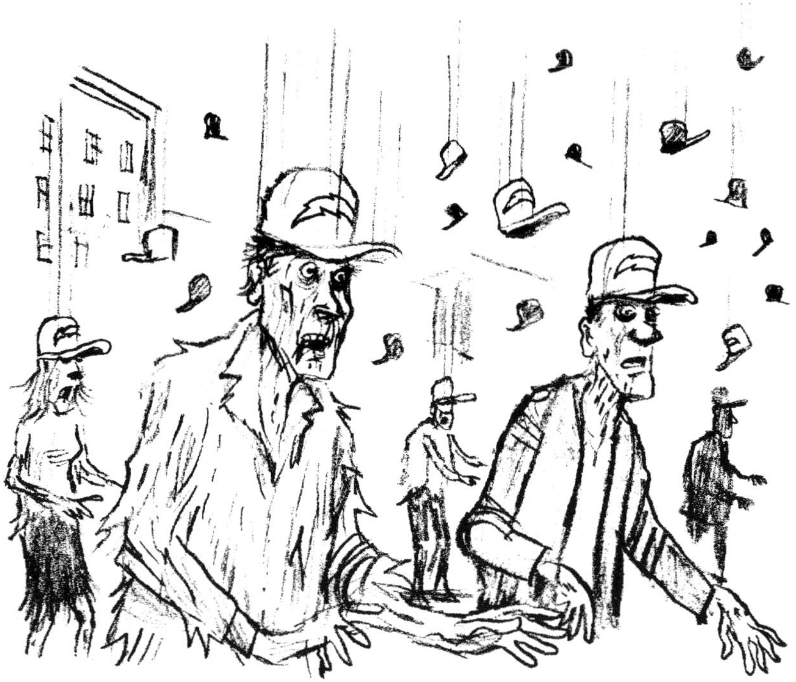

Raiders fans do the rest.

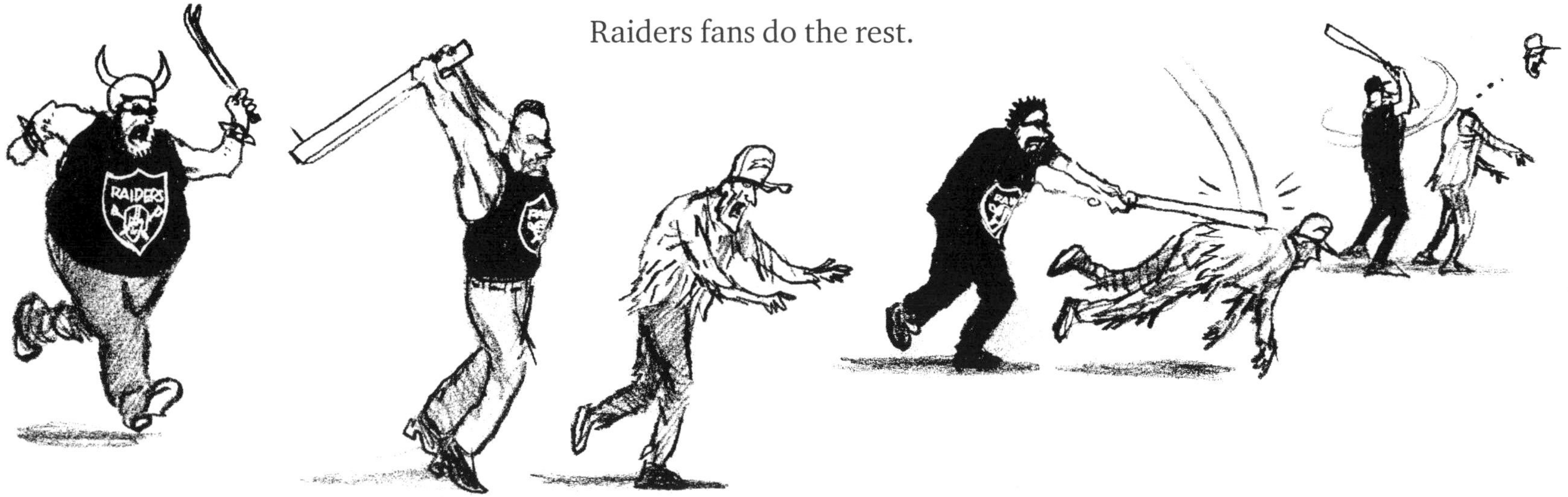
RAIDERS

(Also works with Packers caps dropped over zombie-infested parts of Chicago, Red Sox caps dropped over the Bronx, etc.)

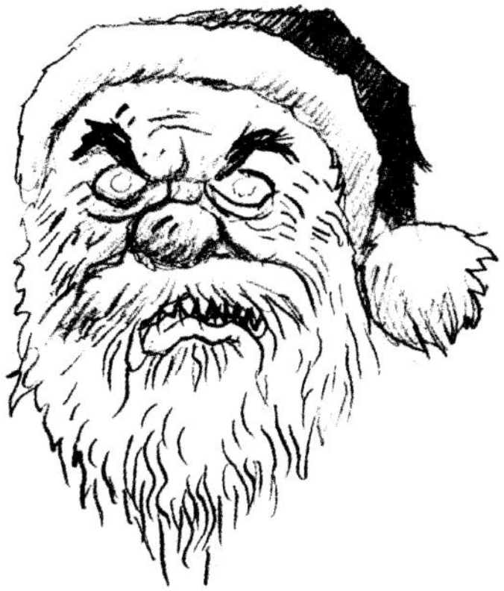

ZOMBIES, ZOMBIES EVERYWHERE!

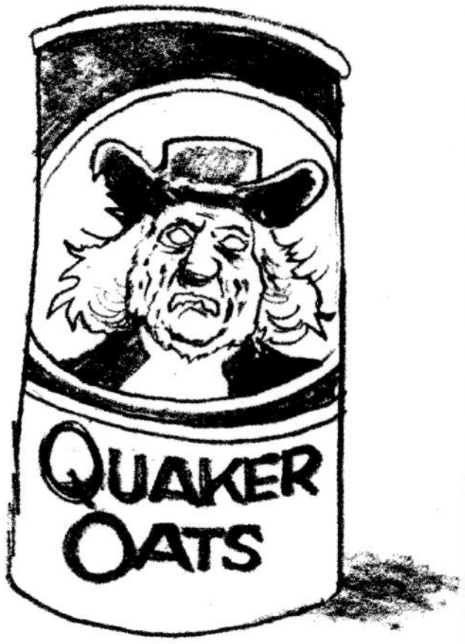
QUAKER
OATS

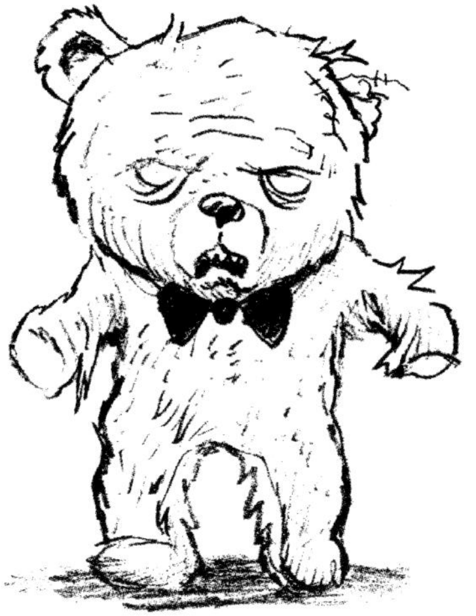

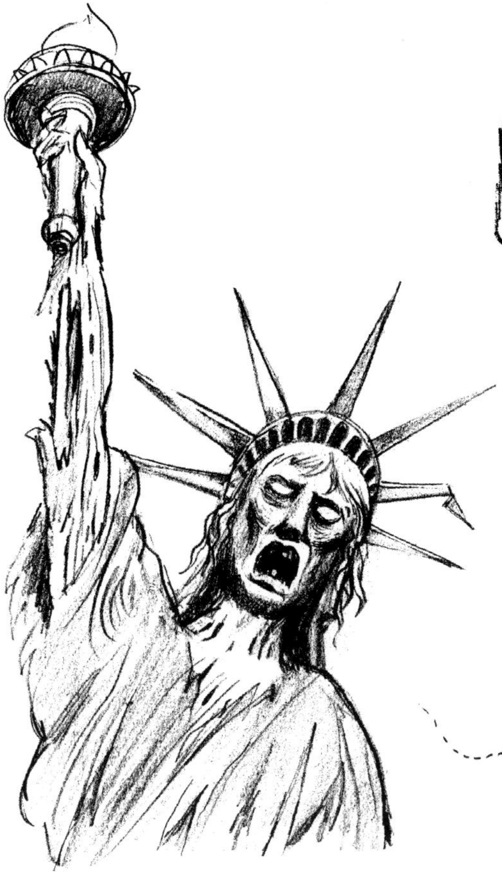

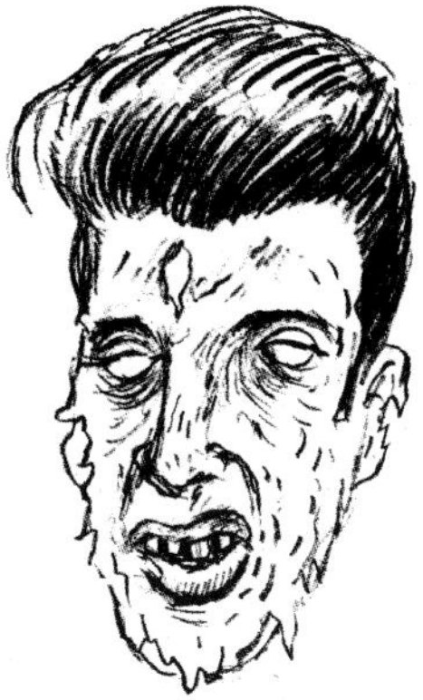

ZELVIS
(ZOMBIE ELVIS)

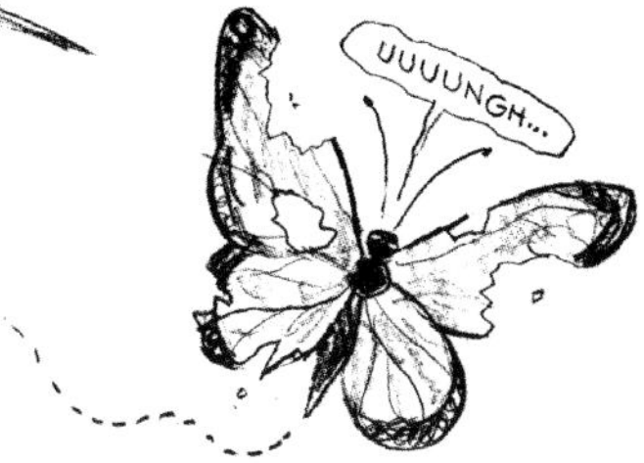
UUUUNGH...

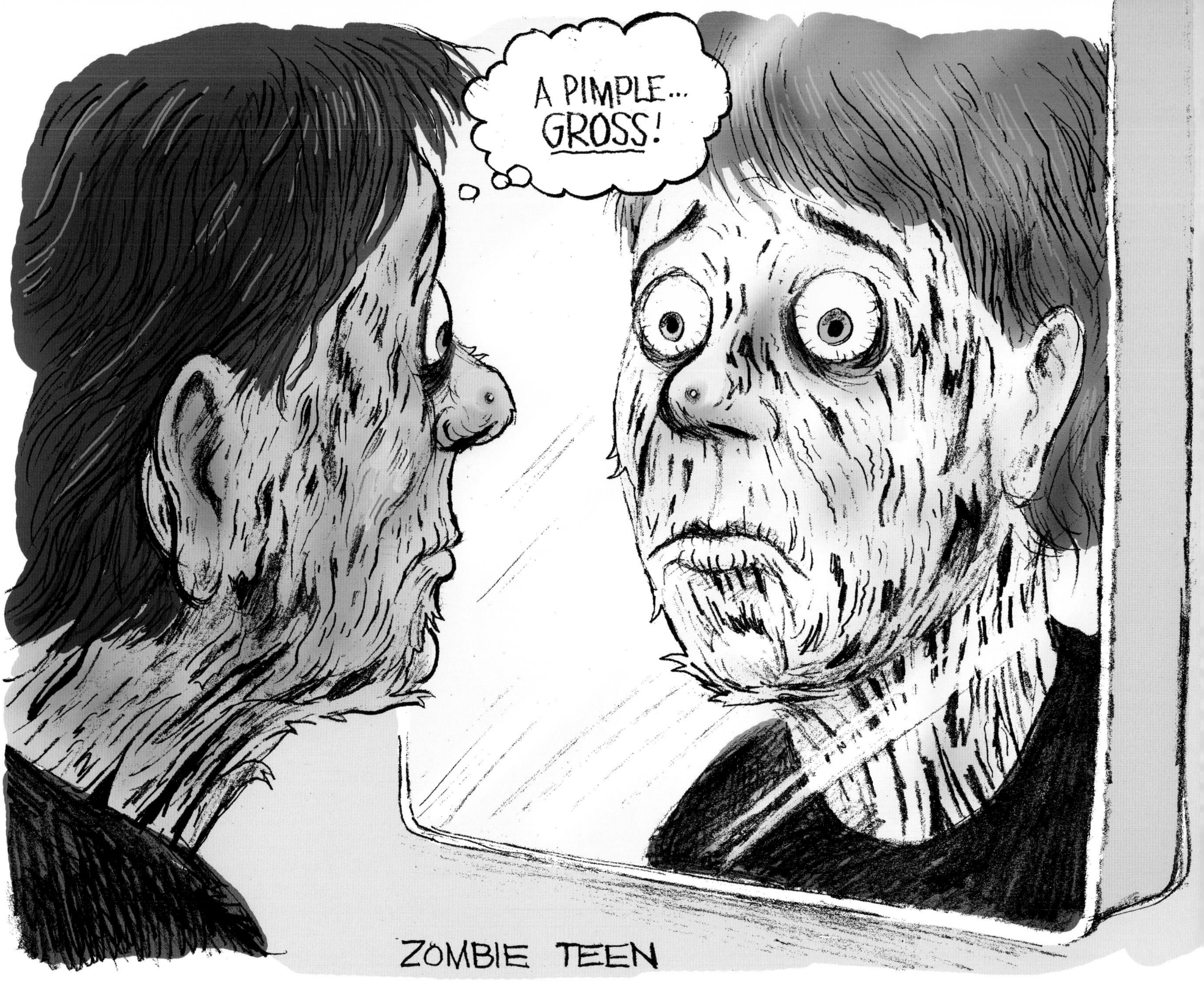
A PIMPLE...
GROSS!
ZOMBIE TEEN

FAMOUS PEOPLE

Like zombies, our culture is obsessed with celebrities. My kids know way too much about these stars from TV, supermarket tabloids, etc. Granted, we probably consume more pop culture than your average family but, still, do they *really* need to know where Ben Stiller owns a vacation house or who Lady Gaga is dating? Where does this fascination come from? I don't know. What I do know is it's totally fun drawing Betty White punching out a silverback gorilla.

Uppercut!

47

BIGFOOT

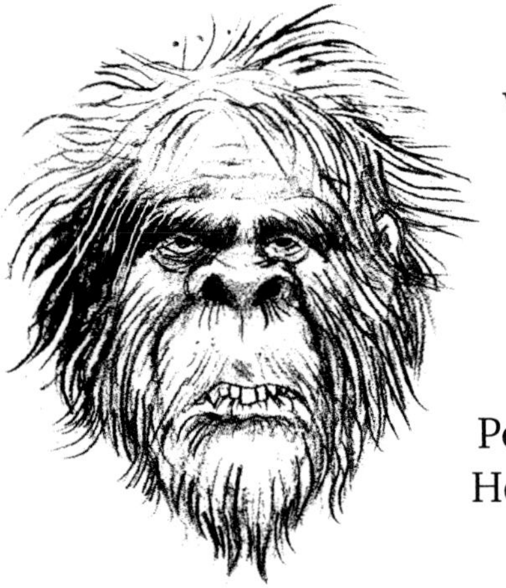

We included Bigfoot in this chapter on famous people because he's a true celebrity. You can't tell us Bigfoot wouldn't be mobbed for autographs walking through Times Square. The thing is, though, he'd never visit New York. It's not his style. He's too much of a recluse…

Perhaps he wouldn't be such a social outcast if he tried a new 'do? Here are a few suggestions for the big guy:

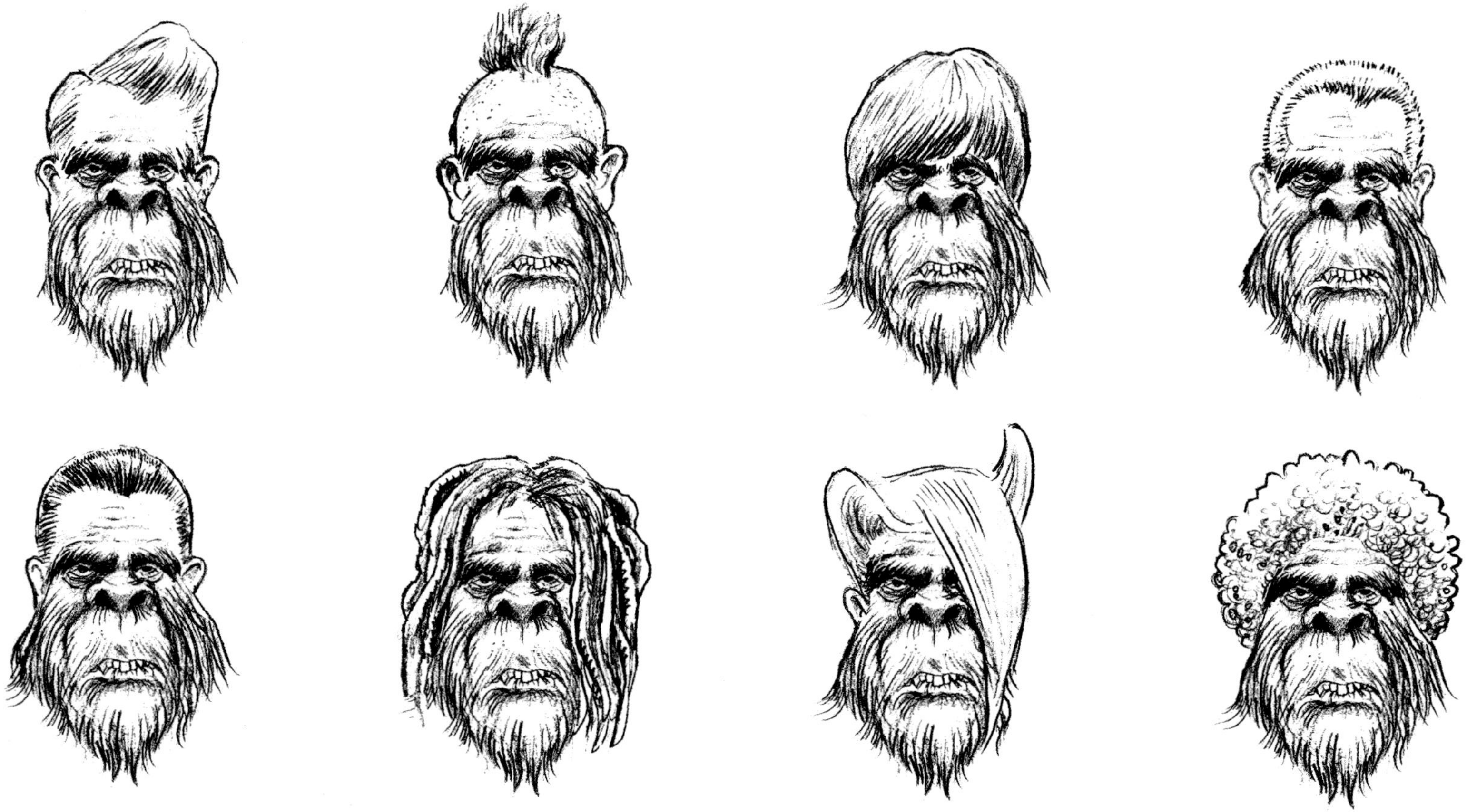

BIGFOOT VS. ZOMBIES

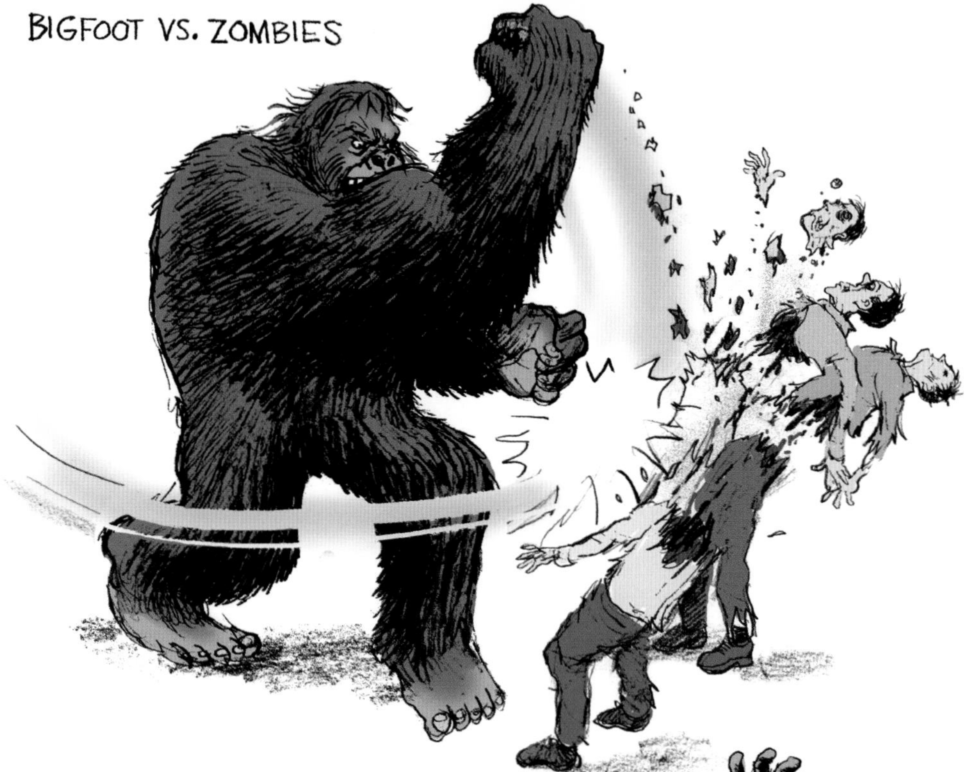

BIGFOOT VS. CHUCK NORRIS

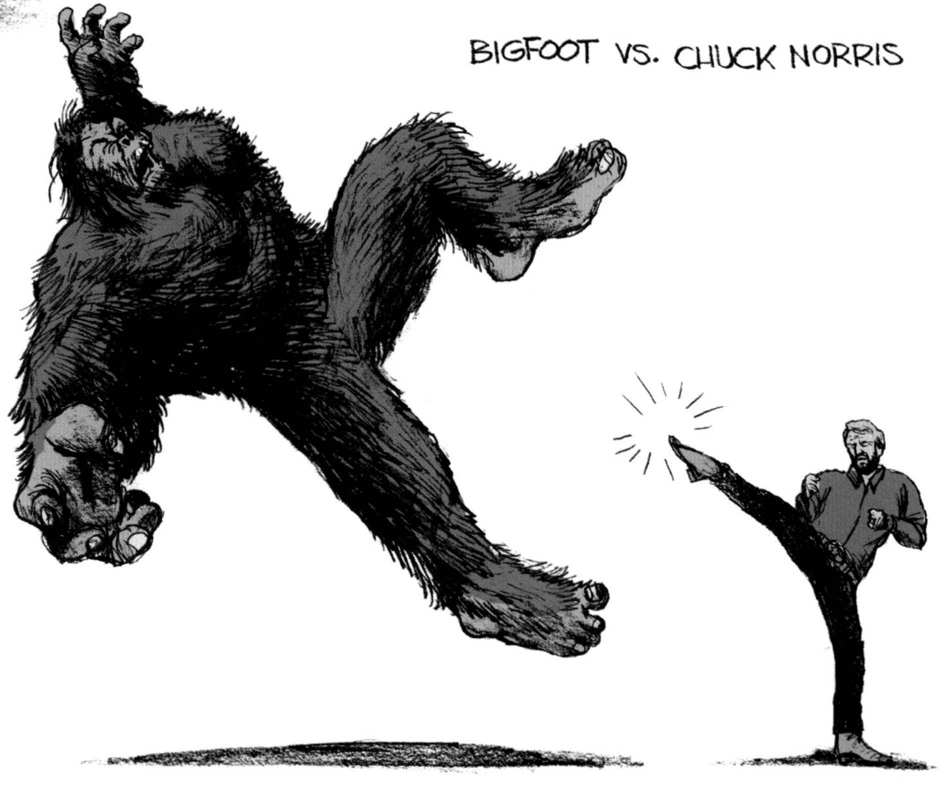

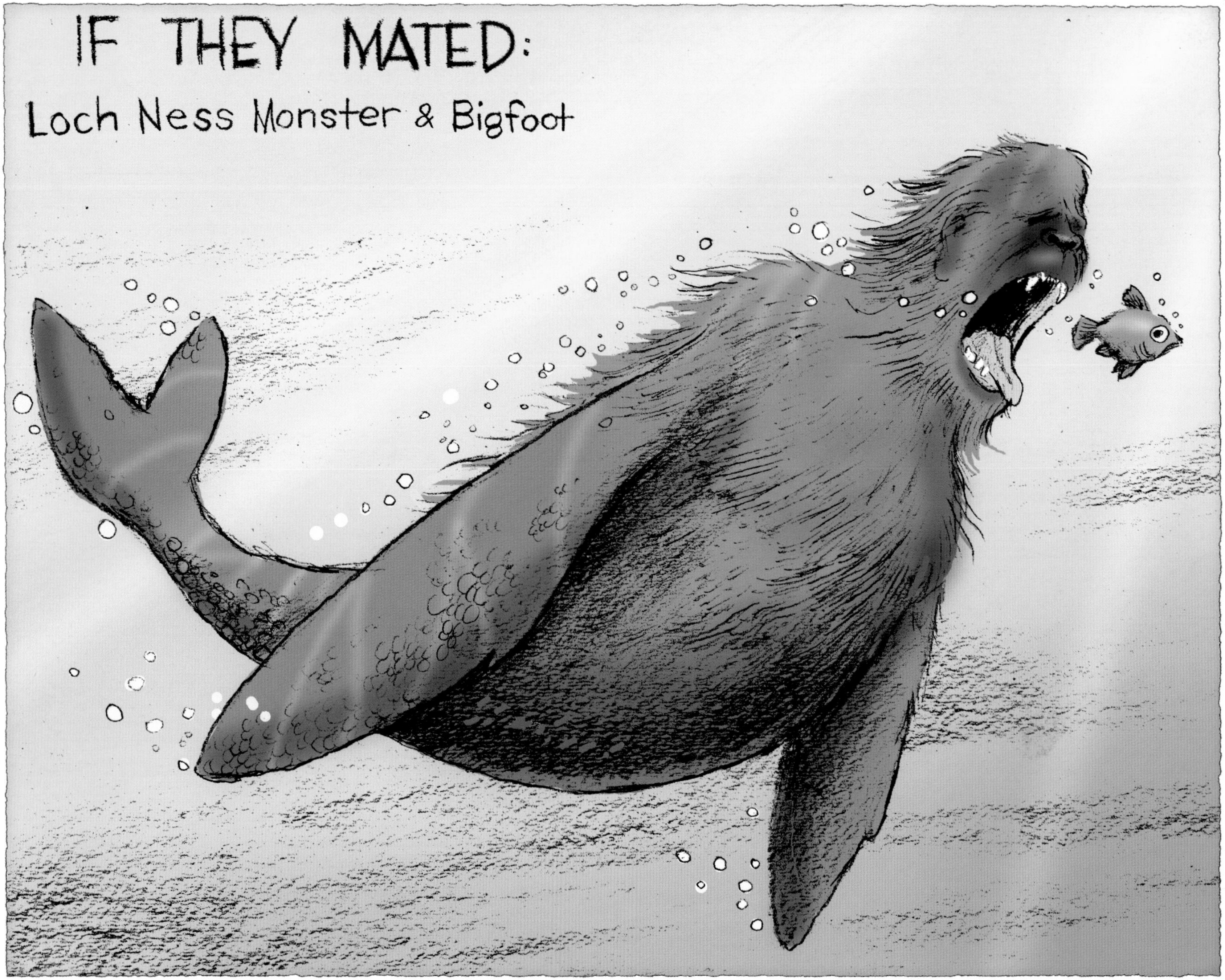
IF THEY MATED:
Loch Ness Monster & Bigfoot

"Nesquatch"?

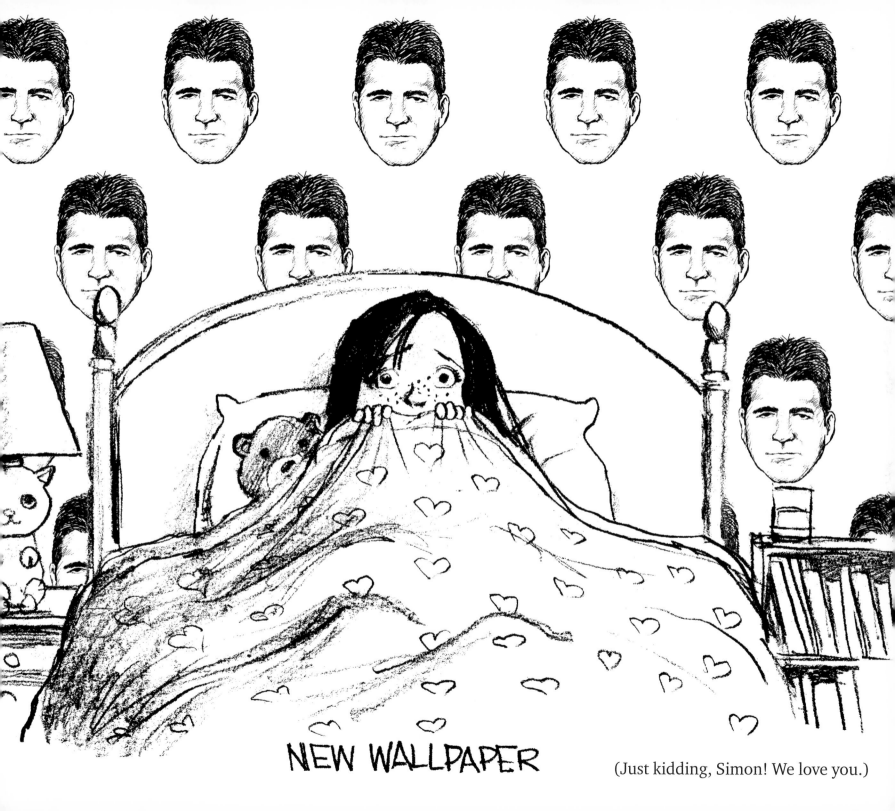

NEW WALLPAPER

(Just kidding, Simon! We love you.)

TARGOYLE

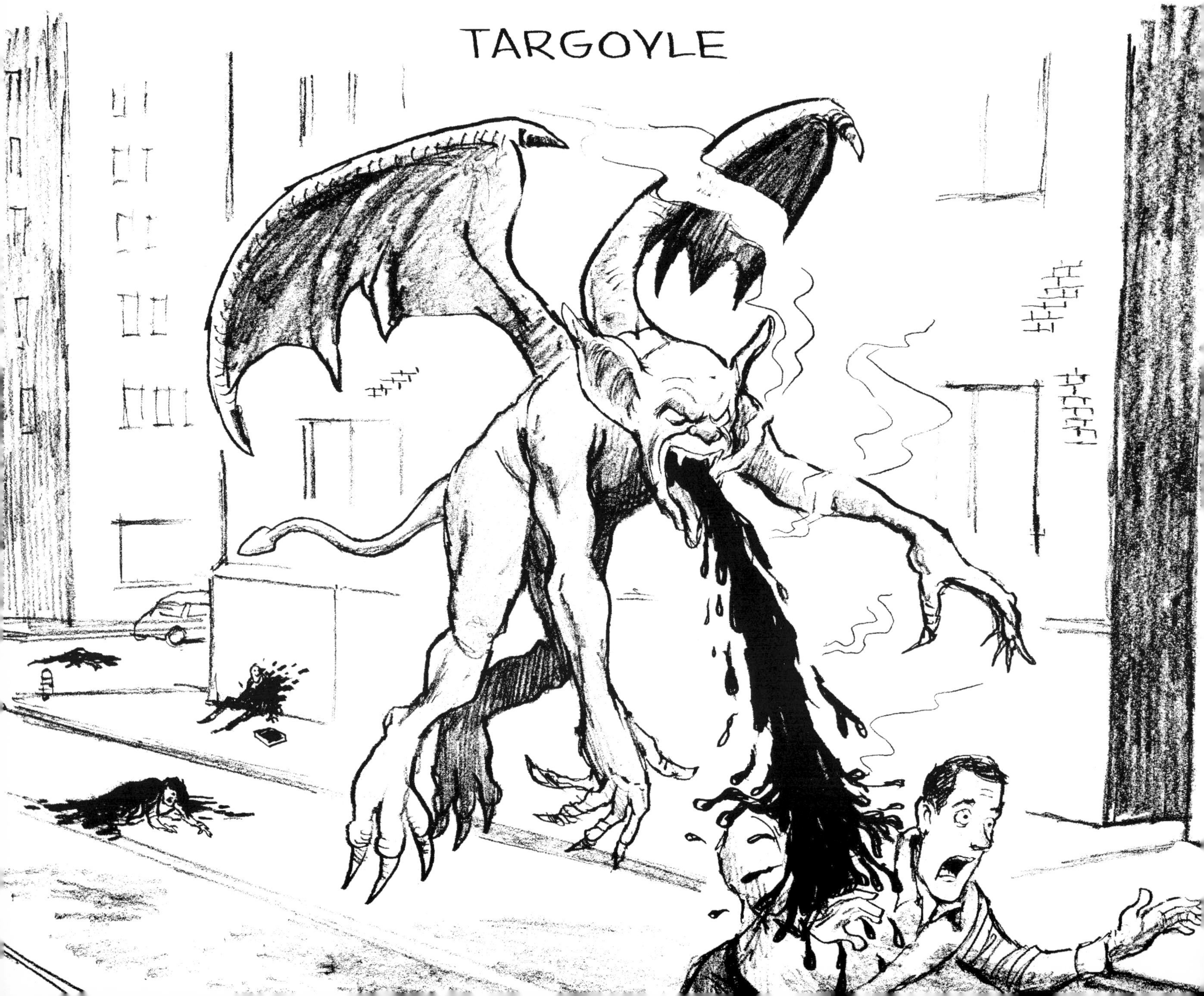

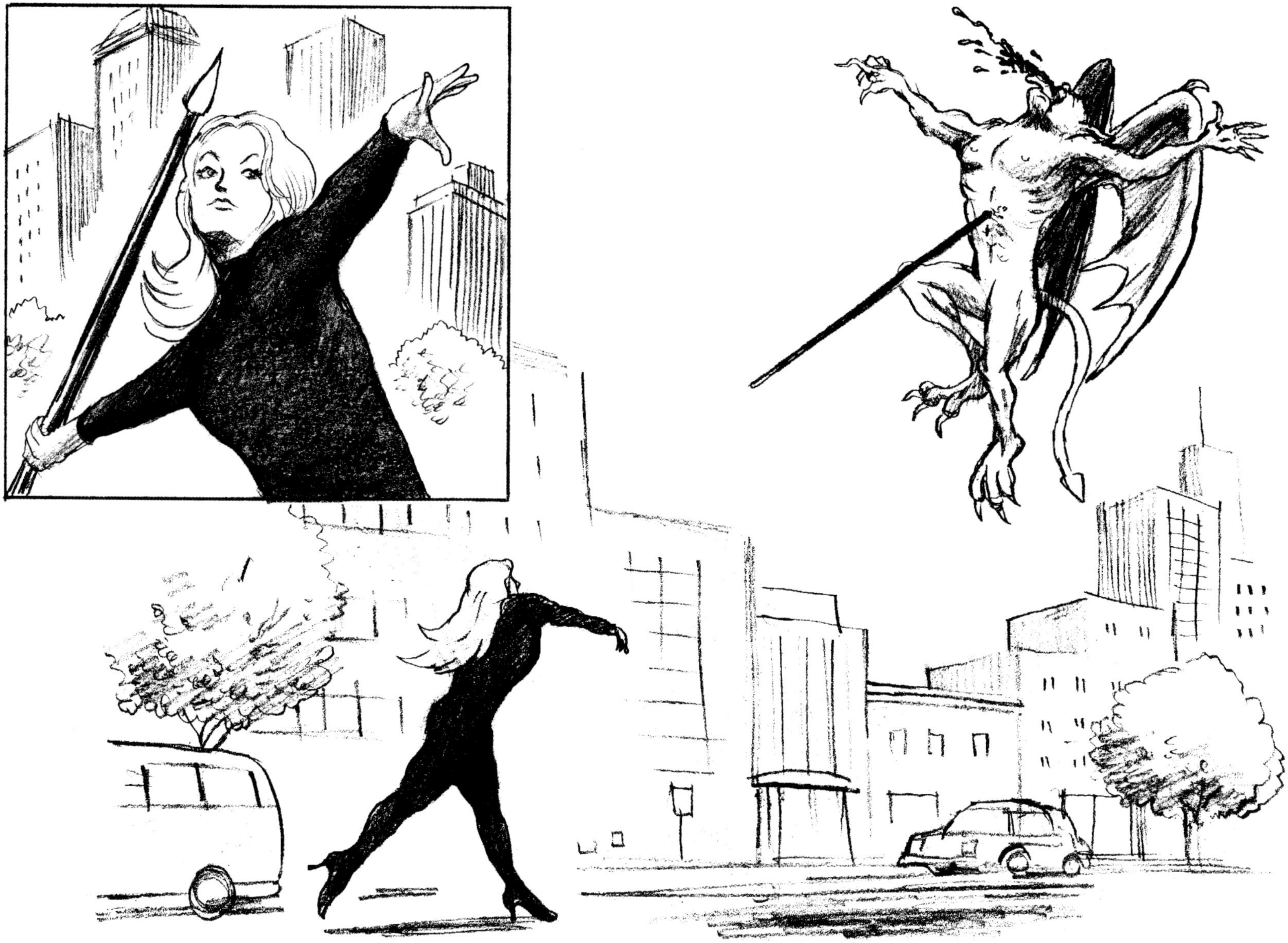

BRITNEY SPEARS

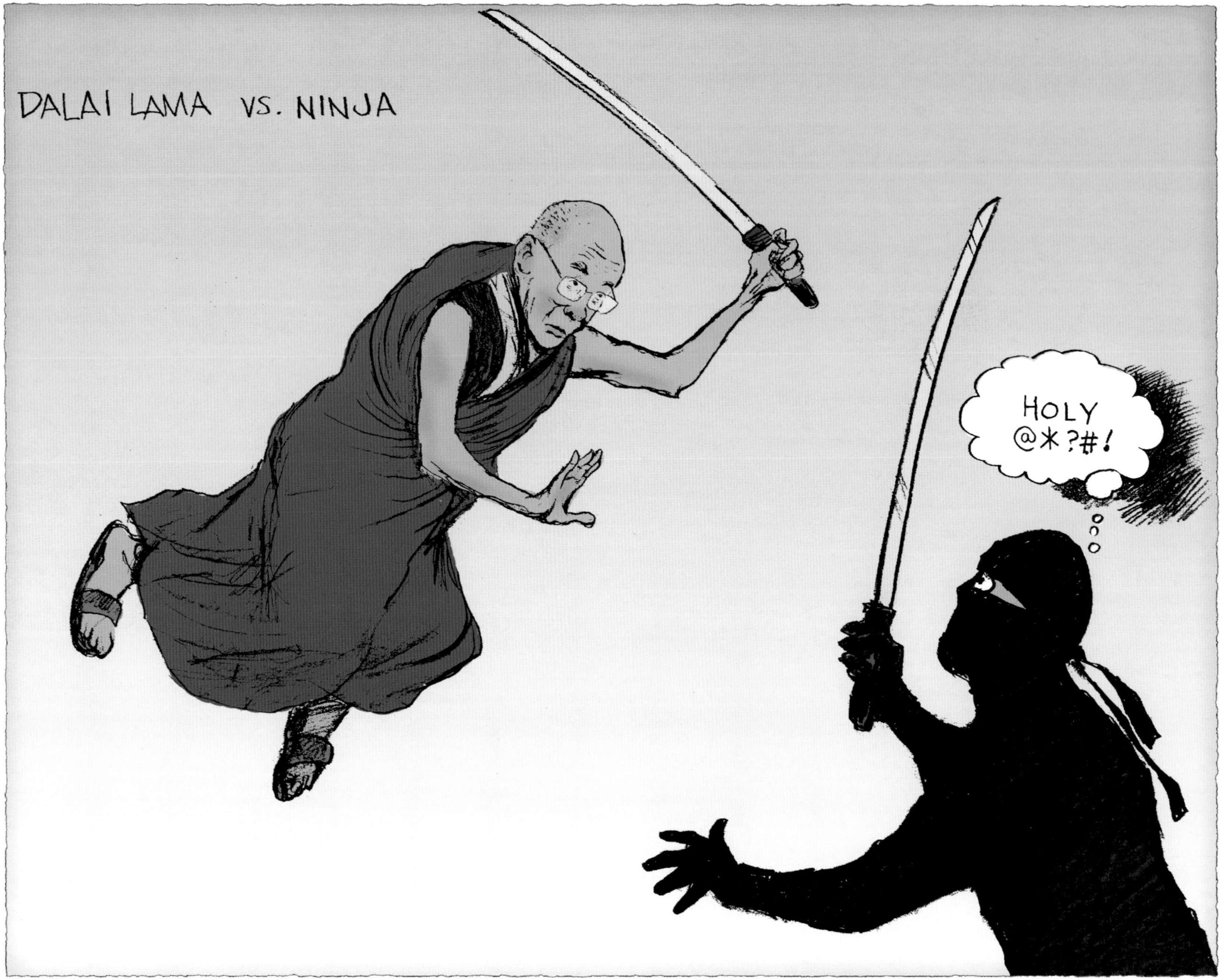
DALAI LAMA VS. NINJA
HOLY @*?#!

NAPOLEAN DYNAMITE

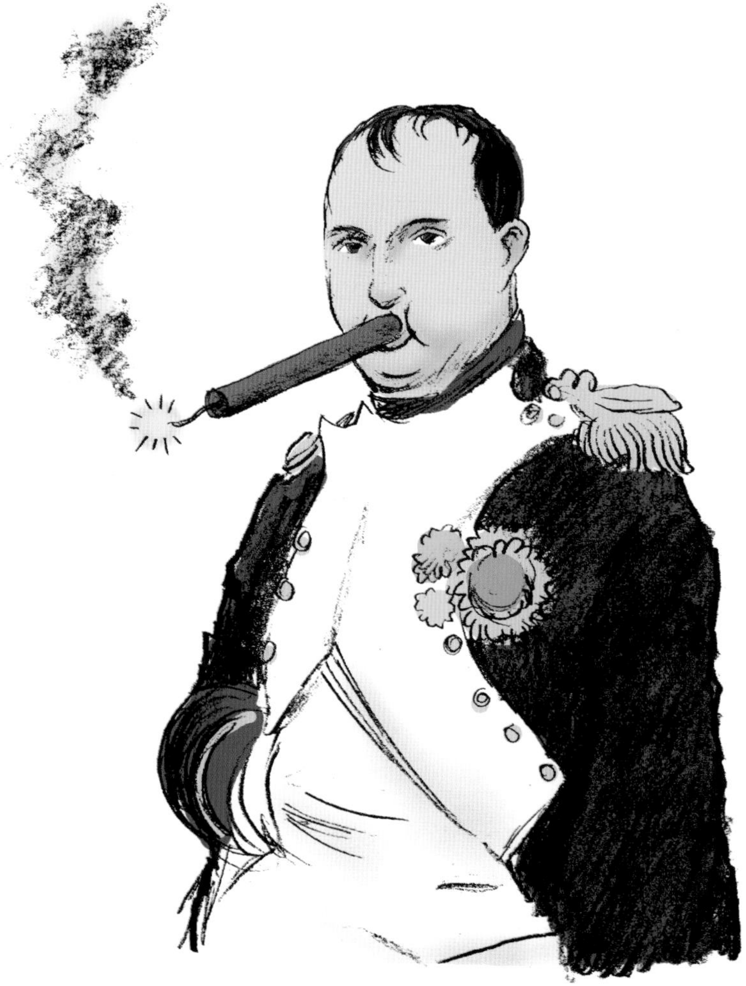

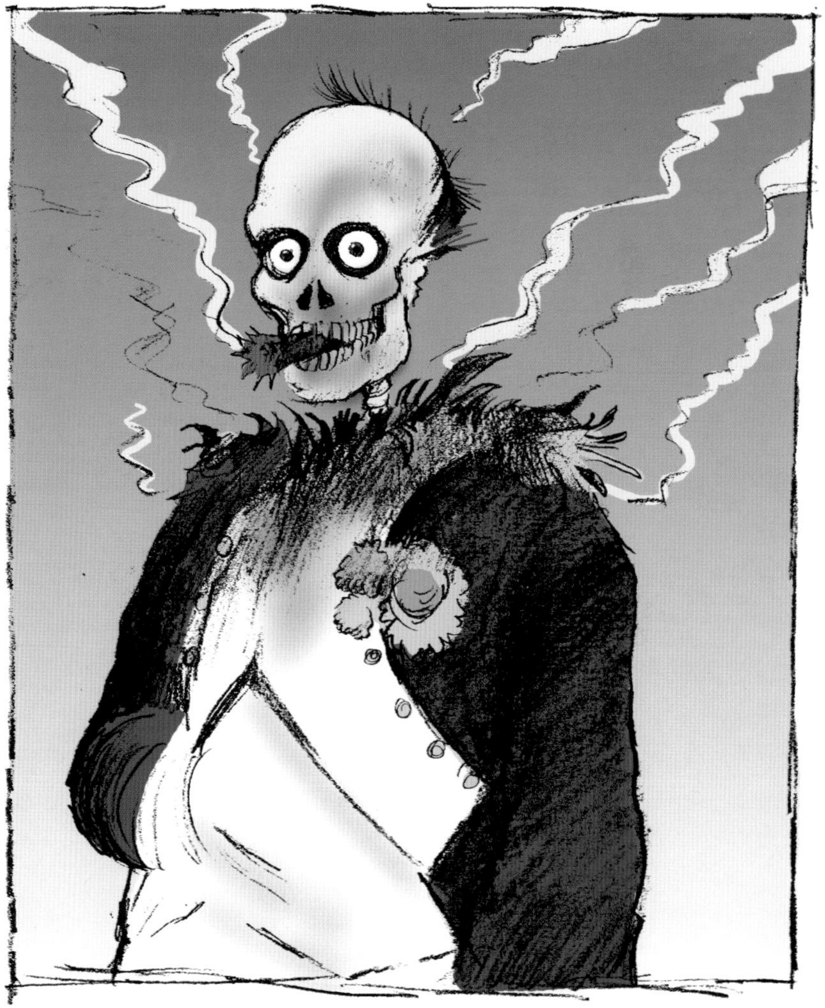

SECRET MUTANT POWERS OF US PRESIDENTS

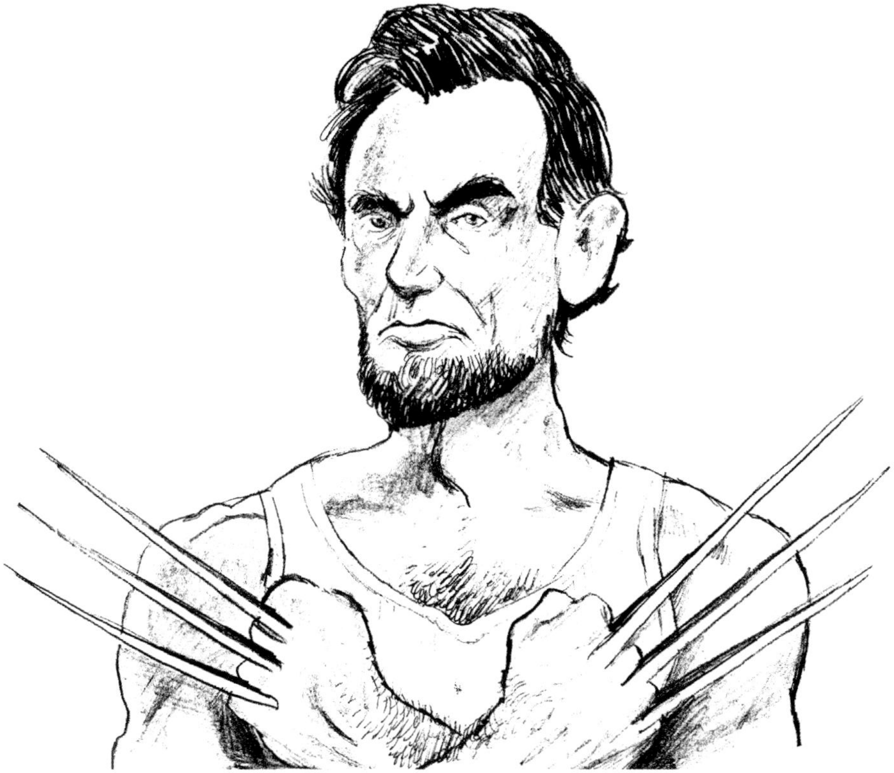

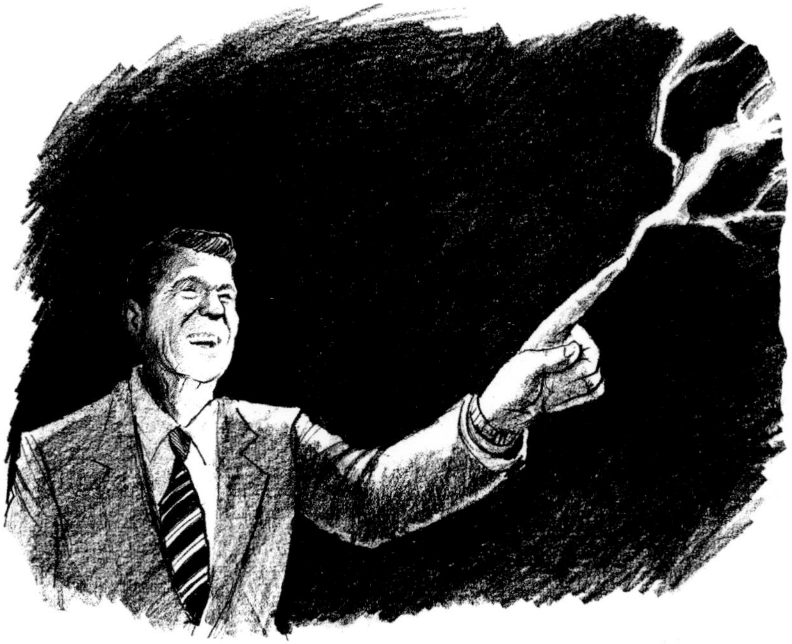

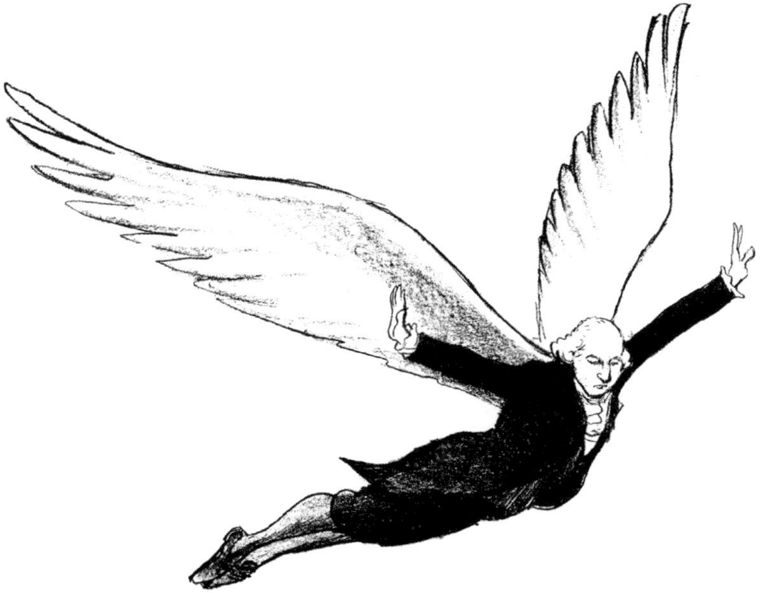

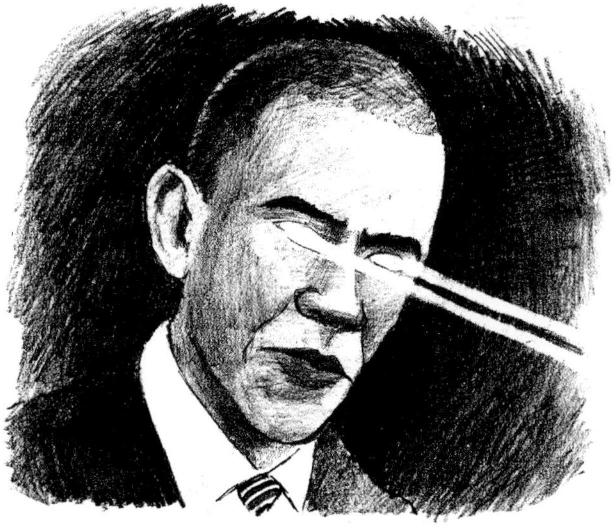

GUESS THE CELEBRITY CYCLOPS

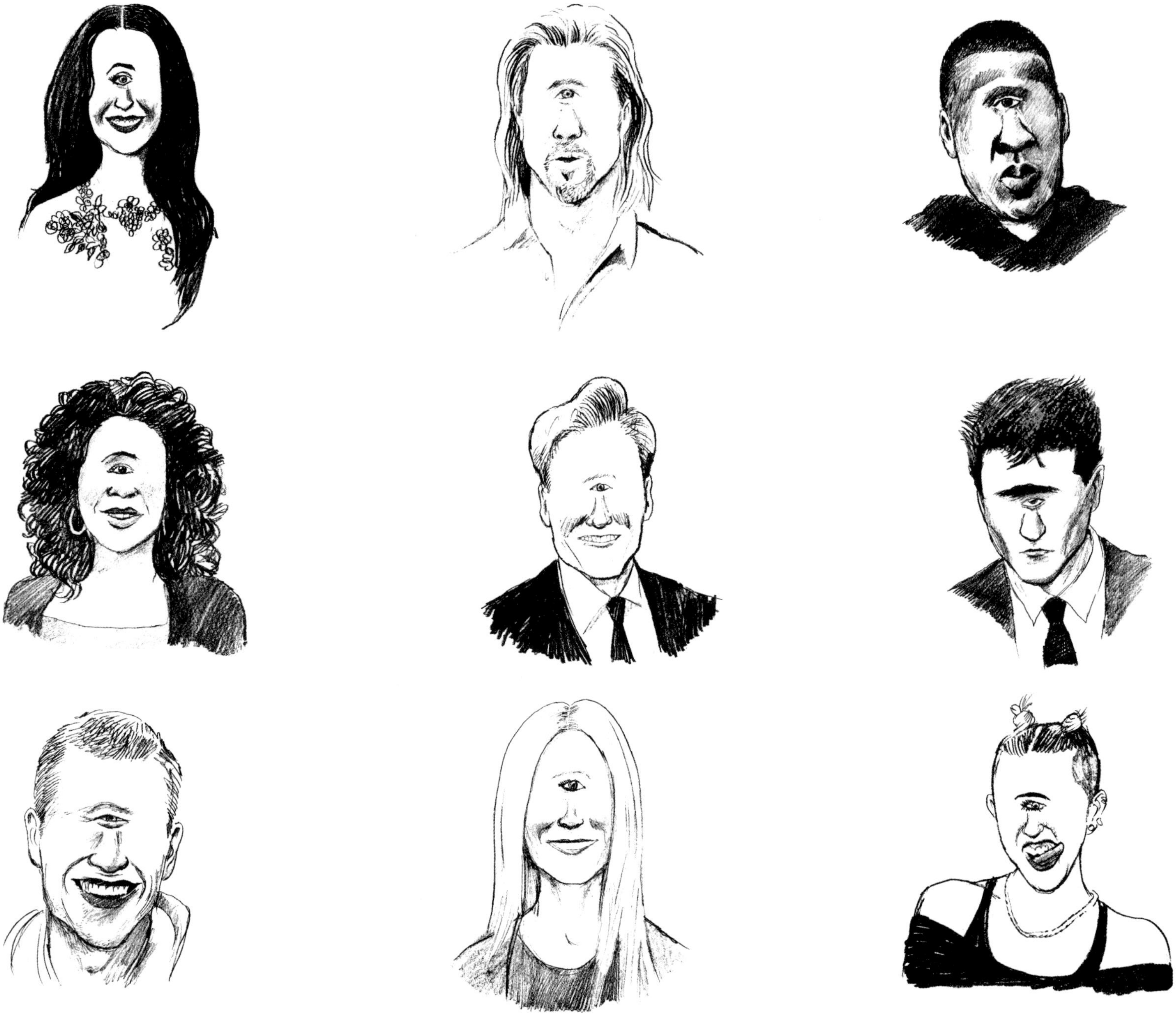

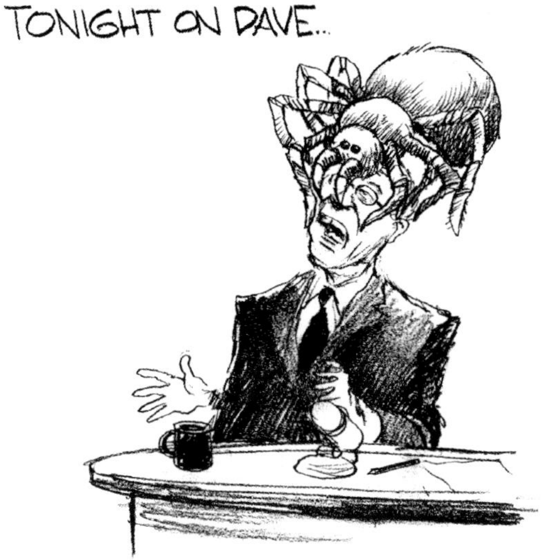
TONIGHT ON DAVE...

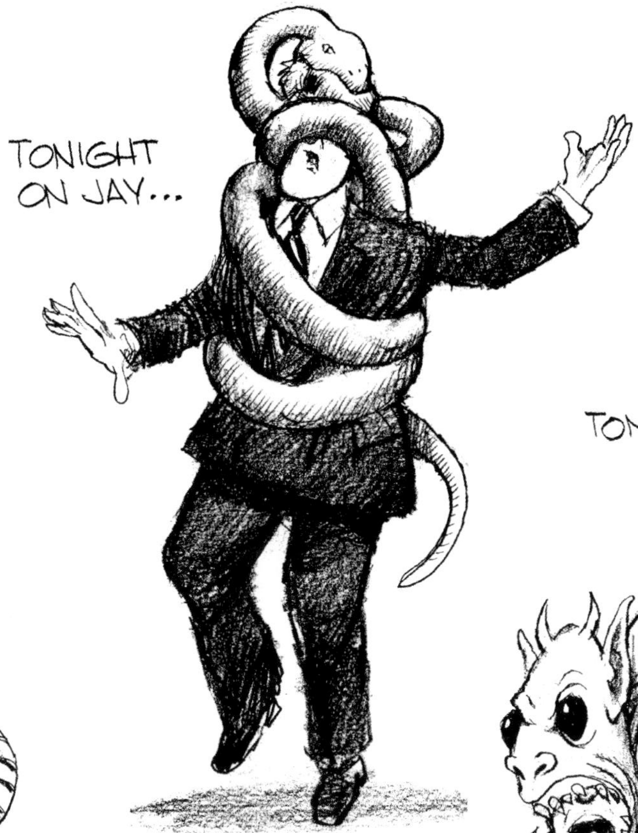
TONIGHT
ON JAY...

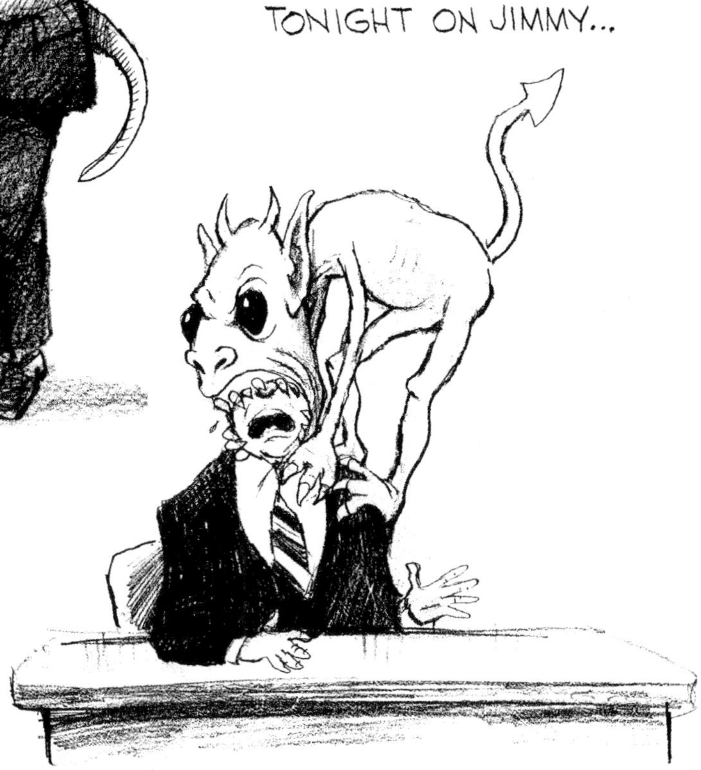
TONIGHT ON JIMMY...

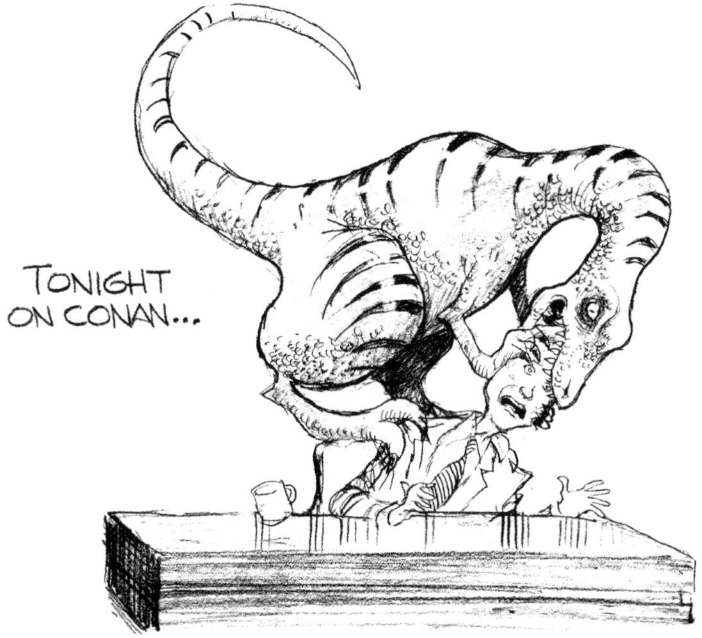
TONIGHT
ON CONAN...

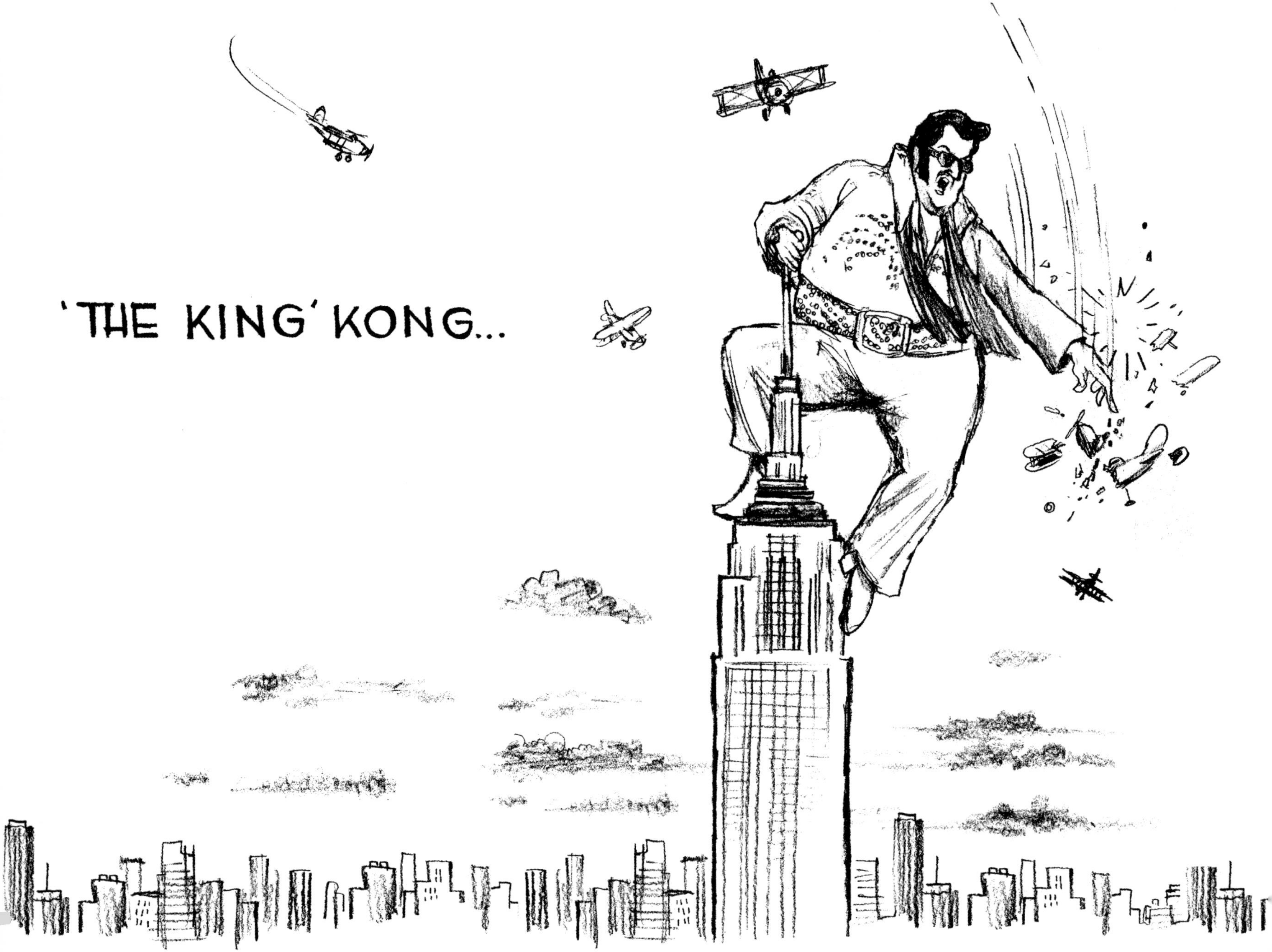
'THE KING' KONG...

SYLVESTER AND TWEETY

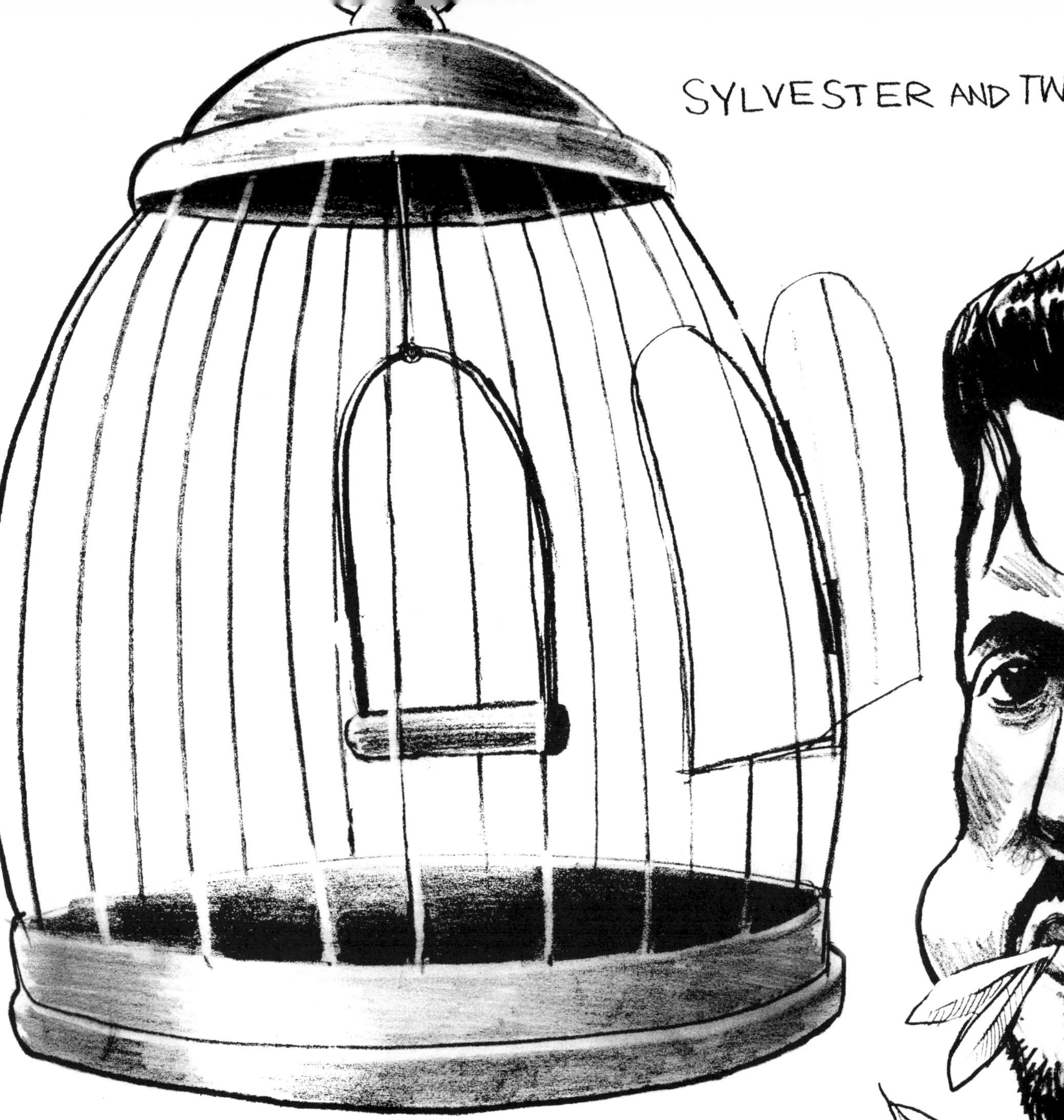

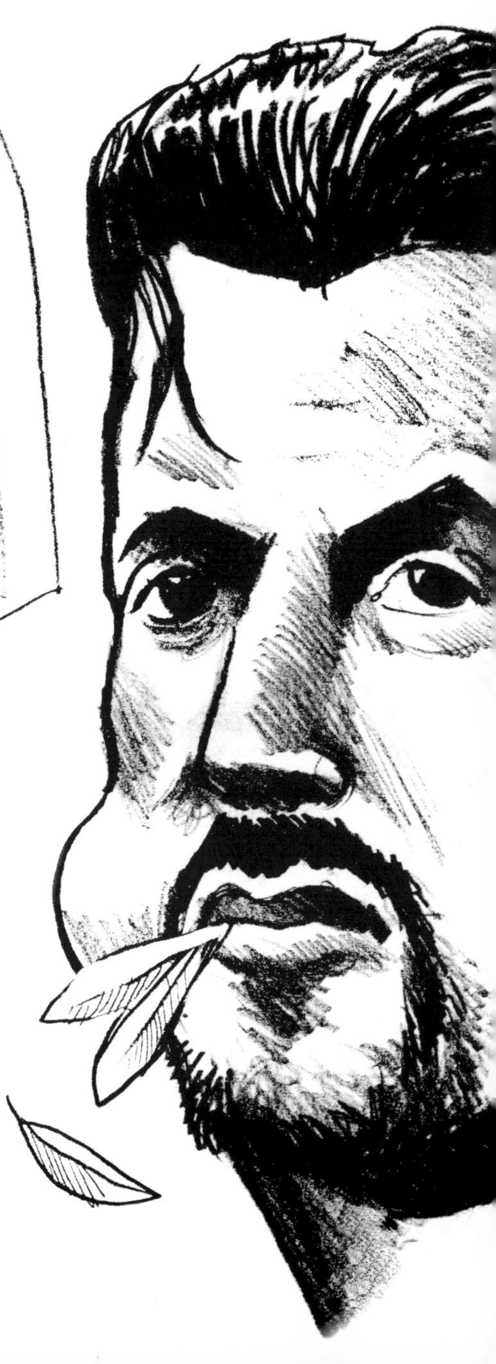

Sly's heyday was a little before my kids' time, but I've shown them all the Rambo movies except the last one (too violent), and all the Rocky movies except *Rocky V* (too lame).

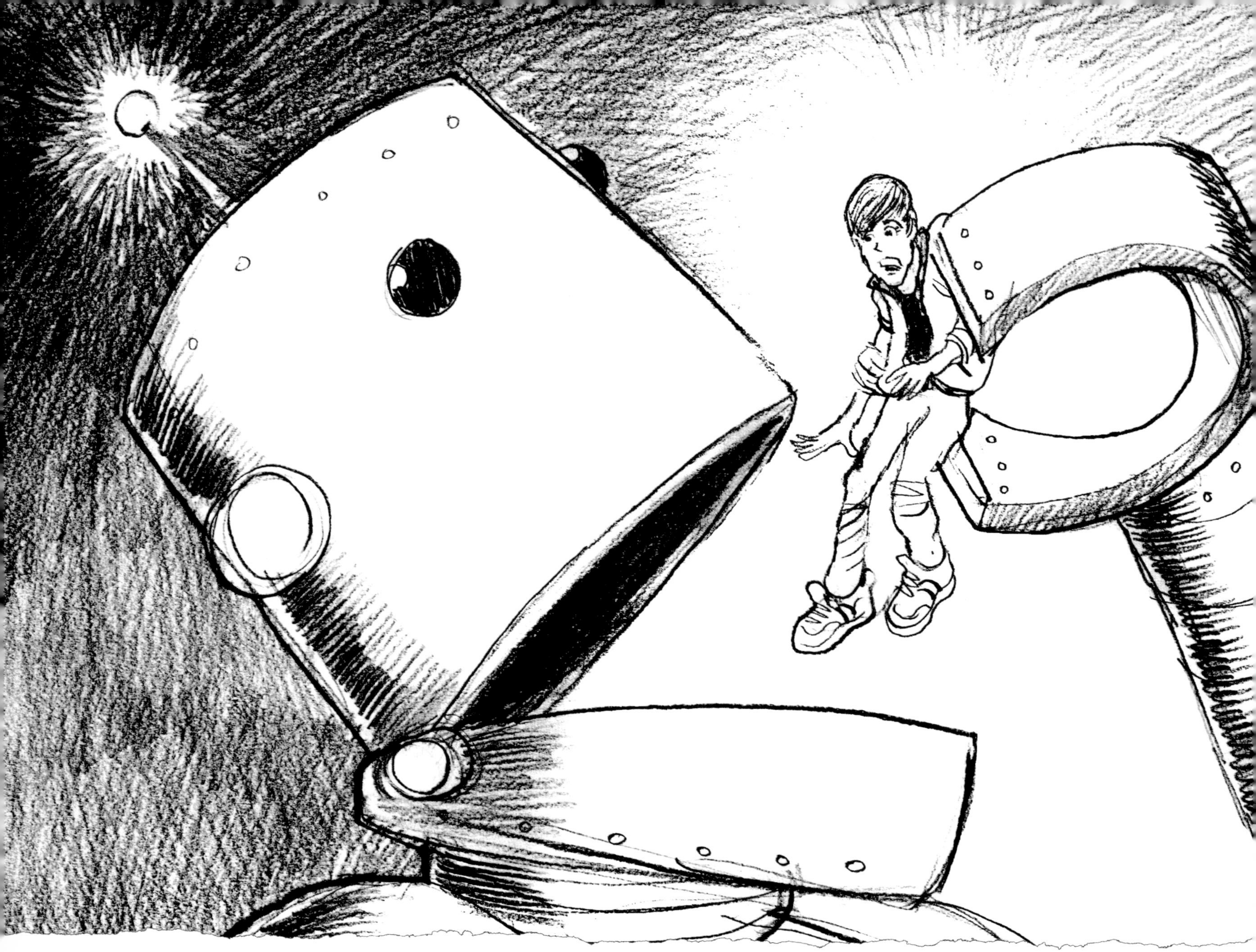

My boys say they don't like the Biebs, but I will sometimes catch them listening to his music. They requested this one a few years ago (notice the old hairstyle).

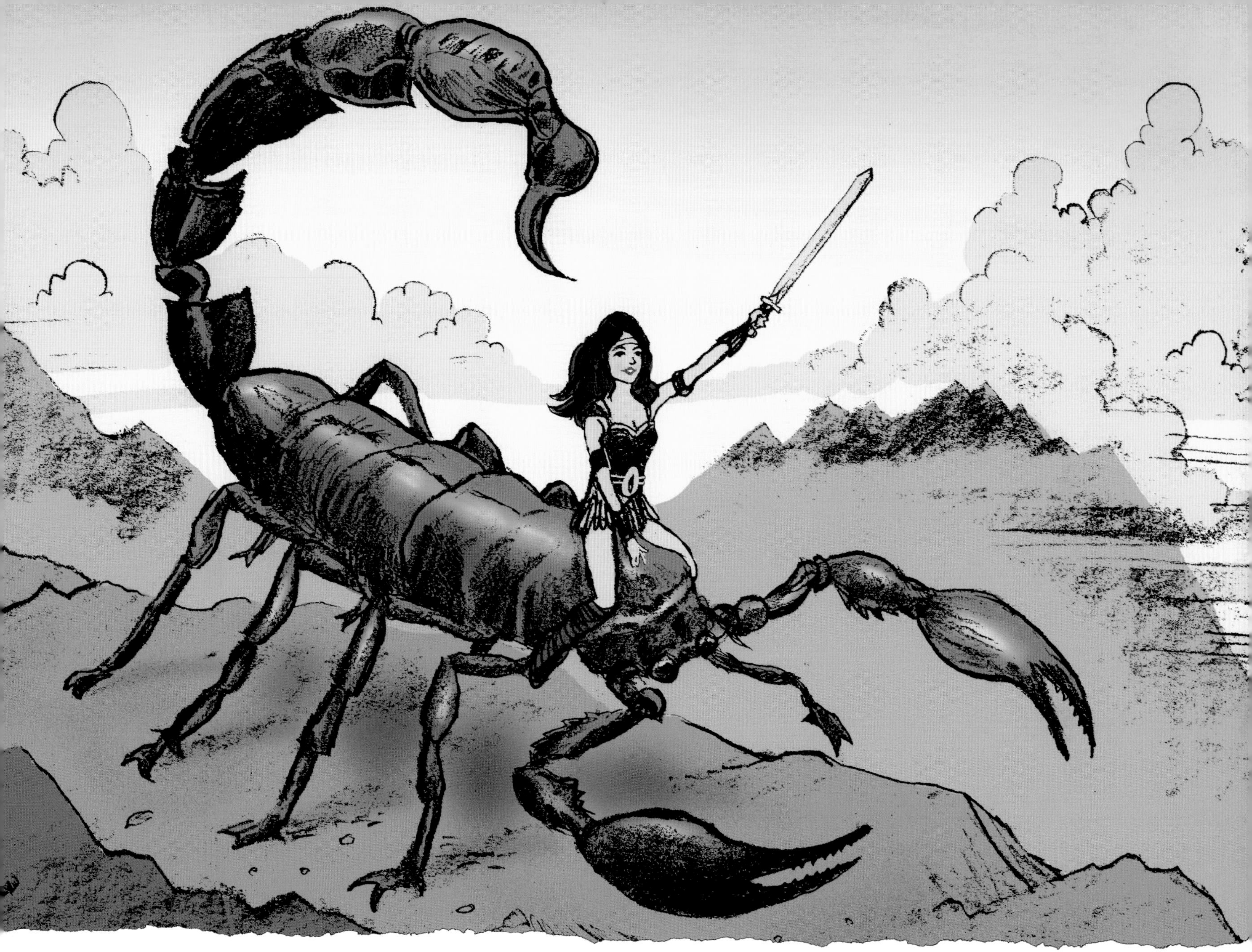

It's a testament to their affection for Selena that they
would request her drawn as a magnificent scorpion princess.

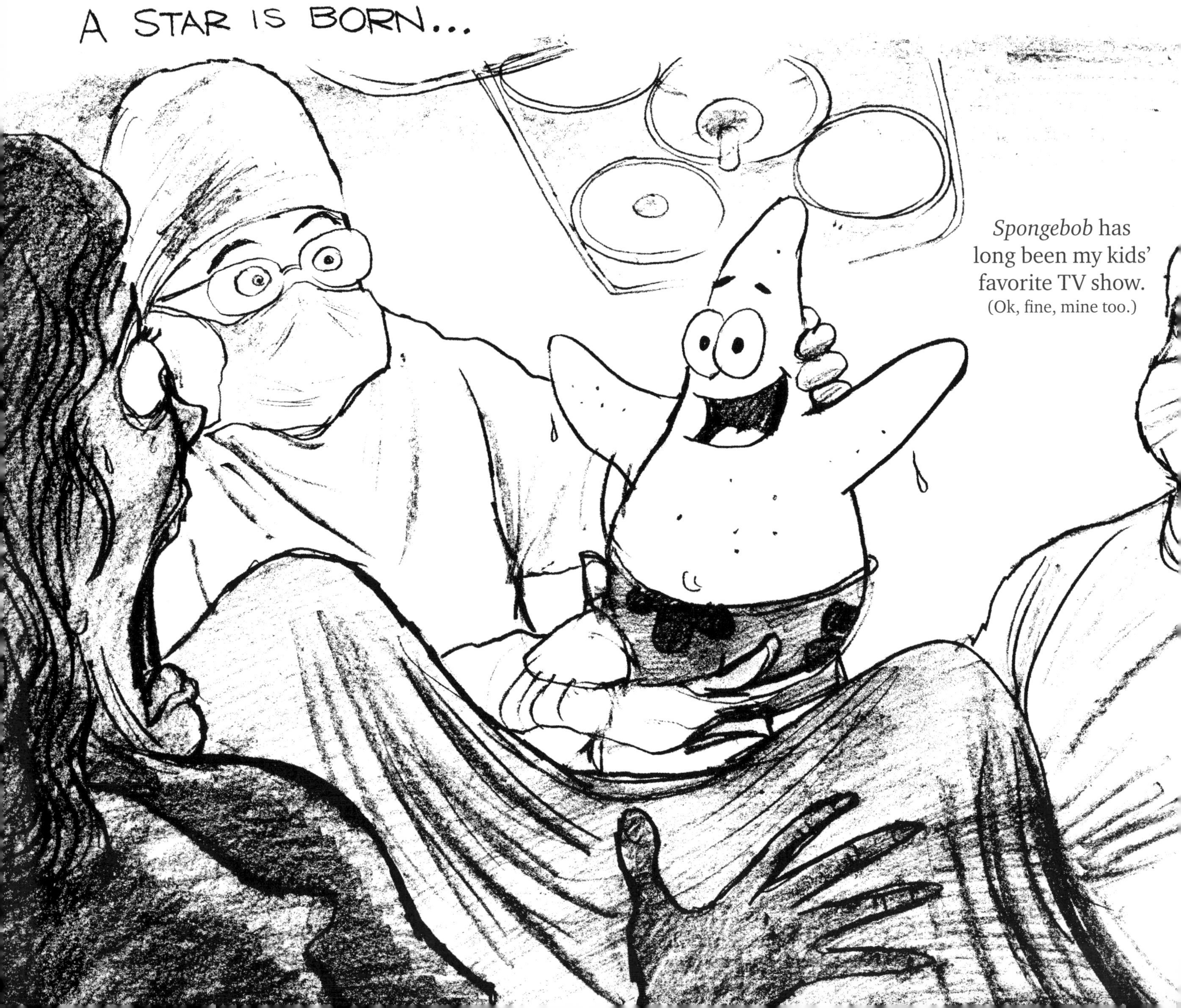
A STAR IS BORN...

Spongebob has long been my kids' favorite TV show.
(Ok, fine, mine too.)

ALIENS, ANIMALS & OTHER CREATURES

This chapter could easily have been a hundred pages long but we've narrowed it down a bit. Aliens are pretty simple to do: Basically, just draw a bald human with an eating disorder and incredibly dilated pupils. And like Napolean Dynamite sketching ligers ("a lion and a tiger mixed . . . bred for its skills and magic"), I too have always loved drawing strange animals doing weird stuff, and I've passed this love on to my kids. But when they tell me they want to be cartoonists, I make them write "I will chose a practical profession with a future" one hundred times.

CONTINENTAL BREAKFAST

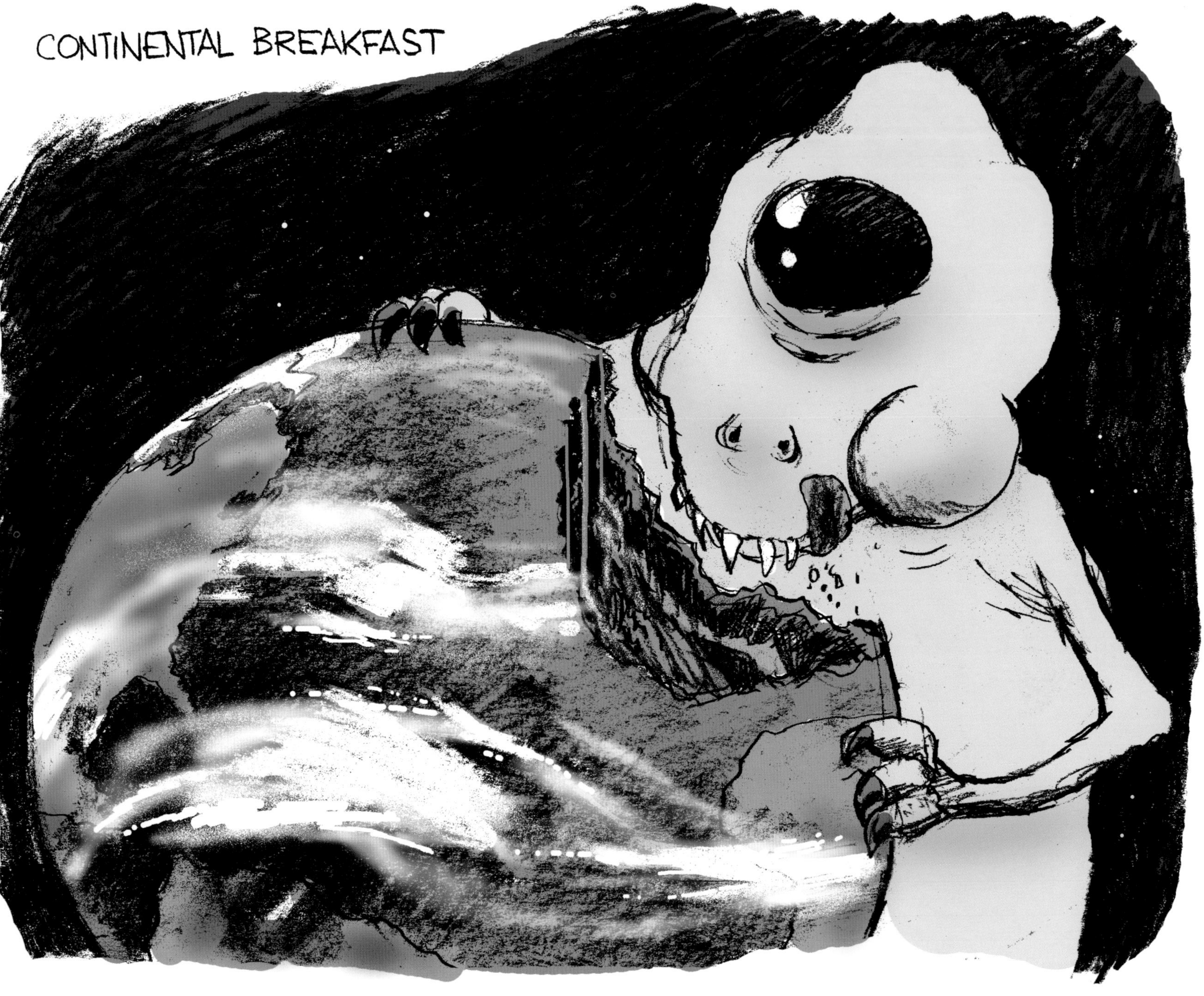

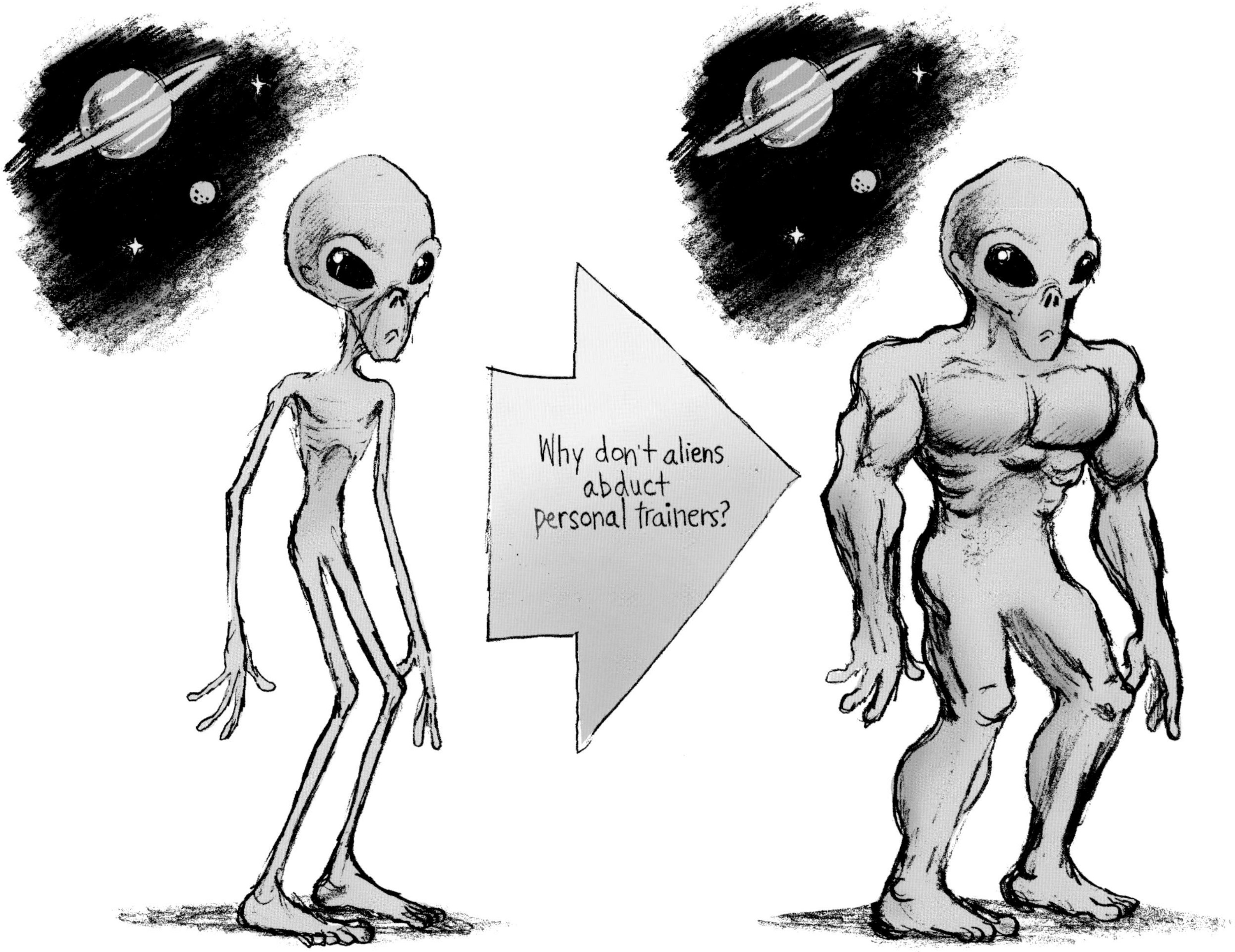
Why don't aliens abduct personal trainers?

You never see muscular aliens. Why is that?

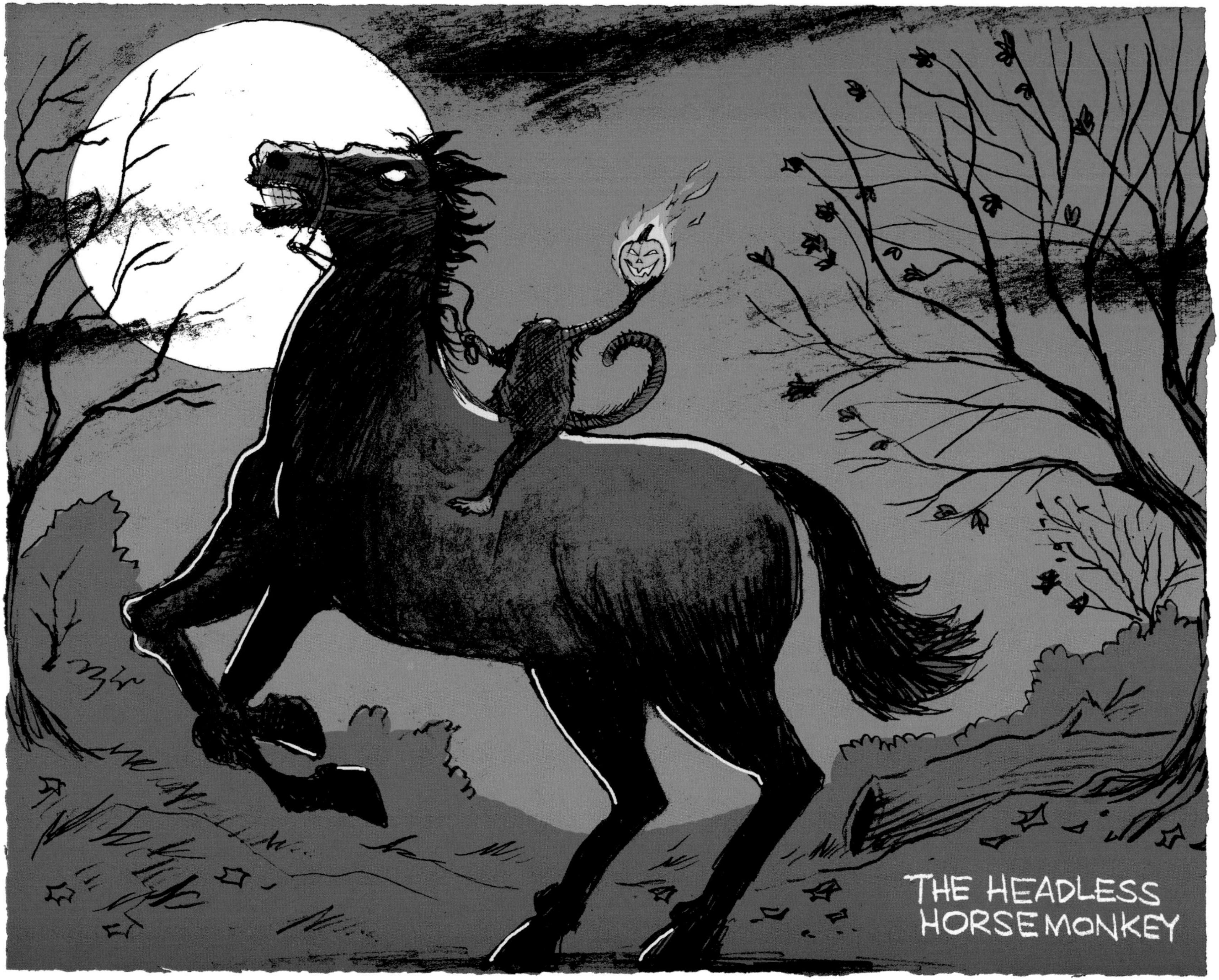
THE HEADLESS
HORSEMONKEY

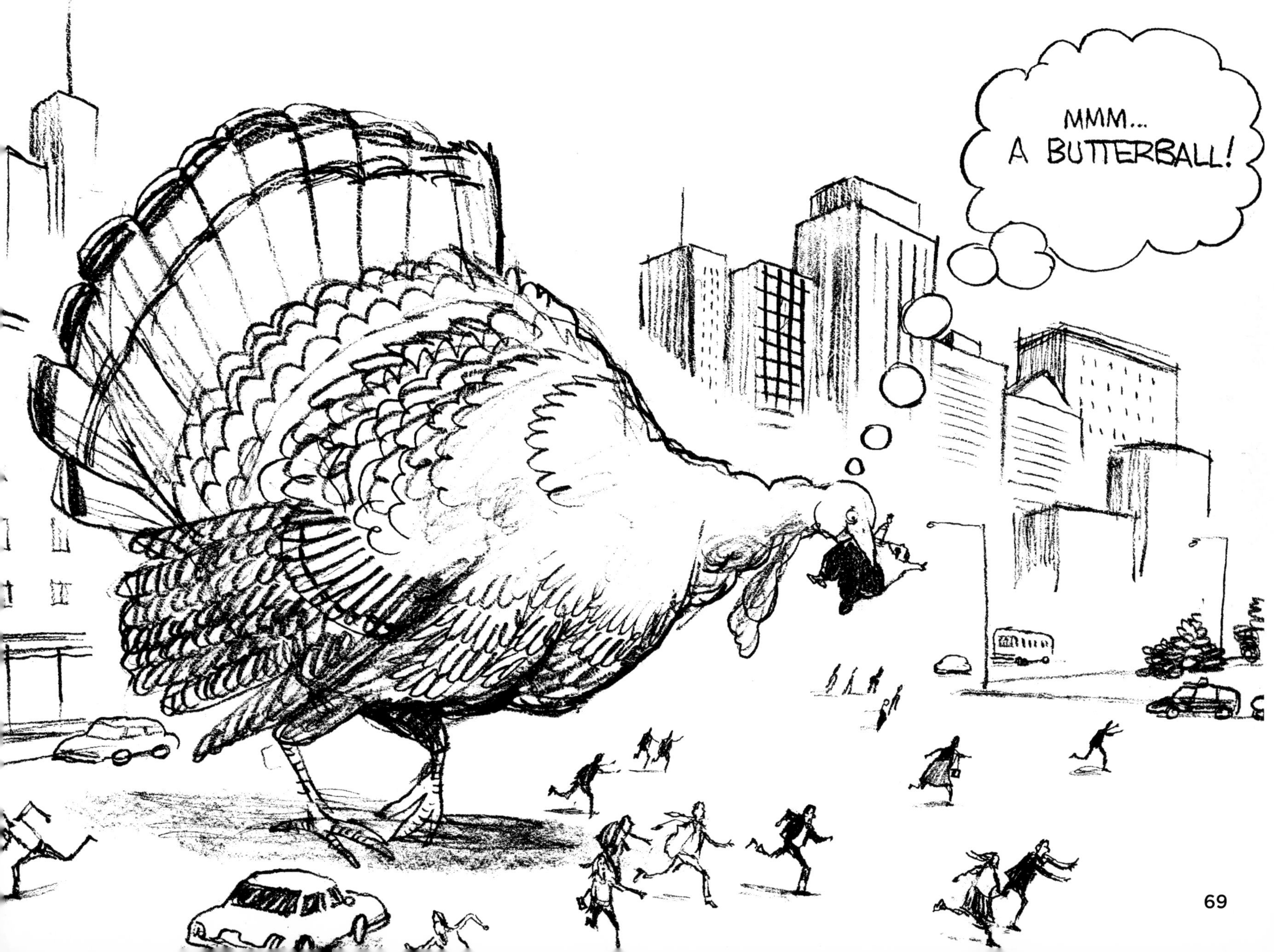
MMM...
A BUTTERBALL!

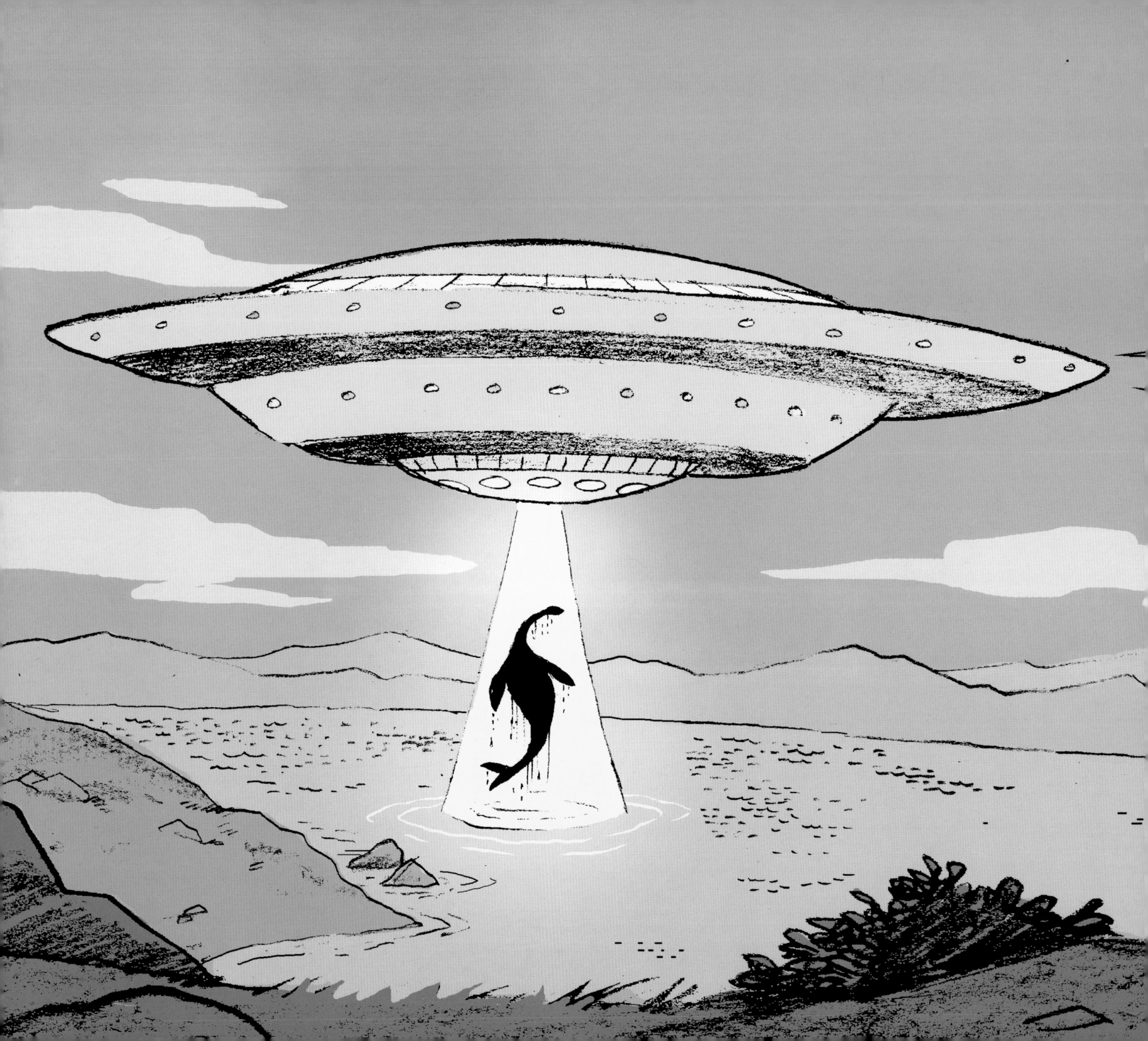

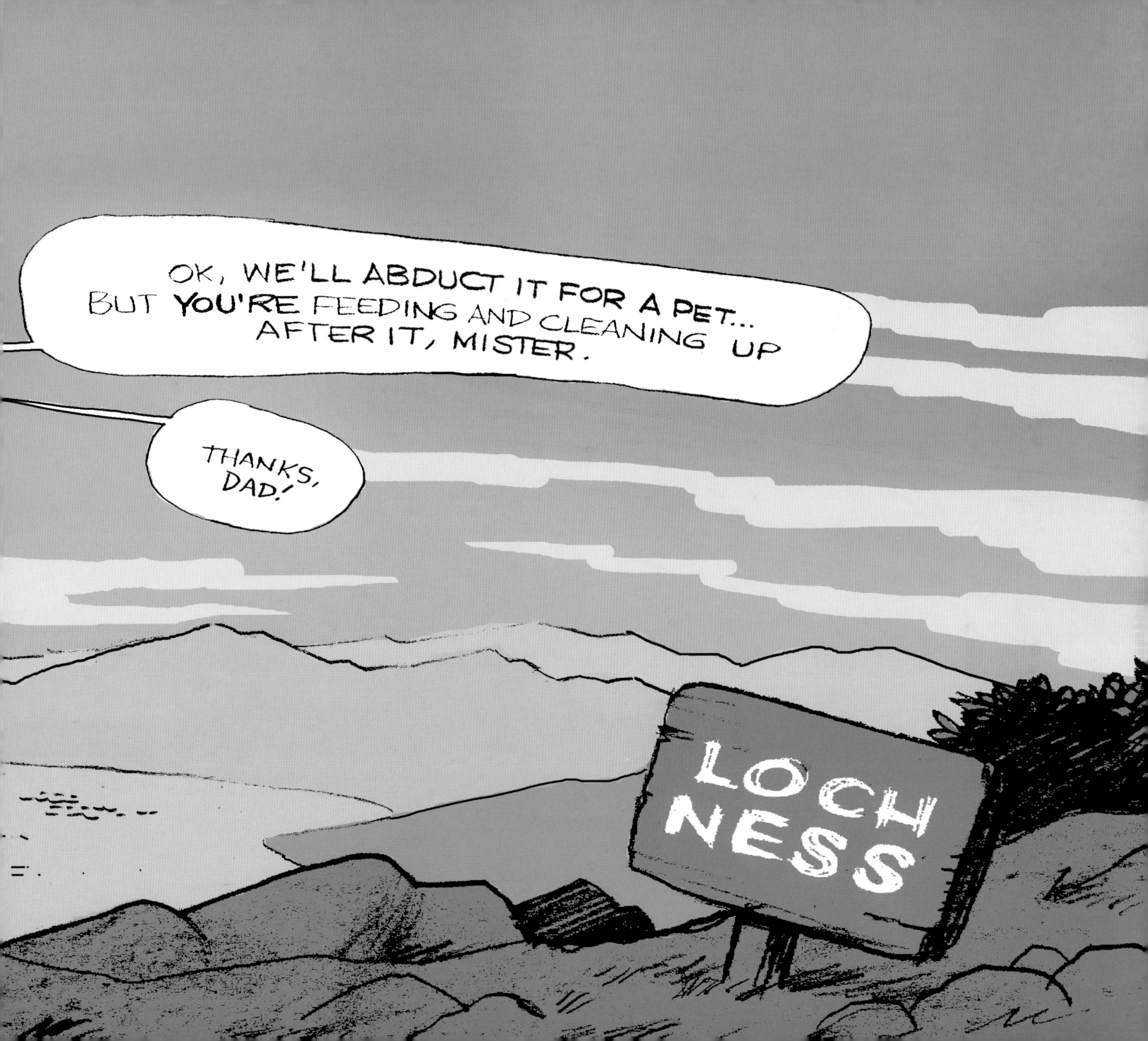
OK, WE'LL ABDUCT IT FOR A PET... BUT **YOU'RE** FEEDING AND CLEANING UP AFTER IT, MISTER.
THANKS, DAD!
LOCH NESS

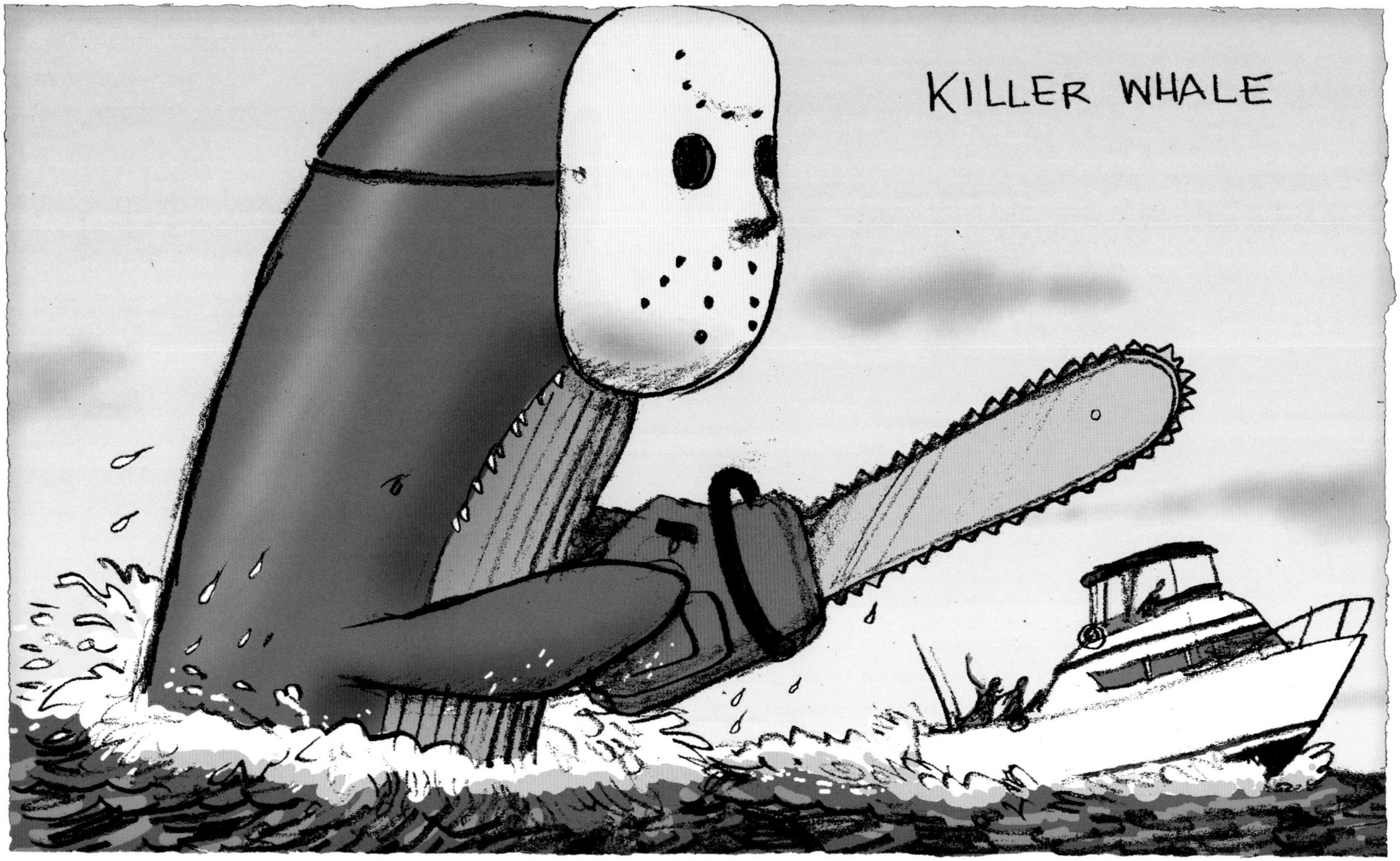
KILLER WHALE

CENTAUR CLAUS IS COMING TO TOWN!

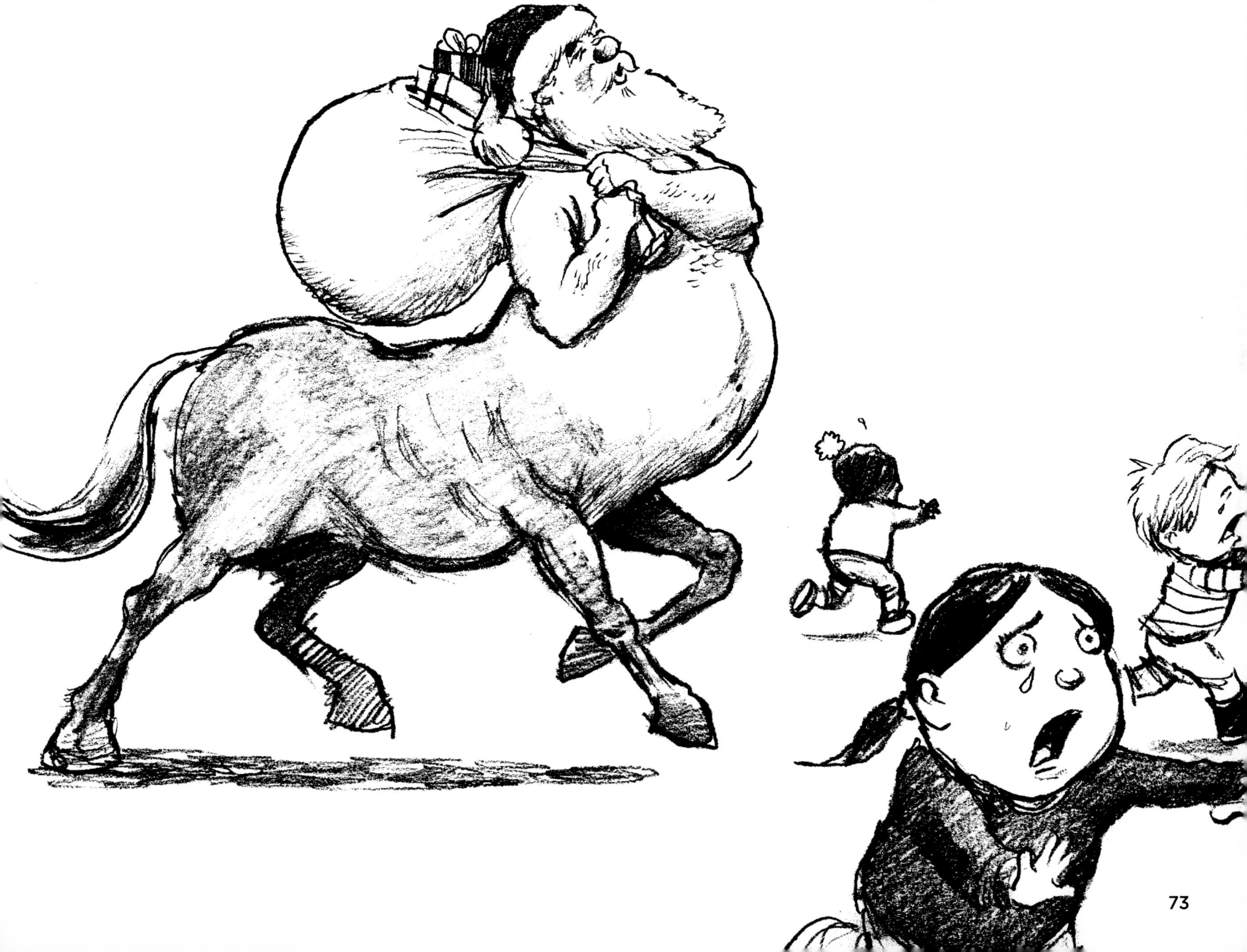

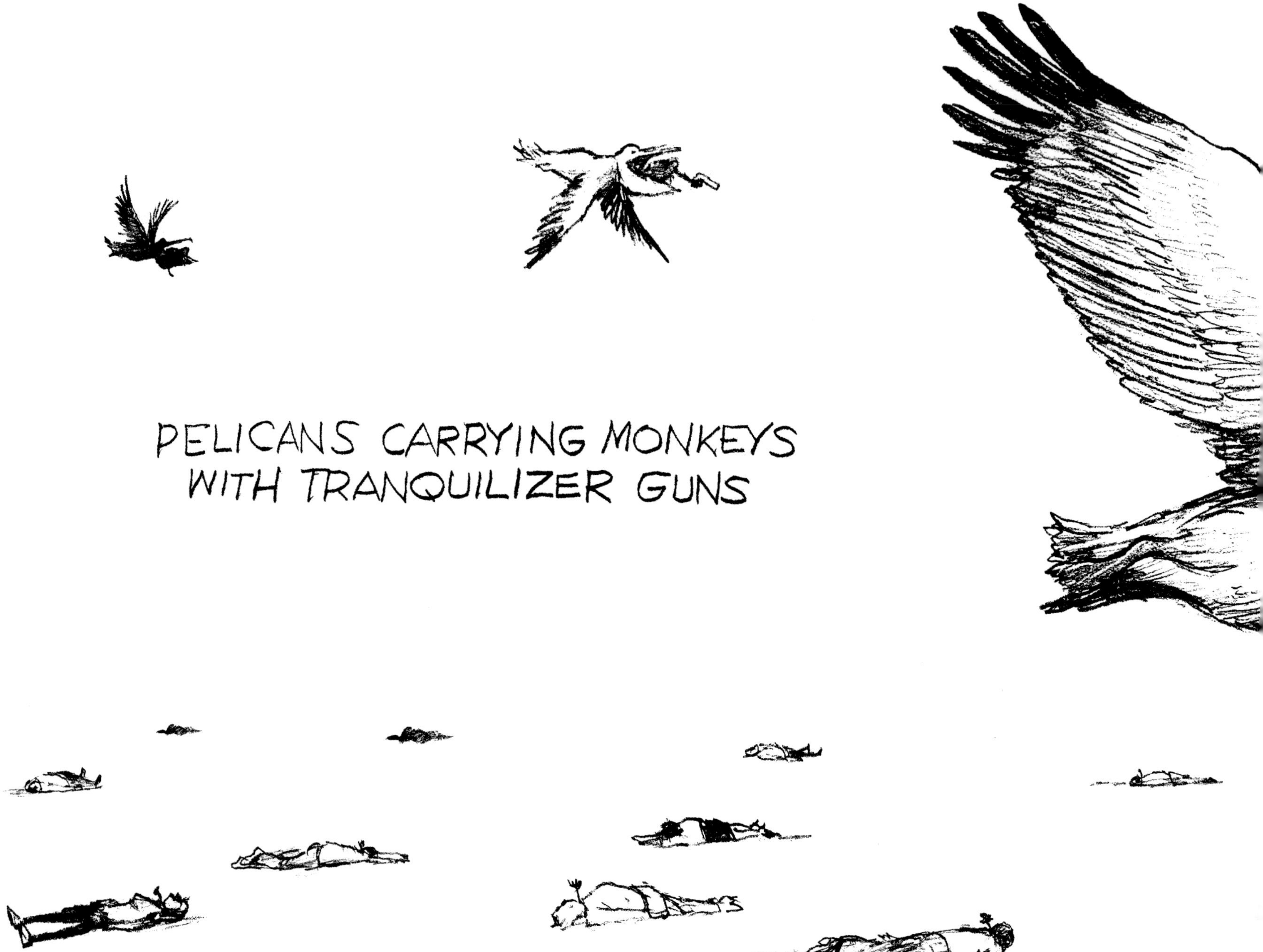
PELICANS CARRYING MONKEYS WITH TRANQUILIZER GUNS

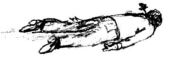

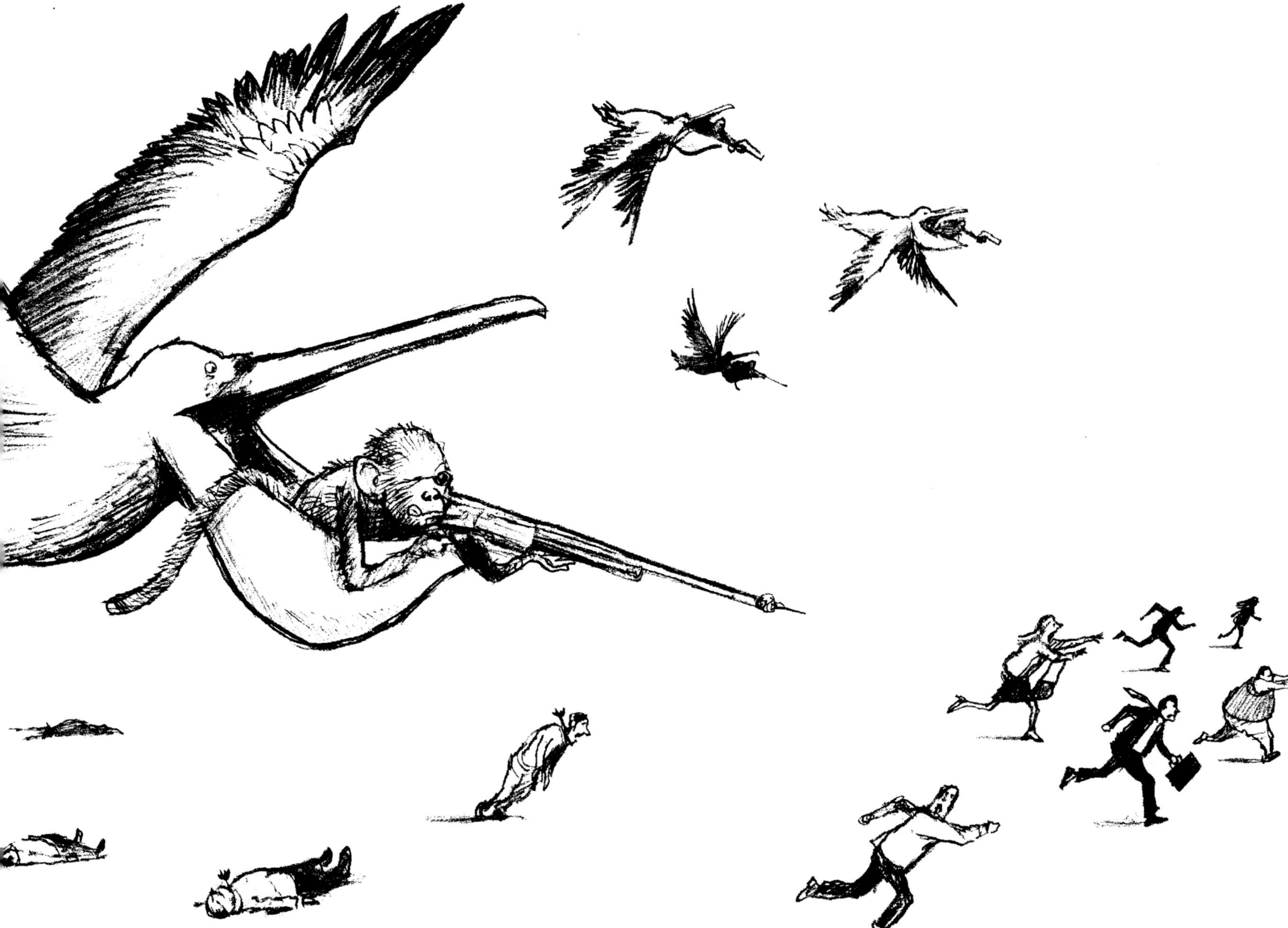

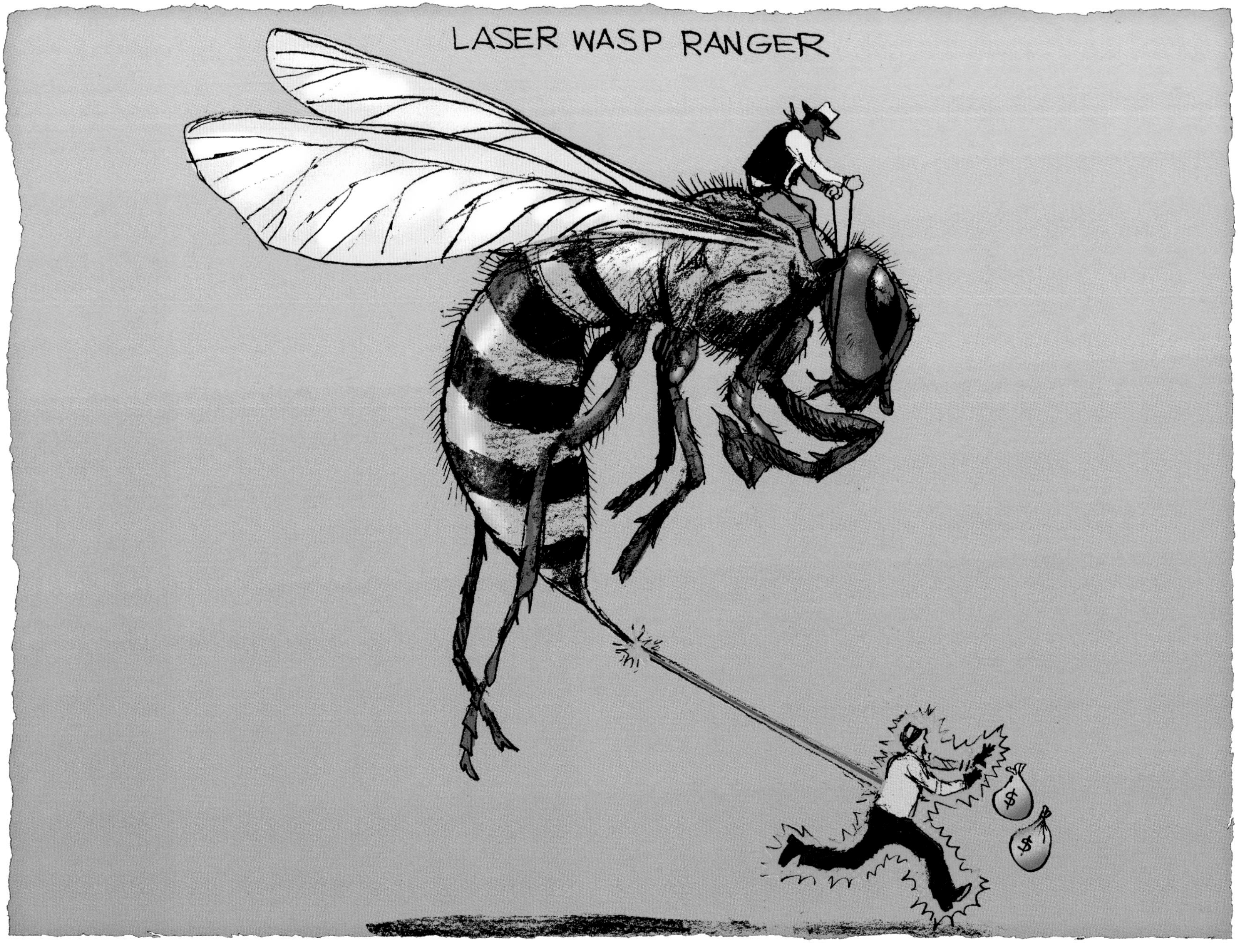
LASER WASP RANGER

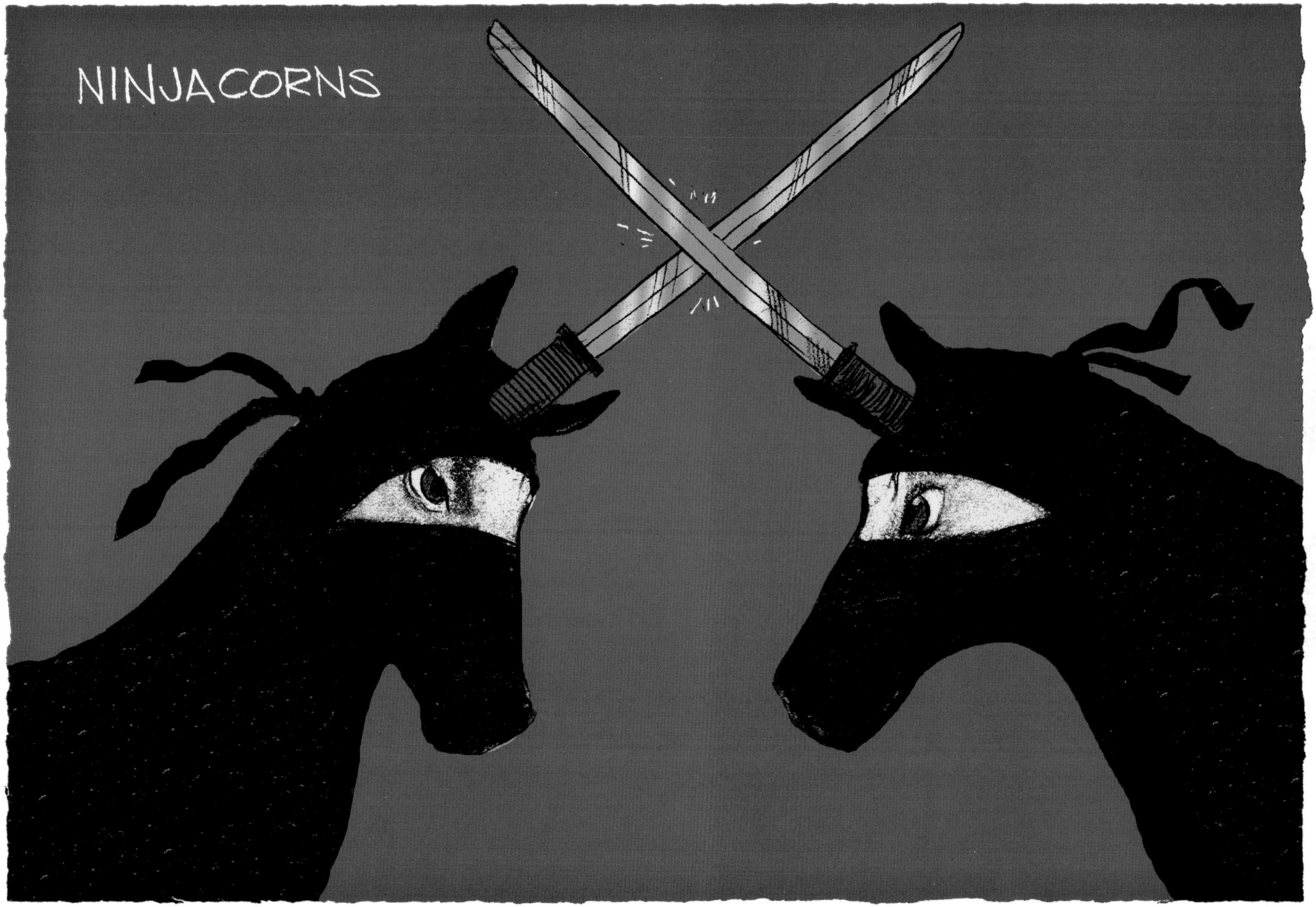
NINJACORNS

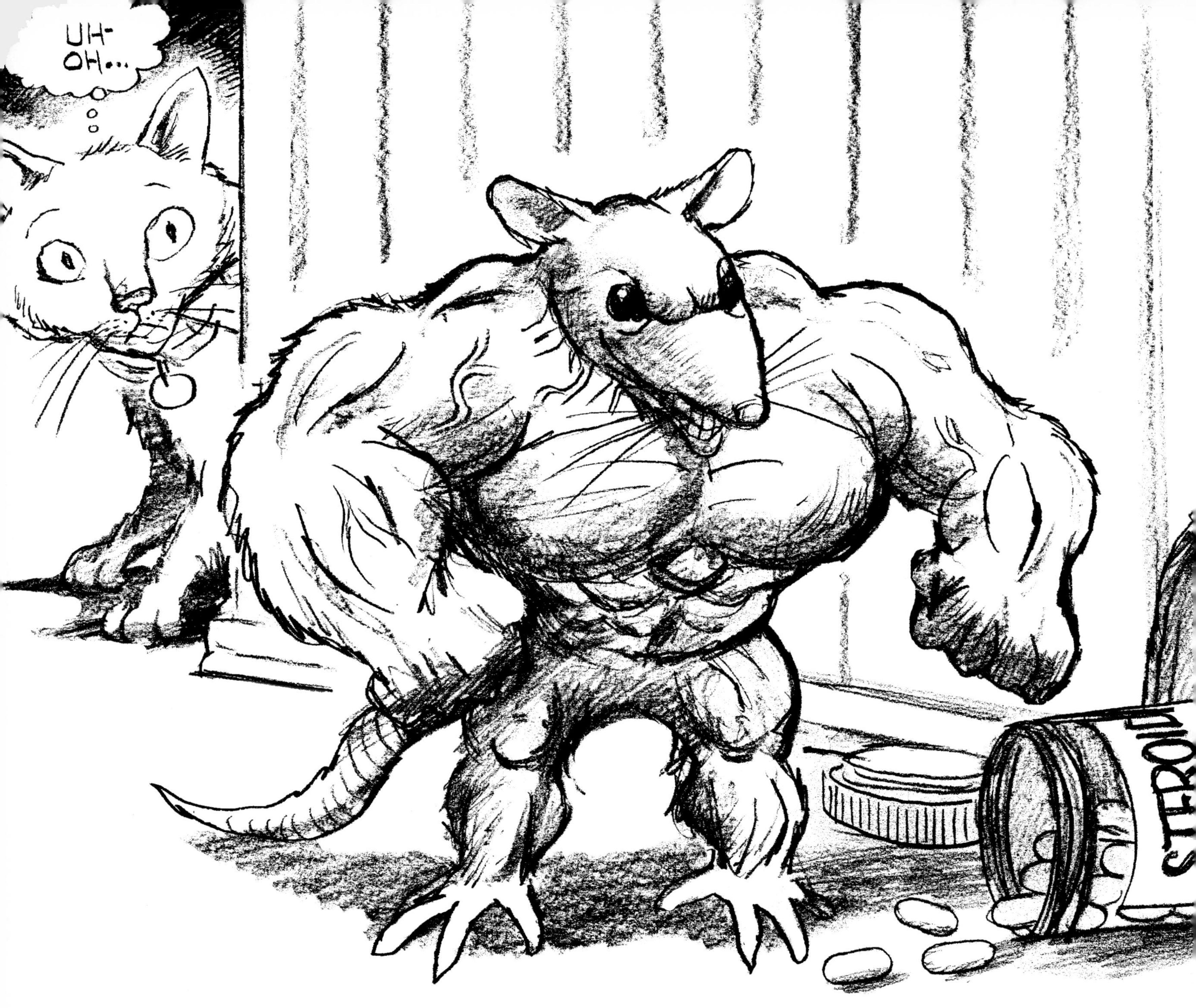
UH-OH...
STEROID

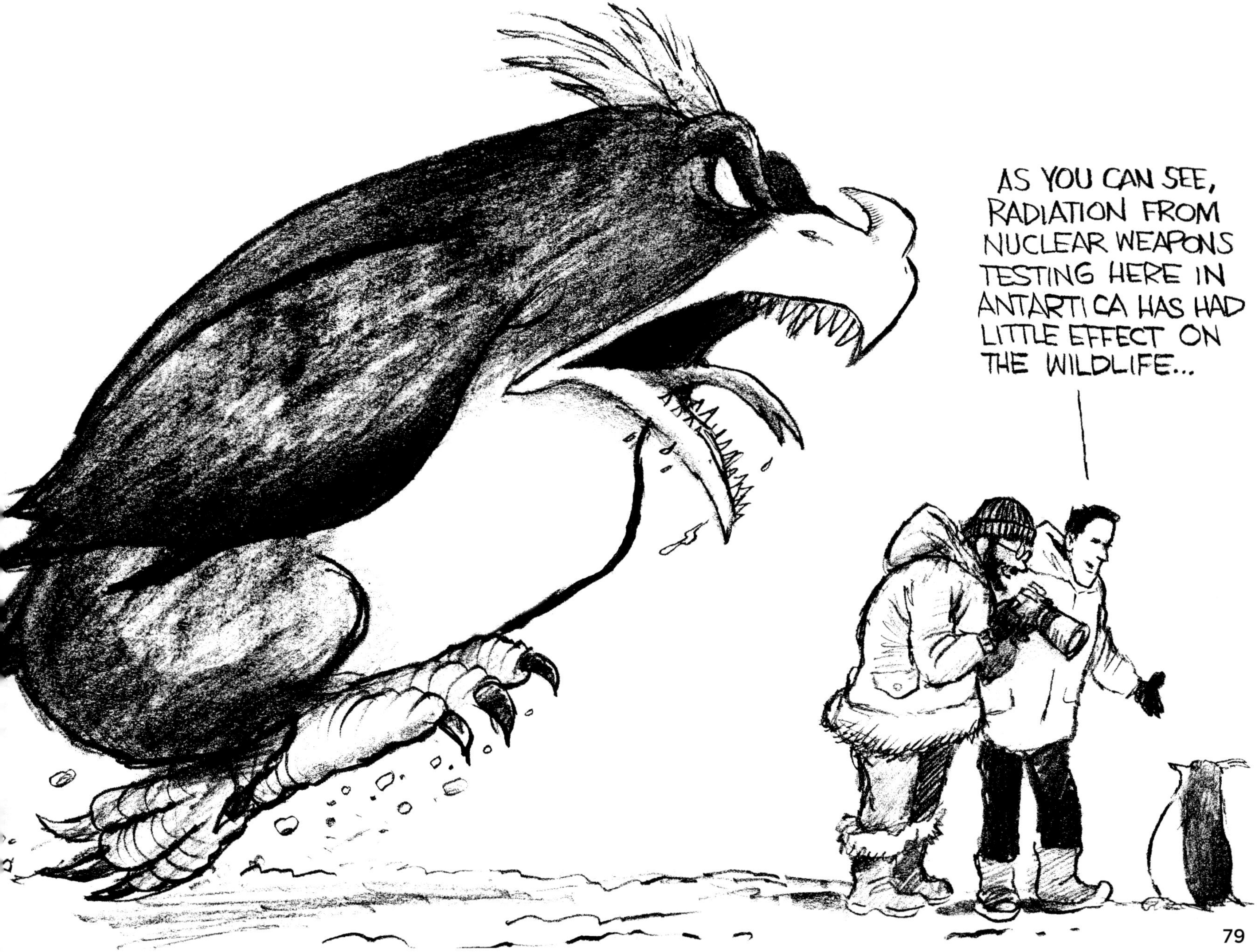
AS YOU CAN SEE, RADIATION FROM NUCLEAR WEAPONS TESTING HERE IN ANTARTICA HAS HAD LITTLE EFFECT ON THE WILDLIFE...

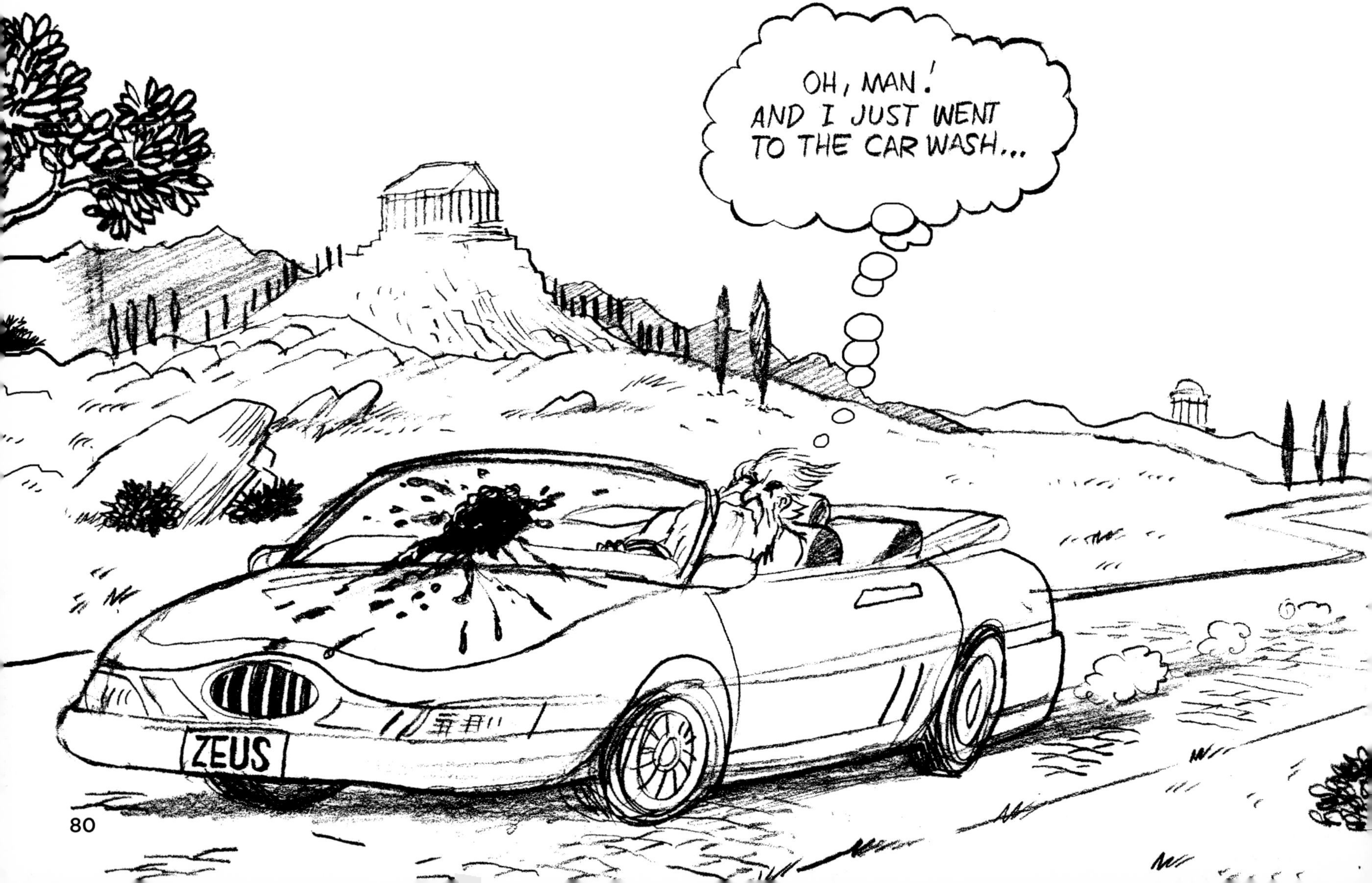
OH, MAN!
AND I JUST WENT
TO THE CAR WASH...
ZEUS

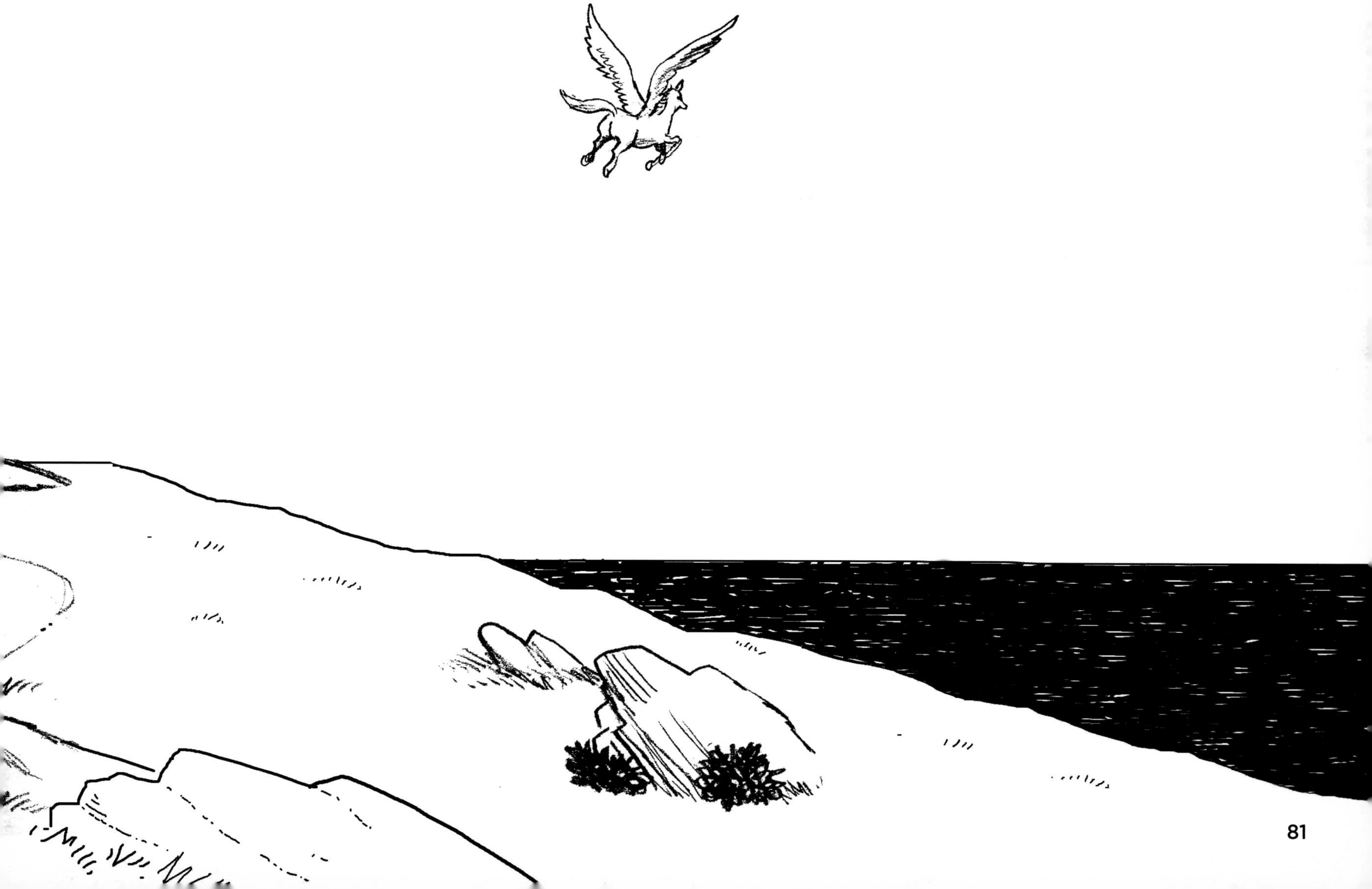

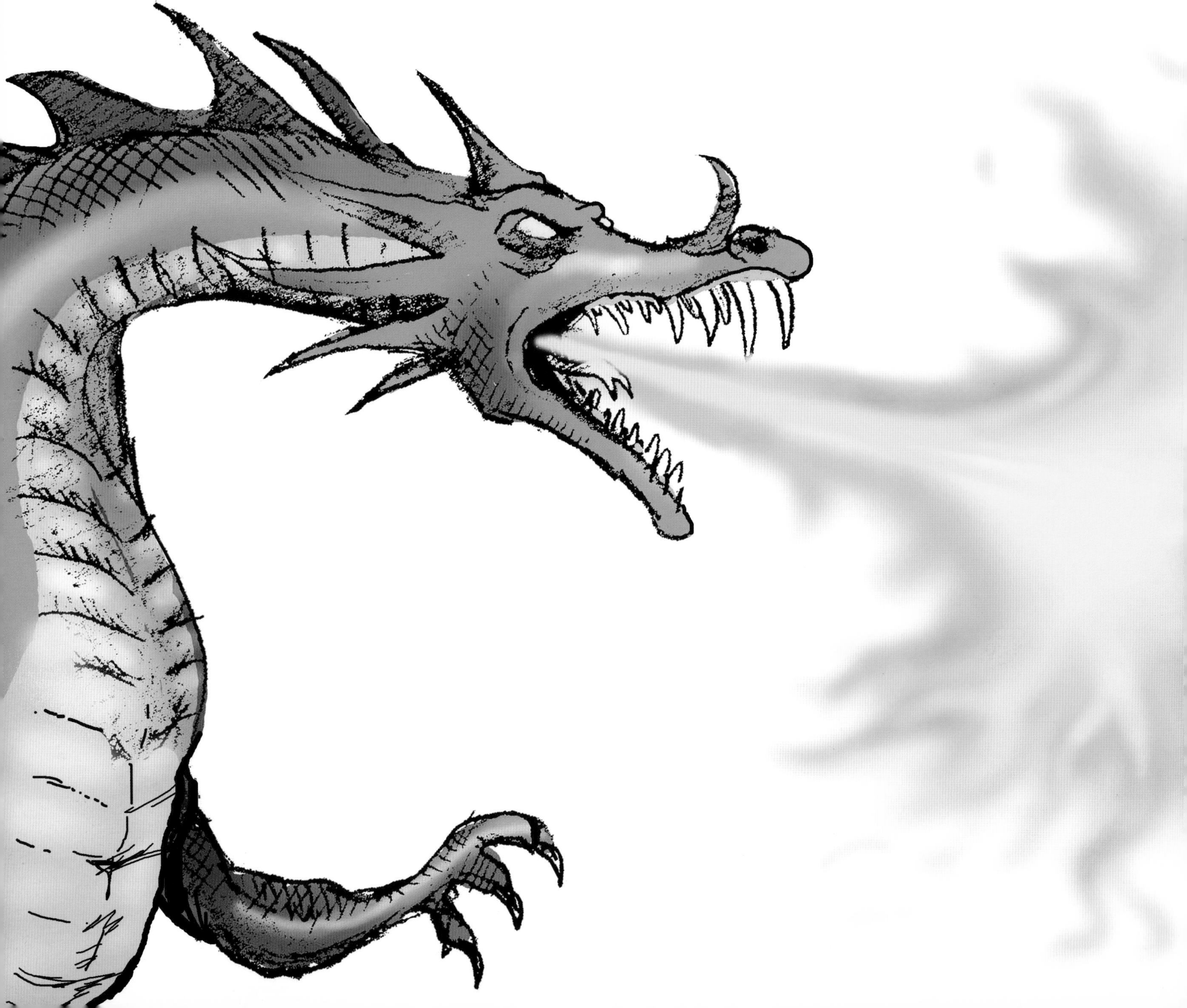

One of my personal favorites.

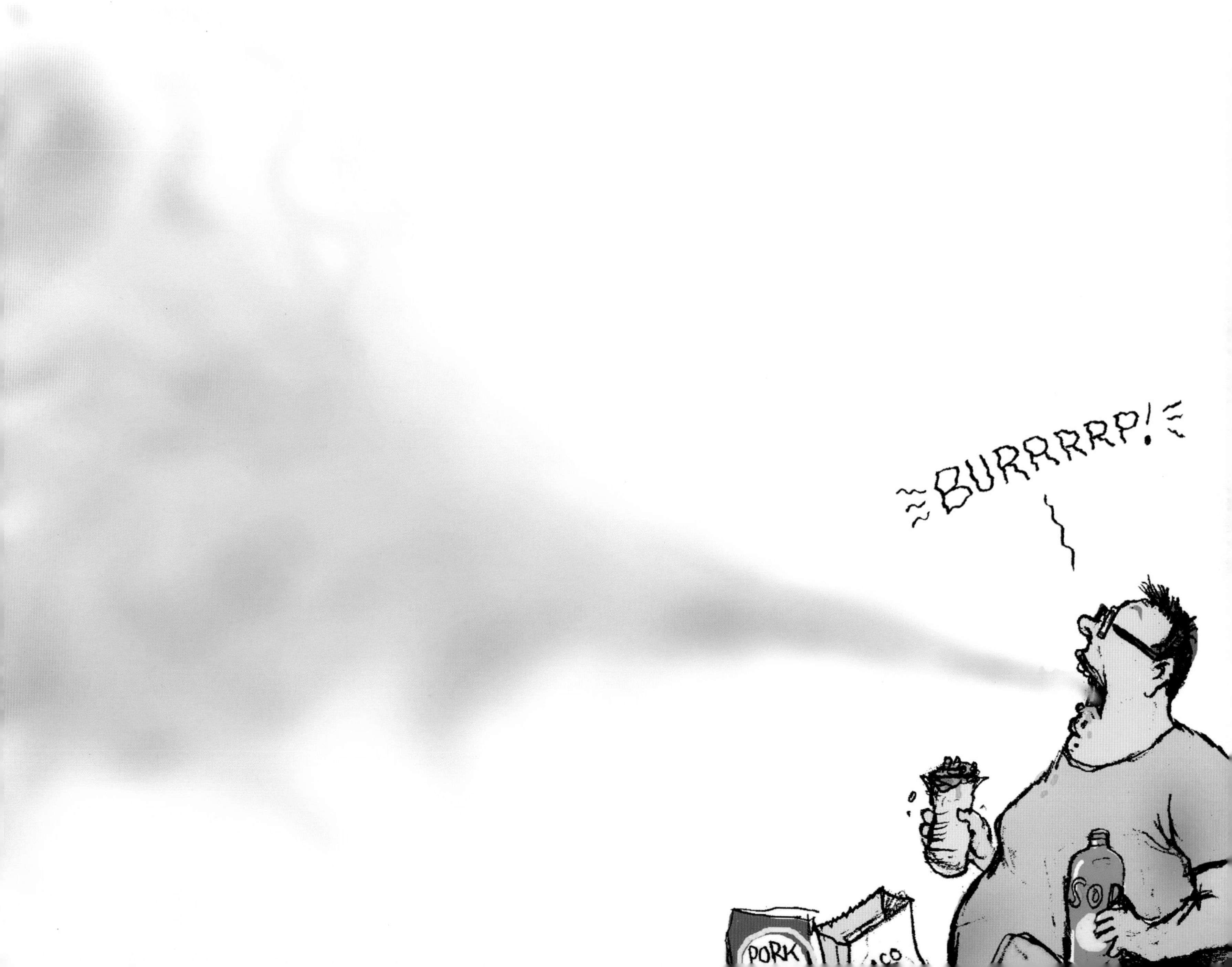
BURRRRP!
PORK

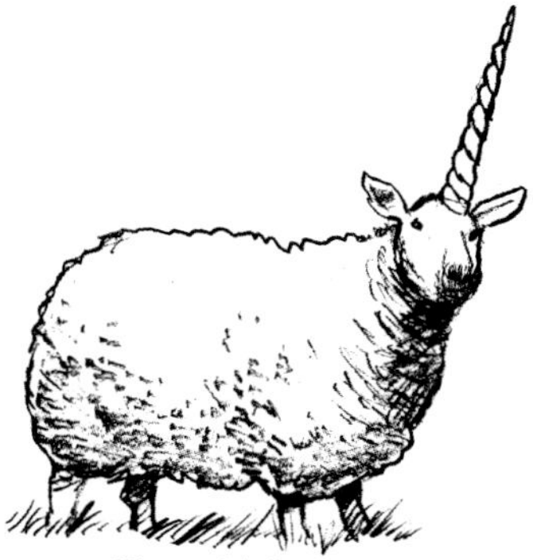

EWE-NICORN

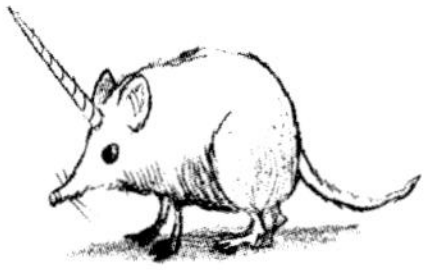

SHREW-NICORN

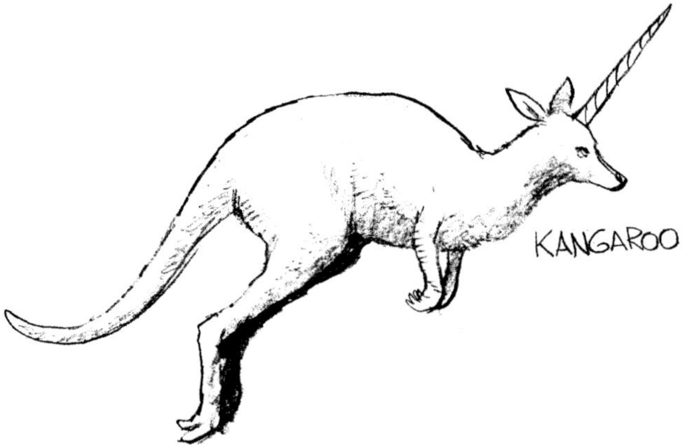

KANGAROO-NICORN

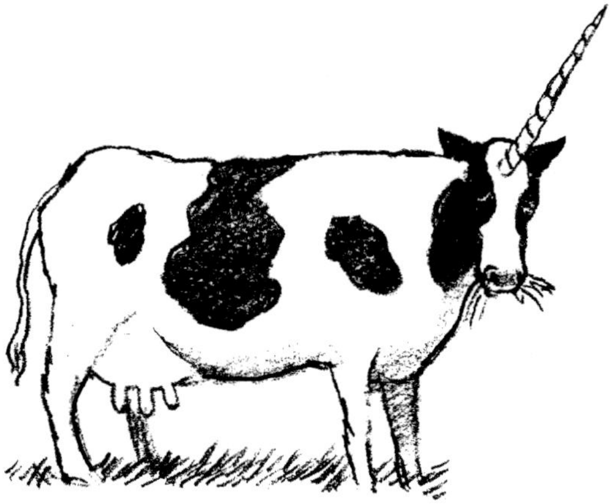

MOO-NICORN

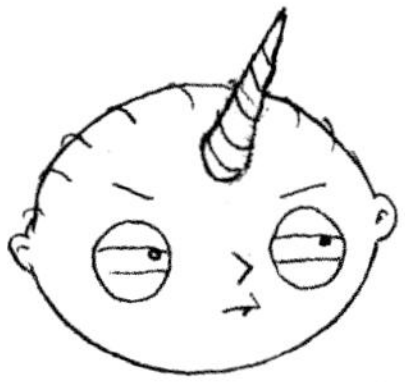

STEW-NICORN

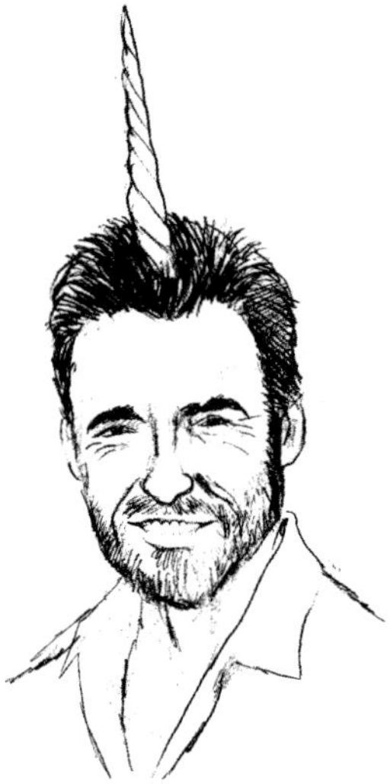

HUGH-NICORN

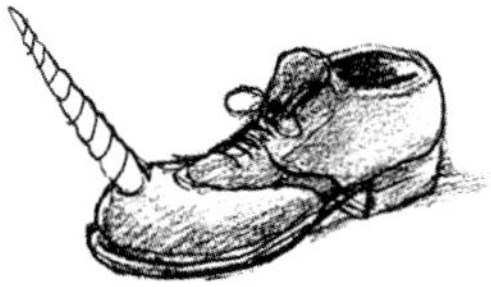

SHOE-NICORN

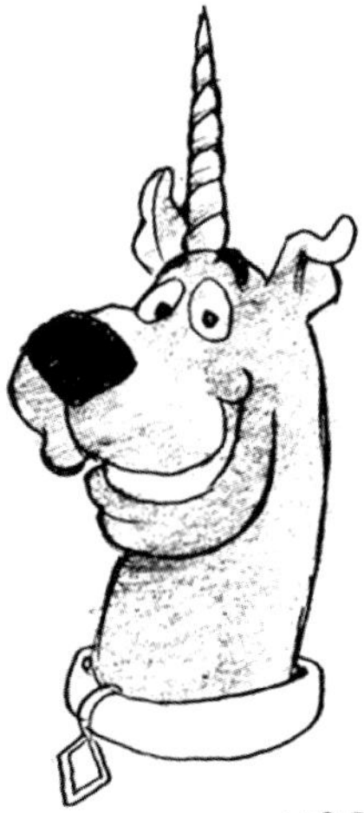

SCOOBY DOO-NICORN

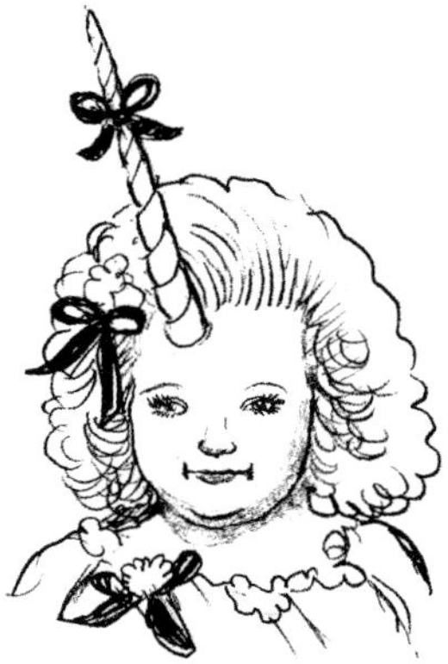

HONEY BOO-BOO-NICORN

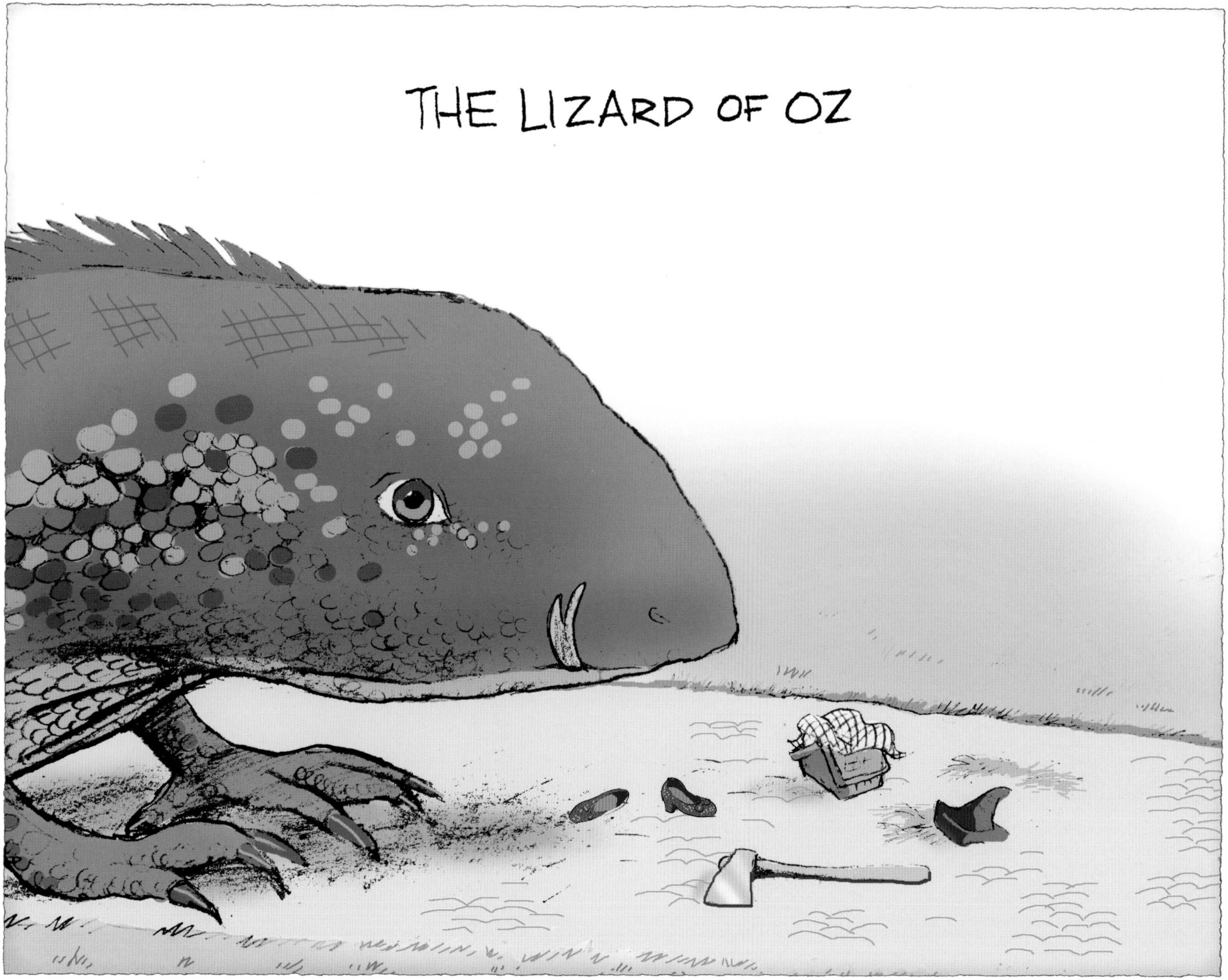
THE LIZARD OF OZ

THE TERMINGATOR

NINJAPUS

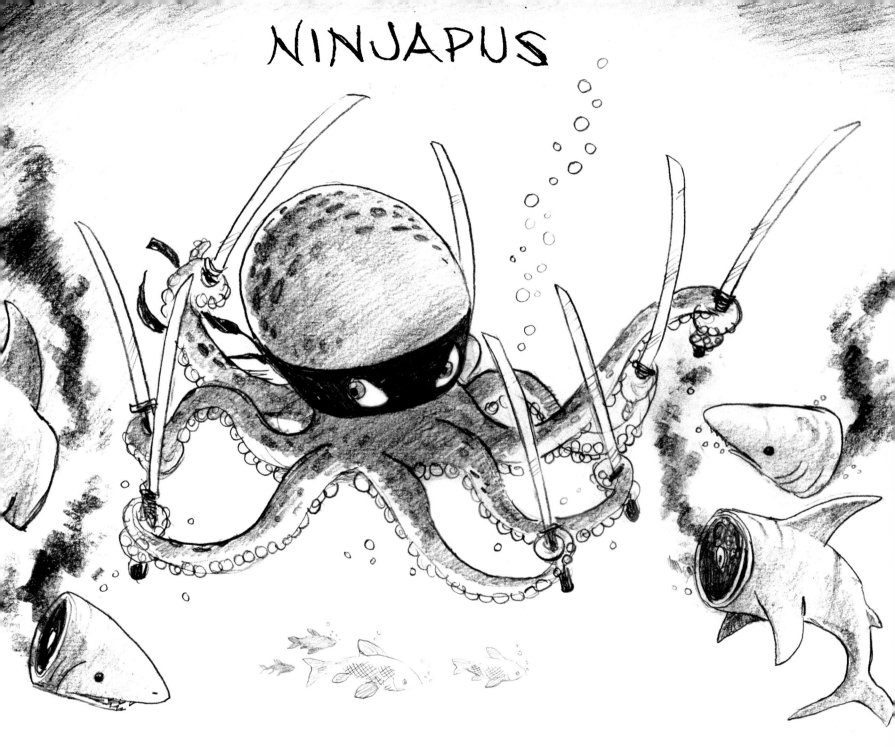

One of my earliest drawings for the boys.

LEGEND OF THE HAMURAI

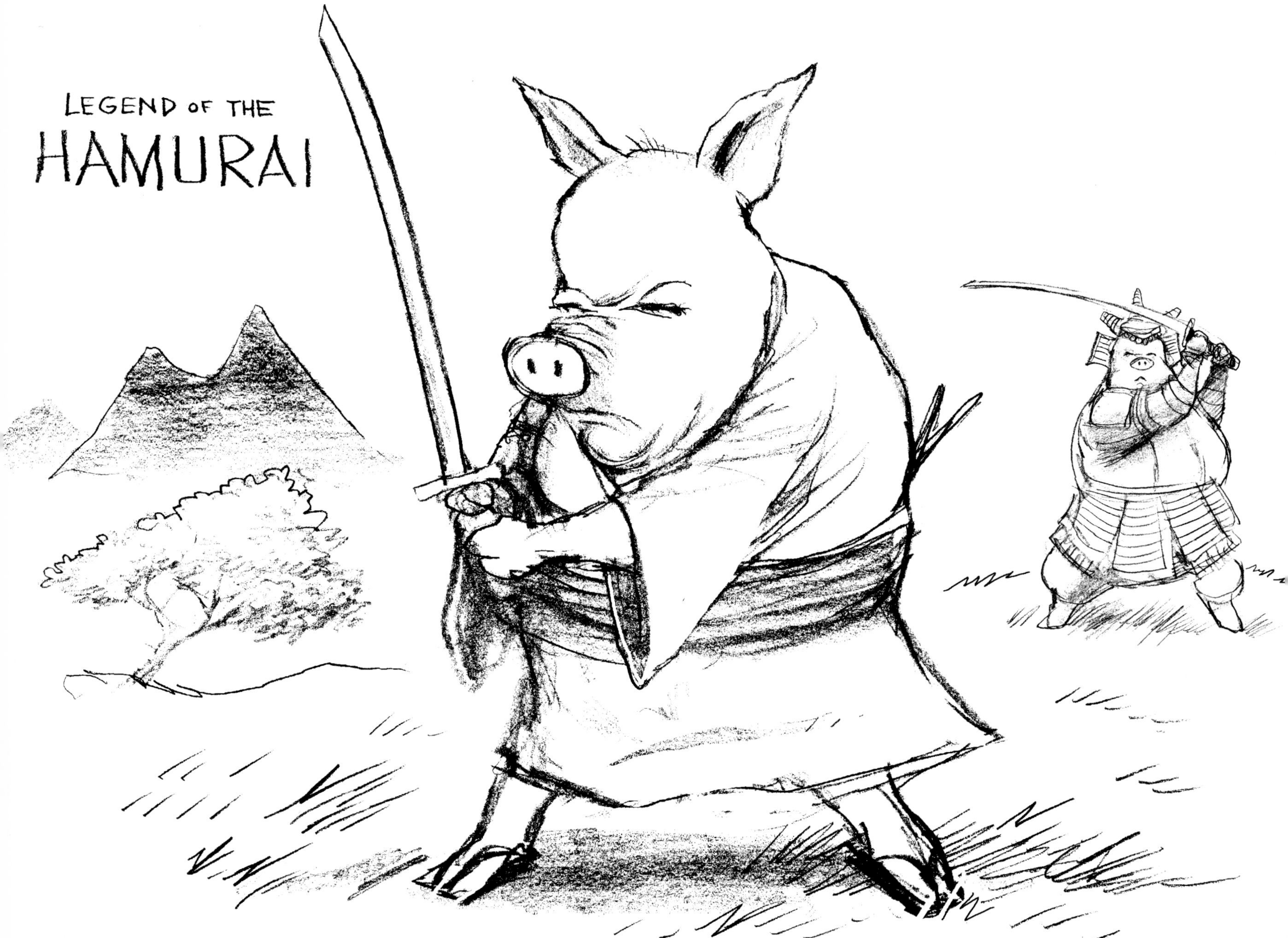

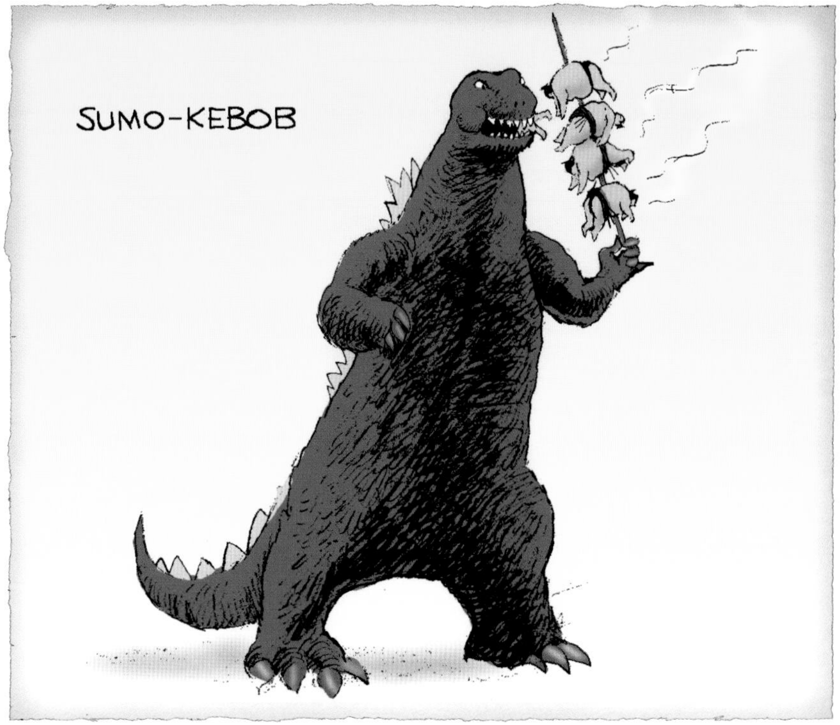
SUMO-KEBOB

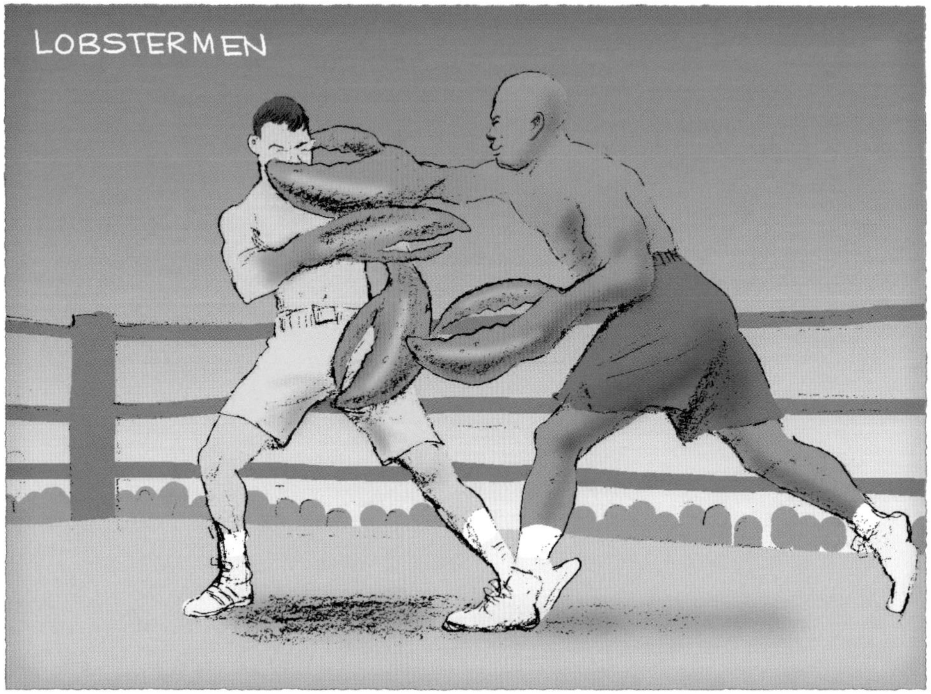
LOBSTERMEN

Genetic engineering could have such an impact on the world of sports and entertainment. Imagine human-canary hybrids competing on *The Voice*. Think of the ratings!

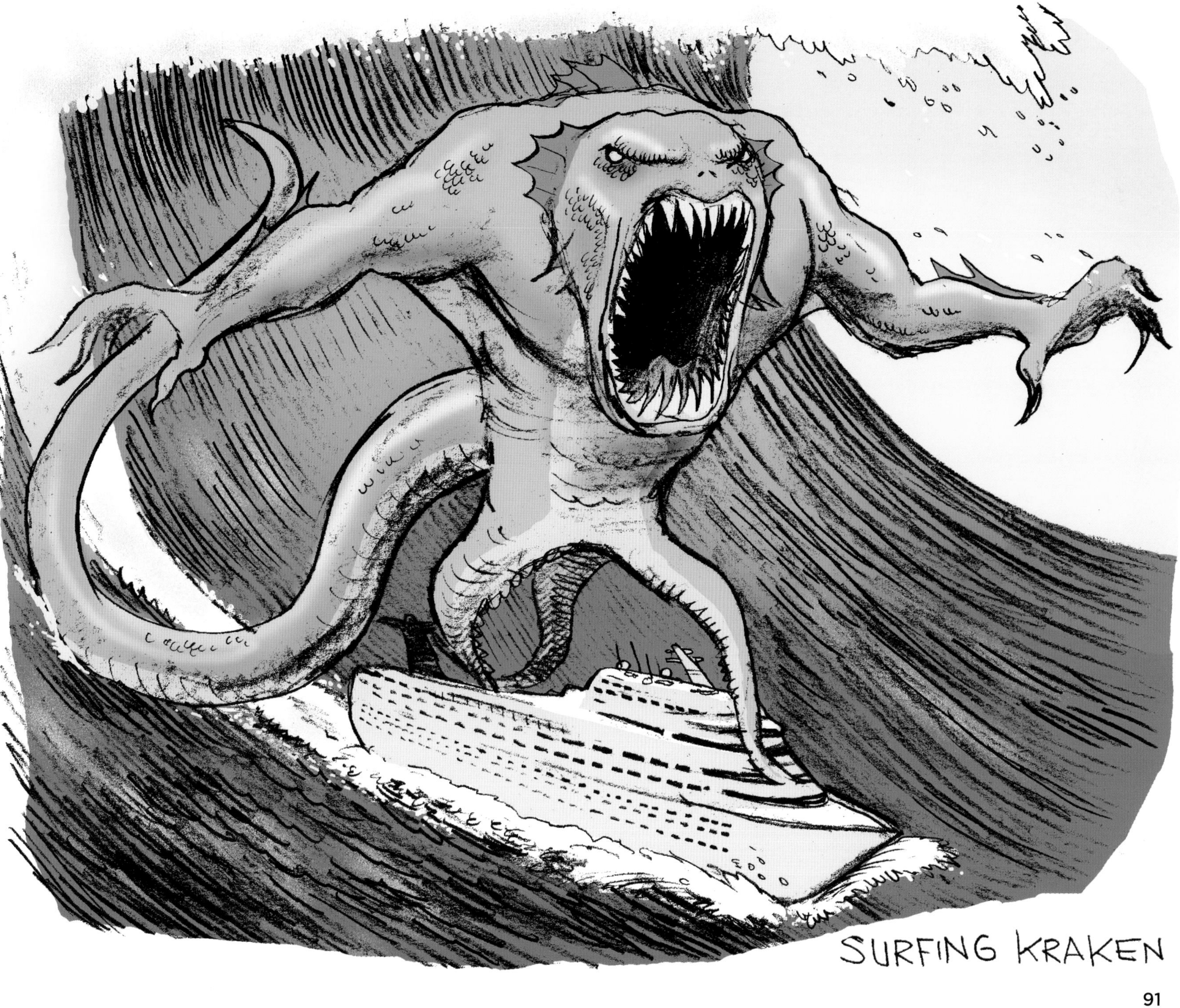

SURFING KRAKEN

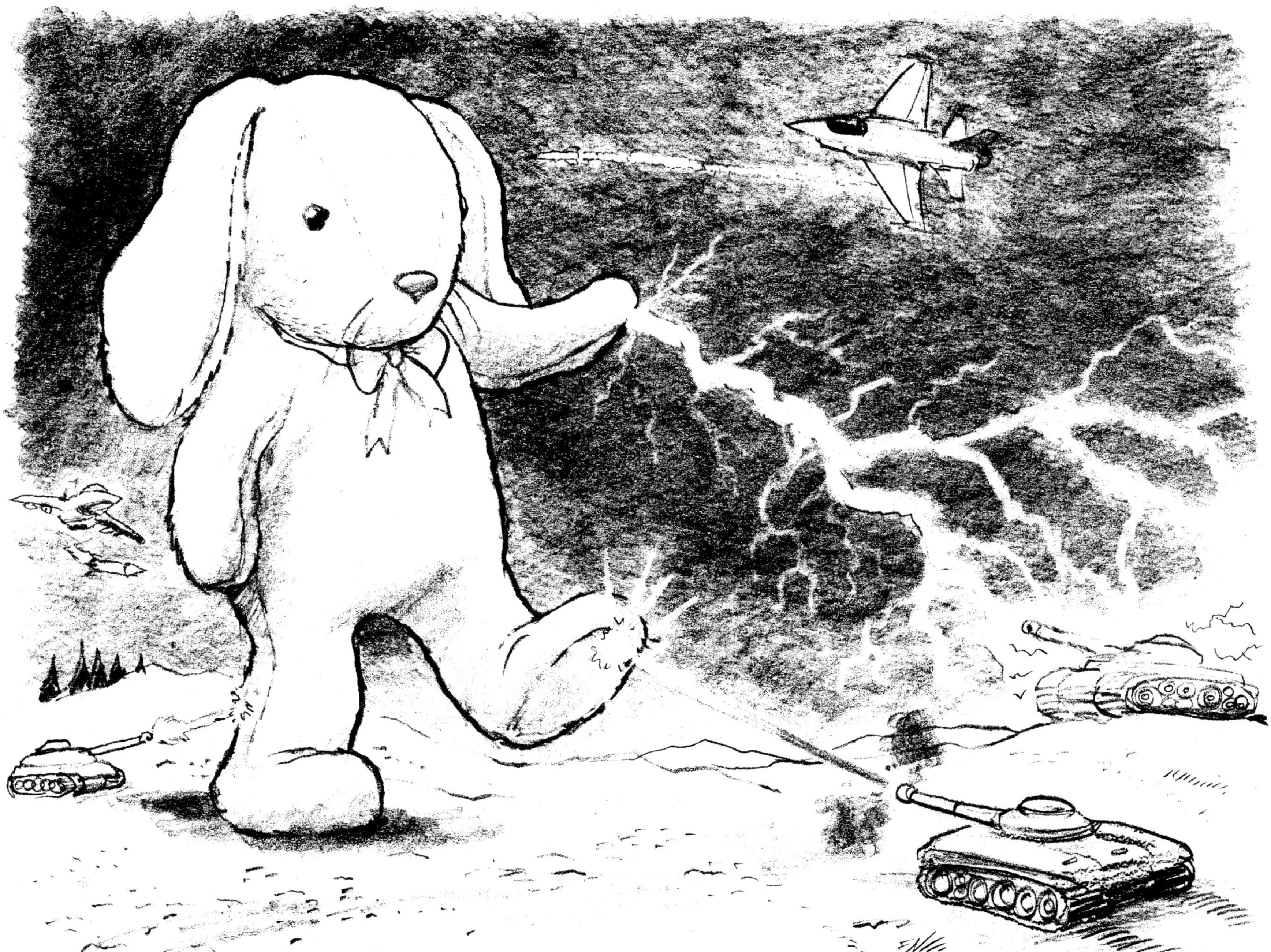

THUNDER BUNNY

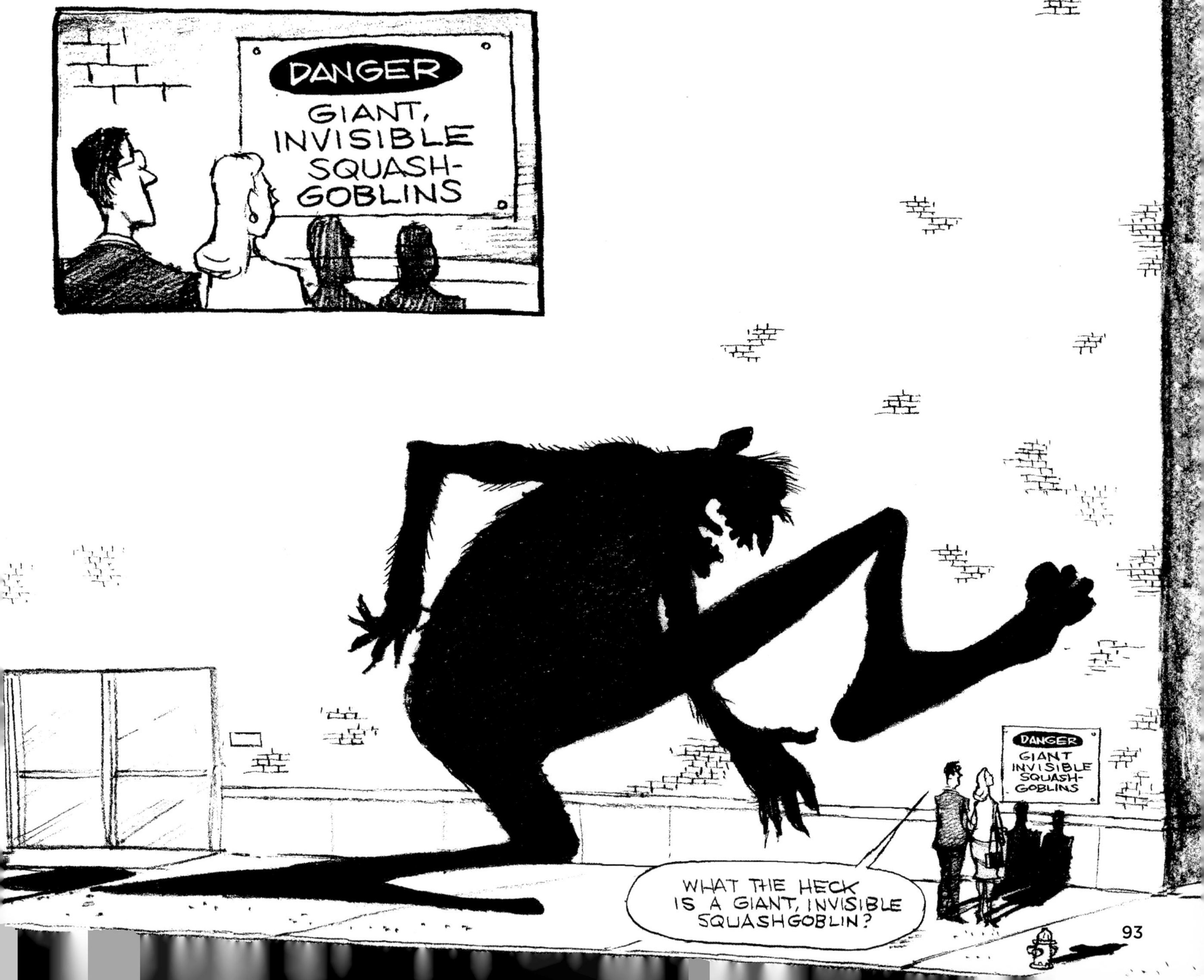
DANGER
GIANT, INVISIBLE SQUASH-GOBLINS
DANGER
GIANT INVISIBLE SQUASH-GOBLINS
WHAT THE HECK IS A GIANT, INVISIBLE SQUASHGOBLIN?

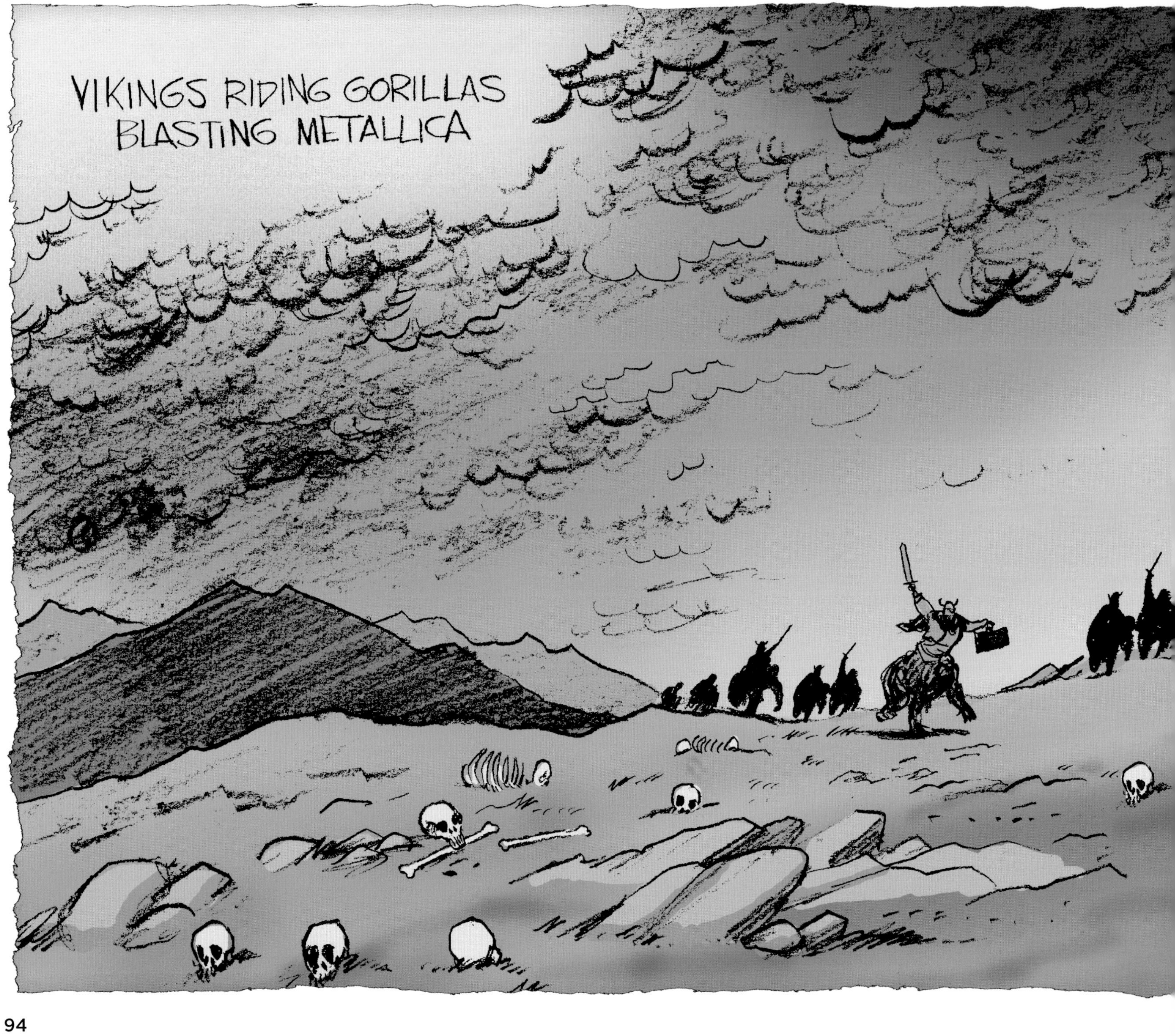
VIKINGS RIDING GORILLAS
BLASTING METALLICA

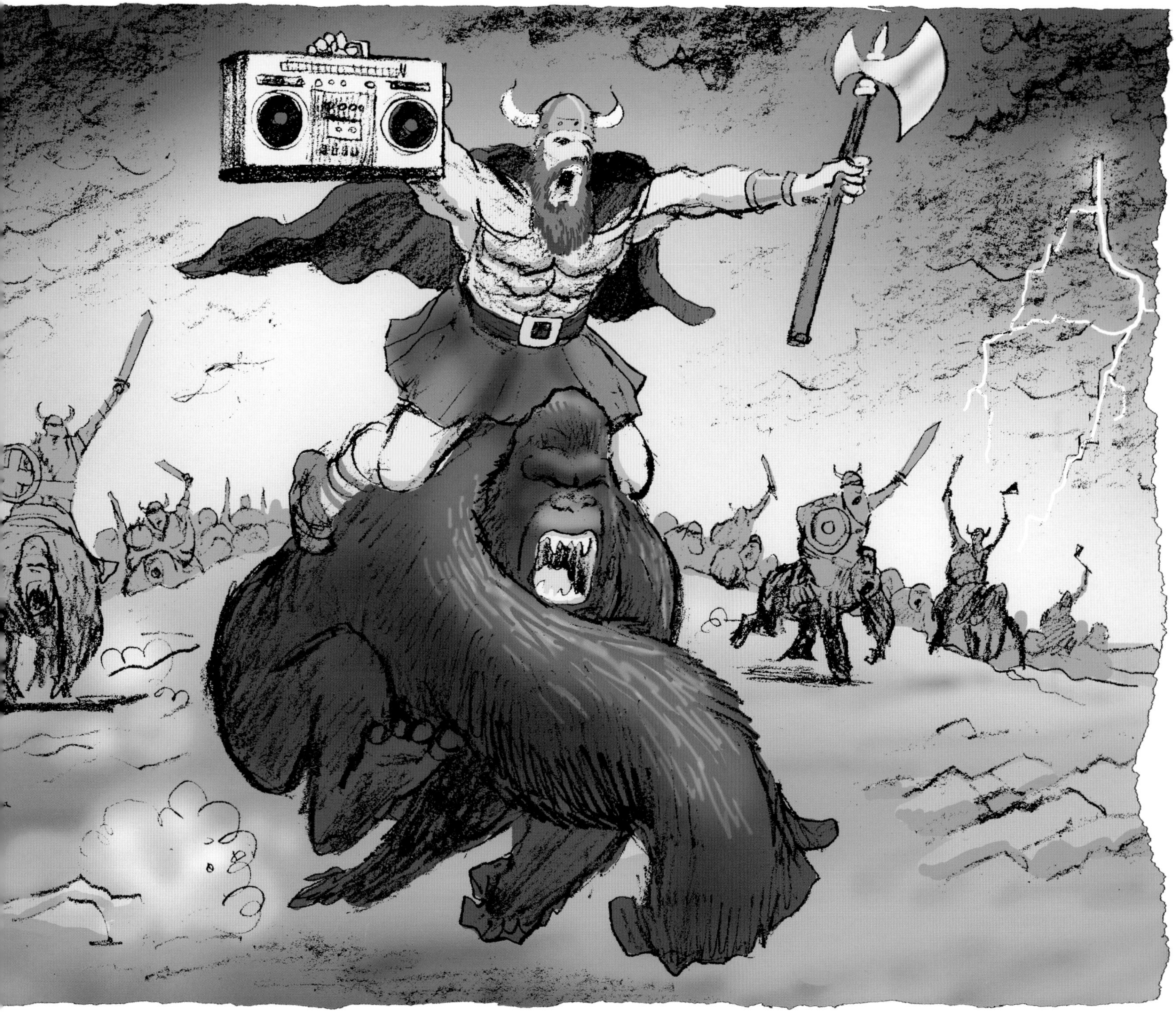

Indonesia should partner with a giant defense contractor and make these. (We get a 10 percent creator's fee.)

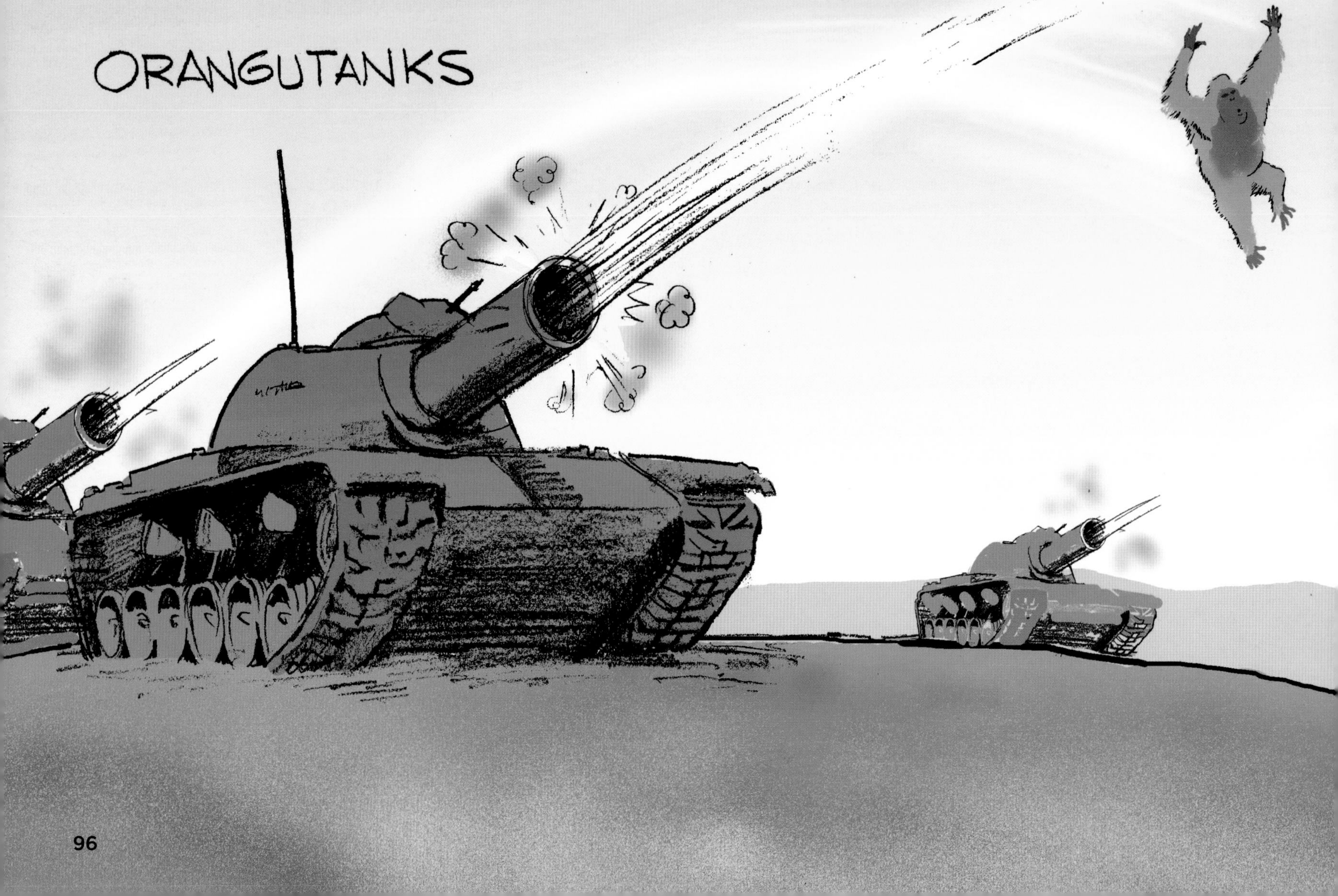
ORANGUTANKS

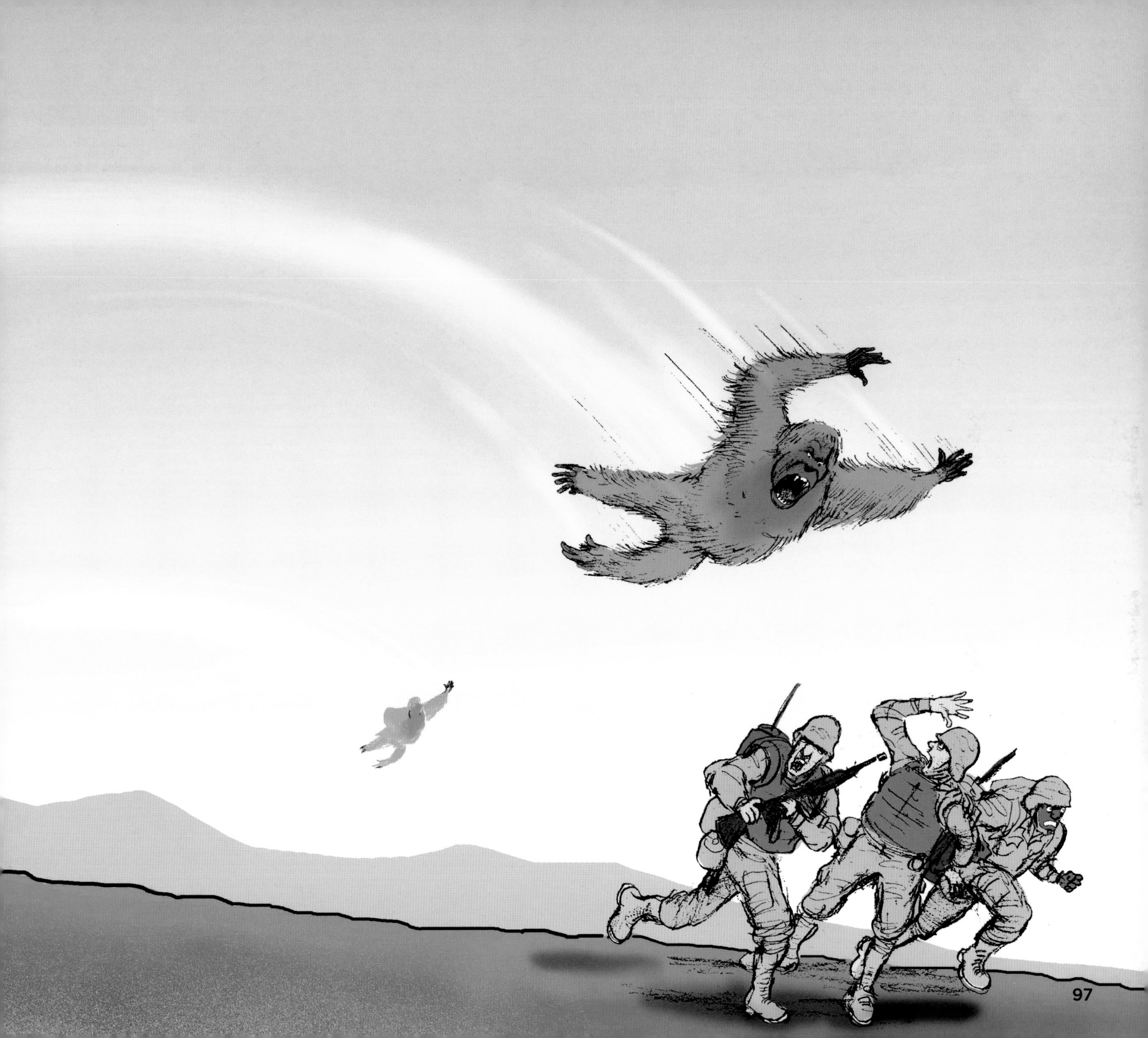

MONKEY JUGGLING
JUGGLING MONKEYS

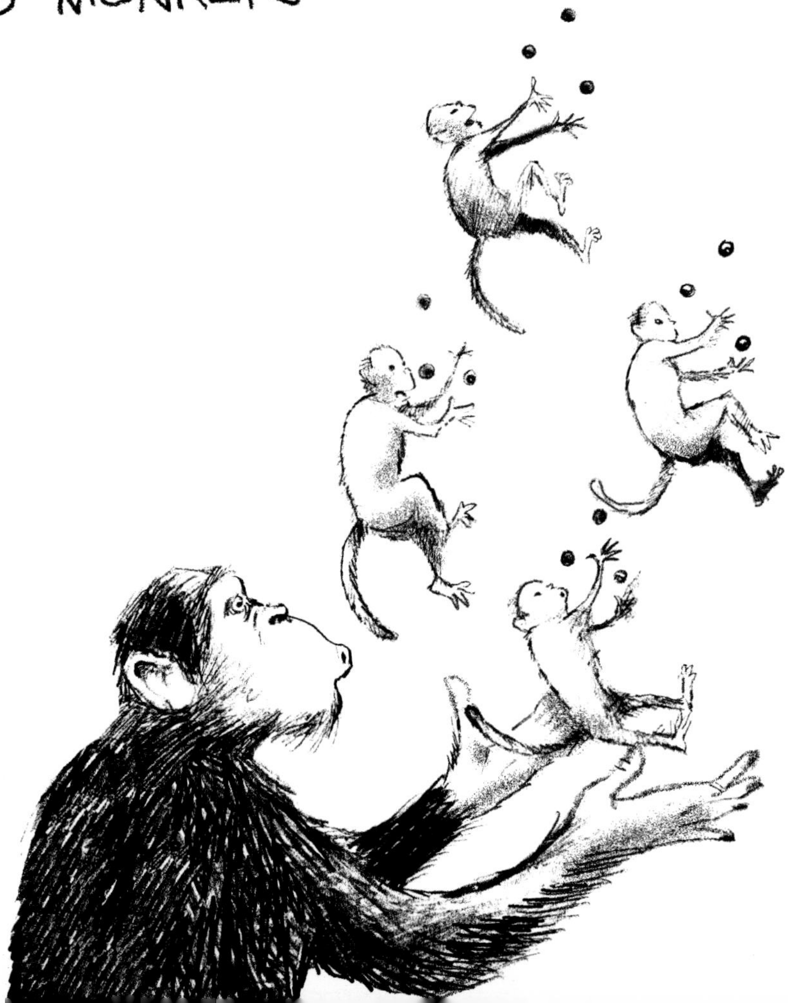

MISCELLANEOUS

I grew up in Orange County, California, and all my friends surfed. I was too afraid of sharks and the cold water. Now my boys surf. I'm happy they didn't get any of my wimpy genes.

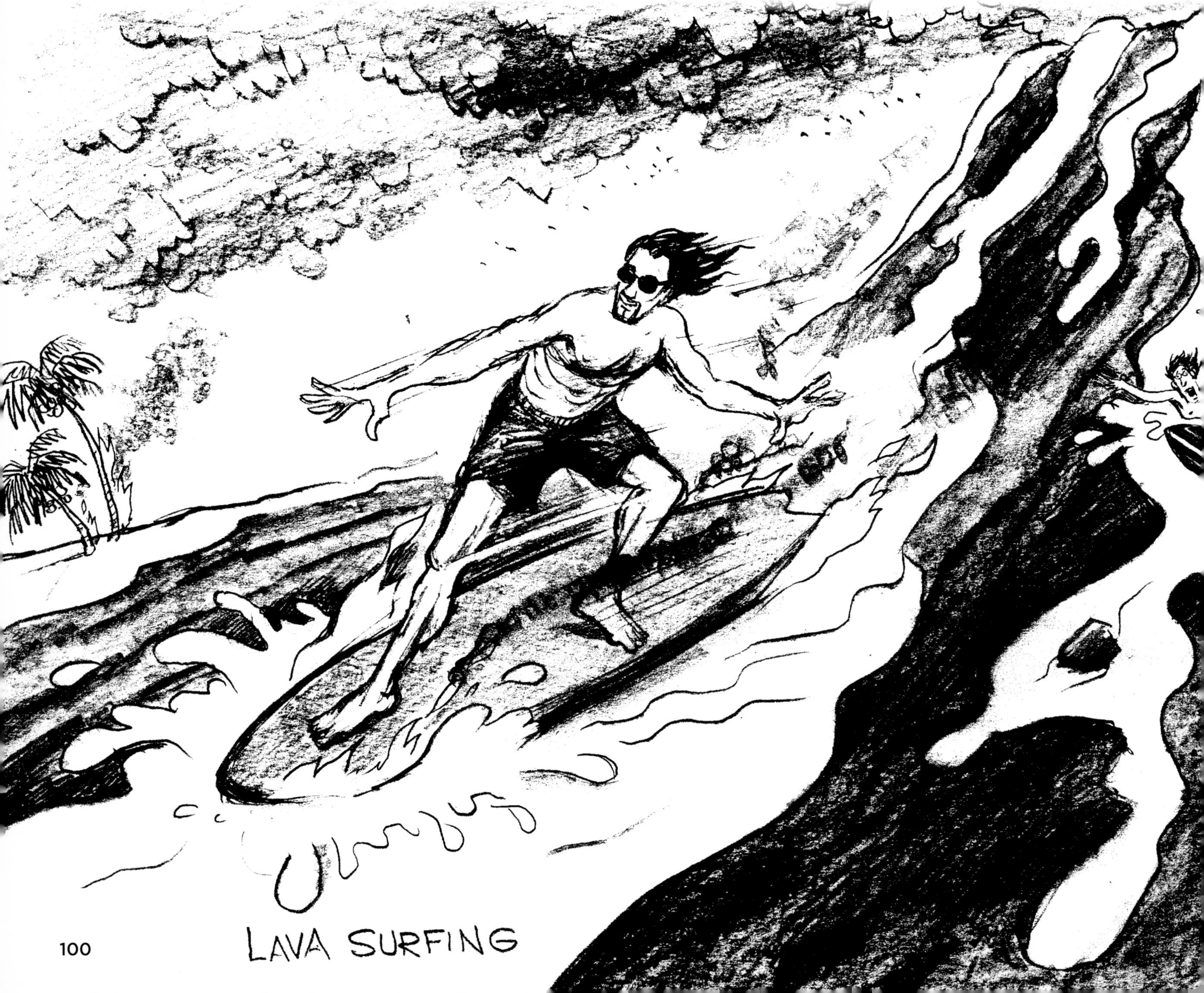
LAVA SURFING

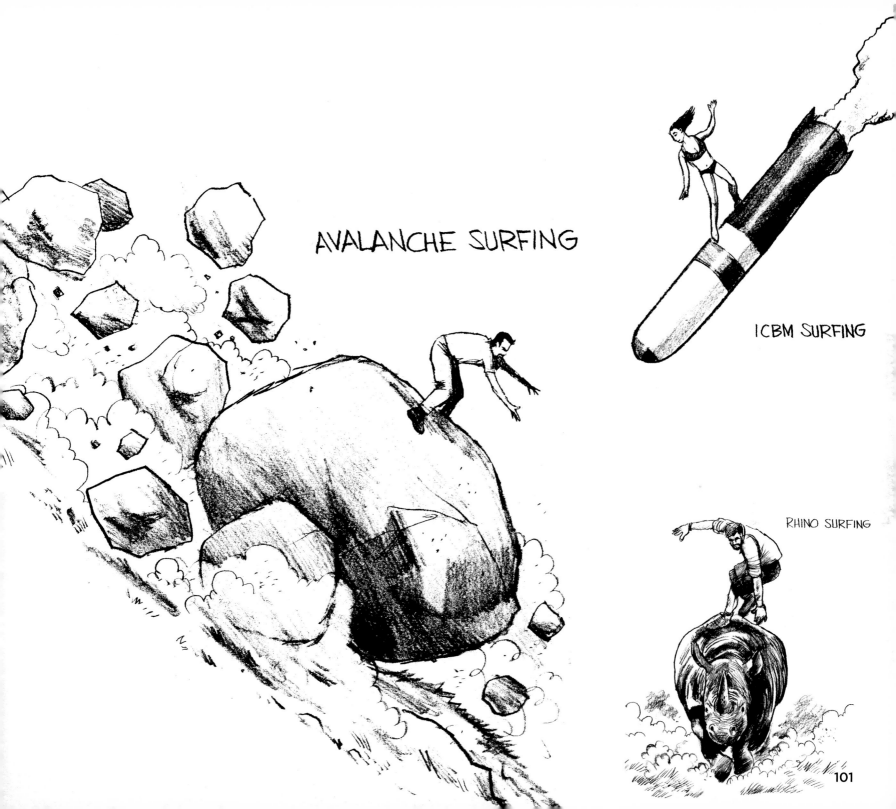

AVALANCHE SURFING

ICBM SURFING

RHINO SURFING

101

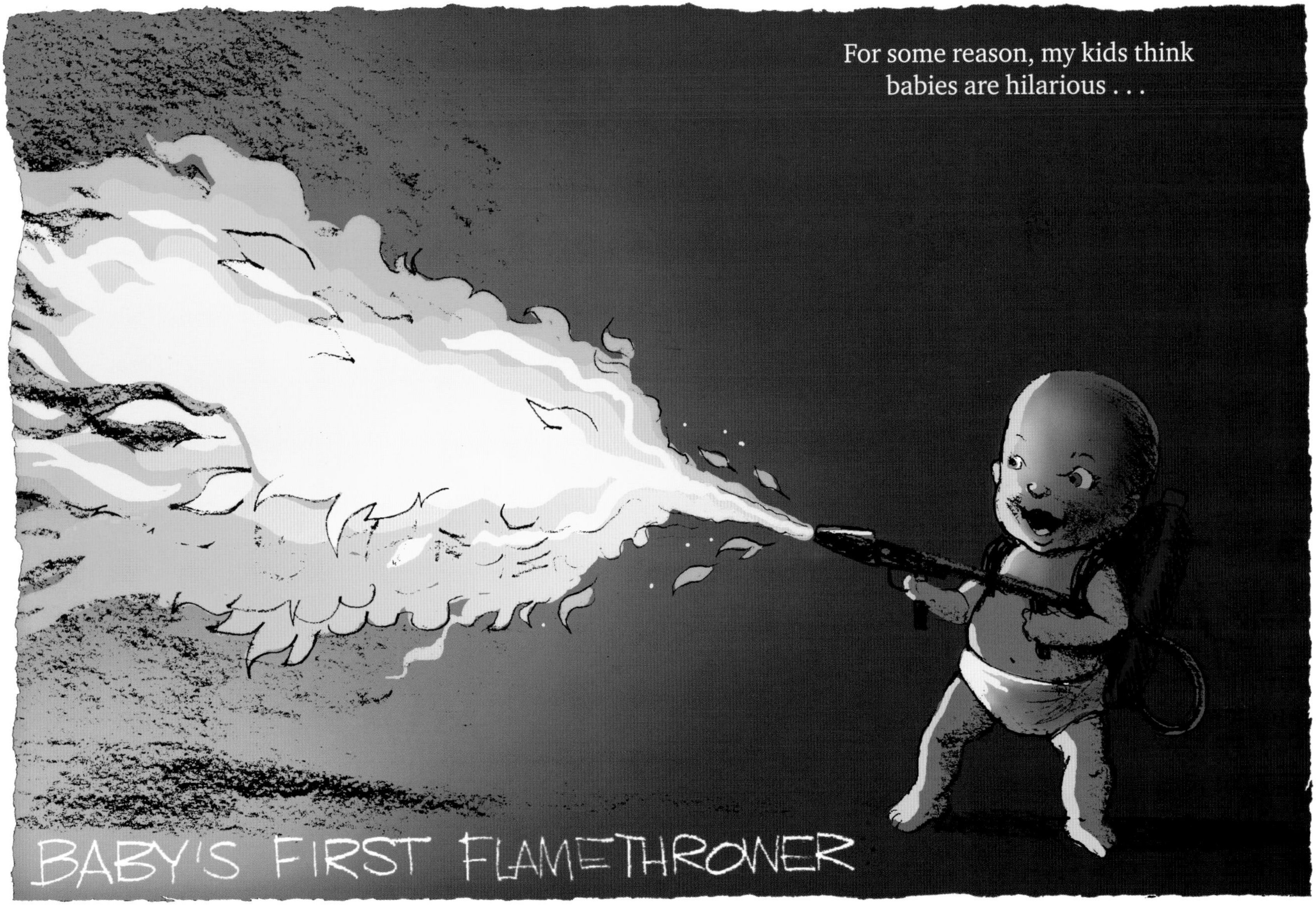
For some reason, my kids think babies are hilarious . . .
BABY'S FIRST FLAMETHROWER

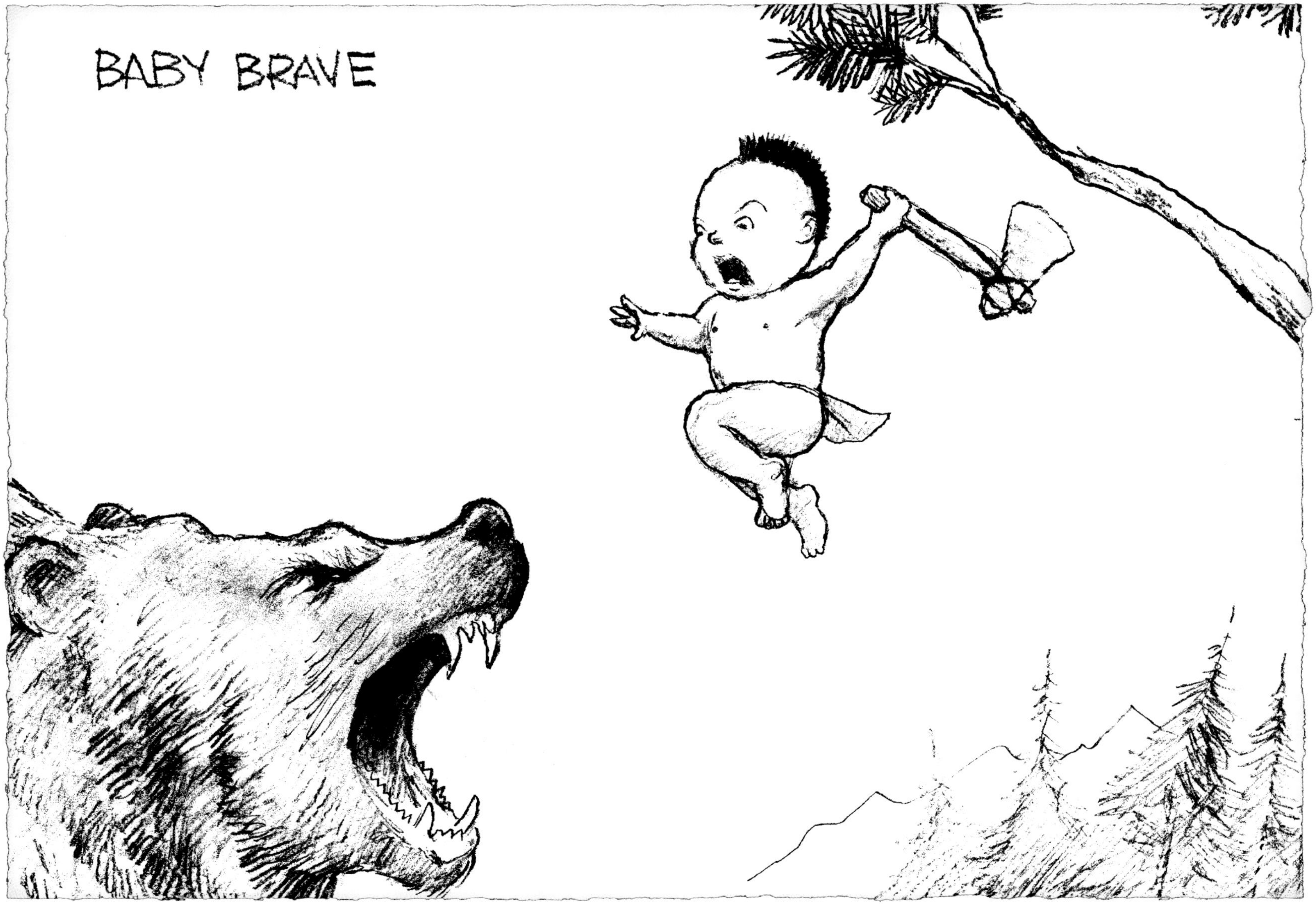
BABY BRAVE

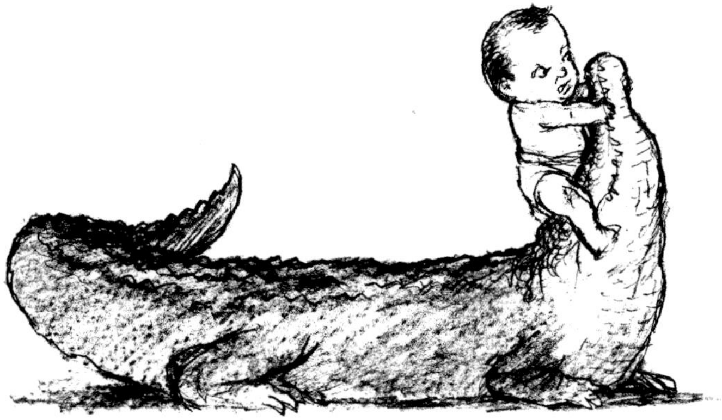

BABY ALLIGATOR WRESTLER

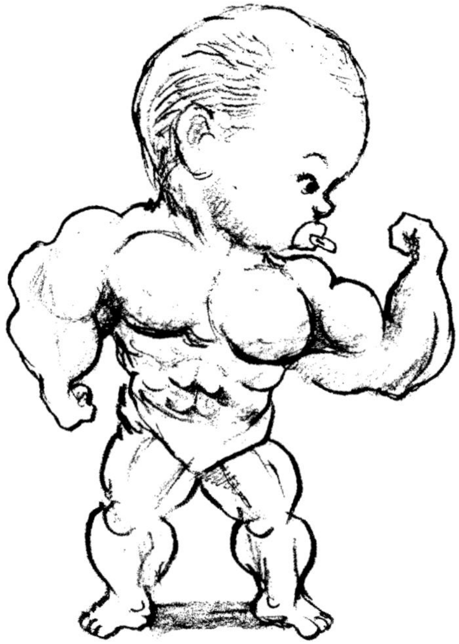

BABY BODYBUILDER

NINJA BABY

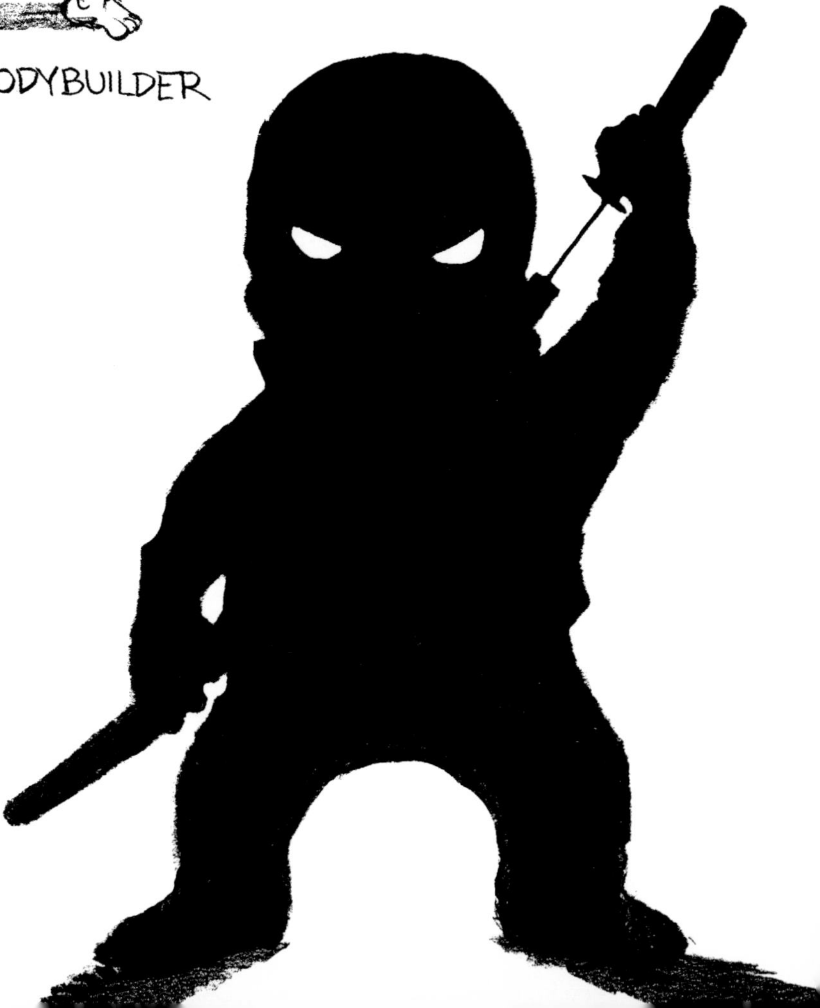

BABY KICKBOXER

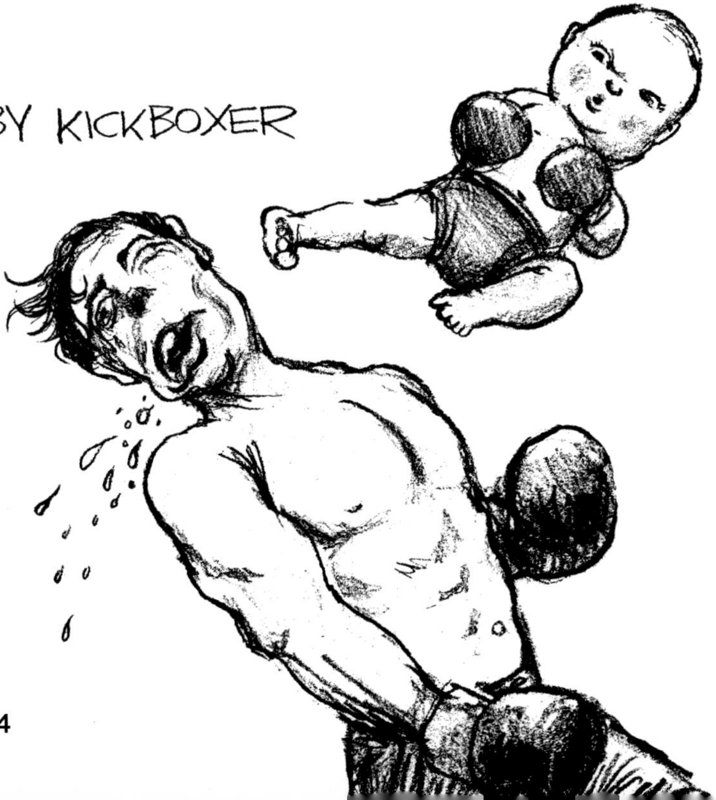

JUST WHEN YOU THOUGHT IT WAS SAFE TO GO BACK INTO THE NURSERY...
BABIES WITH RABIES
PG-13

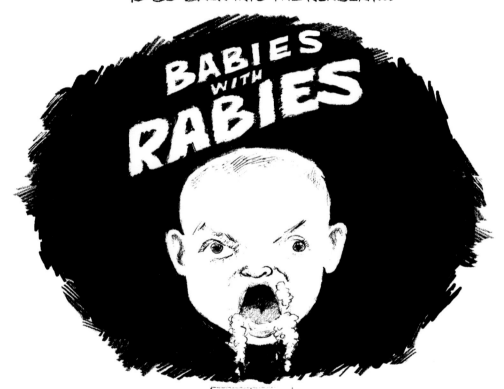

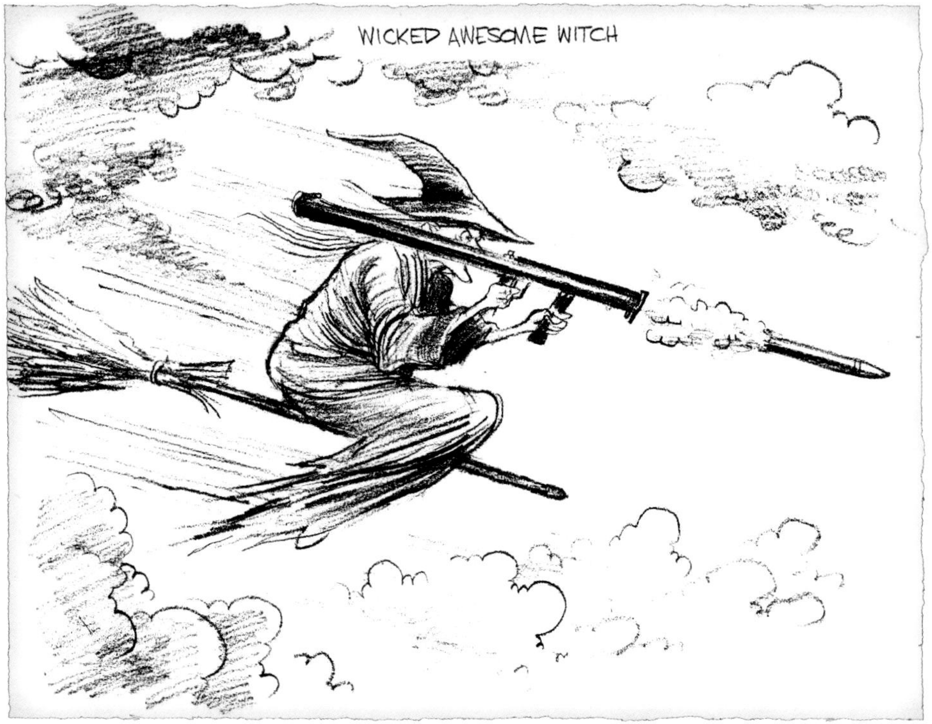
WICKED AWESOME WITCH

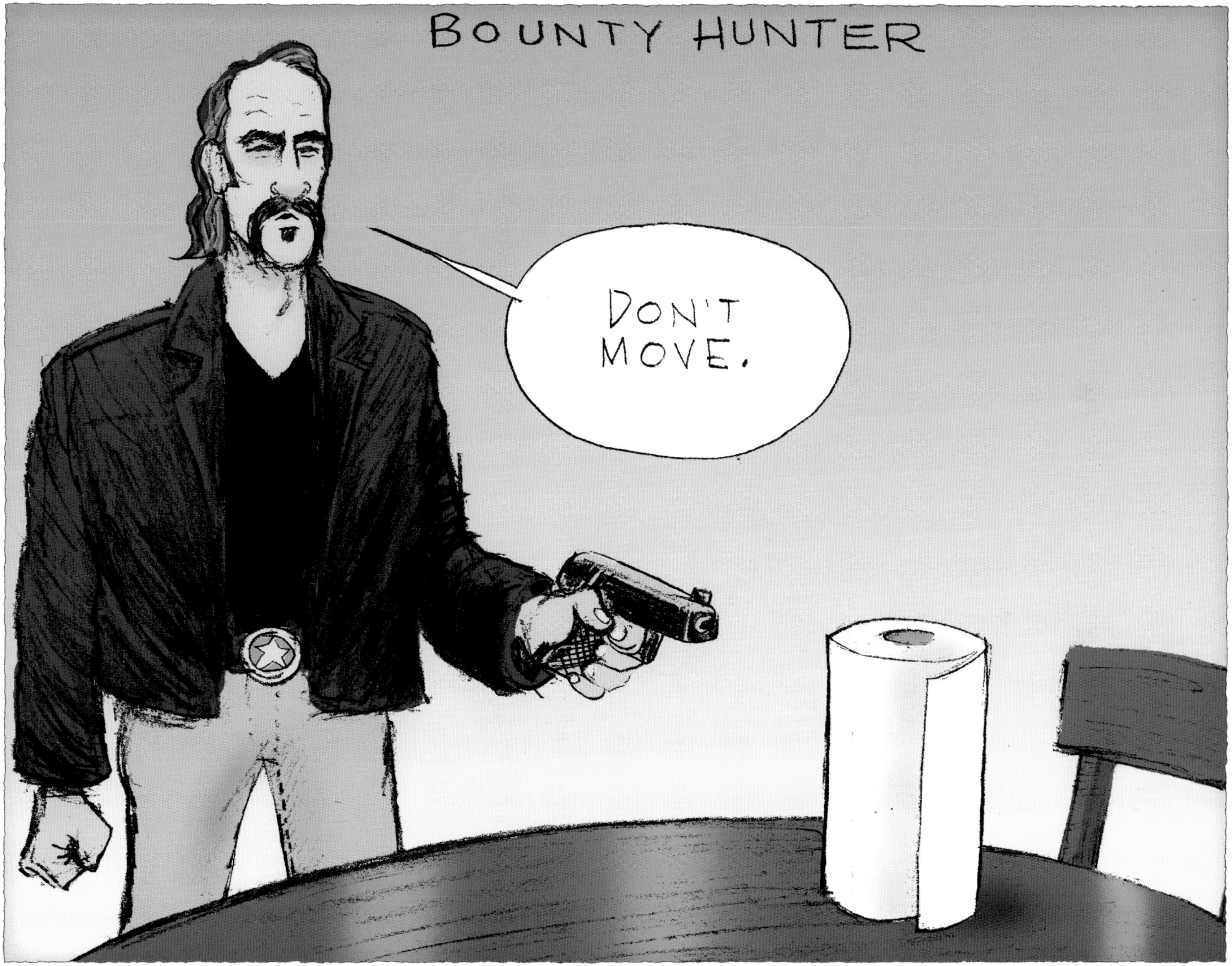
BOUNTY HUNTER
DON'T MOVE.

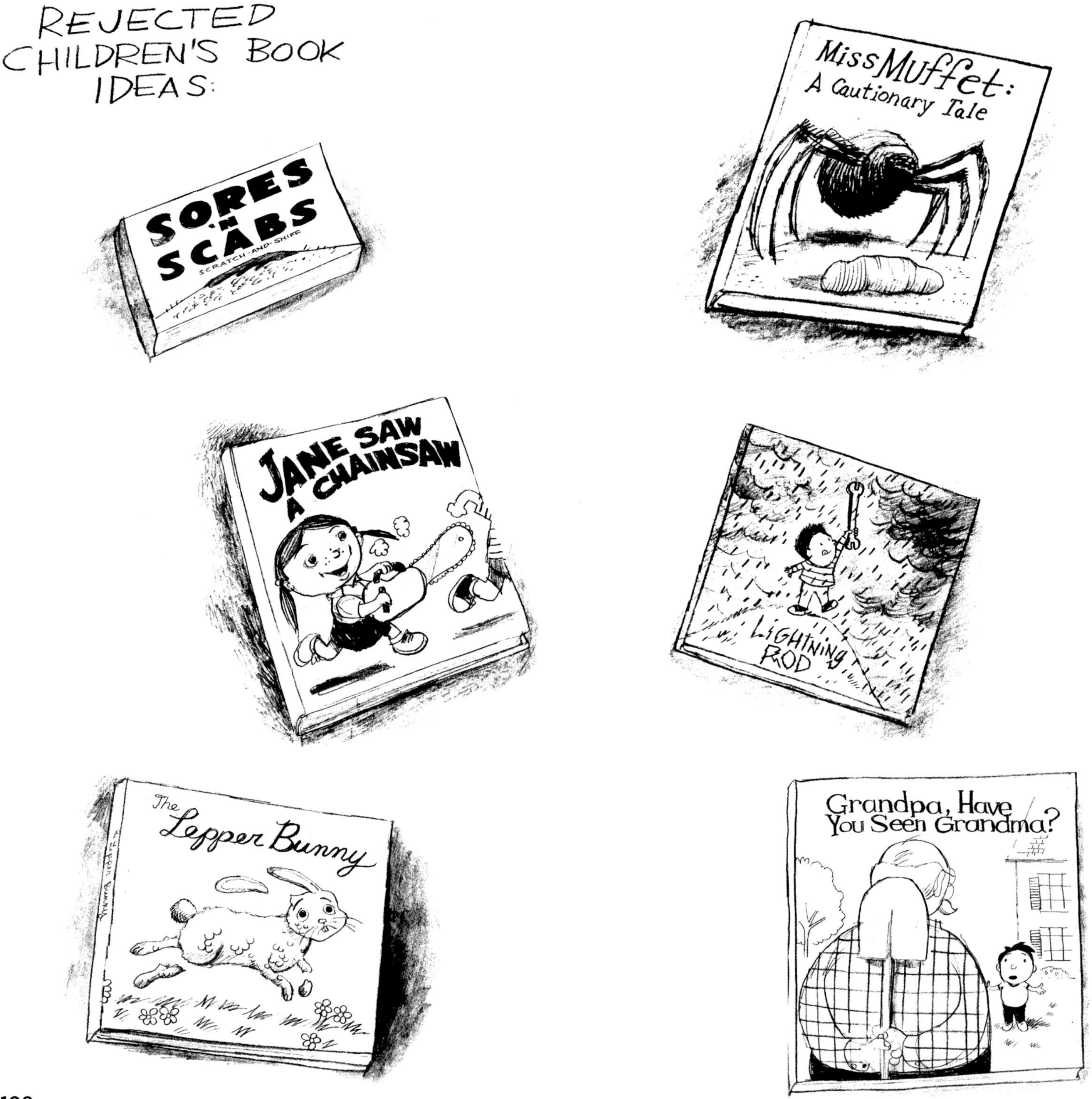
REJECTED CHILDREN'S BOOK IDEAS:
SORES 'N SCABS
SCRATCH-AND-SNIFF
Miss Muffet: A Cautionary Tale
JANE SAW A CHAINSAW
LIGHTNING ROD
The Lepper Bunny
Grandpa, Have You Seen Grandma?

TECHNOLOGY:
Cure for the bullying epidemic

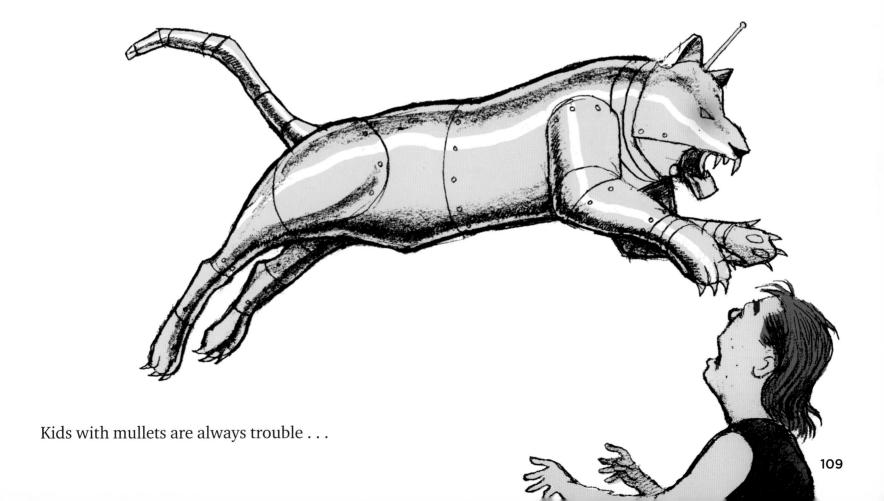

Kids with mullets are always trouble . . .

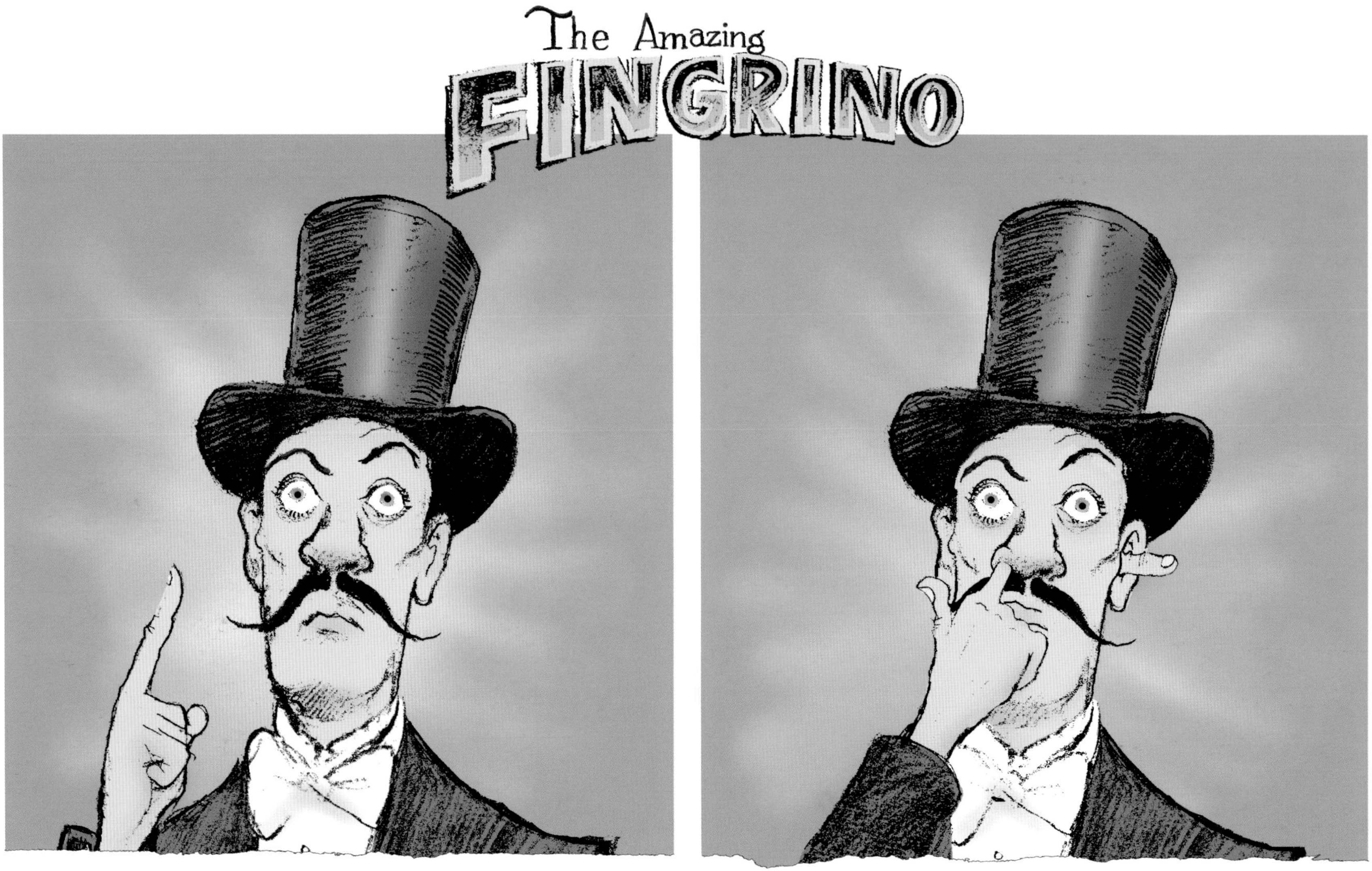
The Amazing
FINGRINO

CELEBRITY DEATH MATCH...

KNOW YOUR CAUTION SIGNS:

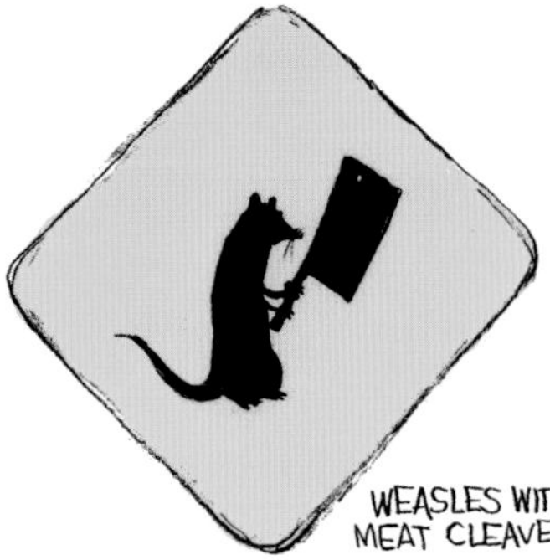

WEASLES WITH MEAT CLEAVERS

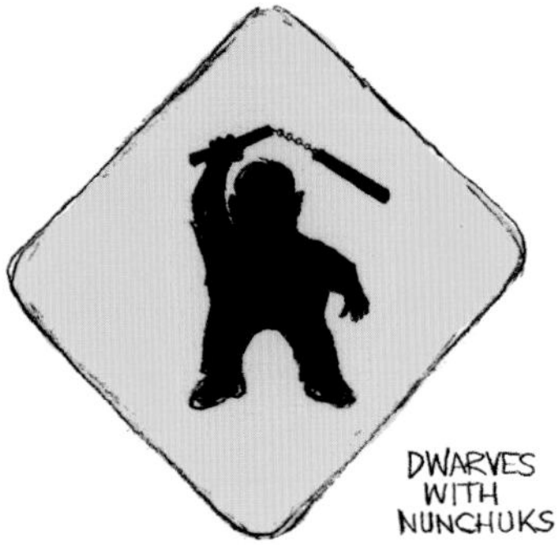

DWARVES WITH NUNCHUKS

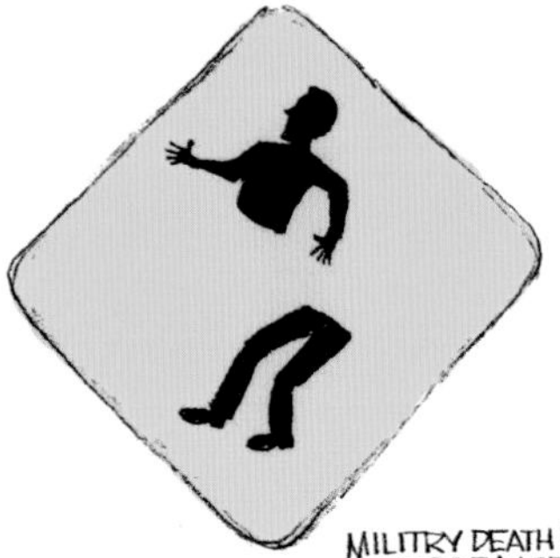

MILITRY DEATH RAY TEST RANGE

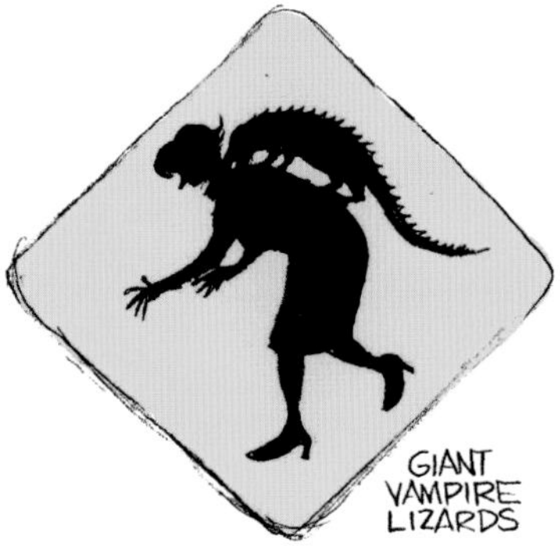

GIANT VAMPIRE LIZARDS

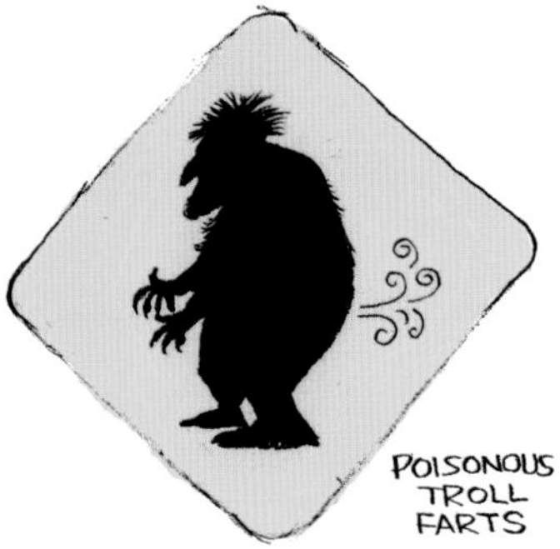

POISONOUS TROLL FARTS

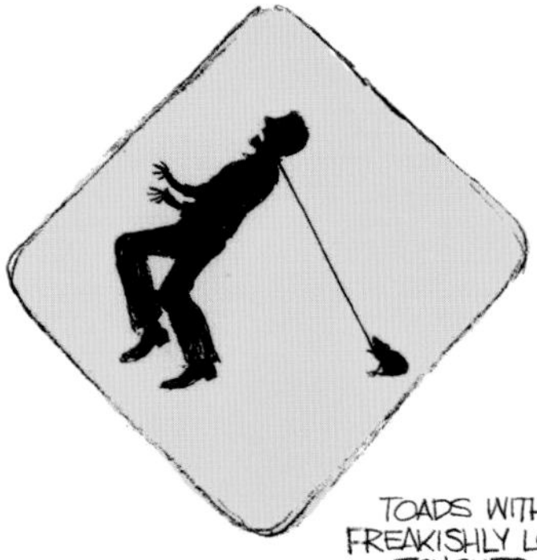

TOADS WITH FREAKISHLY LONG TONGUES

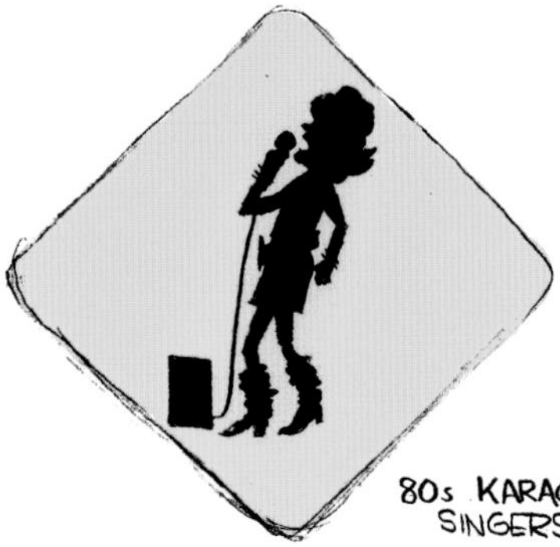

80s KARAOKE SINGERS

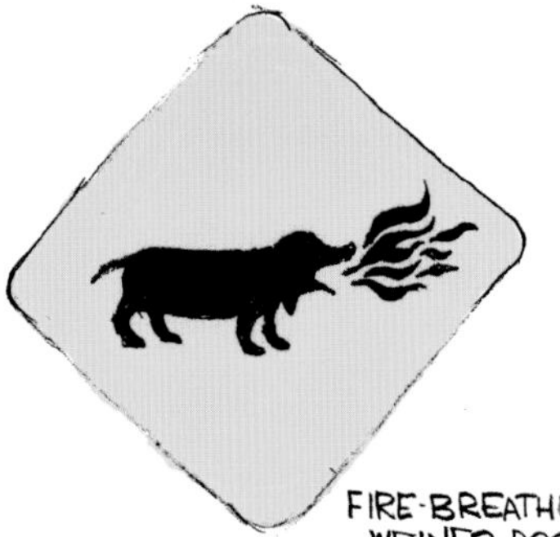

FIRE-BREATHING WEINER DOGS

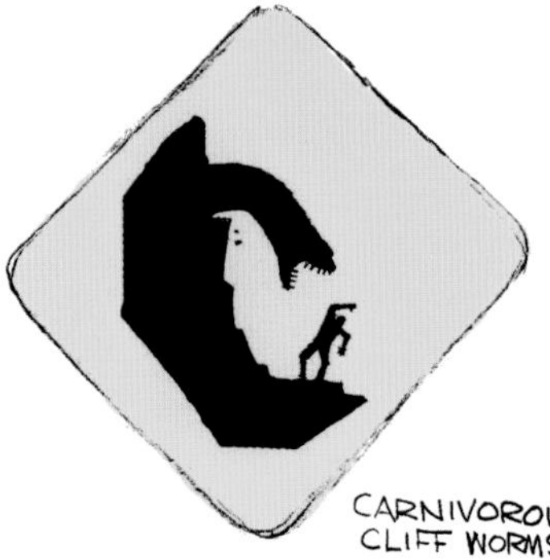

CARNIVOROUS CLIFF WORMS

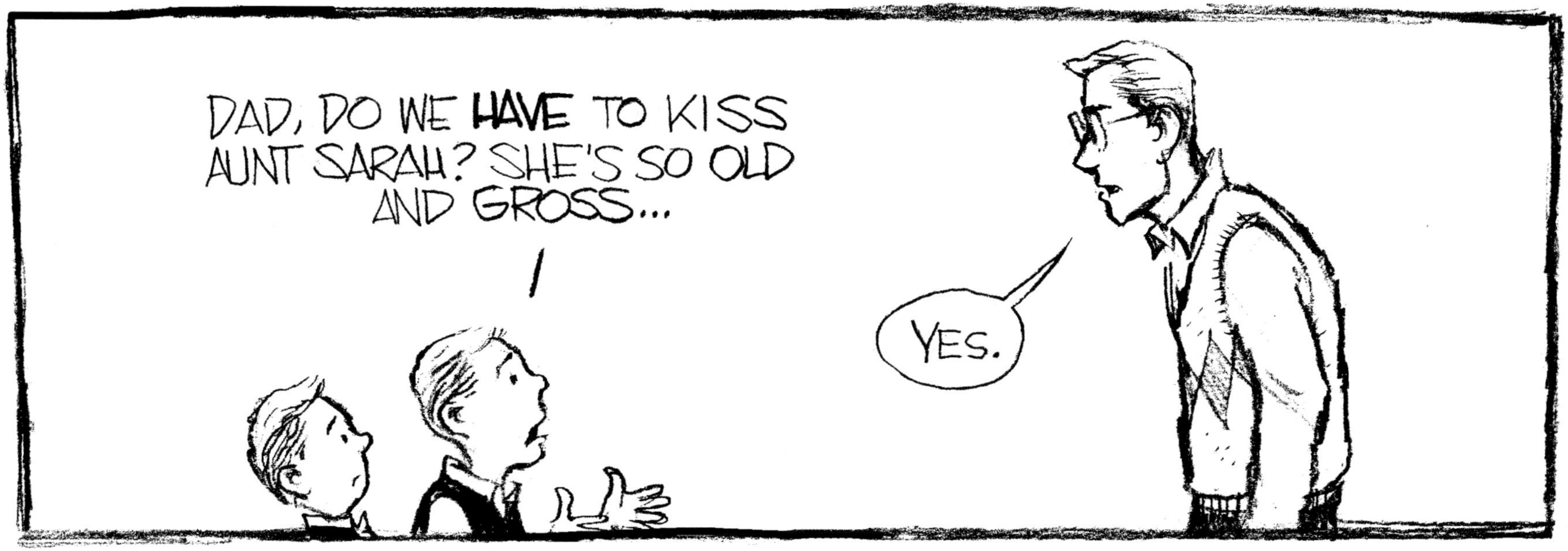
DAD, DO WE **HAVE** TO KISS AUNT SARAH? SHE'S SO OLD AND GROSS...
YES.

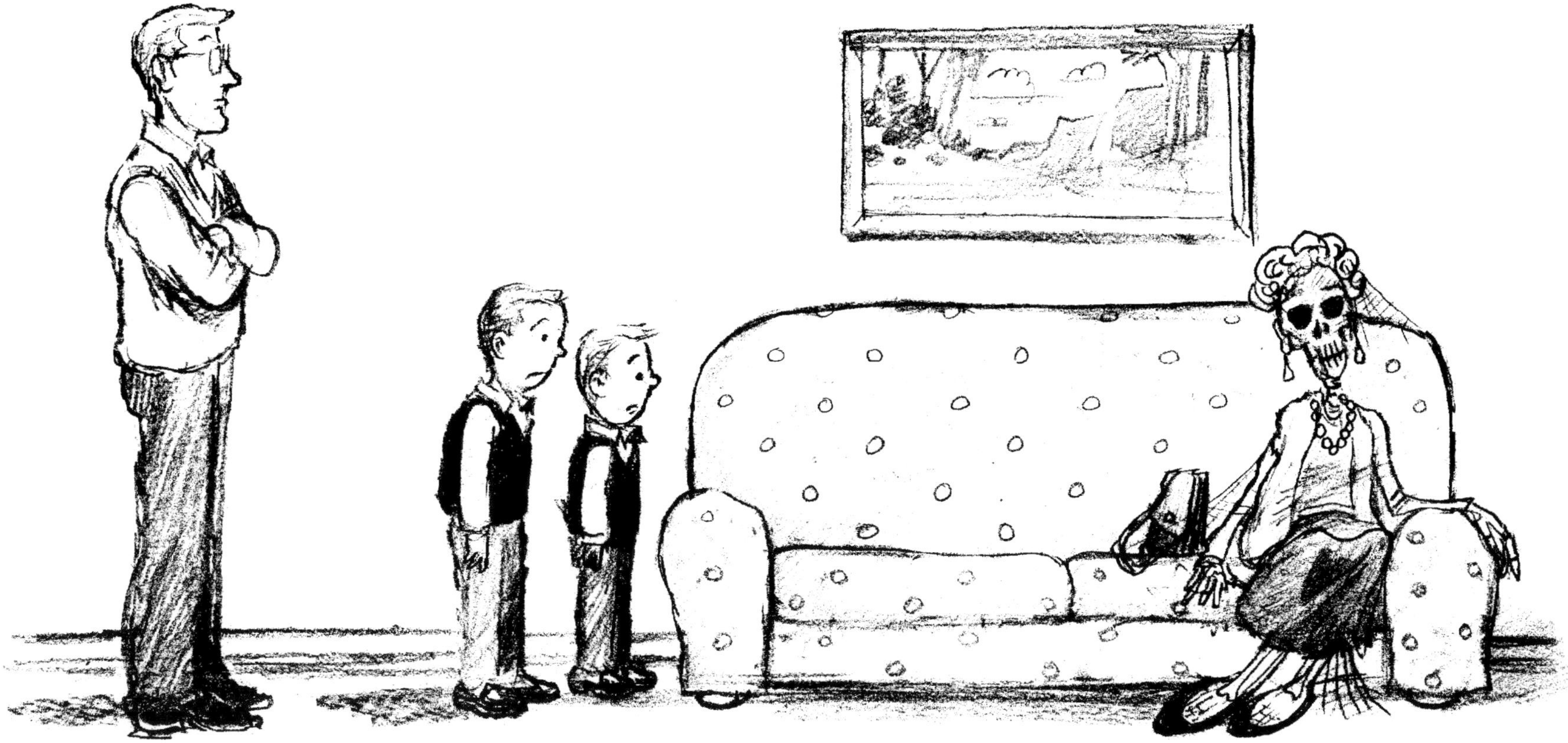

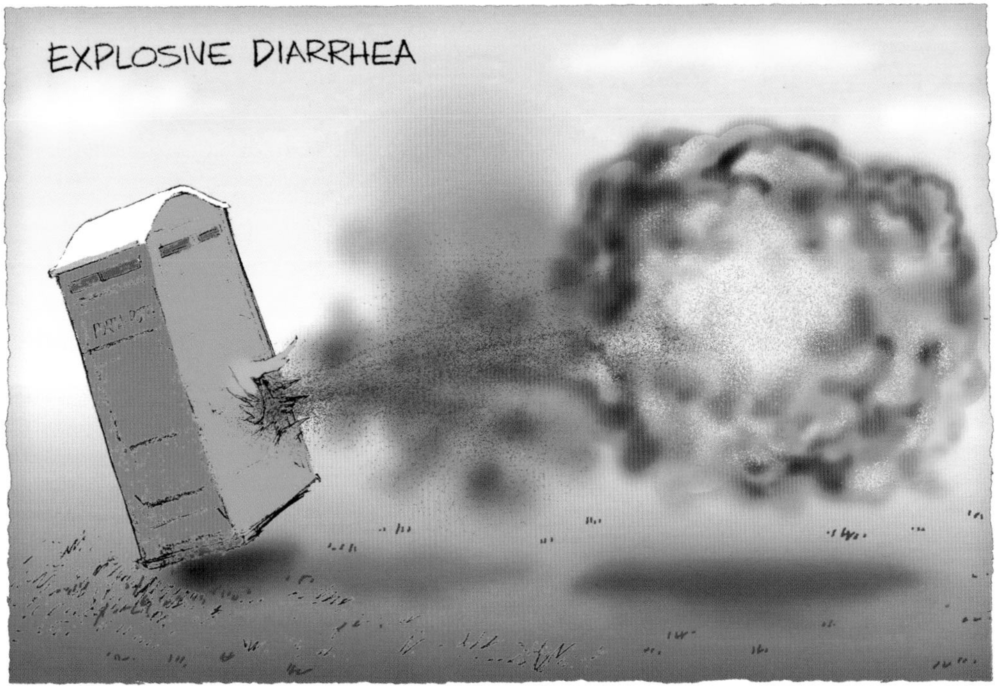
EXPLOSIVE DIARRHEA

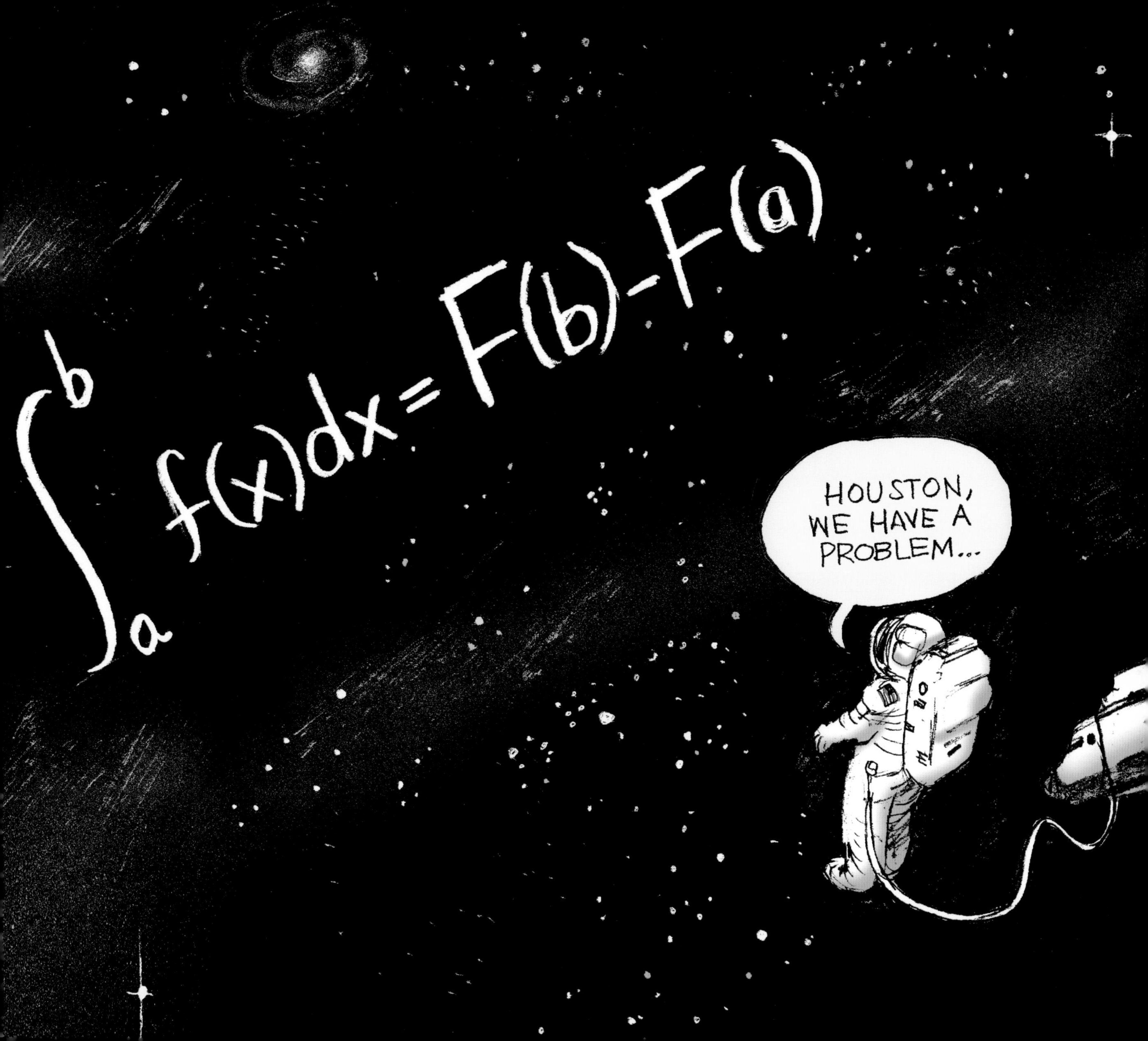

$\int_a^b f(x)dx = F(b) - F(a)$
HOUSTON, WE HAVE A PROBLEM...

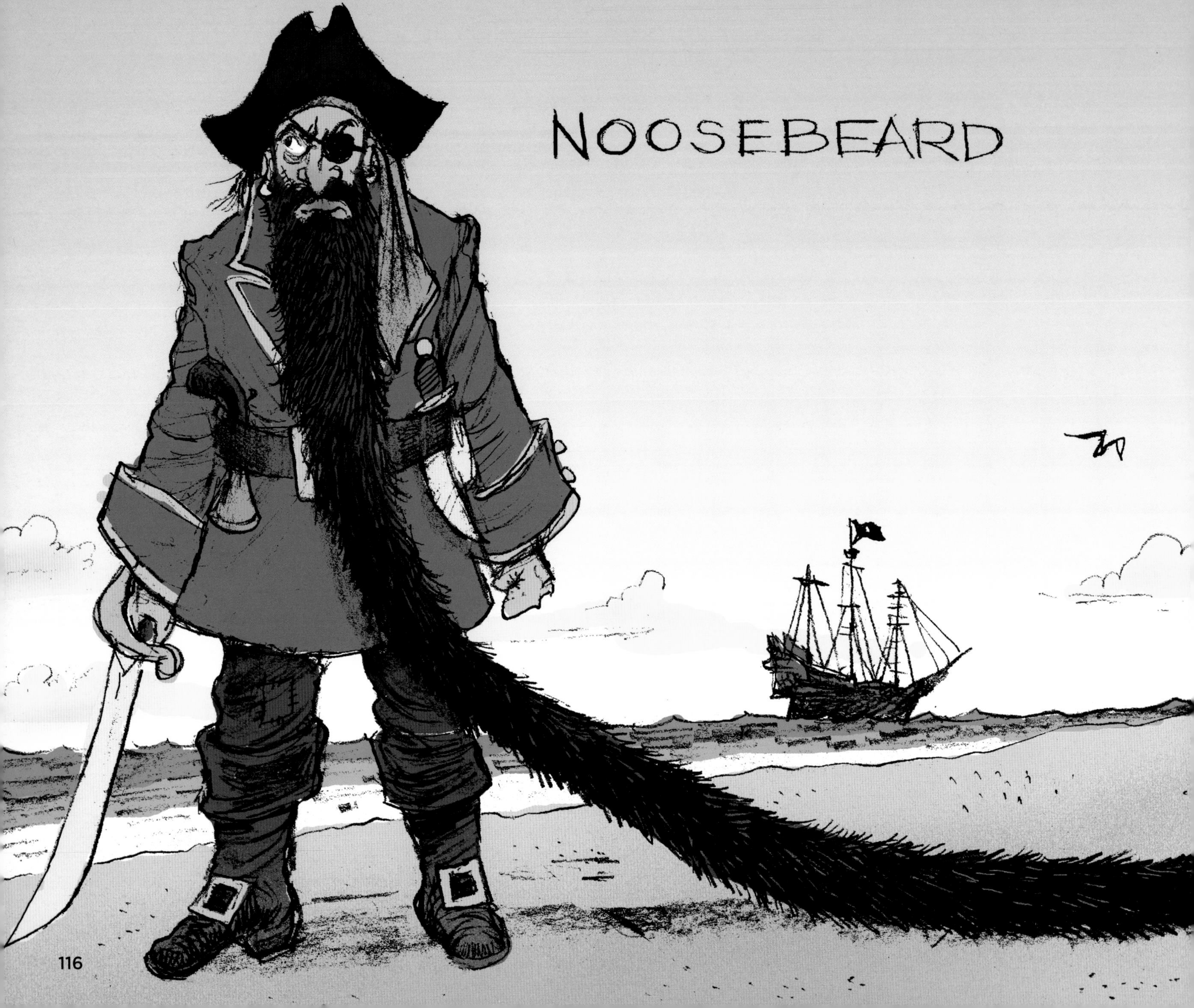
NOOSEBEARD

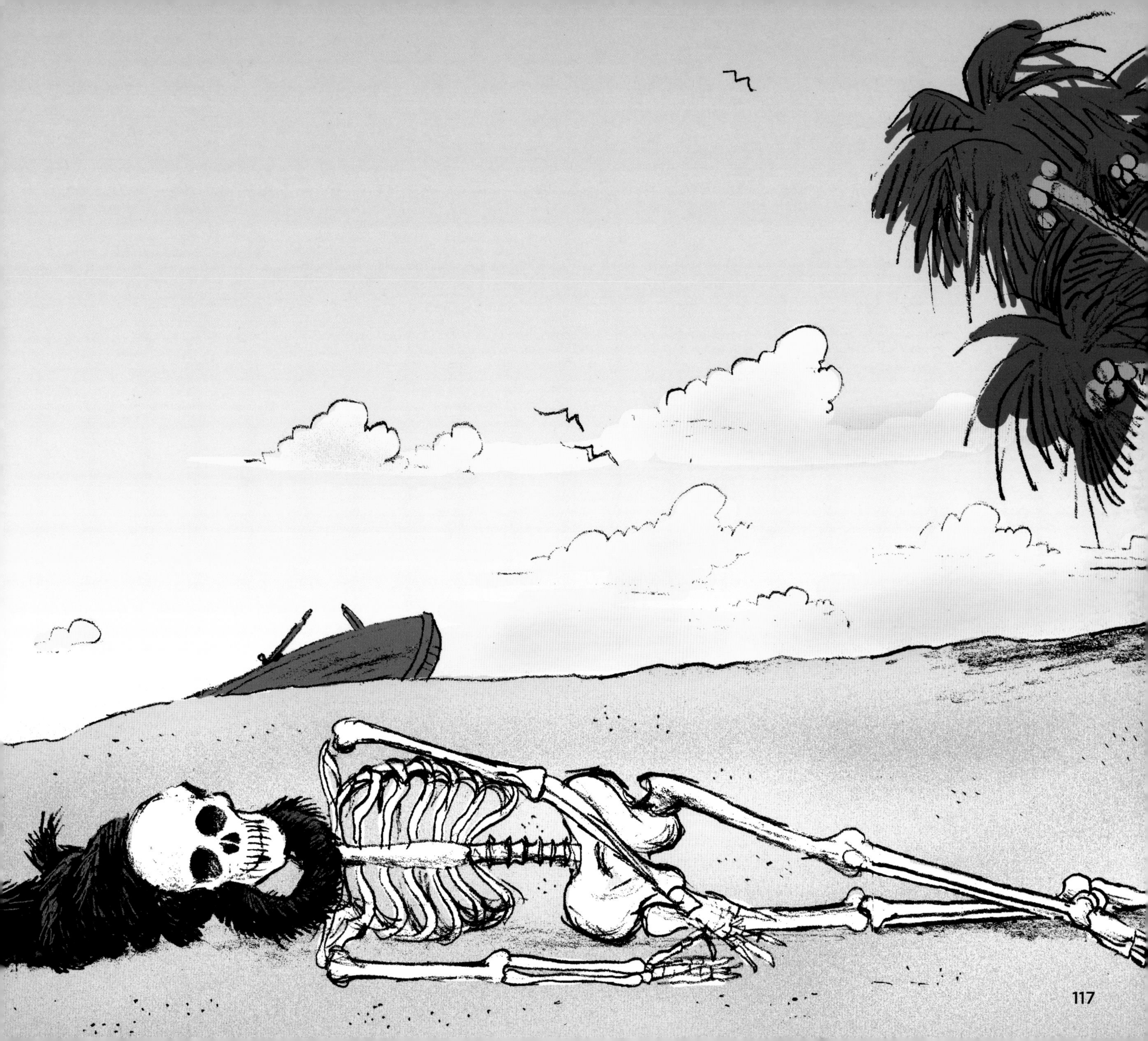

HOW TO MAKE THE OLYMPICS MORE INTERESTING...

OCTOGENARIAN WEIGHTLIFTING

CRACK!

HYDROCHLORIC ACID LONG JUMP

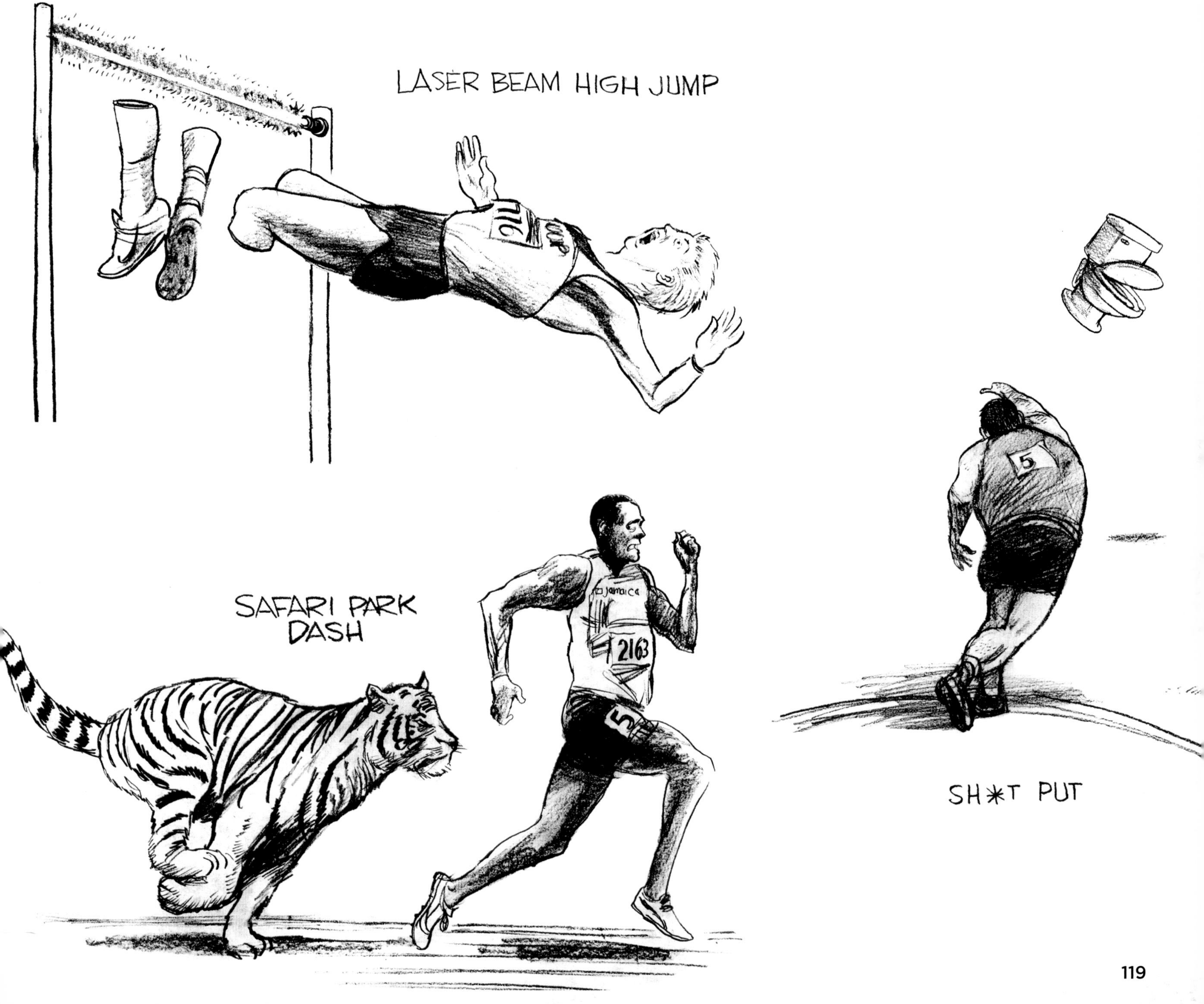
LASER BEAM HIGH JUMP
SAFARI PARK
DASH
SH*T PUT

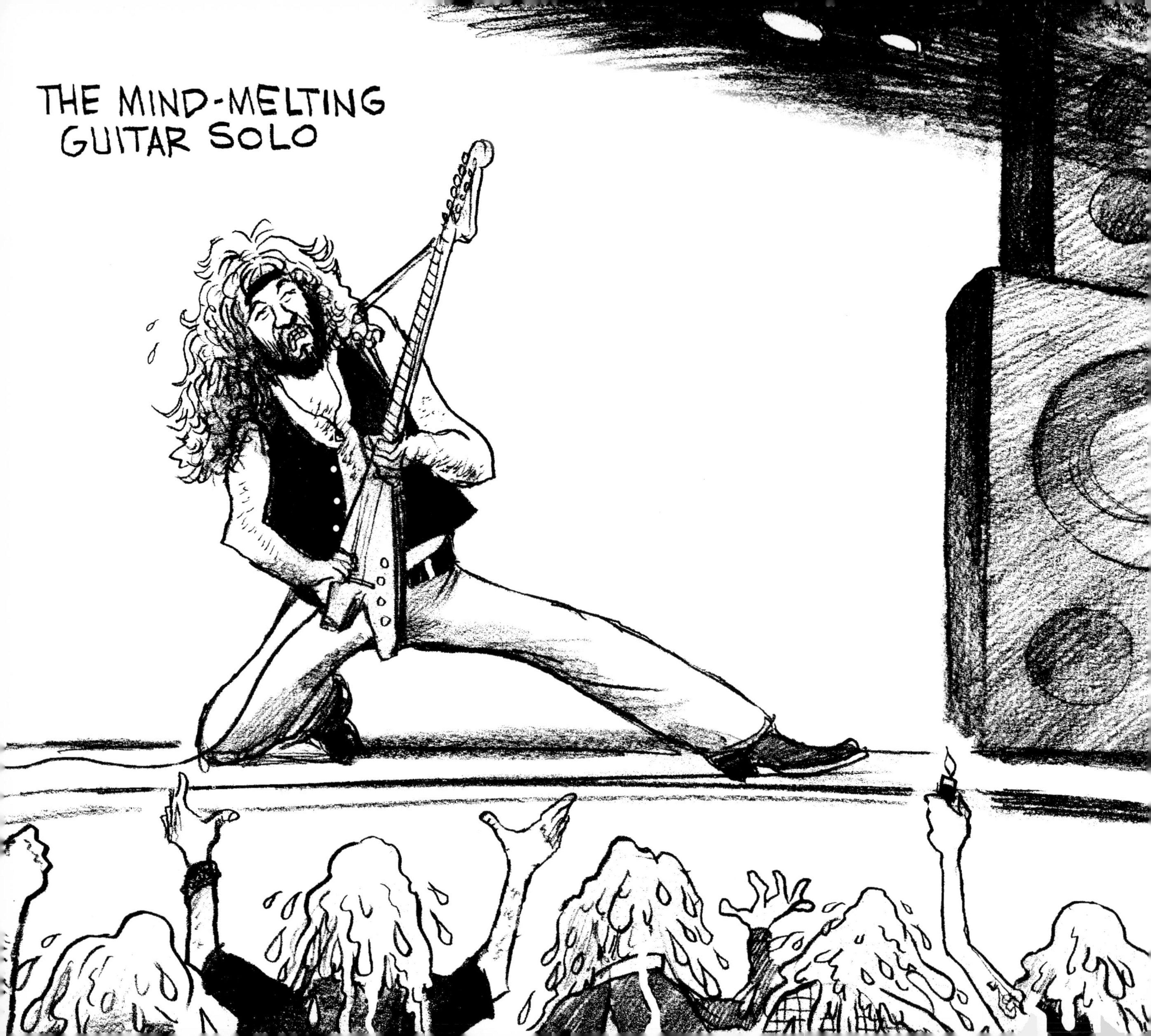
THE MIND-MELTING GUITAR SOLO

VENUS GUY TRAP

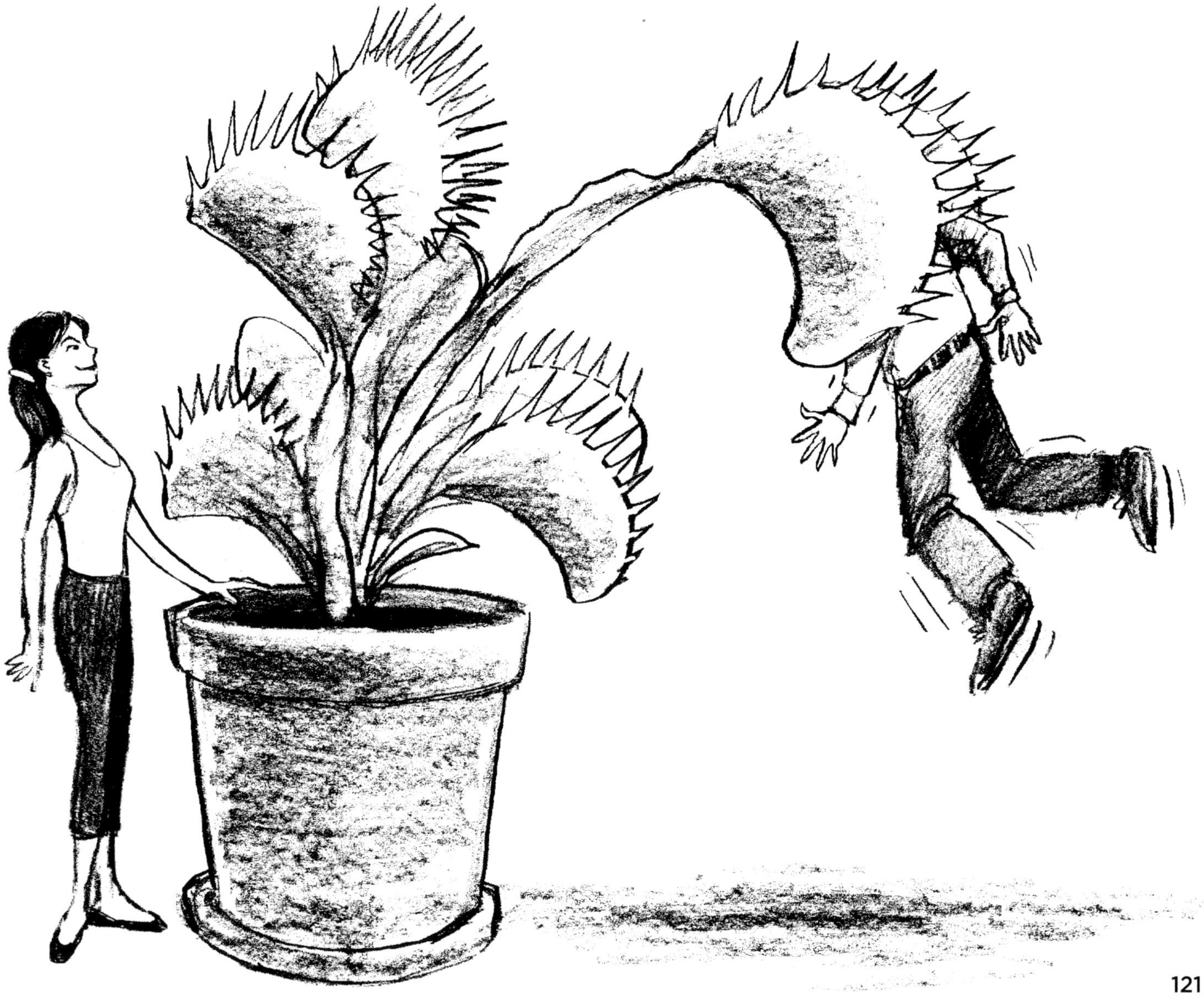

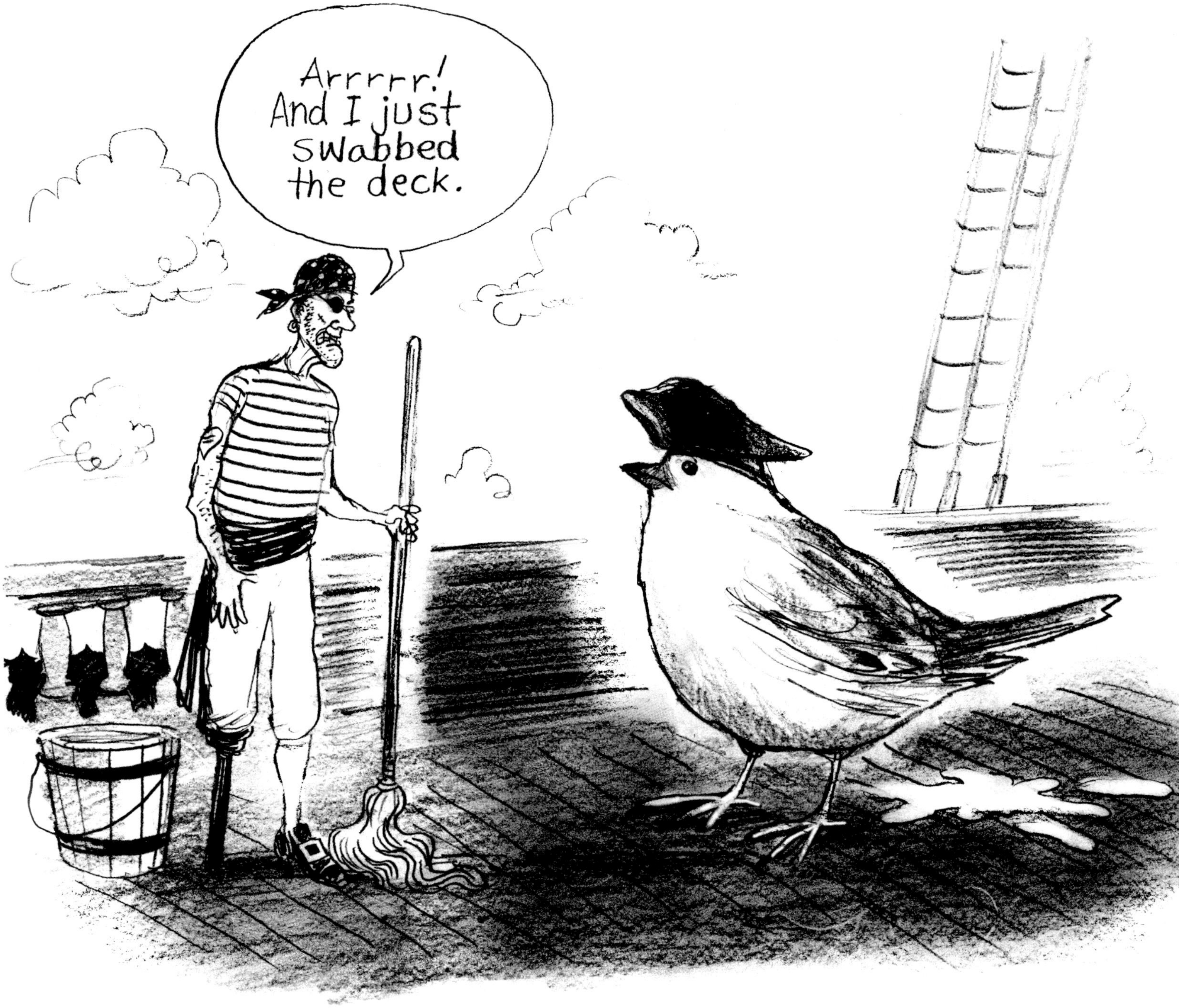
Arrrrr! And I just swabbed the deck.

Jack Sparrow . . .

Schools in nice neighborhoods
play dodge ball . . .

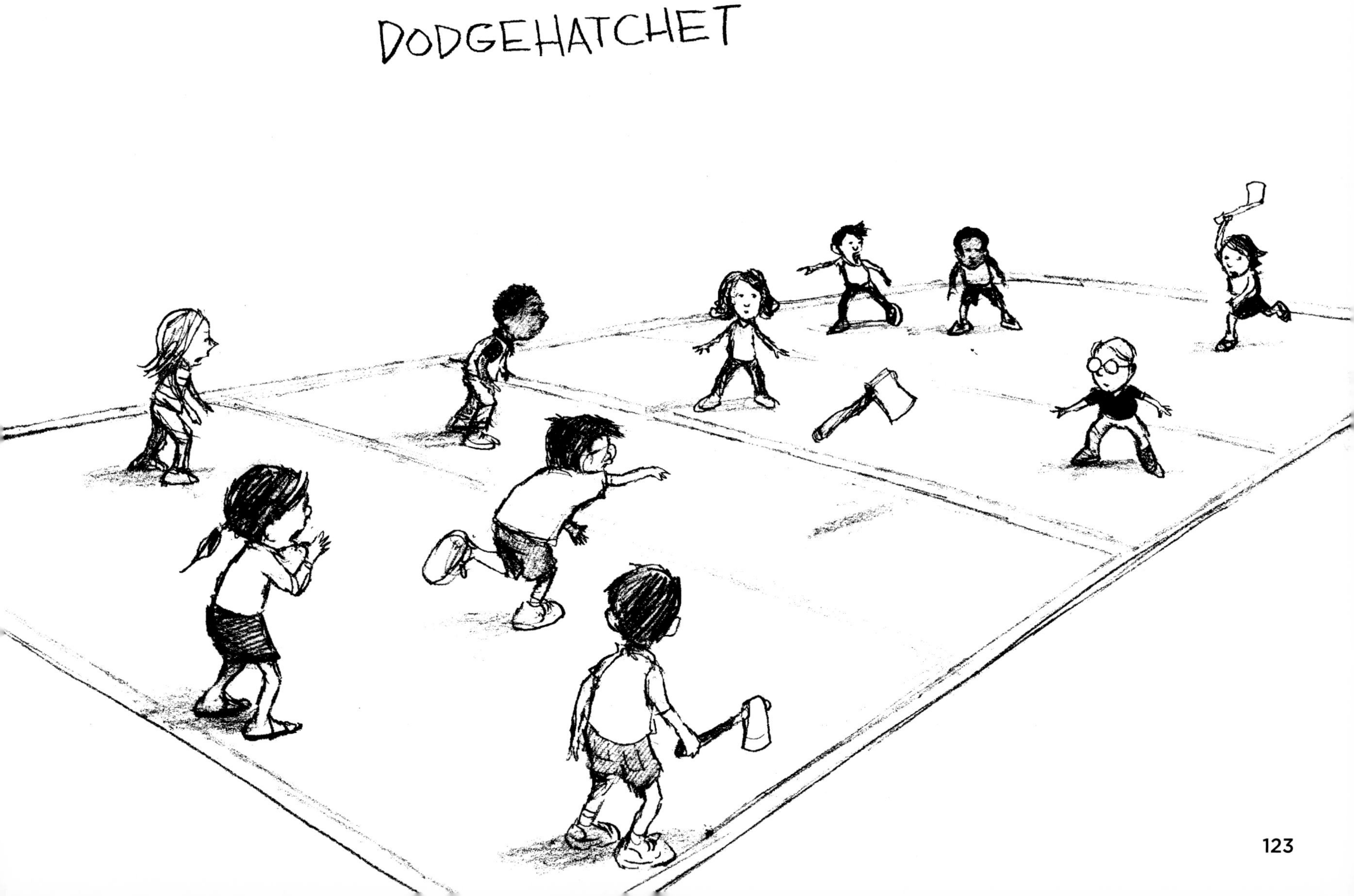
DODGEHATCHET

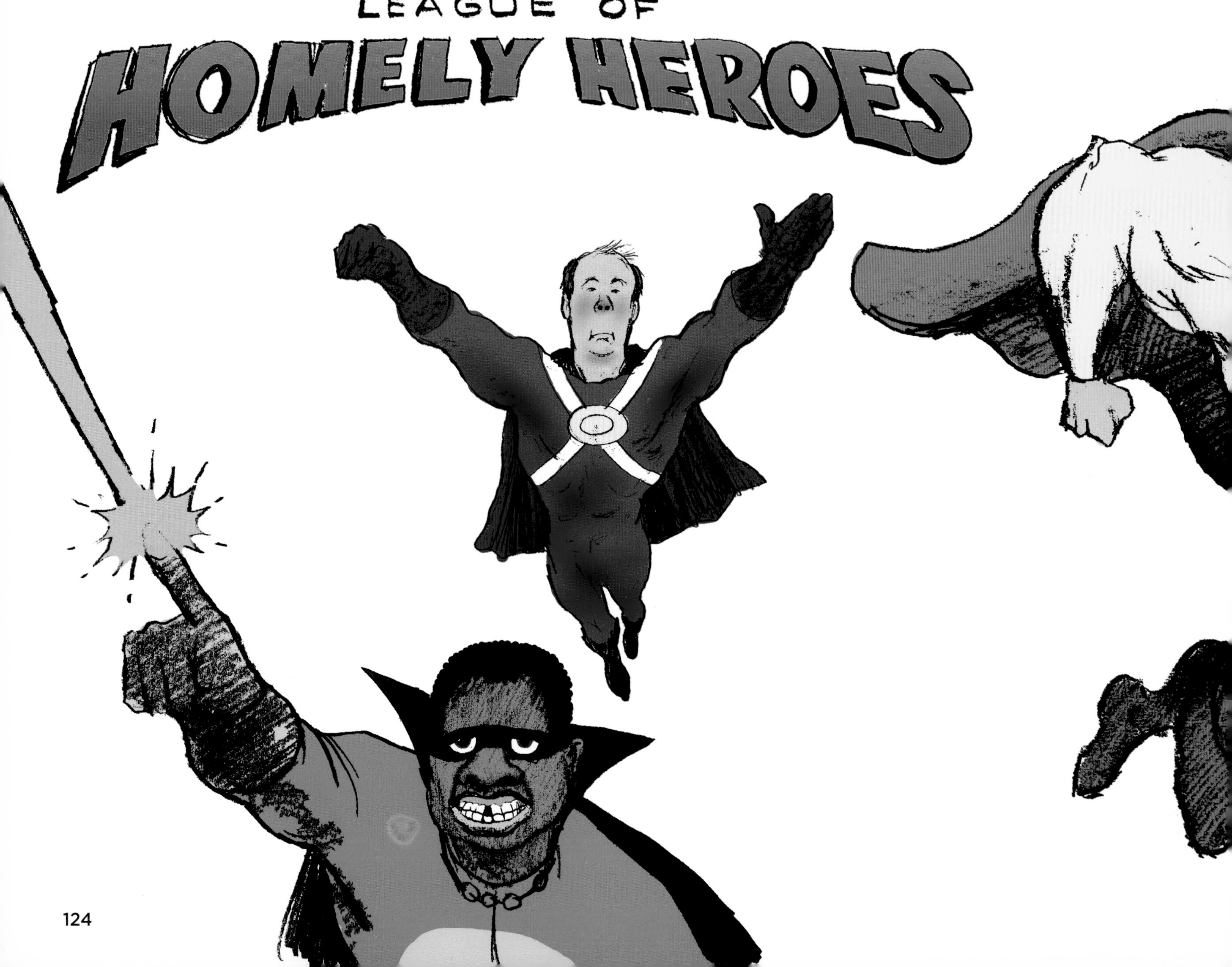
LEAGUE OF
HOMELY HEROES

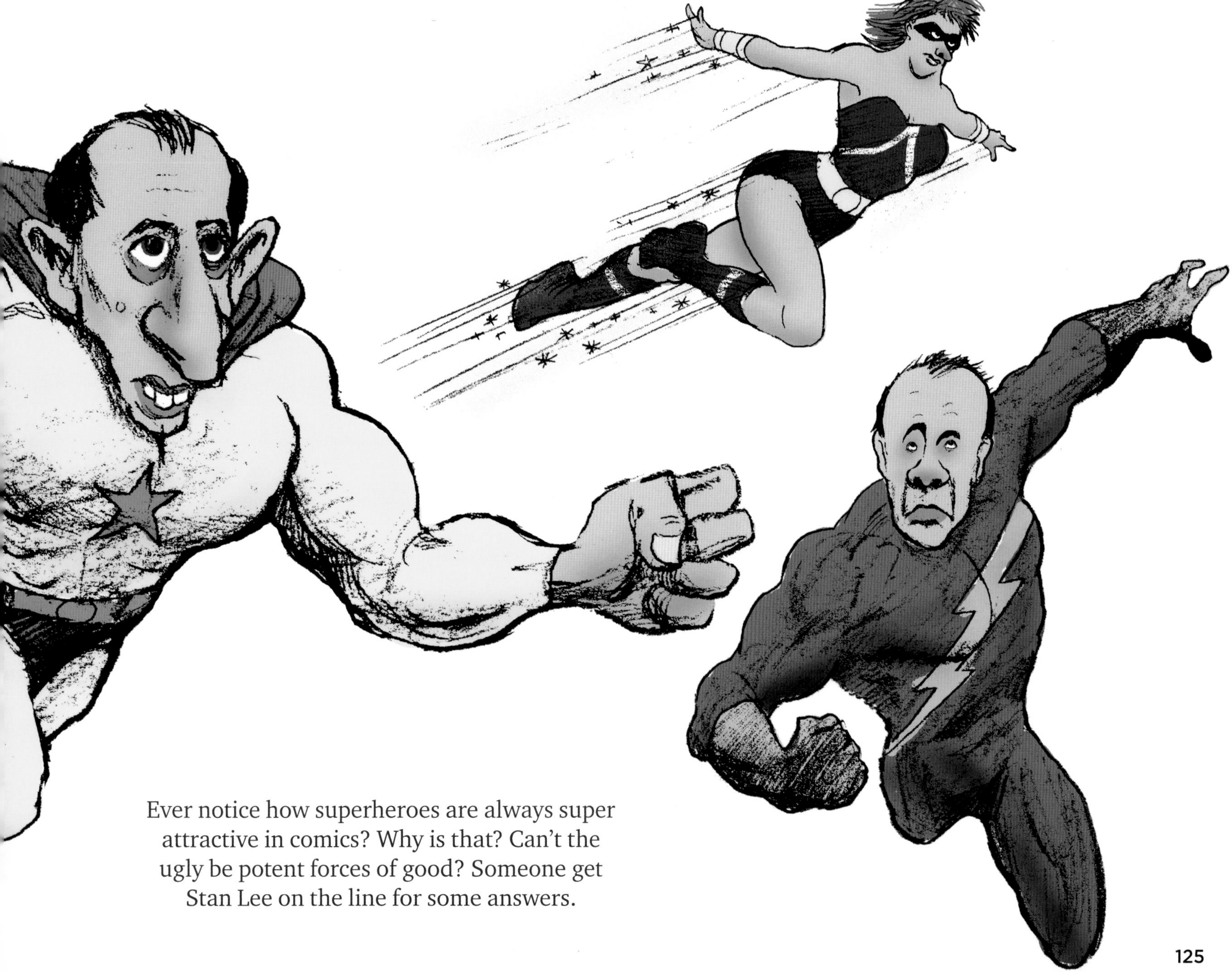

Ever notice how superheroes are always super attractive in comics? Why is that? Can't the ugly be potent forces of good? Someone get Stan Lee on the line for some answers.

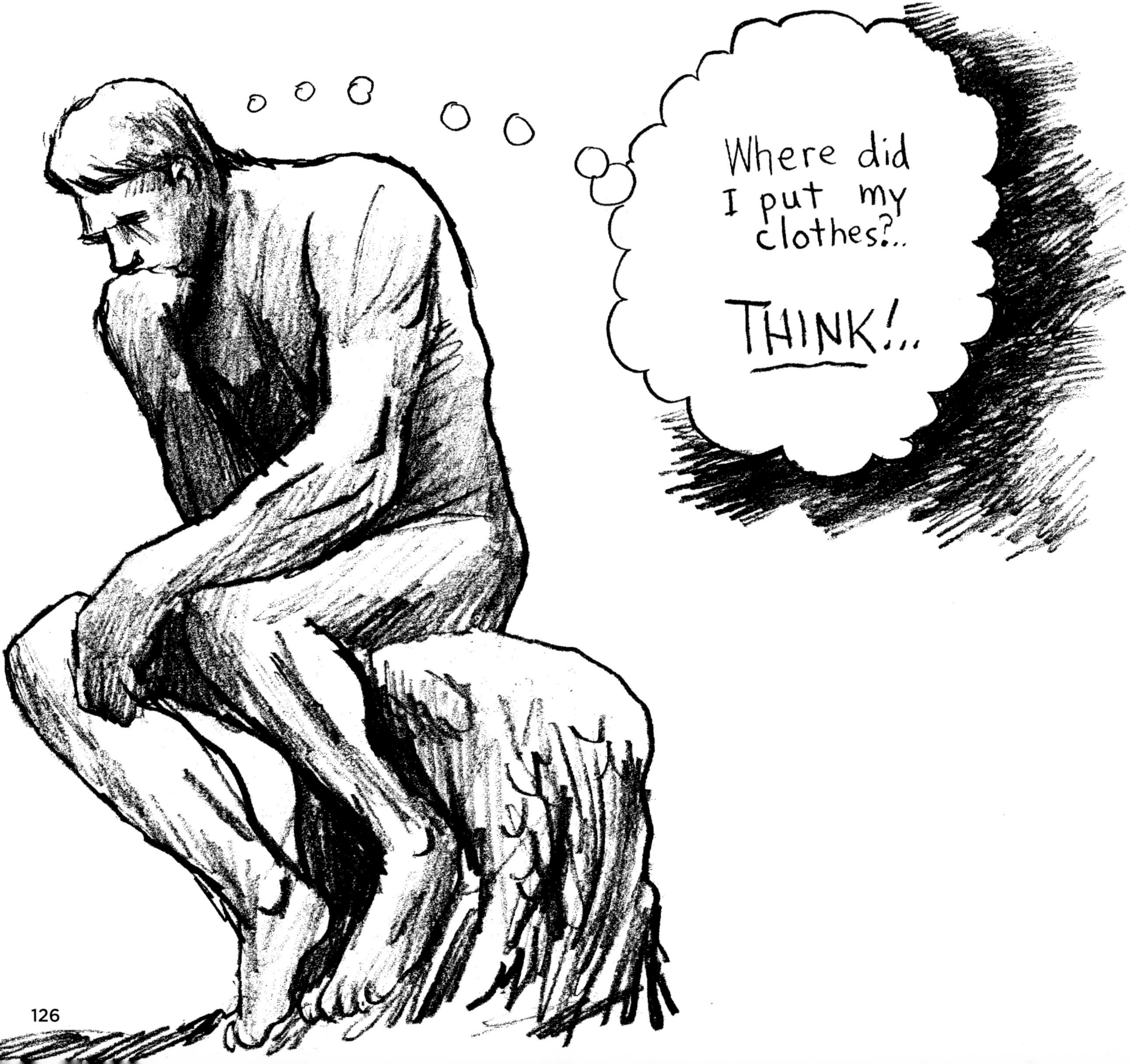
Where did I put my clothes?..
THINK!..

My kids threatened
to do this to me.

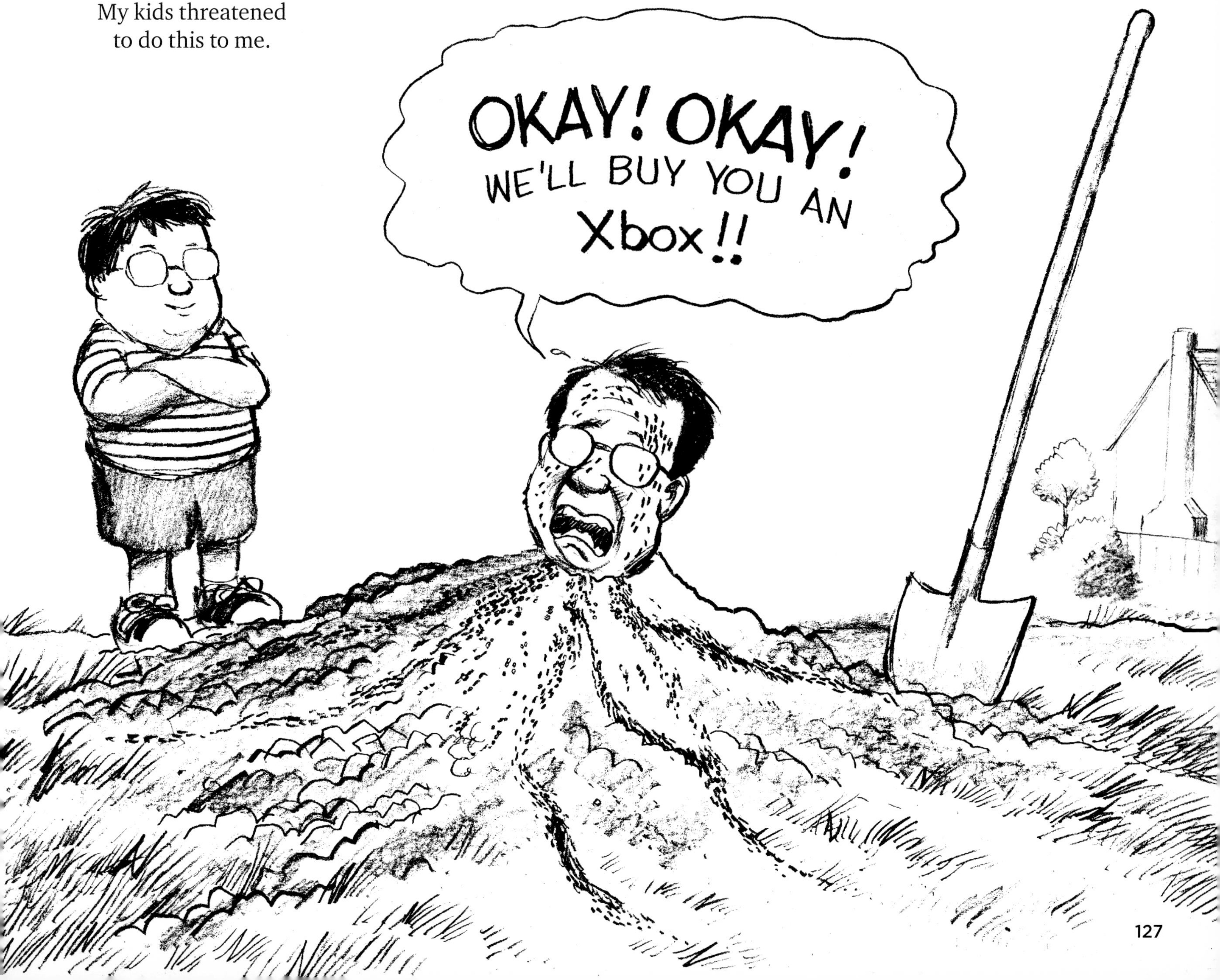
OKAY! OKAY!
WE'LL BUY YOU AN
Xbox!!

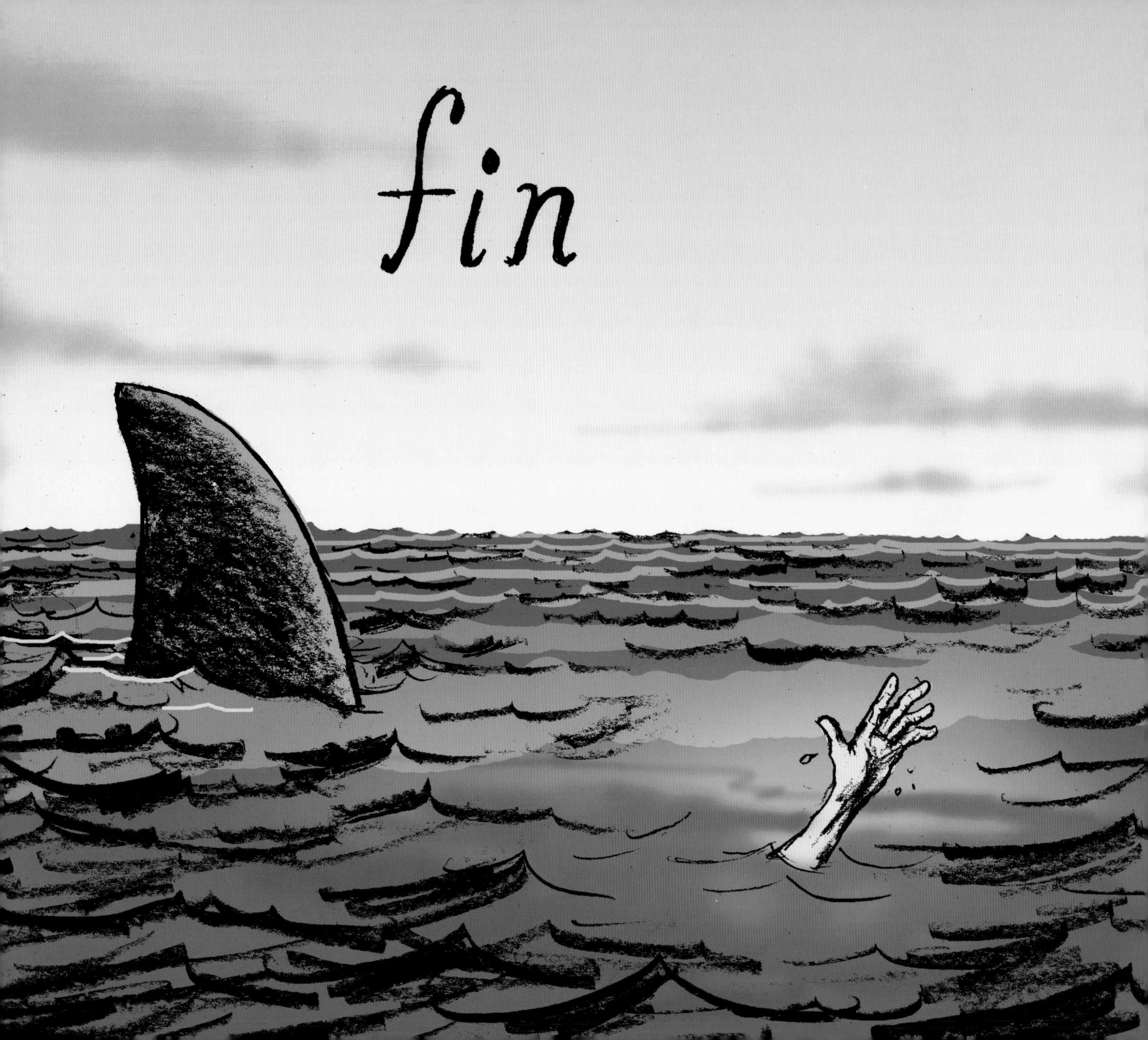
fin

THE WORLD OF THE

PENGUIN

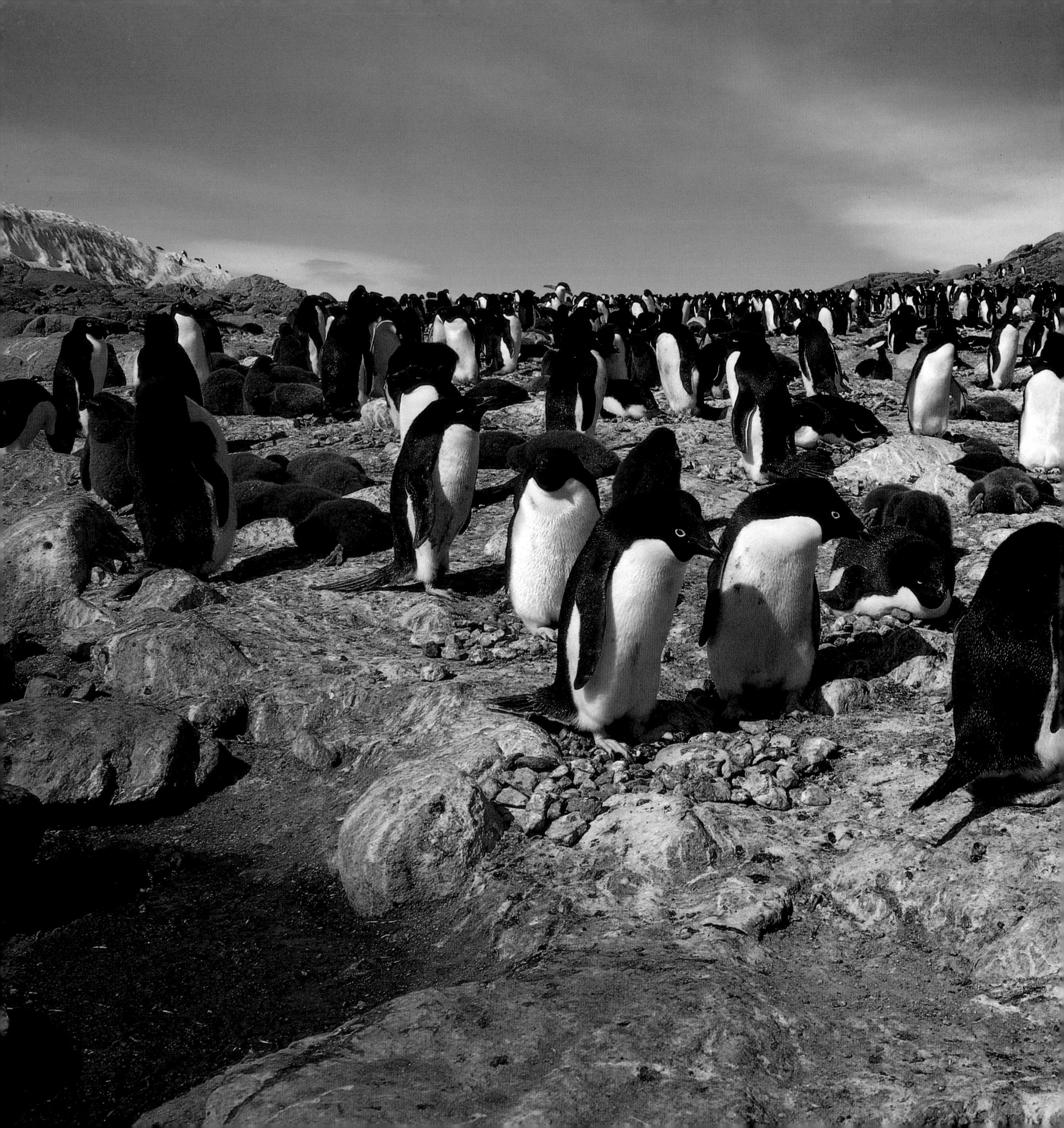

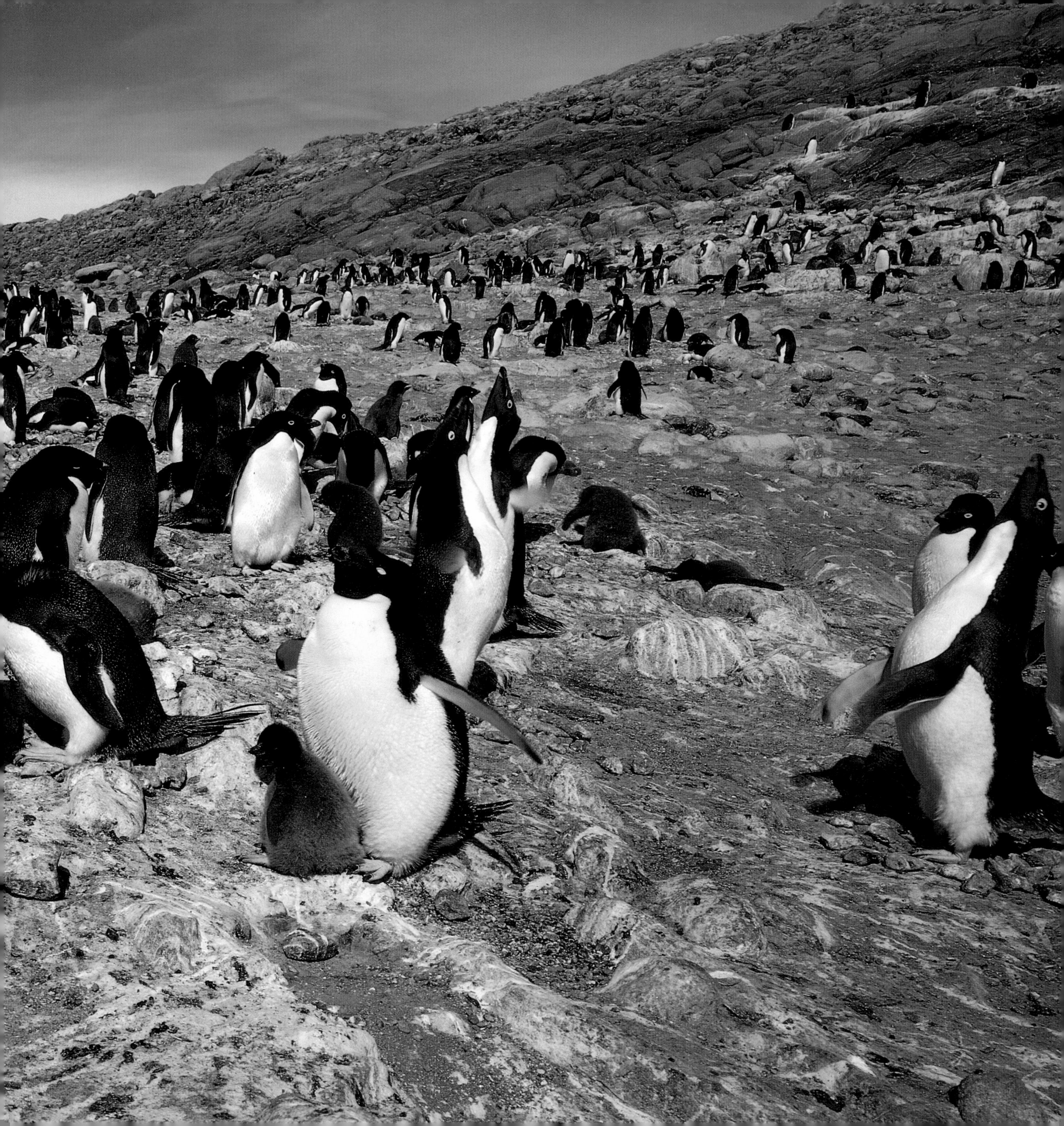

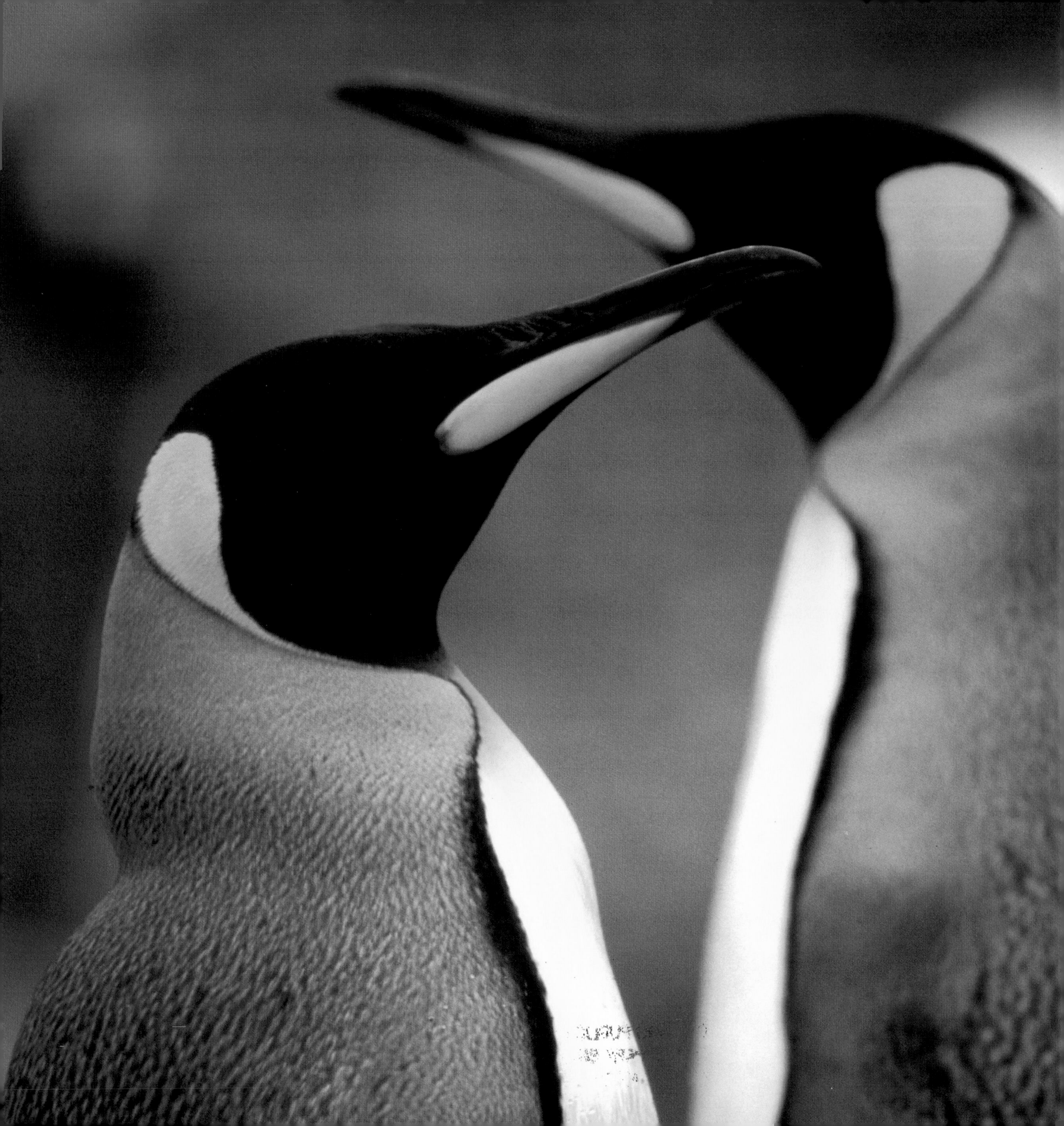

THE WORLD OF THE
PENGUIN

Text and photographs by
JONATHAN CHESTER

Sierra Club Books
San Francisco

The Sierra Club, founded in 1892 by John Muir, has devoted itself to the study and protection of the earth's scenic and ecological resources—mountains, wetlands, woodlands, wild shores and rivers, deserts and plains. The publishing program of the Sierra Club offers books to the public as a nonprofit educational service in the hope that they may enlarge the public's understanding of the Club's basic concerns. The point of view expressed in each book, however, does not necessarily represent that of the Club. The Sierra Club has some sixty chapters coast to coast, in Canada, Hawaii, and Alaska. For information about how you may participate in its programs to preserve wilderness and the quality of life, please address inquiries to Sierra Club, 85 Second Street, San Francisco, CA 94105.

Originally published by Greystone Books, a division of Douglas & McIntyre Ltd.,
1615 Venables Street, Vancouver, British Columbia V5L 2H1.

LIBRARY OF CONGRESS CATALOGING-IN-PUBLICATION DATA

Chester, Jonathan.
World of the penguin / by Jonathan Chester
p. cm.
Includes bibliographical references and index.
ISBN 0-87156-900-0 (cloth : alk. paper)
1. Penguins. 2. Penguins—Pictorial works. I. Title.
QL696.S473C48 1996
598.4'41—dc20 96-17675
CIP

The following publisher has given permission to use quoted material:
From *The Moon by Whale Light* by Diane Ackerman. Copyright © 1992 by Diane Ackerman. Reprinted by permission of Random House.

Front jacket photograph by Jonathan Chester
Back jacket photograph by Jonathan Chester
Jacket and book design by DesignGeist
Printed and bound in Hong Kong through Mandarin Offset

10 9 8 7 6 5 4 3 2 1

For Kirsty

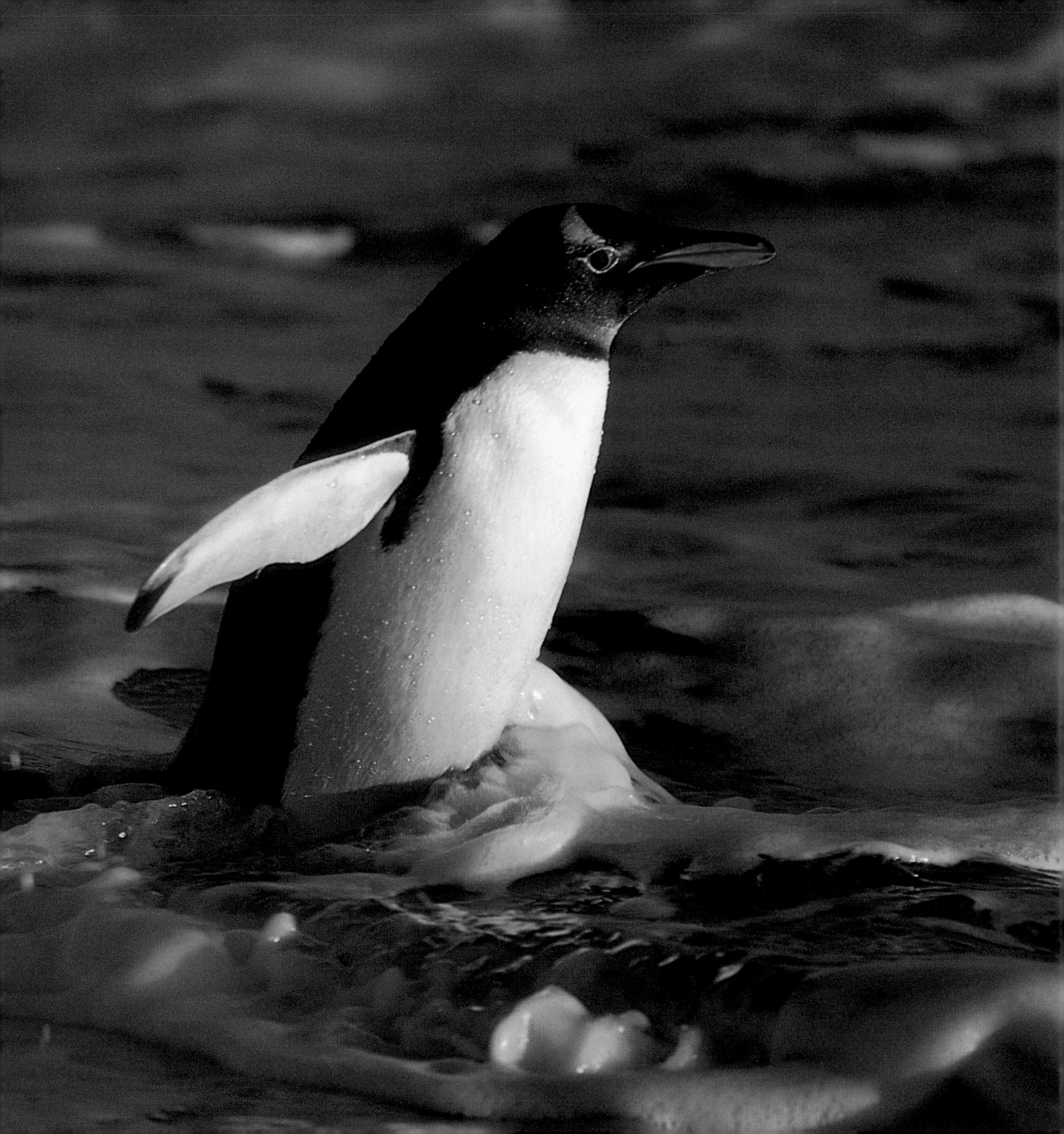

Contents

Acknowledgements

First and foremost, I would like to thank Kirsty Melville, who for years has patiently endured my peregrinations in search of penguin images, tolerated and sometimes even fuelled my collection of penguin memorabilia, and last, but not least, supported my writing and photography in so many ways.

Special thanks also go to Greystone Press, particularly to Rob Sanders, who believed in the book for years and finally found a way to make it happen; Nancy Flight, who endured my comings and goings and who helped shape the manuscript into a much more readable form; and Leah Jahn, who coped with a mountain of images. Many thanks to Sigrid Albert and Gabriele Proctor at DesignGeist for their patience and elegant design. I also wish to thank Tony Williams for reviewing the manuscript.

Steven Broni, Cynthia Cheney, Adam Daragh, Leo Lebon and Rinie van Meurs greatly assisted in obtaining additional images or information. The following organizations also need to be recognized for helping me to reach far-flung parts of the penguin world: Australian National Antarctic Research Expeditions (ANARE), the Falkland Islands Tourist Board, Hedgehog House, Mountain Travel, Sobek, Marine Expeditions and Quark Expeditions.

Finally, many thanks to all my fellow expeditioners and travelling companions who, over the years, have had to put up with the delays and inconvenience caused by my quest for more compelling penguin images.

Author's Note

There is a continuing effort to standardize and simplify species names and common names of penguins, but even the most recent authoritative sources differ in some cases. I have adopted as my guide the nomenclature used by biologist Tony Williams in his book *The Penguins,* while mentioning the historical and contemporary alternatives.

Sizes of penguins given are expressed as "length" because biologists measure from the tip of the bill to the tip of the tail. This measurement is more accurate than height, which varies according to whether the penguin is swimming, walking and so on. Penguin weights also vary greatly, depending on where the bird is in its cycle when it is measured. All birds are much heavier at the start of a period of fasting, whether it is associated with breeding or moulting. Figures for lengths and weights should therefore be used only as a rough guide. The standing height of a bird in the field will always seem slightly less than its stated length.

Penguin populations are also often presented as the number of breeding pairs, since it is difficult to count the actual number of birds; at any point in the breeding cycle, one of the pair may well be at sea feeding. Counts are usually based on the number of nests. Aerial photographs taken from balloons have proved effective for counting species that don't have nests.

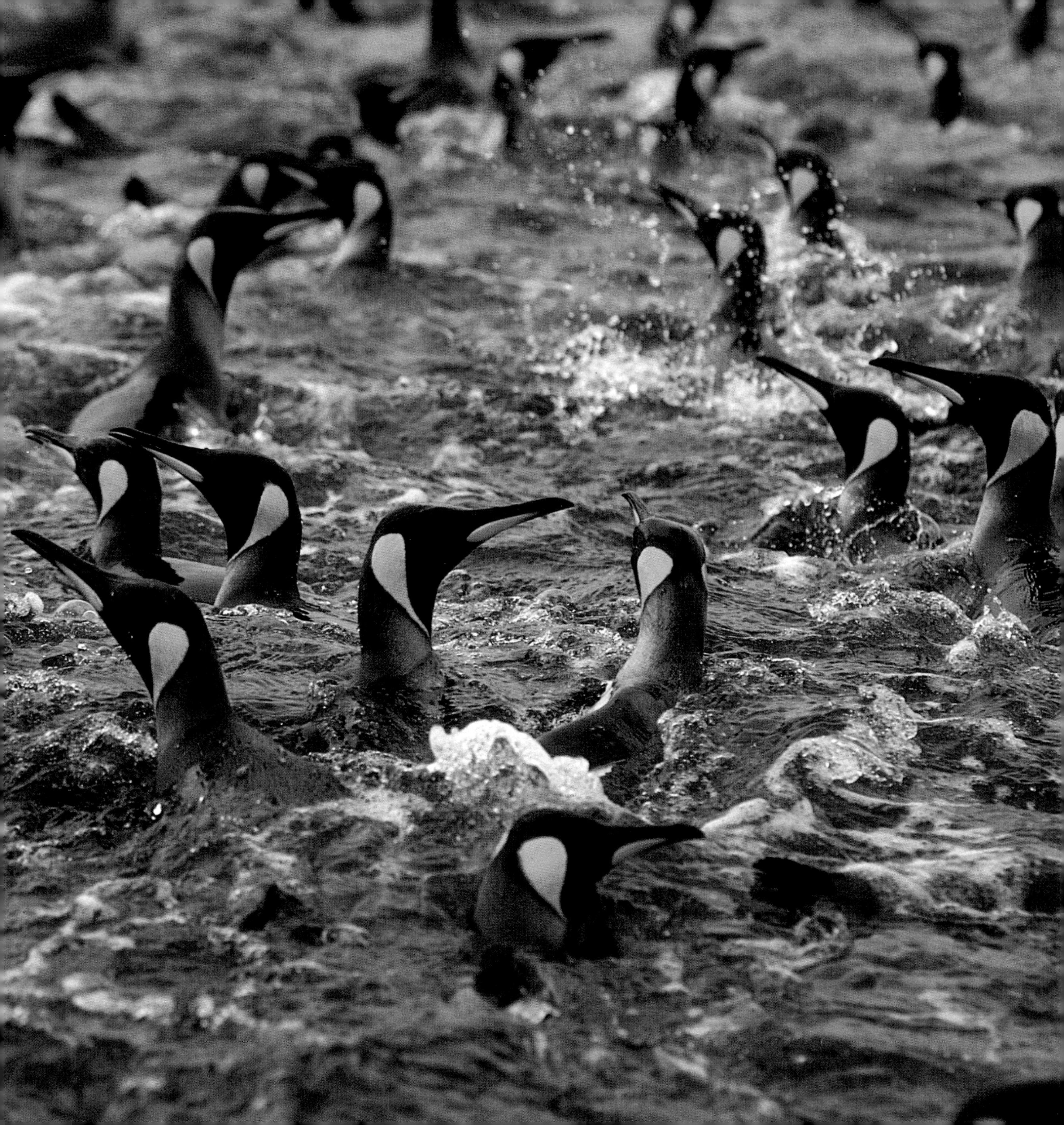

Introduction

The water foamed with the swirl and splash of hundreds of king penguins cavorting around our inflatable boat as we cruised off the shore of Macquarie Island in the sub-antarctic. Inquisitive beyond belief, they were pecking at the pontoons, lifting their heads clear of the water to have a close look at us and then diving under the boat. The scene on the other side of the foaming line of breakers was even more amazing—tens of thousands of the most magnificent penguins, crowded flipper to flipper in a giant rookery on Lusitania Beach. Regulations prohibited us from landing, but there wouldn't have been room anyway.

Although I first became acquainted with penguins as a boy, watching timid little, or fairy, penguins hiding in rocky crevices on the south coast of Australia, where we used to spend our summer holidays, it was not until I reached the Antarctic in 1985 that I became totally absorbed by these fascinating creatures. We were camped on the fringes of the Antarctic continent, at Commonwealth Bay, the site of the remains of Australian explorer Sir Douglas Mawson's huts. There I encountered Adélie penguins for the first time. With an indomitable spirit, they calmly endured what Mawson dubbed "the windiest place in the world." Even in midsummer, fierce katabatic winds would howl down off the icecap for days on end, while the Adélies courted, built rocky nests in the few sheltered spots and raised their chicks.

Since then, I have encountered many other penguin species in my travels, from half a million breeding pairs of chinstraps, sprawling over hectares of slopes like a textured patchwork carpet of black and white, to the amazing rockhoppers, known as jumping jacks, as they hopped hilariously in unison down a slope. To see them clambering up steep rock, having battled ashore through a pounding surf, gave me the utmost respect for the hardiness of these miniature mountaineers.

My fascination with penguins also grew out of a long-standing interest in polar history. Herbert Ponting, the cinematographer on Robert F. Scott's second Antarctic

FACING PAGE: *The sea boils with curious king penguins.*

expedition, was one of the first to capture footage showing penguins as "small amusing black and white people," which forever wedded them to the South Pole in people's minds. Since the Antarctic region is devoid of any large land mammals, such as the polar bear found in the Arctic, penguins have become synonymous with the Antarctic, even though they are much more common in the subantarctic.

Frank Hurley, the Australian photographer and cinematographer, often photographed penguins, first during Mawson's Australasian Antarctic Expedition and later as a member of Shackleton's Trans-Antarctic Expedition. The images of these feathered performers were so important to the documentary about the epic adventures of Shackleton's party that Hurley returned to South Georgia the season after they had been rescued, just to obtain the necessary footage.

These early images reinforced the association of penguins with the Antarctic and also with a certain anthropomorphic quality that continues today. Although not in quite the same league as cats or dogs in the cuteness stakes, penguins have long been favourites of advertisers, copywriters and cartoonists. There is the famous cartoon strip character Opus in *Bloom County*, by Berke Breathed, and a humorous penguin, Mawson, who inhabits daily papers down under. Gary Larson's offbeat *The Far Side* cartoons occasionally feature penguins as well.

Penguins have at times also played minor dramatic roles on the silver screen. A cadre of penguins became extras in *Batman Returns*, albeit portraying rocket-carrying commandos performing evil deeds. Because he was born with so-called flippers instead of hands, the villain was also called Penguin. Hollywood glossed over the fact that his flippers bore no resemblance to an actual penguin's appendages. There were even protests from animal rights activists at several screenings, but perhaps they were protesting the penguins' loss of innocence in the public's eye, rather than any indignities to penguins on screen, for most of the feathered cast seemed to be animatronics. Penguins as villains reached new depths in the delightful Academy Award-winning Claymation cartoon *The Wrong Trousers*. Here the penguin masterminds a diamond heist disguised as a rooster.

As if all this were not enough, marketers continue to find ingenious ways to use penguins to capture our attention. The penguin name has been used by many businesses over the years. The publishing company Penguin Books has made the penguin a household symbol. The name and image was chosen in 1935 by British businessman Sir Allen Lane (at the suggestion of his secretary) as the imprint for the publication of "good quality sixpenny paperbacks of well established hardback books." It embodied "dignified flippancy"—just the tone Lane was after for his audacious series.

A perennial symbol of anything icy or cold, penguins have been helping to sell air conditioners for decades, and a chain of frozen yogurt stores in California trades under the name Penguin. In this vein, penguins were adopted as the signature of the American ice hockey team the Pittsburg Penguins in the 1966-67 season. At the opposite end of the cultural spectrum, perhaps inspired by the preferred dress of classical musicians, is Great Britain's long-standing Penguin Café Orchestra.

This widespread fascination with tuxedoed characters who embody human frailty and humour, combined with my love for and experiences with these amazing birds, inspired me to write this book. But I wanted to go below the surface image of penguins to disclose their "real" nature, including the vital role they play in helping to understand the ecology of the Southern Hemisphere.

This book explores the many incredible aspects of the discovery, biology and behaviour of the seventeen species of penguins around the world. The pressures penguins face today are mostly a result of human interference; the book also explores the degree and extent of these pressures.

I hope that this book conveys how fascinating these charismatic ocean flyers are and that it will help you appreciate why we need to ensure that their natural environment is preserved. Looking after their environment is the only way that we can ensure the future of this family of flightless birds, which are now considered an important indicator of the health of our planet.

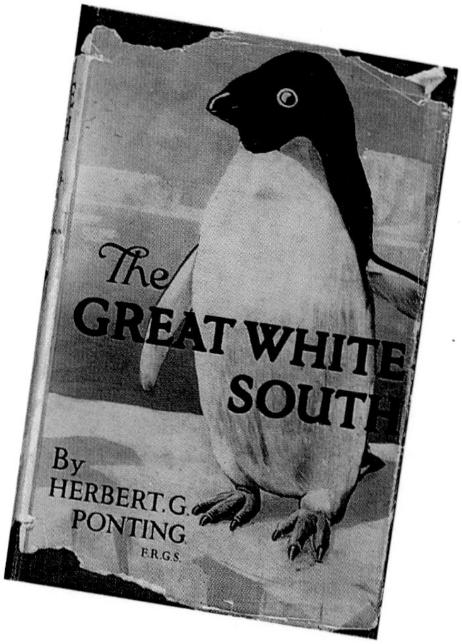
The
GREAT WHITE
SOUTH
By
HERBERT.G.
PONTING
F.R.G.S.

Herbert Ponting, the photographer on Scott's ill-fated expedition to the South Pole, was among the first to capture penguins on film.

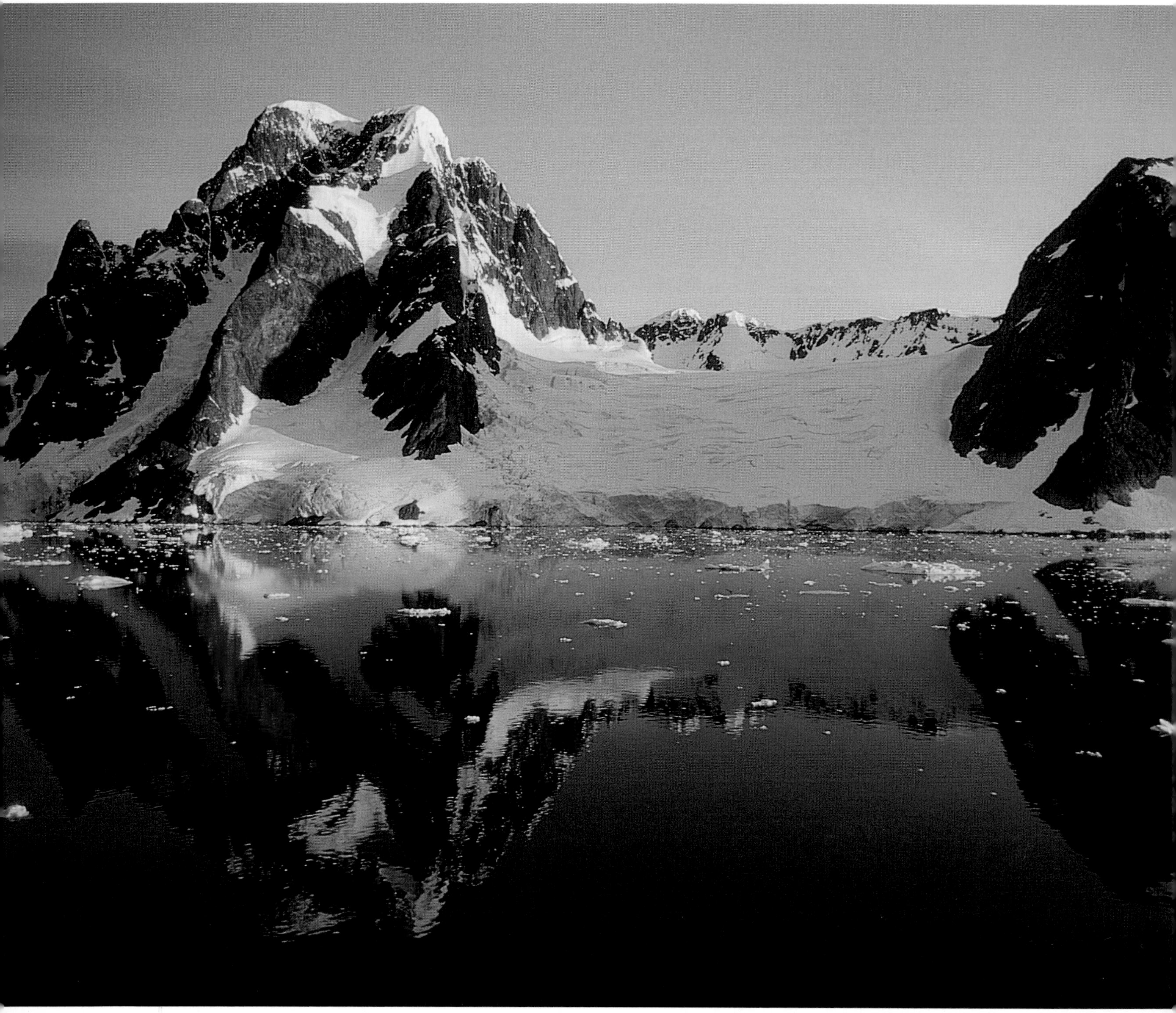

Part I

PENGUINS AND NATURE

Penguins are like icebergs—
a scintillating mystery,
most of which is hidden from view.

—Diane Ackerman,
The Moon by Whale Light, 1992

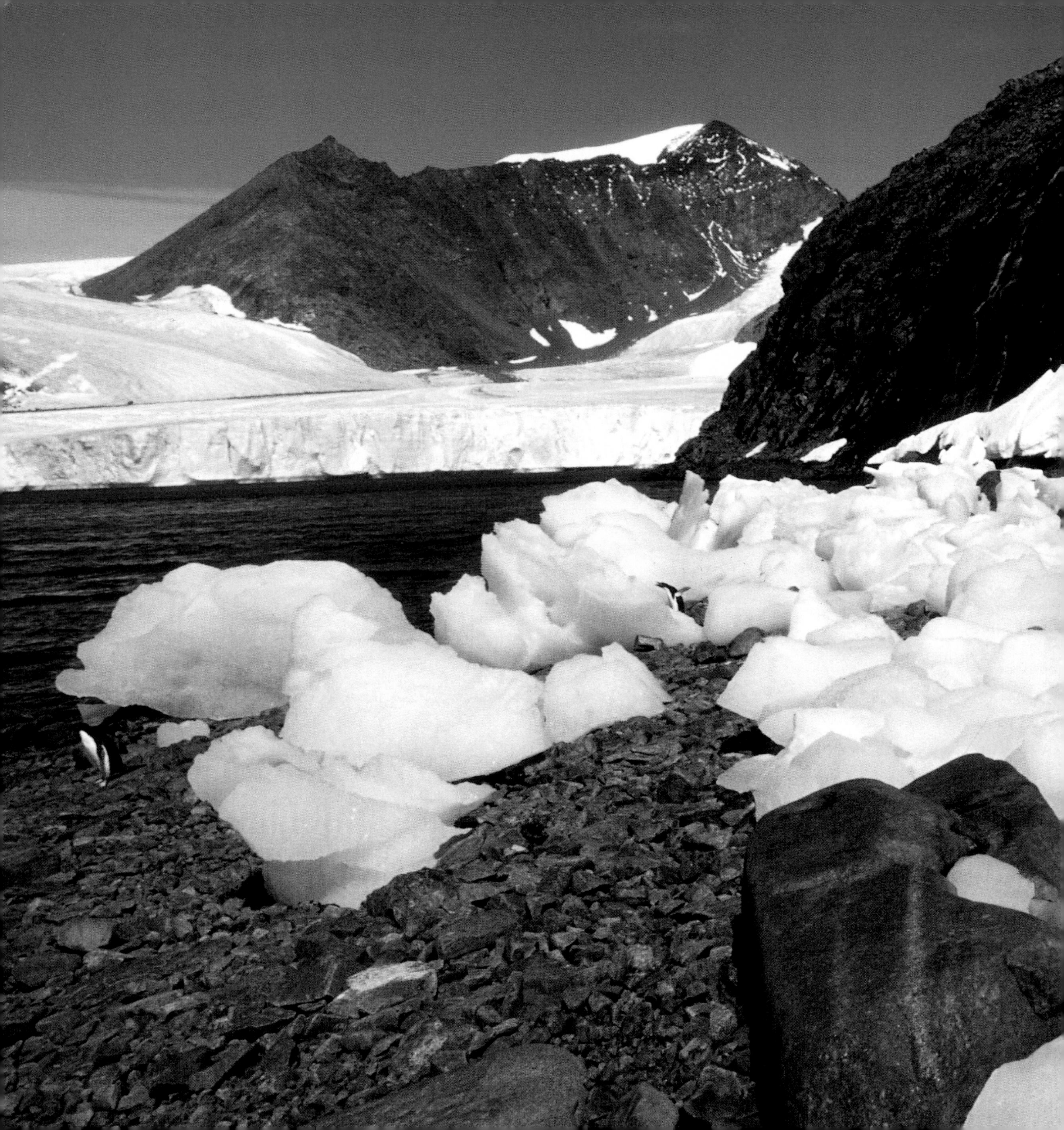

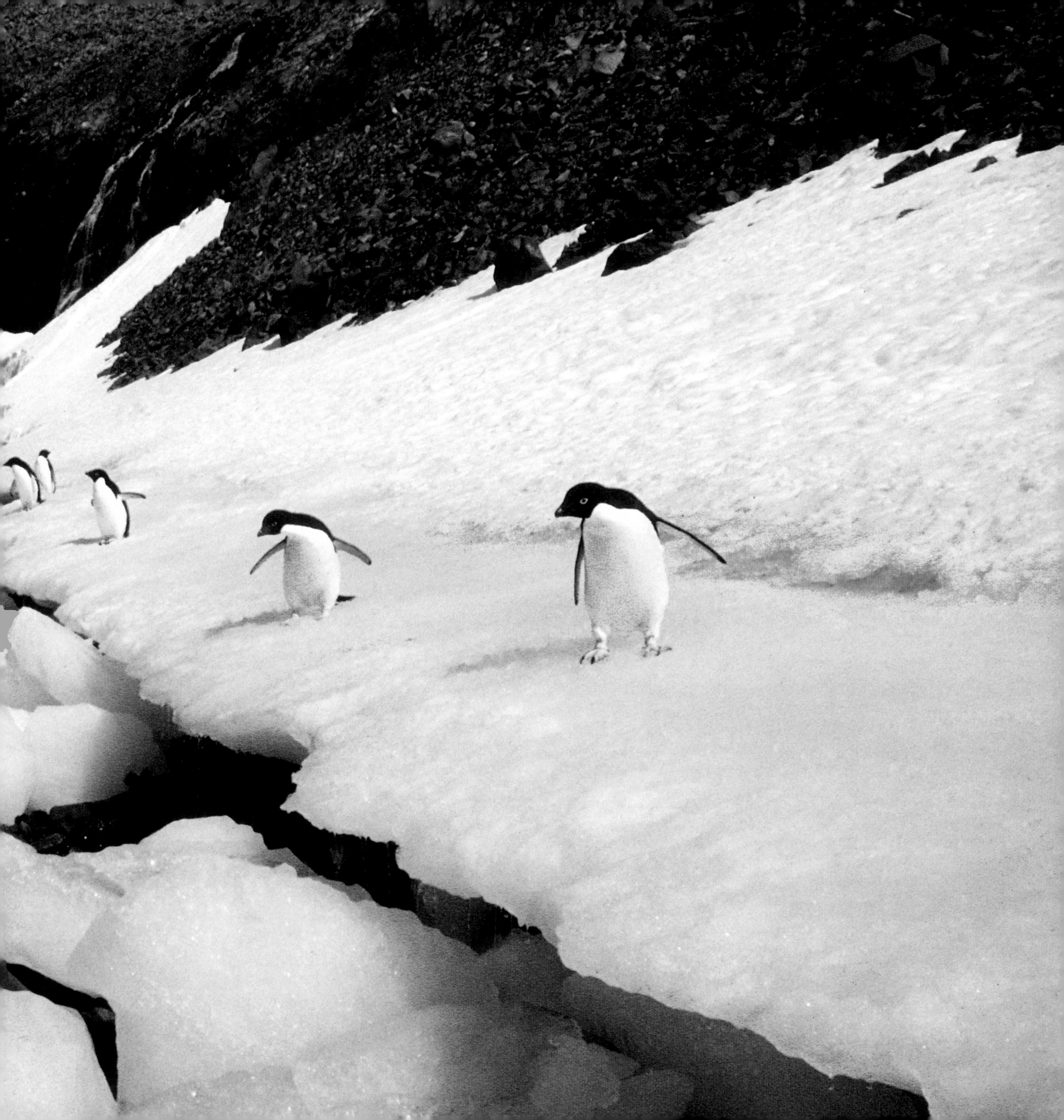

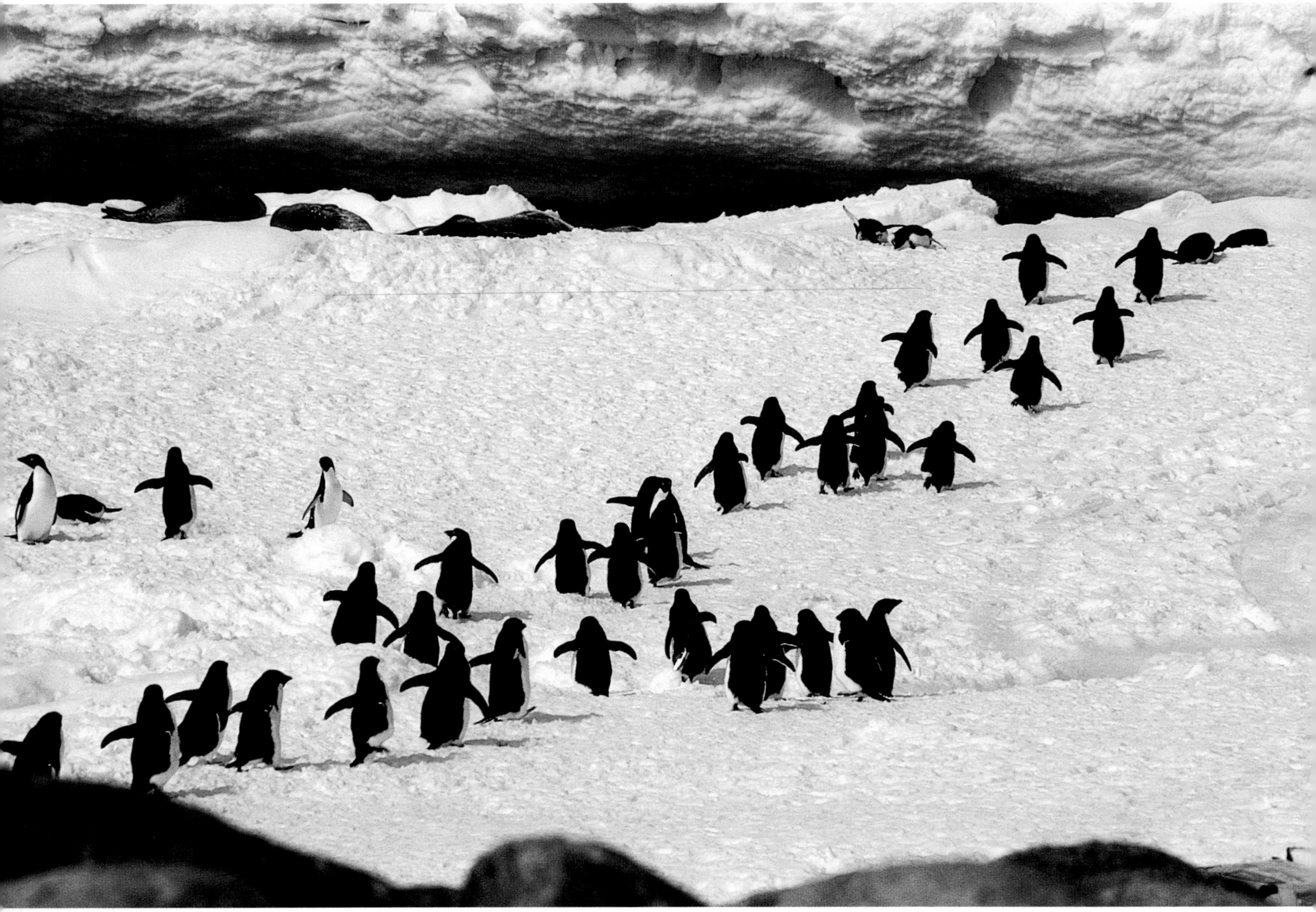

Chapter 1   What Is a Penguin?

There are two kinds of penguins in the Antarctic, the white ones coming towards you and the black ones going away from you.

—Anonymous

Penguins are a family of specialized flightless sea birds found only in the Southern Hemisphere. Most people associate penguins with the South Pole, but they occur mainly in the cool subtemperate oceans north of the Antarctic and comprise an incredible 80 per cent of all bird biomass farther south in the subantarctic region. Because they are warm blooded, like mammals, they can be active in almost any climate. Some species survive year-round in the depths of the Antarctic; others endure the blazing heat of the tropics.

Penguins vary greatly in size—standing at almost a metre (3 feet), the tallest penguin, the emperor, is about three times the height of the smallest, the little penguin—but all penguin species are similar in form. From the chest up, each species has distinctive feather markings, or coloured plumes and skin patterns, by which they can be identified. Like other diving birds, penguins are almost neutrally buoyant, meaning that they weigh as much as the volume of water they displace and so float very low in the water. As a result, the only part visible above the surface of the water, by which penguins may easily recognize one another, is the head and shoulders.

Penguins have complex behaviour patterns that help them deal with their highly social mode of breeding and the severe demands of their environment. Researchers are only now beginning to understand some of these patterns, but many aspects of penguins still remain a mystery. Even the term "penguin" is an enigma.

FACING PAGE: *Penguins have what is known as countershading— dark backs and white undersides, which may afford them some camouflage at sea.*

What's in a Name?

There are several plausible sources of the name penguin. Naturalist Tony Soper suggests that it originated in 1592, when a Welshman sailing with Sir Thomas Cavendish saw these strange creatures at Porto Deseado in Patagonia and called them *pen-gwyn*, which means "white head" in Welsh.

Other accounts, however, suggest that the term "penguin" came from the Spanish *penguigo* and was first applied to the great auk, a now extinct flightless diving bird that used to live in the North Atlantic and that had black and white plumage like that of today's penguins. *Pinguis* is Latin for "fat," which, as the poorly nourished early sailors would have discovered, was a feature of the auk's anatomy. When other Europeans explored to the south and discovered a similar-looking flightless diver, they used the same name—penguin.

The *Shorter Oxford English Dictionary* suggests that the first recorded use of the term "penguin" in the English language was between 1578 and 1588. It also lists a little-used but delightful term: "Penguinery, a place where penguins congregate and breed." The name penguin has also been applied in several other instances stemming from one of the bird's defining characteristics. *Brewer's Dictionary of Phrase and Fable* states: "The name of this flightless bird is applied to training aircraft used on the ground; also, jocularly, to a member of the Women's Royal Airforce, a 'Flapper' who does not fly."

Taxonomy

Long after penguins were first sighted by Europeans, naturalists began to develop the system of classifying all living things and giving them a two-part Latin or Greek name, now called a scientific name.

Penguins belong to the class Aves and, below that, to the order Sphenisciformes, from the Greek, *spheniscus*, meaning "wedgelike," possibly in reference to the shape of the wing or the body. There is only one family, Spheniscidae, which is organized into six genera. It is unusual to have only one family in an order, but taxonomists argue that penguins are unique and thus deserve this distinction.

The six genera of living penguins are: *Aptenodytes* (unwinged diver), *Pygoscelis* (elbow legs), *Megadyptes* (big diver), *Eudyptes* (crested), *Eudyptula* (good little diver) and *Spheniscus* (wedgelike). Some genera also have common names that are somewhat descriptive and so can help to make sense of the myriad of species names. The *Pygoscelis* are called the brush-tailed or long-stiff-tailed penguins because their prominent tail feathers seem to sweep the ground behind them. The *Eudyptes* are known as the crested penguins because they all have coloured plumes above their eyes, and the *Spheniscus* are known as the ringed penguins because of the ring-shaped bands of black or white feathers on their chests and heads.

Even taxonomists have difficulty determining some of the species of penguins. Deciding where variations between populations are sufficient to regard them as separate species is an evolving process, and even eminent scientists can't agree. The consensus is that there are seventeen species of modern-day penguins—some say eighteen, and in the past some held that there were only sixteen. The royal penguin was once considered a subspecies of the macaroni, rather than a full-fledged species, and some taxonomists (particularly in New Zealand, where the subspecies is found), maintain that the white-flippered penguin is a full species rather than a subspecies of the little penguin.

Variations between penguin species occur mostly in their size and in the pattern and colour of markings on their heads. As this rockhopper matures, its yellow eyebrows will become bushier.

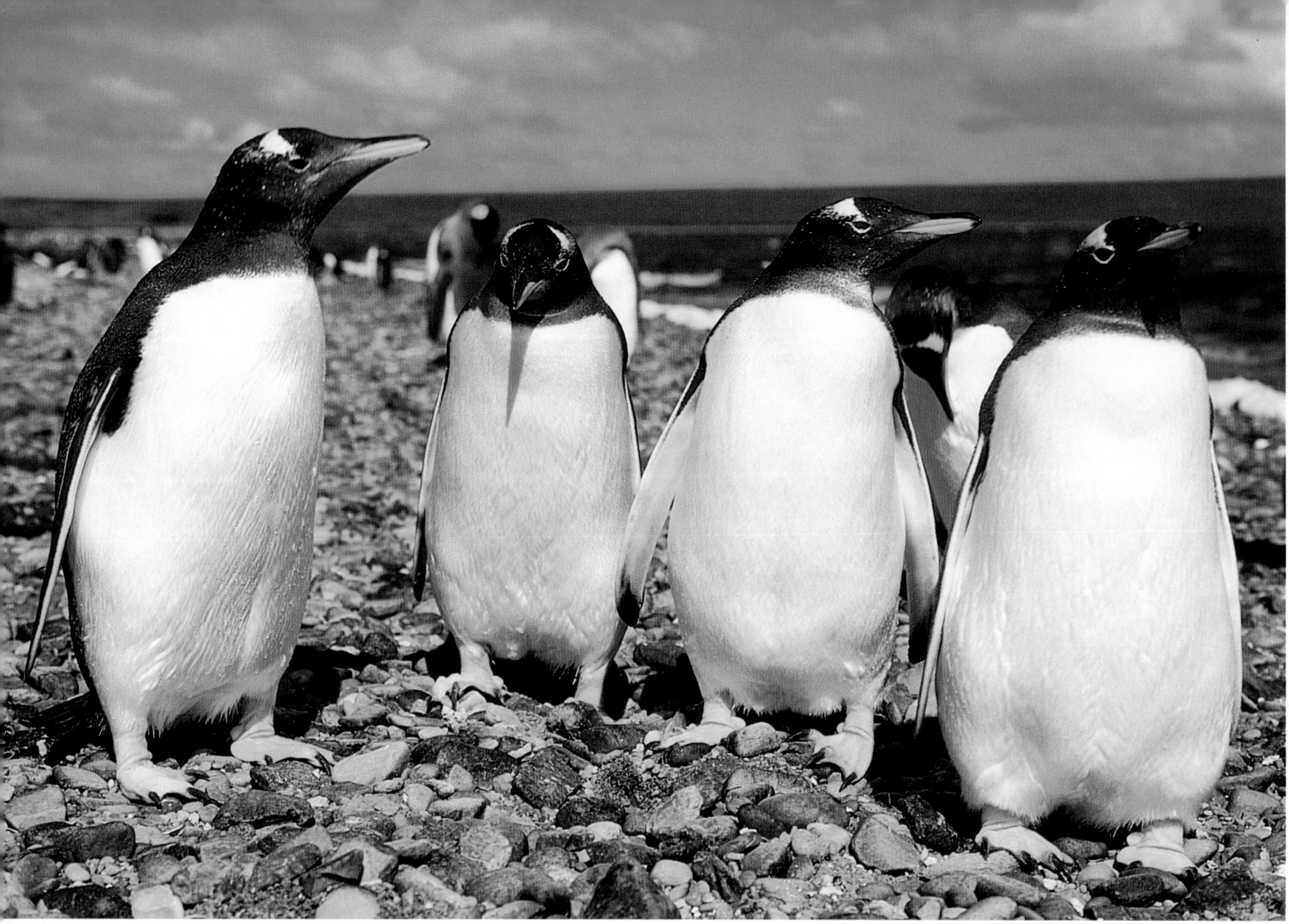

Gentoo penguins, one of the three species of the Pygoscelis *genus—commonly called the brush-tailed penguins—are found predominantly in the Falkland Islands, in the subantarctic and on the Antarctic Peninsula.*

Scientific names are an important way of avoiding confusion, since common names vary so much and the same species may have different names in different regions. The little penguin, for example, is also called the fairy penguin in parts of Australia and the blue penguin, or little blue, in New Zealand. The Humboldt penguin is also referred to as the Peruvian penguin. In addition, different species may share the same common name. The term *jackass penguin,* for example, has been variously used to refer to the magellanic, Humboldt and African penguins.

Ancient Origins

Penguins are thought to have begun to diverge from petrel-like flying birds over 65 million years ago. By the late Eocene, 45 to 50 million years ago, penguins were clearly differentiated from other birds. Fossil records reveal many species of penguins that have long since vanished from the earth. All of these fossils have been found in the Southern Hemisphere, and they consist mostly of two characteristic bones, one from a part of the foot, the tarsometatarsus, and another from the flipper (or arm), the humerus. These bones are the most densely calcified, since they are used in the load-bearing aspects of the bird's walking or swimming, and so are more resistant to erosion. As a result, they survive the process of fossilization better than other, less robust bones. Since these bones are distinctively penguin-like, they are easily recognized and have become the key to determining the proportions and size of fossil species.

The first fossil penguin bone was found by a Maori in New Zealand in 1859 and was sent to England to the naturalist Thomas Huxley for identification. He recognized it as the first known penguin fossil, and since it was unlike any living species, he gave it a new scientific name, *Palaeeudyptes antarcticus*.

Over forty species of fossil penguins have been described so far, from seventeen genera, and they have been found on all the major southern land masses: Australia, New Zealand, South America, southern Africa and the Antarctic. It is widely agreed that earlier penguins were more diverse and much larger than present-day species. Penguin paleontologist George Gaylord Simpson claims that these fossil penguins were the dominant predators of small crustaceans, long before seals and their relatives appeared. The largest species that once roamed the seas, *Pachydyptes ponderosus* (heavy diver), was estimated to be between 143 and 162 centimetres (56 to 64 inches) tall and weighed a massive 81 kilograms (178 pounds).

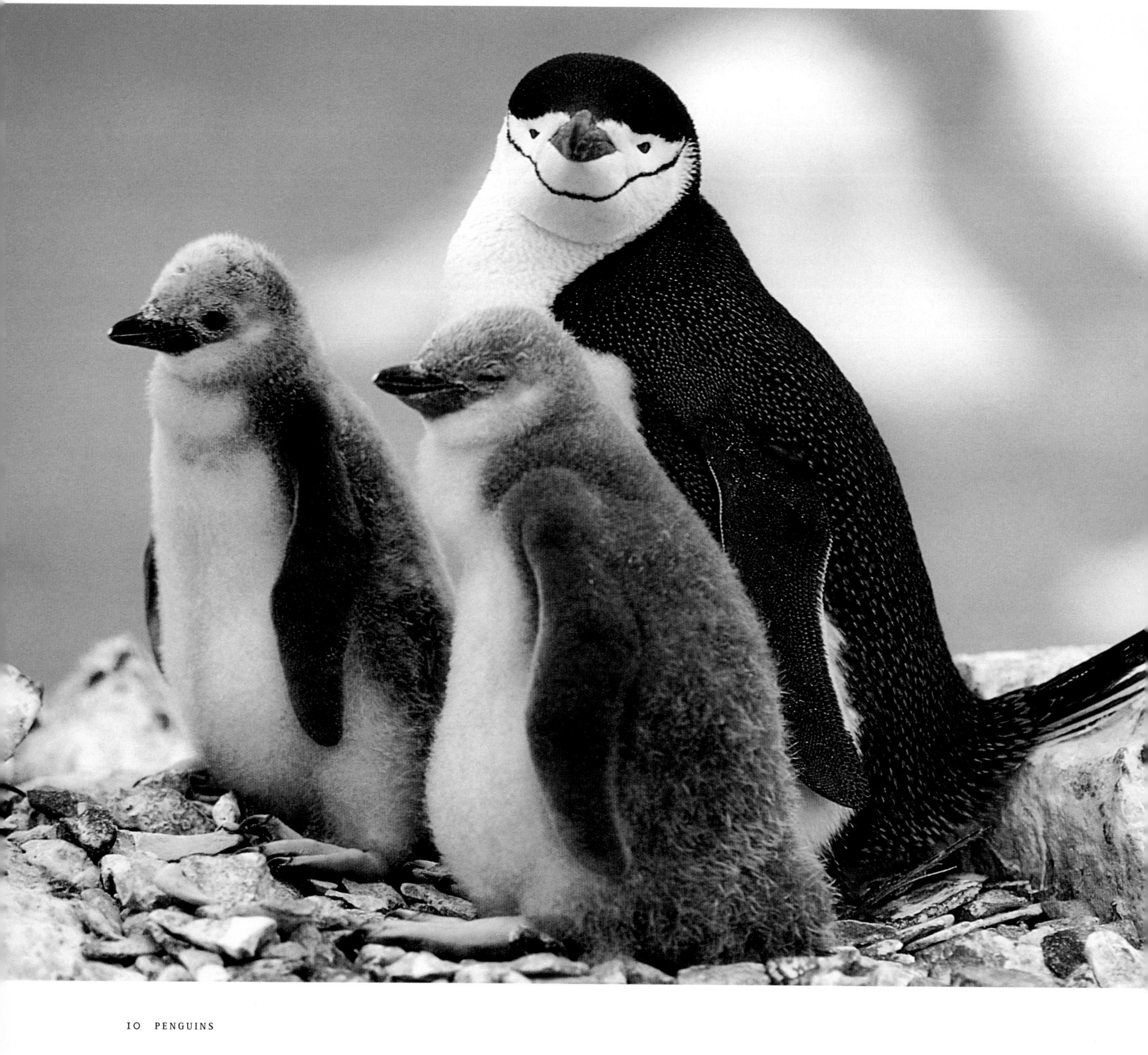

Creatures of the Cold Currents

Sea dominates the southern half of the world, and most penguin species inhabit this great southern ocean that encircles the globe between latitudes 50° and 60° south. In places, this broad band of eastward-flowing, nutrient-rich water sweeps northward on the west coasts of Australia, South America and southern Africa, creating cold currents that extend the range of penguins far to the north. The Benguela Current sweeps northward along the west coast of South Africa, and the West Australian Current sweeps along the west of Australia. The well-known Humboldt Current pushes north as far as the equator along the west coast of South America. Smaller cold currents also extend to the north on the east coasts of New Zealand and the Falkland Islands, enabling various penguin species to inhabit these regions.

At the Antarctic Convergence, or Antarctic Polar Front, the cold Antarctic water meets the warmer, subtropical water of the Indian, Pacific and Atlantic Oceans. This is a zigzag boundary, 30 to 50 kilometres (20 to 30 miles) wide that varies between 48° south and 61° south. The southern, denser water is rich in nutrients from currents that lift minerals from the ocean floor into the lighted layers. Here plankton (free-floating microscopic organisms) proliferates, forming the basis of the food web, which in turn supports krill, fish and squid. Eight species of penguin breed close to or south of the Antarctic Convergence, but they are not uniformly distributed.

It is believed that historically penguins dispersed from the southern temperate zone, in the vicinity of New Zealand, south to the subantarctic and north to the equator. Penguin species are also divided along lines of longitude into sectors: the New Zealand-Australia, South American and African sectors each have unique penguin species.

The only species that breed on Antarctica are the emperor penguin and the Adélie penguin, which are known as the continental Antarctic penguins. Both species are found around the continent. The Adélie penguin is also found along the Antarctic Peninsula.

The maritime Antarctic penguins are the gentoos and the chinstraps, which nest on the Antarctic Peninsula and the so-called Scotia Arc—the chain of islands that sweeps northeastwards from the tip of the Antarctic Peninsula. These include the South Shetland, South Orkney and South Sandwich Islands. The gentoos and chinstraps also extend northward into the subantarctic near the Antarctic Convergence.

Subantarctic penguin species that breed in this transition zone on subantarctic islands (South Georgia, Bouvetoya, Heard and Macquarie Island) are the king, rockhopper, royal and macaroni.

FACING PAGE: *Chinstraps, another of the brush-tailed penguins, are one of the seventeen species of penguins recognized today. Some forty fossil species have also been unearthed.*

NEW ZEALAND
North Island
South Island
AUSTRALIA
Snares
Auckland Islands
Campbell Island
Macquarie Island
PACIFIC OCEAN
Circumpolar Ocean Currents
West Australian Current
Balleny Islands
Scott Island
Ross Sea
Ice Shelves
INDIAN OCEAN
Amundsen Sea
Antarctic Peninsula
Antarctic Convergence
Heard Island
South Pole
Galapagos Islands
Humboldt Current
ANTARCTICA
South Shetland Islands
Iles Kerguelen
Weddell Sea
Cape Horn
Patagonia
South Orkney Islands
Chile
Peru
Falkland Islands
South Sandwich Islands
South Georgia
Bouvetøya
SOUTH AMERICA
Cape of Good Hope
Benguela Current
South Africa
AFRICA
ATLANTIC OCEAN

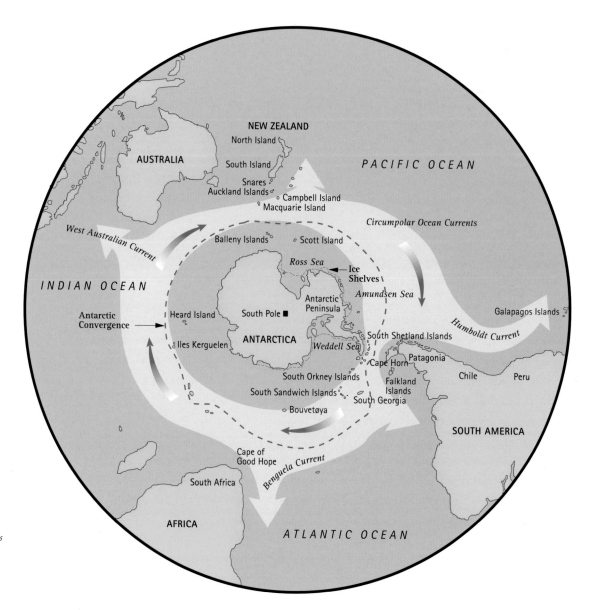

Cold currents in the Southern Hemisphere. Adapted from Chris Gaskin and Neville Peat, The World of Penguins, *p. 6.*

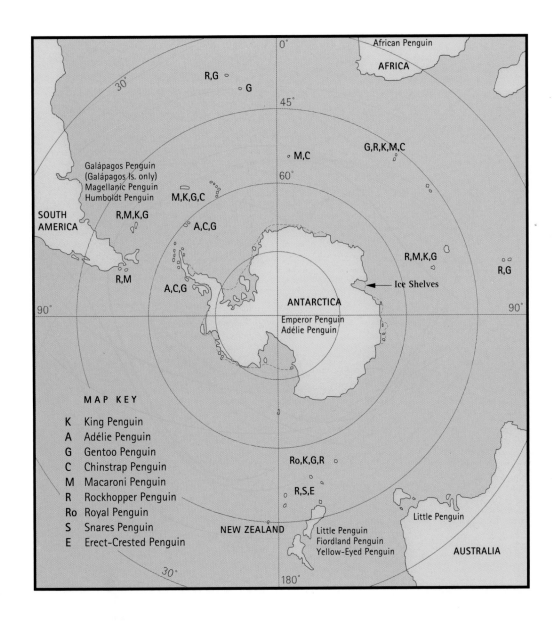

Inside the map:

0°
African Penguin
AFRICA
R,G ∘ ☐
∘ G
45°
G,R,K,M,C
∘ M,C
60°
Galápagos Penguin
(Galápagos Is. only)
Magellanic Penguin
Humboldt Penguin
M,K,G,C
SOUTH
AMERICA
R,M,K,G
A,C,G
R,M,K,G
R,G
R,M
A,C,G
Ice Shelves
ANTARCTICA
Emperor Penguin
Adélie Penguin
90° 90°

MAP KEY

K   King Penguin
A   Adélie Penguin
G   Gentoo Penguin
C   Chinstrap Penguin
M   Macaroni Penguin
R   Rockhopper Penguin
Ro Royal Penguin
S   Snares Penguin
E   Erect-Crested Penguin

Ro,K,G,R
R,S,E
Little Penguin
NEW ZEALAND
Little Penguin
Fiordland Penguin
Yellow-Eyed Penguin
AUSTRALIA
30°
180°

Distribution of today's penguin species. Adapted from Tony D. Williams, The Penguins: Spheniscidae, *Fig. 1.2.*

North of the convergence is the temperate subantarctic zone, which is occupied by the magellanic penguin in South America and is home to the Snares, erect-crested, rockhopper, Fiordland, yellow-eyed and little penguin in the New Zealand area. Penguins of the temperate region include the African penguin and, in the South American sector, the Humboldt, magellanic and Galápagos penguins. The Galápagos is in fact a tropical species, occurring only in the Galápagos Islands, which straddle the equator.

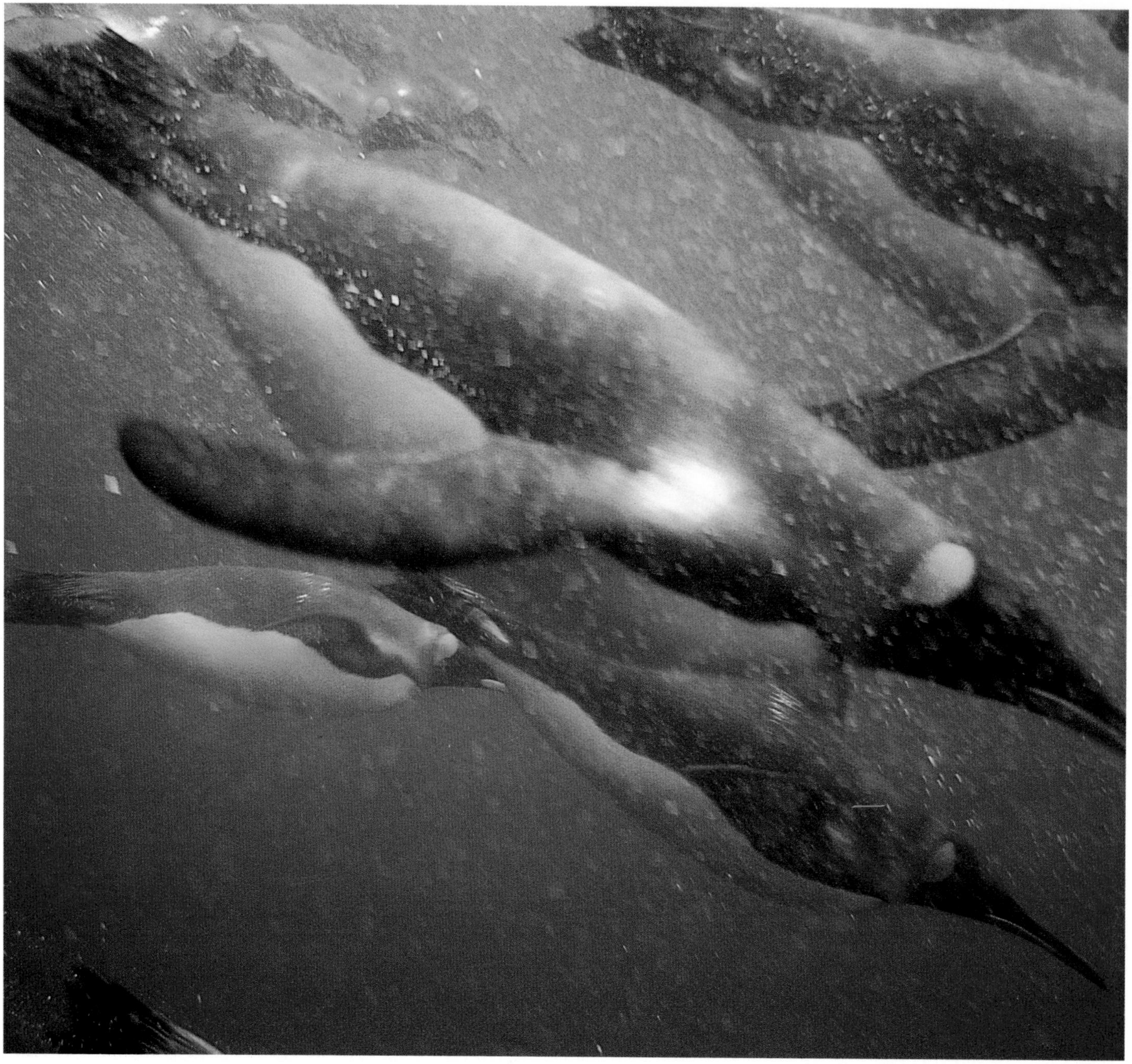

Chapter 2 Adapting to Life in the Sea

Who would believe in penguins,
unless he had seen them?

—Conor O'Brien, *Across Three Oceans*

When penguins lost the ability to fly in air, they evolved into a form that gave them great mastery in another medium—the sea. Penguins have very compact, streamlined bodies and short, extremely stiff wings, which are attached to strong muscles and which they use as paddles; their feet and stubby tails together form a rudder. Most other diving birds propel themselves through the water by using their feet, but penguins thrust themselves forward on the upward stroke of their wings, or flippers.

Their legs are positioned low down on their bodies to minimize drag in the water, but this position means that when penguins are on land they have an upright stance. With such short legs, they seem to be clumsy and awkward, though they are, in fact, quite agile. The most southern species often resort to tobogganing on their chests on snow, rowing themselves along with their flippers and pushing with their feet. In this manner, they can outpace a human over a short distance. Emperor penguins regularly waddle and toboggan hundreds of kilometres over the fast ice—the frozen sea that is connected to the Antarctic continent—to get to and from their breeding colonies.

Penguins have strong webbed feet, each with three hooked toes that are used for gripping slippery rocks and ice. Going up a steep rock or ice slope, penguins can often be seen using their bills to give them a third hold on the rock or ice. Rockhoppers are regular mountaineers, able to bound and claw their way up very tortuous slopes. Penguins are

FACING PAGE: *Masters of the oceans, penguins literally fly under water, using the upstroke of their powerful flippers to propel themselves.*

also incredibly tough. The rockhoppers especially withstand a tremendous battering when they land on a rocky coast in heavy surf. Their thick layer of blubber and feathers cushions them against the pounding they regularly receive. Besides offering physical protection, their feather coats have markings that offer some camouflage in the sea.

Most penguins have black backs and white fronts. The exception is the little penguin, which has a bluish back and white front. This black and white colouration is known as countershading and is a feature that penguins share with other species, such as cormorants, and killer whales, or orcas. The part of the creature that receives the most sun is dark, and the part that receives the least sun is light. There is believed to be an ecological advantage in this colouration for penguins. It is suggested that when the birds are in the water, they blend with the inky depths when seen from above, and to a predator looking up from below, their white underside blends with the light of the sky or the underneath of the pack ice. When on land, penguins also make use of this countershading to help control their temperature. Depending on whether they are hot or cold, they can put their backs to the sun or face the sun and thus help control their temperature.

Penguins have adapted to the widest range of climates of any species on earth. The differences in the species at the extremes of the climactic range, the Galápagos penguins in the north and the emperors in the south, show how natural selection has enabled penguins to adapt physiologically and behaviourally to a vast range of climates.

As one moves farther south, penguins become larger, with less surface area to volume, facilitating heat retention. Thus, for example, the emperor penguin is the largest species, whereas the Galápagos penguin is one of the smallest. Less skin is also exposed to the environment in Antarctic species. Adélies, for example, have feathers covering most of their faces, leaving only a very small portion of the bill exposed. Humboldt penguins, in contrast, have an extensive area of bare pink skin at the base of their bills that helps them radiate heat and keep cool.

A thick layer of fat, or blubber, provides insulation and serves as an energy store in species that fast for long periods. The male emperor penguin, for example, must fast when it is incubating an egg, and all species fast when they undergo their moult. The birds' densely packed feathers also provide insulation. Each short, stiff feather has a separate downy shaft at its base that creates a second layer of trapped air close to the skin, beneath the true feathers. This double layer provides 80 to 90 per cent of a penguin's insulation, but the feathers have to be kept in excellent condition to maintain their waterproof qualities. Cold water draws off heat ten times faster than air, and penguins can rapidly suffer from hypothermia if they lose their waterproofing.

Penguins spend many hours every day preening themselves, especially when they leave the water. The Gálapagos penguin has been observed passing an average of three

FACING PAGE: *Penguins can make use of their countershading to help control their temperature by turning their backs towards the sun or away from the sun.*

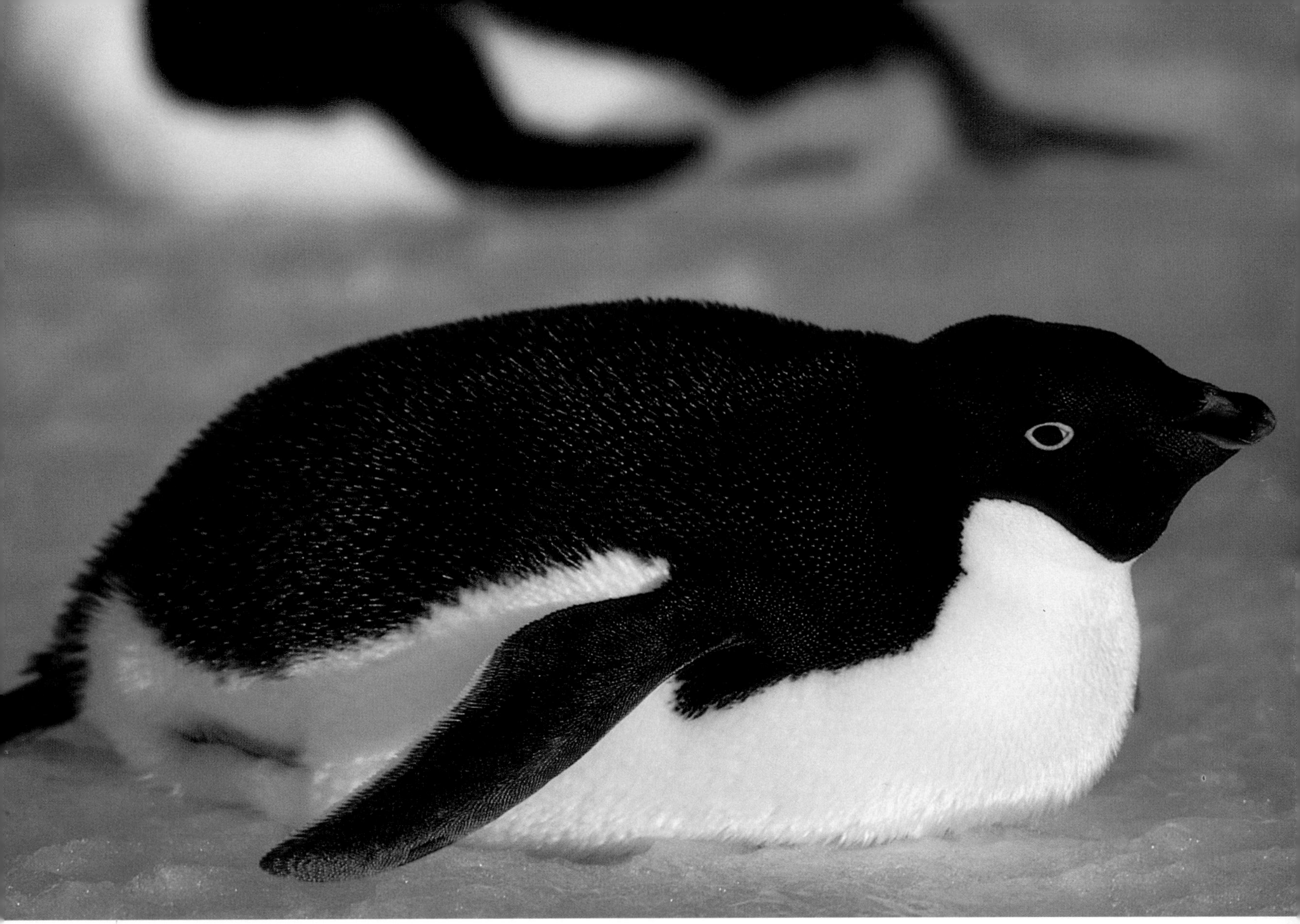

A moulting king penguin chick seems quite dishevelled. Until penguin chicks fledge, they are unable to take to the sea. King penguin chicks look so different from their parents that early explorers at first believed they were a different species.

hours a day on feather maintenance. Using its bill, it replenishes the oil layer on its coat from a gland just above its stiff tail feathers. The penguin applies oil to its feathers and to the edges of its flippers and then uses its flippers to transfer the oil to its head. Penguins will also preen in water. In some species, such as the rockhopper, one penguin will preen another; this practice, called allopreening, occurs between the sexes, male to female, and is believed to have more to do with courtship than with waterproofing. Two penguins of the same sex will also preen each other.

As a rule adult penguins moult once a year. The exceptions are the Galápagos penguin and some populations of African penguins, which may moult twice in a year. Moulting is necessary to replace worn and damaged feathers that no longer provide a waterproof shield. In most penguin species, moulting takes place after the breeding season. In preparation for this period of great physiological stress, which includes fasting for two to four weeks, penguins spend several weeks at sea feeding continuously. This prolonged feeding also enables them to store up enough energy to produce the new feathers. The first stage of the development of the new plumage is the forming of feathers under the skin, which begins while the penguins are still at sea. After they come ashore, they begin to shed their old plumage. Until they have a complete new coat, they are unable to go to sea, since they no longer have a waterproof shield. During this period the species inhabiting the temperate region are highly vulnerable to land-based predators because they can't escape into the water.

Being warm blooded and very well insulated, penguins can easily overheat, even in Antarctica. They control their body temperature by various mechanisms, which include holding their wings out at a 45-degree angle and fluffing up their feathers. In this way, they allow the most air to flow over their body and the underside of their flippers, obtaining maximum cooling. Penguins also control the blood supply to their unfeathered areas, such as their feet, the underside of their flippers and, in some species, parts of their faces. When their feet are in contact with the ice and snow and they are cold, they restrict the blood flow to their feet; when they are hot, they do not restrict it. On a sunny day in the Antarctic, penguins, especially chicks, will lie prone, exposing their feet to the air to cool them. Penguins also possess a heat exchange system in their nasal passages whereby they can reduce the heat lost to the environment in very cold conditions.

In contrast to many other species of birds, there are few observable differences between males and females in penguins. It is especially difficult to determine males from females in the wild. The main indications are subtle differences in body size and bill dimensions, the male being slightly larger.

Masters of the Deep

Penguins are very efficient swimmers and divers. When travelling fast, they can achieve speeds of up to 12 kilometres per hour (6.5 knots), but most species average around 4 to 8 kilometres per hour (2.2 to 4.3 knots). At this speed they can travel enormous distances. When swimming rapidly, some species will leap clear of the water every few metres, a technique called porpoising that enables them to breathe and decreases their chances of being taken by a predator. At the same time, their feathers become coated with a layer of air bubbles that helps to reduce drag.

Antarctic penguin species have also developed the ability to leap out of the water to a substantial height, enabling them to reach raised ice edges or rock ledges. Penguins have also been recorded at great depths. The larger species (*Aptenodytes* genus) can dive deeper than smaller species because they have larger reserves of oxygen in relation to the needs of their muscles. Emperors have been recorded at over 400 metres (1300 feet), and one was timed as staying submerged for eighteen minutes. Even the little penguin has been recorded at almost 70 metres (230 feet). Typically, most species' dives are much shorter and to depths of less than 100 metres (328 feet).

Because penguins breed on land yet forage under water, they have to be able to see well in both mediums, which have very different physical properties. Penguins have a relatively flat cornea, which minimizes the effect of moving from air to water, and they also have the ability to change the shape of the lens. Their large eyes are adapted to the low light they experience when they are hunting in deep water.

FACING PAGE: *Penguins can obtain fresh water from the sea by excreting excess salt from their nasal glands. Some species, such as the royal penguins here on Macquarie Island, drink from streams when they are breeding.*

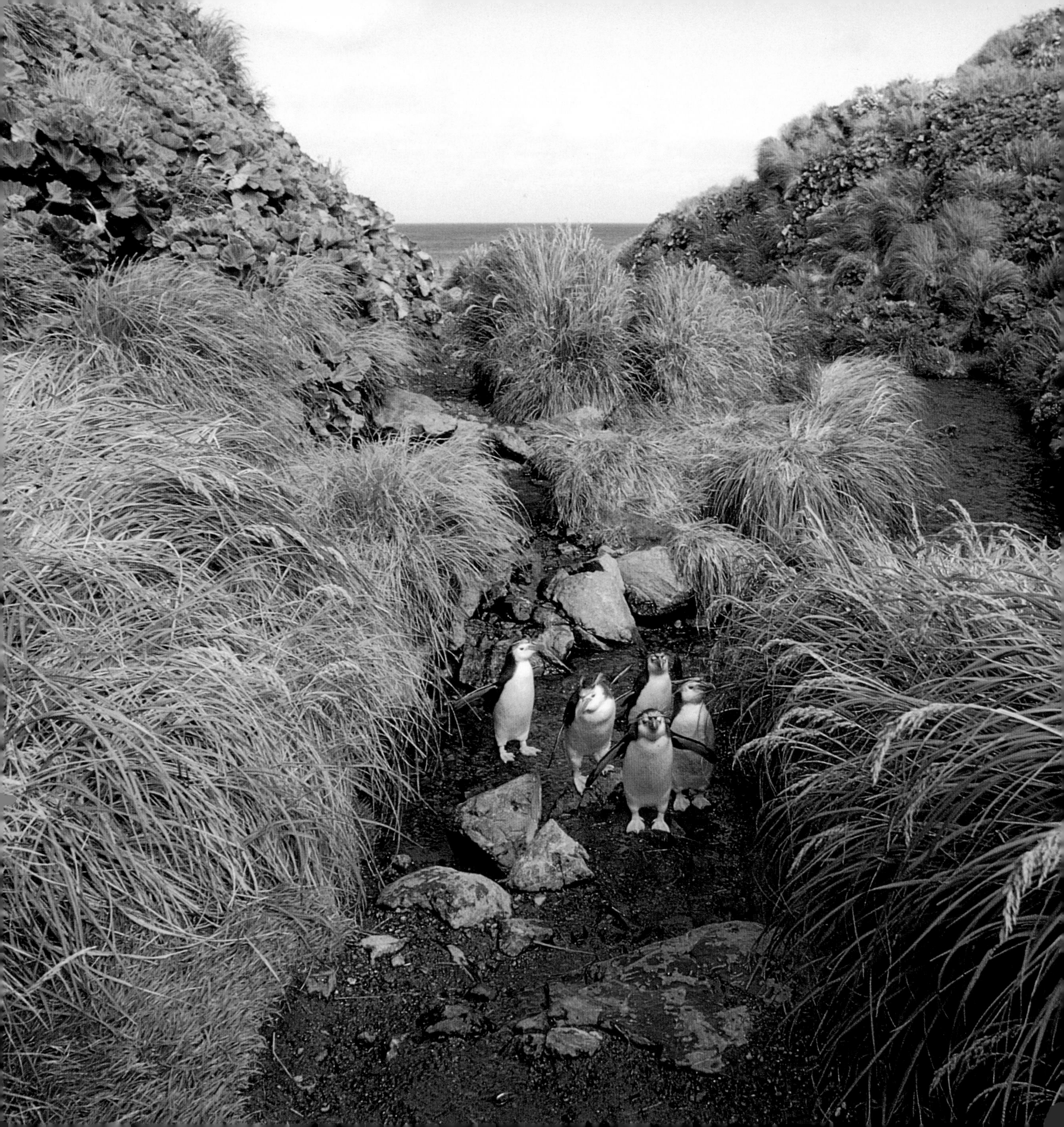

Krill Chasers

Penguins are carnivores that obtain all their energy from the ocean. They feed on crustaceans—the most common being krill—fish and cephalopods, such as squid, that abound in the cold, nutrient-rich southern waters.

Each species has different food preferences and forages in a particular way, allowing more than one species to occupy the same region without directly competing with each other. Most prey species occur in patches, swarms or schools, but penguins do not filter feed, or strain their food out of mouthfuls of water. They dart to and fro, catching individuals and swallowing water as well. The crested penguins feed mainly on swarming crustacea; the ringed penguins and the little penguins feed on pelagic schooling fish, such as anchovies and sprats; and the brush-tailed species prey equally on krill and fish. King penguins seem to specialize in lantern fish, and emperor penguins feed mostly on ice fish and krill.

Penguins' mouths are lined with backward-pointing, gristly spines, enabling them to grasp and swallow wriggling prey, and they can take whole fish up to some 25 centimetres (10 inches) long. Fish are caught side on and then rotated in their bills to be swallowed head first. Little penguins and Humboldts have been observed to circle a body of fish, driving them into a dense pack before diving in for the kill.

Some species have prodigious appetites. The emperor, for example, can eat up to 14 kilograms (30 pounds) at a time. Besides food, penguins seem to have a taste for less nourishing morsels. Pebbles and stones are often taken from penguins' crops when they are dissected. Up to 4.5 kilograms (10 pounds) of stones have been found in an emperor's stomach. Although they may help grind up the food to facilitate digestion, the stones are most probably swallowed to reduce buoyancy and enable the bird to dive more easily. When penguins are carrying a lot of blubber, which is not very dense tissue, they are more buoyant. By picking up stones in their gullets, they add weight and so dive more easily.

It is also possible to determine how long a bird has been ashore and what it has eaten, to a certain degree, by the colour of its excreta. It is said that the guano is white if penguins have recently dined on fish or squid, and pink if they have been eating krill; but if the birds have been fasting for three days or more, then their excreta is greenish.

Like albatrosses and most other sea birds, penguins have nasal glands at the base of their bills that excrete excess salt from the sea water taken in with their food. This is usually detected as droplets coming off their beaks as they shake their heads. Some species eat snow or drink from freshwater streams and puddles, especially when they are breeding.

Dangers at Sea

Penguins spend most of their lives in the sea, and consequently this is where they are most at risk from predators. Most of these are mammals. Menacing leopard seals prowl the shore near penguin colonies waiting to snare a meal. On land the seals pose no threat, but in the water any hint of them is enough to make penguins extremely nervous. With razor-sharp teeth and powerful jaws, they can quickly dispatch an adult penguin with a few bites. They grab the penguin by the head and, while on the surface, thrash the unfortunate bird from side to side, quickly skinning their prey. They often play with dead birds. The other main predator in the far south is the orca, or killer whale.

Farther north, fur seals prey on crested penguins and sea lions take yellow-eyed and gentoo penguins. Other predators in northern areas are sharks and whales.

On land in the temperate regions, such as the Falkland Islands, the striated caracara, turkey vultures and some gulls will hang around colonies trying to steal eggs or pick off injured chicks. Introduced predators (feral cats, dogs, stoats, weasels, foxes) are also a very significant problem for the temperate penguin species.

Although adult penguins on land in Antarctica are not usually threatened, weak and sickly chicks or those on the periphery of the colony are at risk from several species of birds. Skuas, the raptors of the south, often work in pairs to steal eggs and chicks. Sheathbills, scavengers that can be found around penguin colonies in the subantarctic, charge penguins while they are feeding, causing the penguins to spill their food, which the sheathbills promptly scoop up. Giant petrels are the main predator of emperor penguin colonies, accounting for over 30 per cent of chick losses, and they prey on king penguin colonies in the subantarctic.

The balance between predator and prey in nature has been achieved over millions of years of evolution, but in many instances human behaviour has disrupted this delicate relationship. After the decimation of the Antarctic baleen whale population in the nineteenth and early twentieth centuries, more krill became available and so Antarctic penguin populations have been expanding since then.

Leopard seals are one of the main predators of penguins at sea in the Antarctic. They skin their victims by thrashing them from side to side on the surface. GORDON COURT/ HEDGEHOG HOUSE

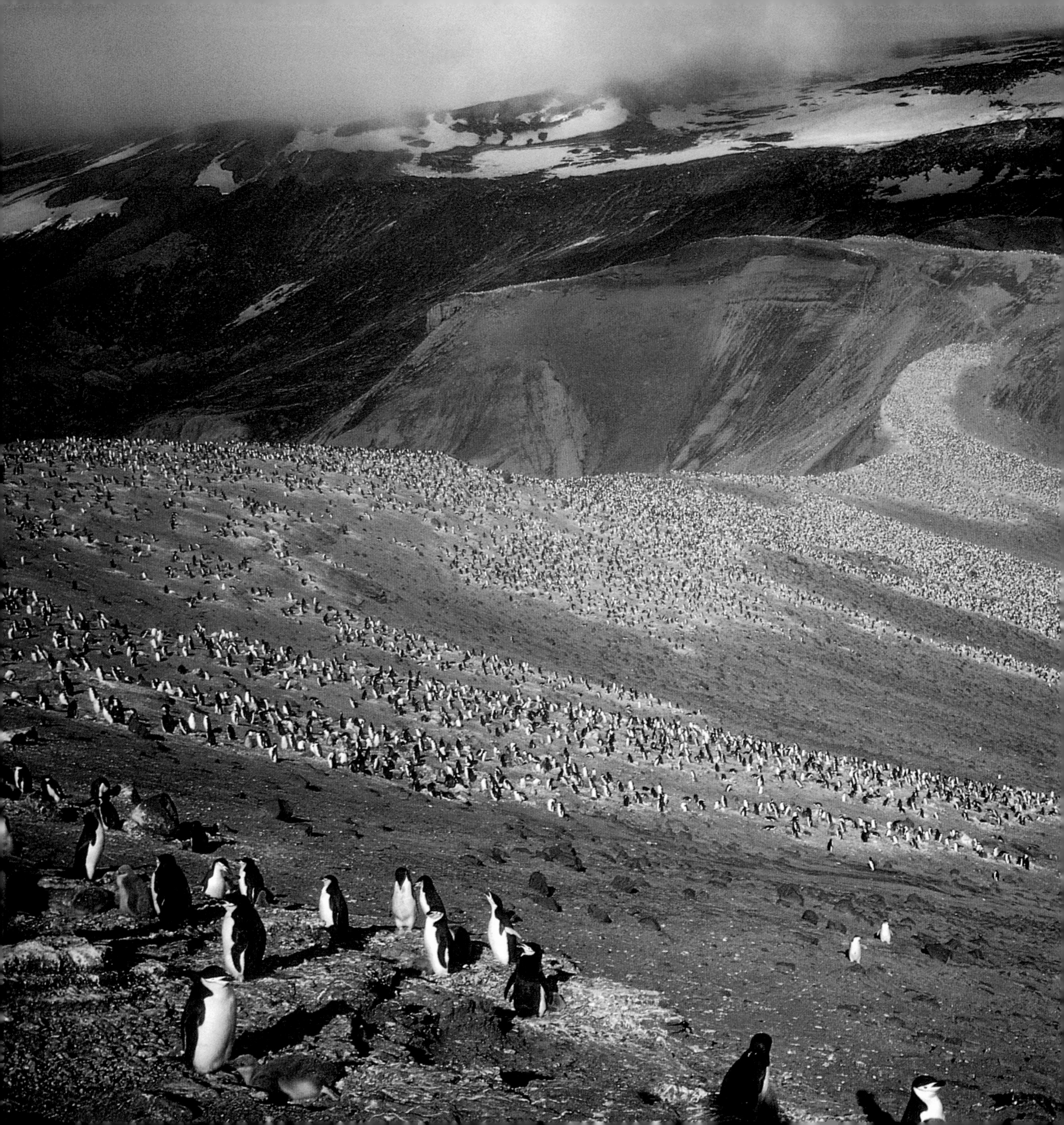

Colonial Breeding

All penguins have a similar structure and form, and most species reproduce in a similar manner. The *Aptenodytes* and the *Spheniscus* do vary substantially in some aspects (nesting behaviour, timing of breeding and breeding strategy) in order to cope with the great differences in their environments. But the typical breeding behaviour of penguins illustrates the remarkable way that they have taken advantage of their ecological niche in the Southern Hemisphere.

Penguins live a long time, as a rule, and some individuals have been recorded as still breeding at seventeen to twenty years of age. Most species do not begin to breed until they are at least three years old, and for the emperor penguin, the average age of first breeders is five years and may be as old as nine years.

Penguin pair bonds are often long-standing. Some species, like the gentoo, stay together throughout the year, whereas others return to the same breeding area at the end of winter (displaying what is called site fidelity) and meet their mates there. If their mate does not arrive in time, they will choose another. Should the original mate arrive later, a battle usually ensues. When both mates do show up, the union is not always assured. Changes in partners occur about 13 to 18 per cent of the time.

Most penguins breed in colonies, some as large as a million pairs. The exception is New Zealand's yellow-eyed penguin, which is a solitary breeder. Mating pairs usually share the task of nest building. In rockhopper, chinstrap and Adélie colonies, nests are tightly packed together, whereas in gentoo colonies they are more loosely scattered. When birds are only a pecking distance apart, they fiercely guard their territory and the rock collection that forms their nest. Stealing nesting material is a perennial pastime for some species.

Nests help to stop the eggs from rolling away and can raise them above the level of the surrounding terrain to allow for better drainage. Thus, when snow melts, or when it rains in more temperate regions, the eggs will stay dry and warm. For some colonial species, especially chinstraps in the Antarctic, the prime nesting sites are high on steep hillsides. These hillsides are the first to lose their winter snow cover, giving the birds the longest period to nest and breed successfully.

Most penguin species lay two eggs in a rudimentary nest. In the Antarctic there is little but rocks, bones and feathers to use as building materials. The more northerly species have twigs and grass. The temperate species—the little penguin and the ringed penguins—nest in burrows or in crevices, which help them to escape from the heat of the sun and afford some protection from predators. The species also use beds of feathers, grass and sticks as nests.

FACING PAGE: *Chinstrap penguins, seen here on Deception Island in the South Shetlands, are one of the many species that breed in very large colonies.*

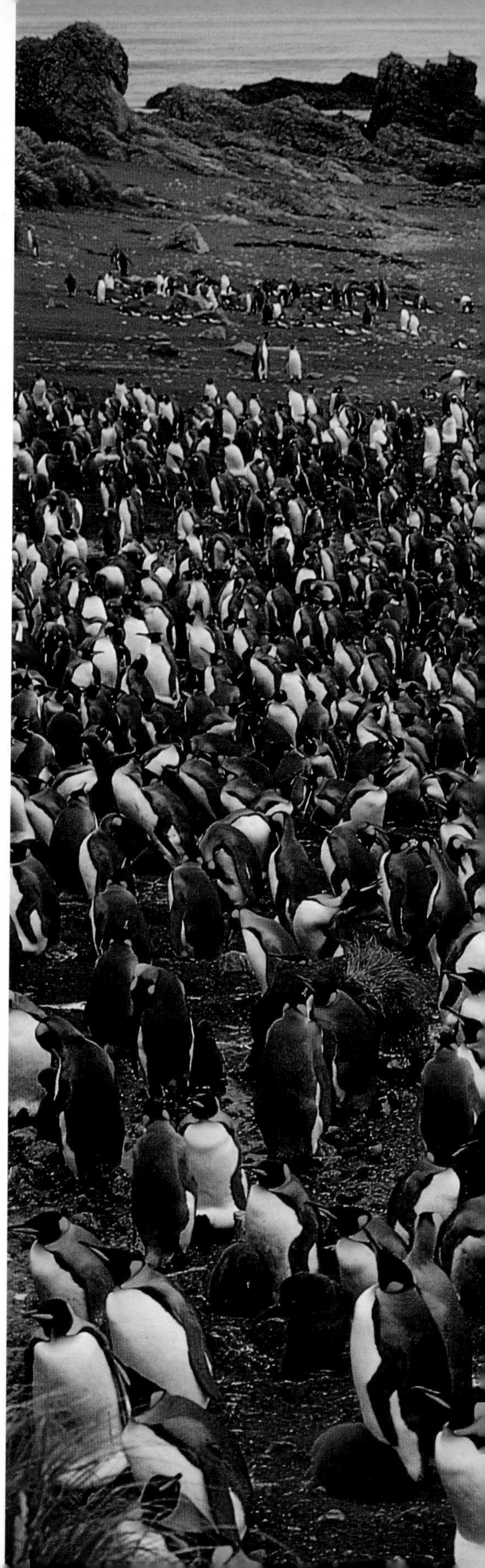

King penguins on Macquarie Island can be seen year-round in vast colonies. Because they balance a single egg on their feet, they do not need to maintain a nest or much territory.

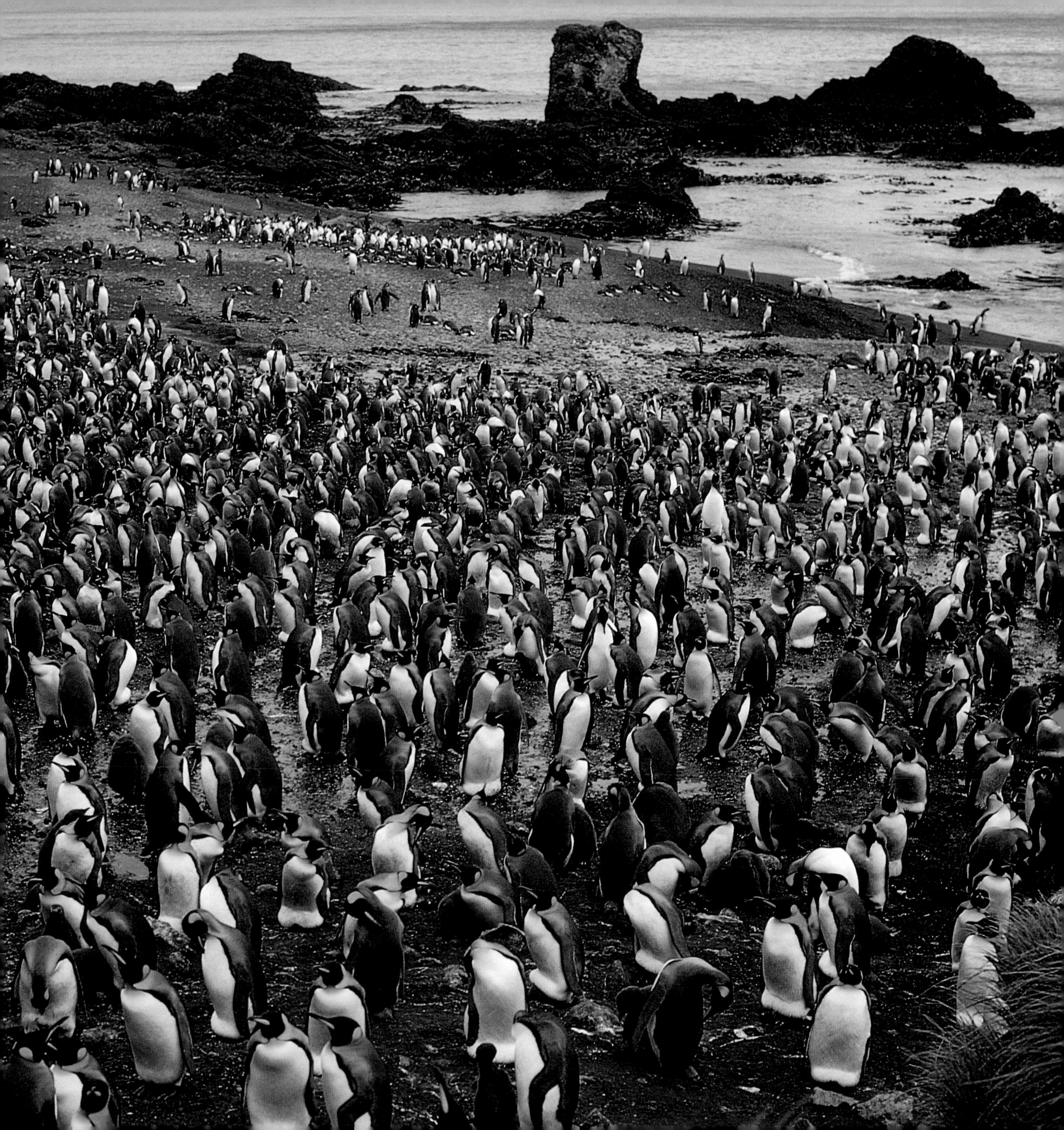

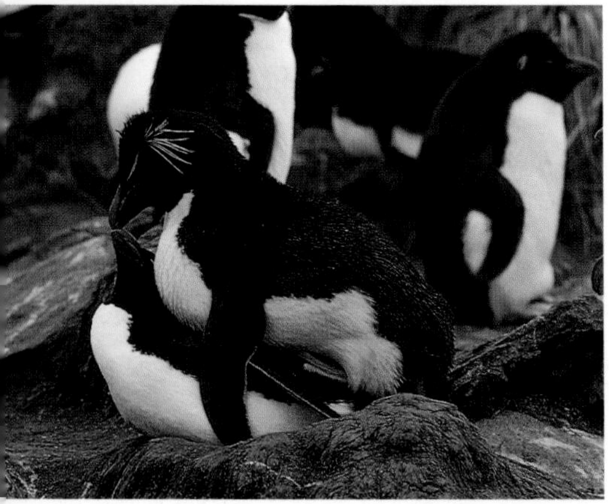

The exceptions to this nesting behaviour are the emperor and the king penguins, which are both members of the genus *Aptenodytes.* These species lay a single egg, which they incubate balanced on their feet under a protective roll of their abdomen. This technique enables them to move around somewhat and thus minimize their exposure to the elements. The emperor is also unique in that only the male incubates the egg. In all other species, both parents share in this task.

Large colonies or rookeries are very noisy, smelly places with a distinctive odour that can be detected a considerable distance downwind. In poor visibility, a penguin colony can often be smelled long before it can be seen or heard. Penguin guano has a fishy, ammonia-like odour and the same sites are colonized year after year, so they become deeply caked with guano. The nests invariably become a quagmire following a storm, or when the snow melts.

In some species, when conditions are poor, only the stronger chick (usually the first-born) will survive. Even when conditions are good, the crested penguins (eudyptids) often discard the first egg, since the second egg is always larger. It is believed that there may not be that much extra energy required to lay two eggs, and the extra egg is a form of insurance against the failure of the larger egg to hatch or the first hatched chick to survive. Even if two eggs hatch, crested penguins rarely raise two chicks.

With most Antarctic species, breeding is synchronized to a narrow time frame that corresponds to opportune weather and feeding conditions, but in temperate regions it is spread over a longer period. Breeding all at the same time affords safety in numbers. Nesting in the centre of a colony has been shown to be more successful than on the periphery, where there is a greater chance that an egg or a chick will be taken by a predator.

It is impossible to deal with the breeding behaviour of each species in detail, but the main features of breeding in the archetype penguin, the Adélie, apply to most other species. Major exceptions are dealt with species by species in the next chapter.

Adélie penguins come ashore in October to their traditional colonies on islands, beaches and headlands all around the Antarctic coast. Rookeries of hundreds of thousands of birds are not unusual. The males arrive first, staking out a territory and advertising themselves. Courtship and mating rituals include "ecstatic displays," in which, typically, an unattached male pumps his chest several times and, with his head stretched upwards and flippers akimbo, emits a loud, harsh braying sound. This display can cause a mass trumpeting by other males, which is believed to help synchronize the breeding cycle within the colony. Mating takes place once the pair has established a rocky nest. The older birds tend to stake nesting sites in the middle of the colony. There is fierce competition for nesting sites, especially on the higher, well-drained ground.

The first eggs are laid in early November, but if they are left unattended for more

When mating, the male penguin mounts the female in what is a delicate balancing act. RINIE VAN MEURS

FACING PAGE: *Penguin chicks grow rapidly. By the time the chicks are three or four weeks old, both parents must go to sea to obtain enough food for the downy balls that gather together in creches or nursery groups.*

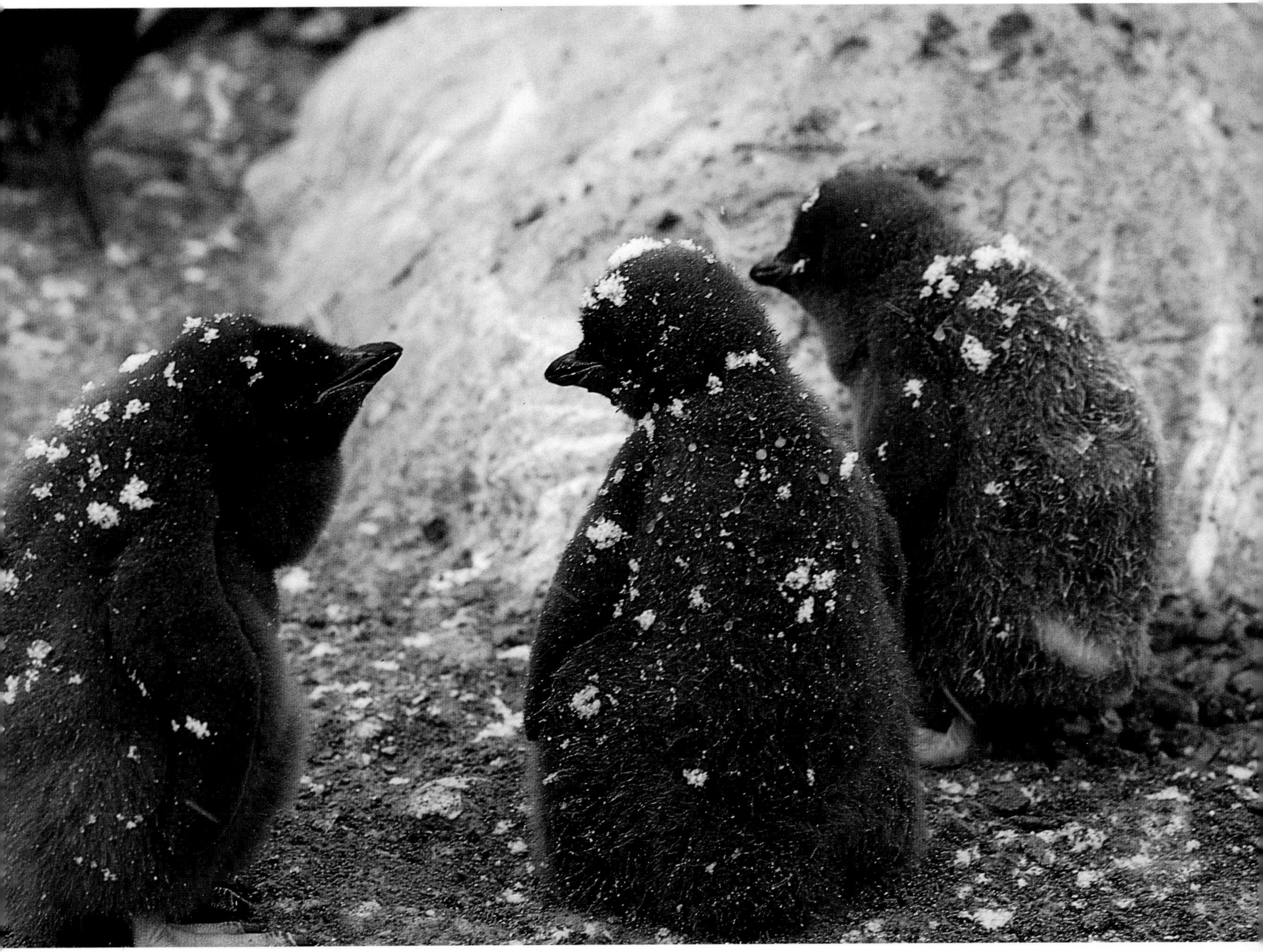

Adélie penguin chicks are fed regur-
gitated krill and fish by whichever
adult is present at the time.

than an hour or two, they will cool and become infertile. If nests are abandoned, the eggs are easy prey for skuas. The male and female Adélies take turns incubating the eggs by sitting or lying on top of them. The eggs are in contact with a part of their lower chest called the brood patch, which is bare of feathers and so transmits body heat more effectively to the egg. The parents also periodically turn their eggs to keep them evenly warm.

The female Adélie returns to the sea after laying, leaving the male to stand alone for up to ten days while his partner feeds. Most pairs produce two eggs, separated by an interval of two to three days, and incubation takes about thirty-five days. The two chicks hatch almost simultaneously. Inevitably one chick is stronger and consequently is able to win more food from its parents. The second usually does not survive. To help cope with the brief three-month Antarctic breeding season, the Adélie chicks are the fastest growing of any species.

The chicks are fed from the crop of whichever parent is present at the time, and their appetite is considerable. They are tended closely by their parents for the first two to three weeks during the so-called guard period. Growing rapidly, the chicks soon develop a thicker woolly grey down and quickly become almost as large as their parents. During the third or fourth week, they join other chicks in creches or nursery groups, leaving both parents free to go to sea to feed in order to satisfy their chicks' increasing demands.

A parade of adults can regularly be seen moving between the colony and the ocean. These birds congregate at the water's edge in large numbers, waiting for the appropriate moment to take the plunge. No penguin wants to be first, in case a leopard seal is lurking in the vicinity, but eventually there is enough jostling from behind that one or two are pushed off the edge. If these survive the first few strokes, then an avalanche of birds follows. Within seconds, the entire flock is heading offshore at a fast pace.

The chicks are ready to fledge around seven to eight weeks of age, and by late March most Adélies have left the colony to spend the winter in the comparative warmth of the pack ice to the north. Very little is known about their behaviour at sea during the austral winter months.

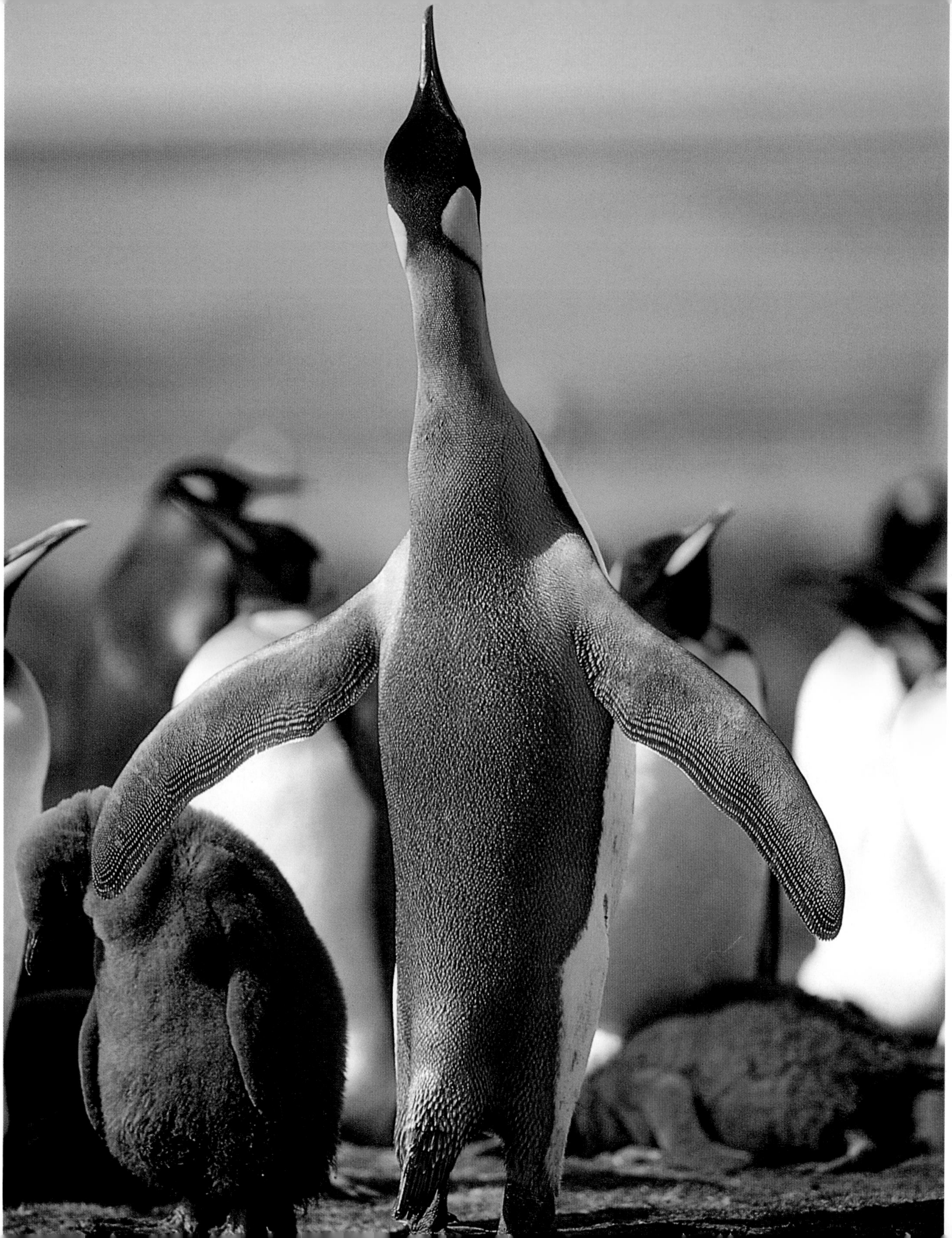

Trills and Trumpeting

Penguins, like all creatures, exhibit a wide range of ritualized behaviours as part of their daily and yearly life cycle, including courting, mating and territorial displays. They communicate by complex behaviour patterns such as head and flipper waving, calling, bowing, gesturing and preening. Territorial disputes lead to aggressive postures such as stares, pointing and even charging. The ecstatic displays already discussed are only one example of a repertoire of courting behaviours.

Penguin vocalizations are distinctive and vary greatly from species to species. They range from the scratchy cooing of the Adélie—not unlike the sound of a high-pitched cackling hen—to the jerky trumpeting and beautiful trills of the emperor penguin. In the 1920s a farmer on the Falkland Islands noted that massed rockhoppers sounded "as if thousands of wheel barrows all badly in need of greasing are being pushed at high speed." Because the harsh sounds of the *Spheniscus* genus resemble the braying of a donkey, it is not surprising that many of them were commonly called jackass penguins. Their "song" is a repetition of short honking notes, alternating with sudden intakes of breath and reaching a crescendo with a drawn-out howl that rises and falls in pitch as it dies away. Penguin calls are particularly important, because it is by call that adults and chicks recognize one another in the vast crowds of large colonies when the parents return from fishing expeditions.

FACING PAGE: *A king penguin performs an ecstatic display by raising itself up on its haunches and trumpeting loudly. This behaviour usually indicates that a male is advertising for a potential mate and warning off other males.*

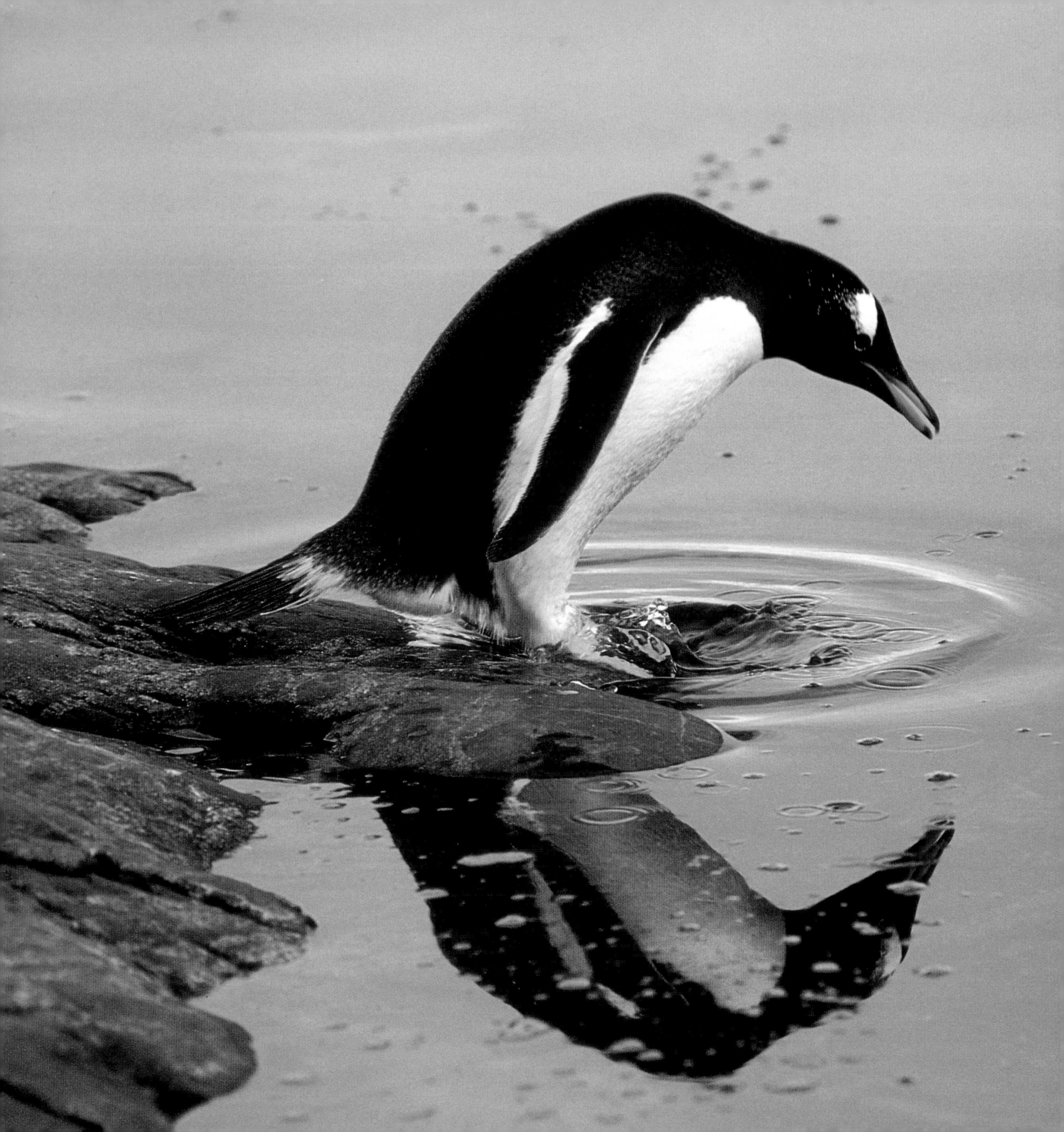

Chapter 3 # Symbols of the South

....

Penguins are the real inhabitants of the South Land.
The proud, stately Emperors—with their courtly, pol-
ished manners—are the upper classes, the aristocrats
of the eternal snows; but the Adélies are the multi-
tude, the bourgeoisie. It is said when Anatole France
first saw warm-water penguins he wept. One wonders
what the famous littérateur would have done if he
had seen Adélies. He might have wept still more—
with laughter.

—Herbert Ponting, *The Great White South,* 1921

Beginning with the species that live in the Antarctic and moving northwards, this chapter describes the seventeen species of penguin, which can be identified by broad biogeographic regions and temperature zones.

FACING PAGE: *When coming and*
going to feed, gentoo penguins pre-
fer to enter and leave the water at
gently sloping beaches.

Species below the Antarctic Circle

The species most commonly associated with the Antarctic are the Adélie penguin and the much larger emperor penguin, both of which breed predominantly on the continent proper.

ADÉLIE PENGUINS

Since the heroic days of polar exploration, which helped focus the world's imagination on the Antarctic through the work of Herbert Ponting and his peers, we have come to know the Adélie better than any other penguin species. The Adélie is the classic "little man in evening dress," though it is more like a cutaway morning suit than a typical tuxedo. The Adélie's most distinctive marking is a white ring around the eyes that beams out of an otherwise all black head. Adélies are not timid and will take on a 2-metre (6-foot) human who has strayed within their territory as readily as another penguin. Having your leg pummelled by one of their tough flippers can result in a nasty bruise.

Adélie penguins, *Pygoscelis adeliae,* one of the brush-tailed species, average 70 centimetres (28 inches) in length and weigh 3.7 to 4 kilograms (8 to 9 pounds). The designation Adélie comes from Adélie Land, which was named by French explorer Admiral Dumont d' Urville in honour of his wife.

The Adélie is the most widely distributed penguin inhabiting the Antarctic. It is estimated that there are some 2.5 million pairs around the continent, breeding mostly within the Antarctic Circle (66°30' S). For their size, the birds are well insulated against the rigours of cold and blizzards, and they are one of the toughest species. They feed mostly on krill, up to 50 kilometres (30 miles) offshore and to depths of 75 metres (250 feet). Experiments have revealed that Adélies navigate by the sun. This finding suggests that they have a biological clock that can calculate the sun's changing position throughout the day.

EMPEROR PENGUINS

The emperor penguin, *Aptenodytes forsteri* (featherless diver), is found only in the Antarctic and has one of the most amazing lives of any creature on the earth. From the time of the earliest explorers, these creatures have fascinated all who cross their path. Its species name, *forsteri,* was bestowed on it in 1844, in honour of the German naturalist, Johann

FACING PAGE: *Adélies are good divers, but they wait in groups at the water's edge for just the right moment before plunging in to avoid potential predators such as the leopard seals that often lie in wait offshore.*

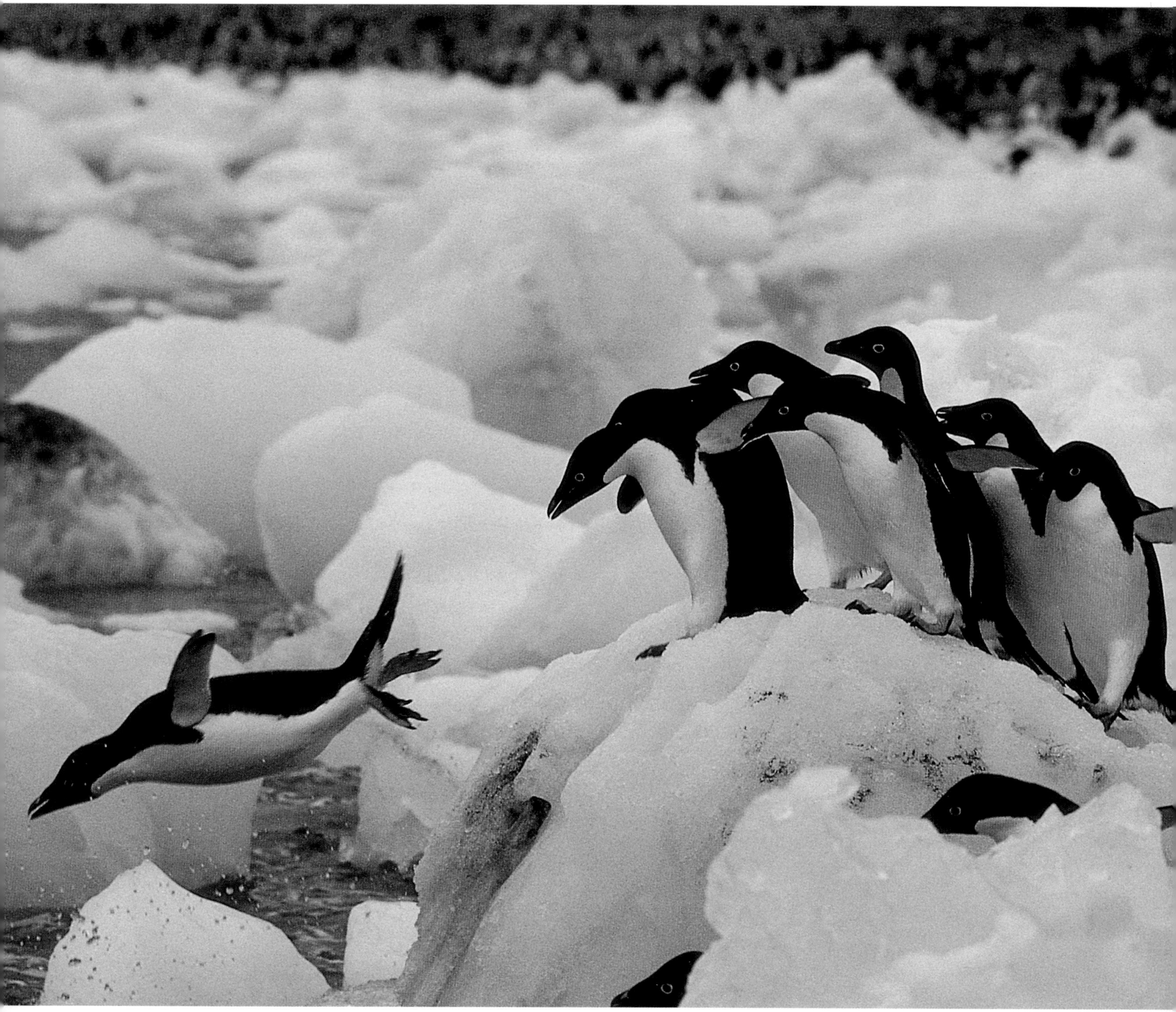

Emperor penguins are found in some forty colonies around the Antarctic continent. They breed on sea ice in the depths of the freezing winter so that by spring the chicks, shown here, are very large and almost ready to fledge.

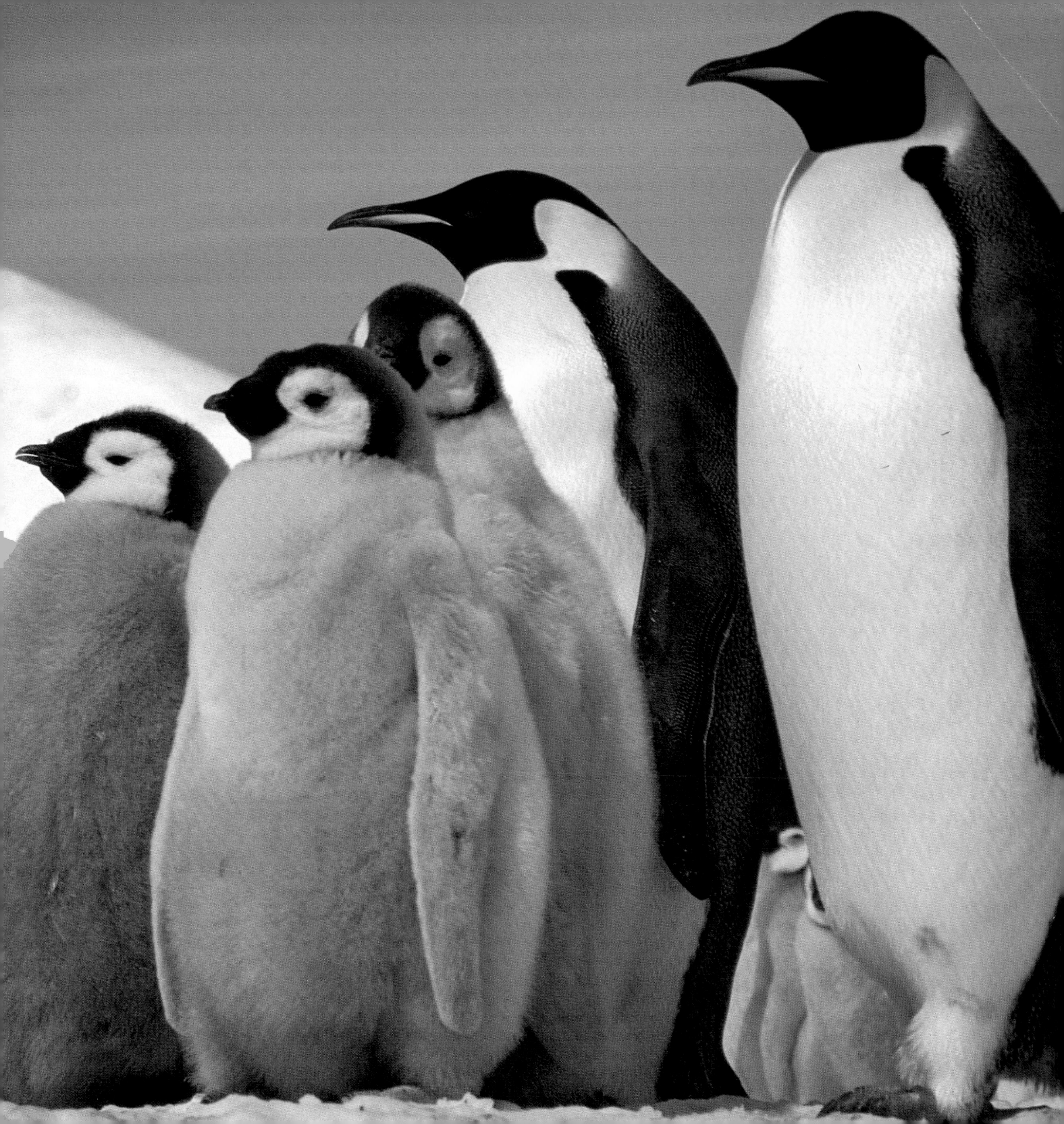

Reinhold Forster, who, during his voyage with James Cook from 1773 to 1775, described four new species of penguin.

Emperor penguins are the largest and most biologically interesting of the southern species. As of 1993, there were an estimated 195,000 of these regal birds in some forty-two rookeries scattered around the continent—most of which are located on fast ice.

Adults are 1 to 1.3 metres (39 to 51 inches) long and weigh from 30 to 38 kilograms (66 to 84 pounds). Though considerably larger than the king penguin, the emperor penguin has proportionally smaller wings, feet and bill, enabling it to retain heat more easily.

Breeding through the Antarctic winter, emperor penguins endure the harshest weather of any species on the planet. Pairs gather in the autumn, having walked up to 200 kilometres (120 miles) across fast ice to get to their traditional breeding colonies. The female lays a single egg in May. She then passes the egg over to her mate and goes to sea to feed. The male incubates the egg for another two months, holding it on top of his feet, where it is completely covered by a thick roll of his belly. During this period the males huddle together for added warmth and protection against the bitter blizzards and subzero temperatures. These huddles, known as turtles, gradually move about, as birds on the windward side start to chill and slowly edge around the perimeter to escape the full brunt of the wind.

By the time the female returns, the chick will have just hatched. The male will have lost up to one third of his body weight. The female then takes over the care and feeding for a six-week period. The male may now have to waddle and toboggan up to 100 kilometres (60 miles) to get to open water to feed himself, having fasted for 115 days. Again he returns to help with feeding the chick. Once the young are old enough to survive away from their parents, they join other chicks in a creche. Come December, the sea ice begins to break up and the colony disperses. By this time, the chicks have moulted and are able to fend for themselves. Those chicks that are slower to shed their down may hitch a ride on ice floes drifting north. In the high austral summer, there are seldom any emperors to be seen on the continent, but occasionally a stray juvenile will come ashore to moult.

The emperors are believed to have developed this winter breeding pattern to allow chicks to grow to independence at a time when food is most plentiful. The adults are large enough to withstand the winter without regular feeding.

Chinstrap penguins are among the most pugnacious of the penguin species. They breed on the Antarctic Peninsula and islands of the Scotia Arc.

The Maritime Antarctic Species

The maritime Antarctic, which includes the Antarctic Peninsula and adjacent islands, is home to two species of penguins. These species, the chinstrap and the gentoo, are also members of the *Pygoscelis* genus.

CHINSTRAP PENGUINS

The chinstrap penguin, *Pygoscelis antarctica,* ranges from 71 to 76 centimetres (28 to 30 inches) in length and from 3.9 to 4.4 kilograms (8½ to 9½ pounds) in weight. Though similar in appearance to the Adélie penguin, the chinstraps are slightly smaller and more aggressive. They are named for the distinctive narrow band of black-tipped feathers that extends from ear to ear under their chins, like the strap of a guardsman's helmet. Their diet is similar to that of the Adélie penguin, consisting mainly of krill and a few species of fish. On the Antarctic Peninsula, the two species can often be found breeding side by side. Chinstraps hatch later than the Adélie and gentoos, but their growth rate is faster.

Chinstraps are found mostly in the subantarctic, but there are also large colonies on the Antarctic Peninsula. They may be the most numerous penguin, with a population estimated at 12 to 13 million. They often select lofty sites that are the first to become snow free to ensure the maximum amount of time to raise their chicks.

GENTOO PENGUINS

Gentoos, *Pygoscelis papua,* are slightly larger than Adélies and chinstraps, standing 75 to 90 centimetres (30 to 35 inches) tall and weighing 6 kilograms (13 pounds). They can be recognized by their orange beaks and the flecked white marking above their eyes. Gentoos are found around the globe between 50° and 60° south and on the scattered subantarctic islands. The Antarctic Peninsula is the southernmost extent of their breeding range.

The origin of the name gentoo is uncertain. One source suggests it is derived from the Portuguese *gentio,* a religious term meaning "not of the faith," or gentile. Gentoo used to be a popular name in the nineteenth century, when it was used to describe Hindus in those parts of Anglo-Indian society where Muslims predominated. The Hindus wear a white cotton cap, and gentoos also have a white cap—a band of feathers extending across the top of the head.

Writer Dianne Ackerman suggests that the name gentoo was the result of a ruse by

a British Museum man, who received a gentoo skin from an Antarctic explorer, thought it was a new species of bird, and decided to hide the information for a while. Later, he went off to Papua New Guinea, and when he returned, he described the bird as if it were one of the local species, naming it after the Gentoo, a religious sect on Papua New Guinea.

The scientific species name, *papua,* originated from his description, lending credence to this explanation.

Until the 1930s the gentoo was generally known in the Falklands as the Johnny penguin. Gentoo penguins are present in the Falklands year-round, breeding on gently sloping ground (usually on grass) near the sea. They return to the same region but move plots every year. By the end of the summer, the whole area is trampled flat and covered with guano, which fertilizes the ground and encourages the grass to grow back. Colonies are divided into "clusters" of nesting penguins, and the largest colonies can have up to ten of these.

Gentoos are thought to fish deeper than other species (with the exception of king and emperor penguins), diving to at least 100 metres (300 feet). Sea lions prey on gentoos, and the inshore approaches to most colonies are patrolled by large males, or bulls. Gentoo colonies around the Falklands are often some distance inland, probably because in the past, when there were many more sea lions on the beaches, they were known to wade into colonies and take penguins.

FACING PAGE: *Gentoo penguins, the largest of the brush-tailed species, are found around the Antarctic and subantarctic.*

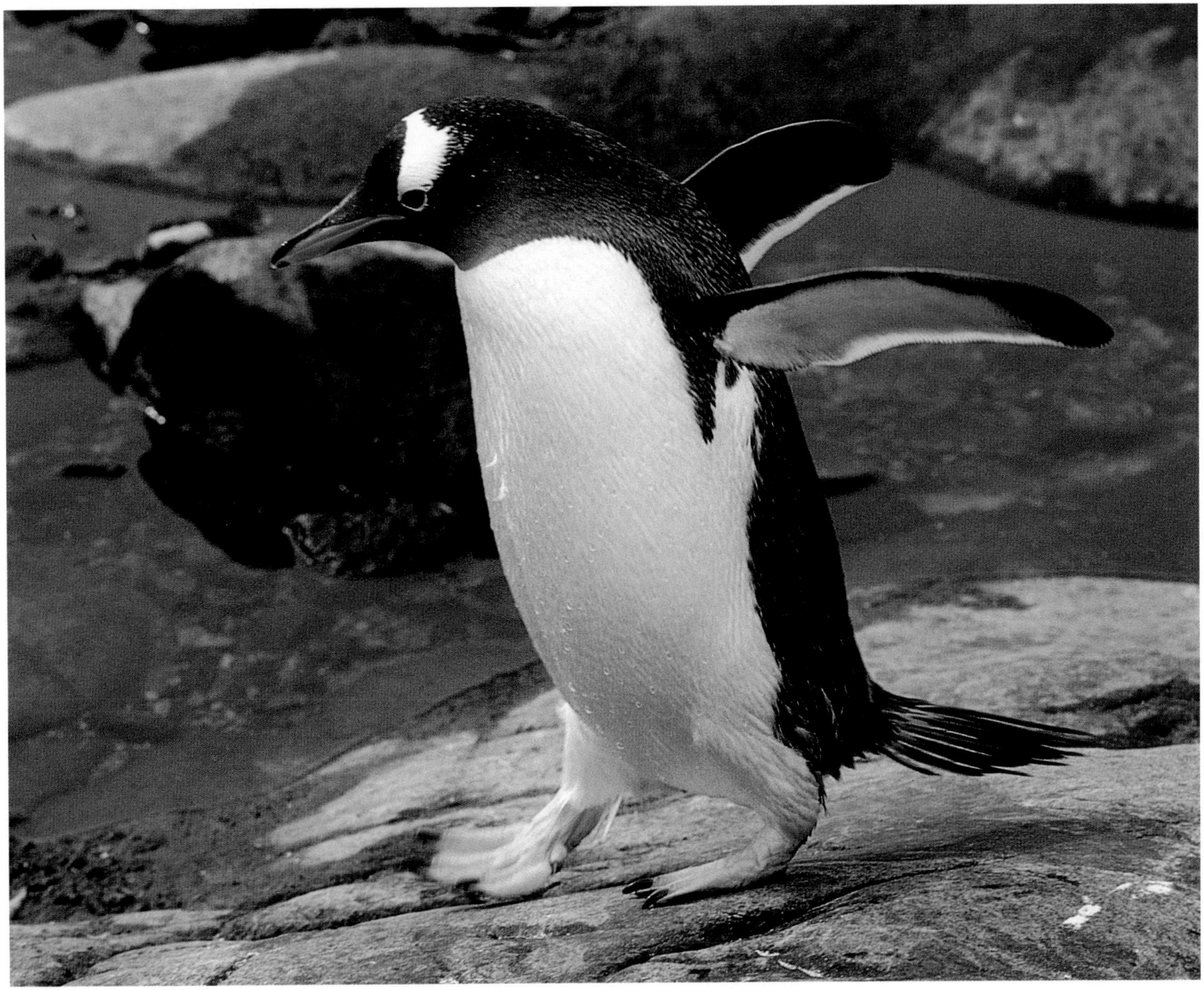

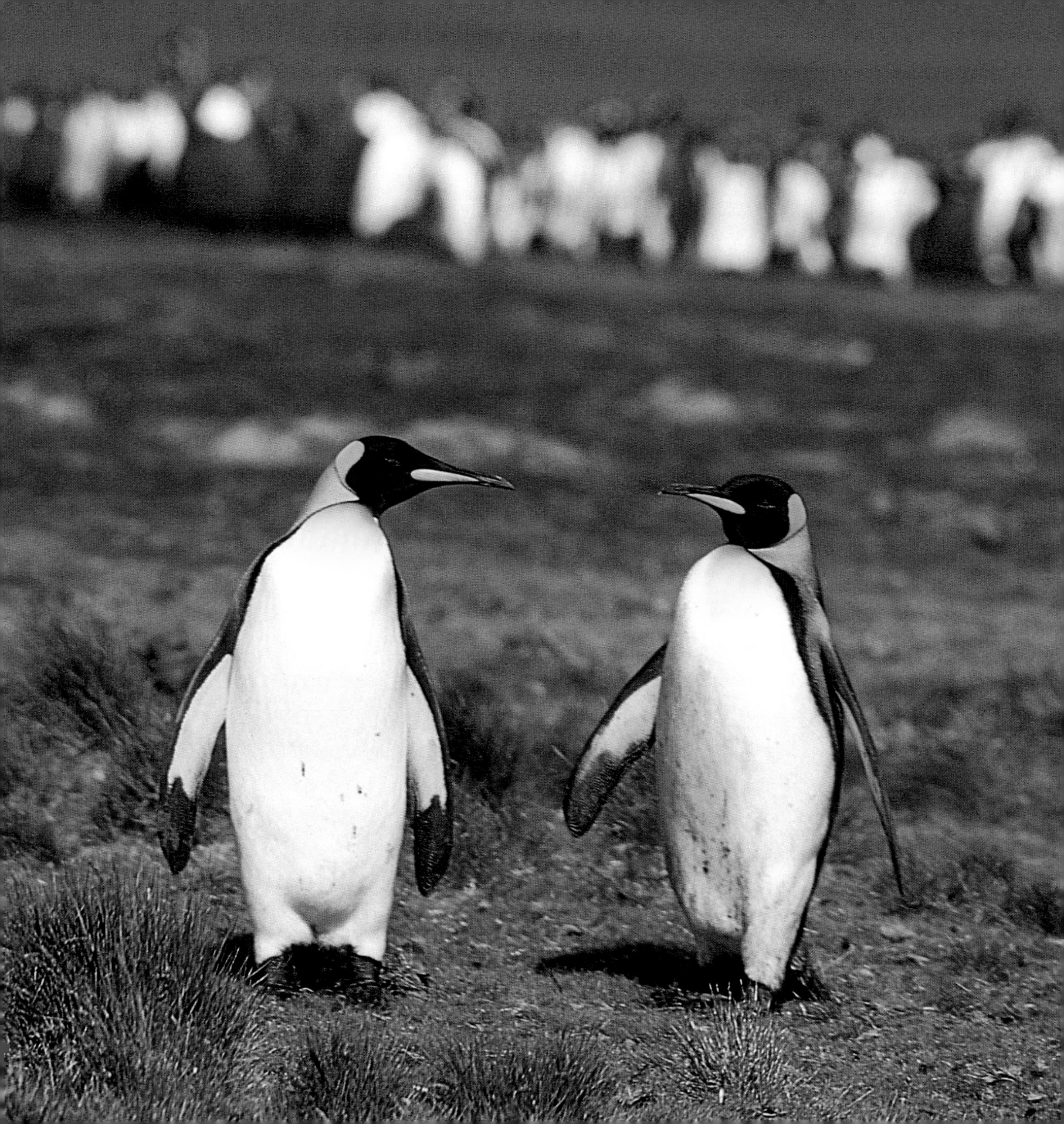

Subantarctic Species

KING PENGUINS

King penguins, *Aptenodytes patagonica,* are the most beautiful and stately penguins of all. With their silvery-grey backs and orange patches flaming on their cheeks, they are extremely photogenic. They range in length from 85 to 95 centimetres (34 to 37½ inches) and weigh 12 to 14 kilograms (26 to 31 pounds), about half the size of emperor penguins. Kings are predominantly a subantarctic species, breeding on islands between 46° and 55° south. Small populations also occur as far north as the Falkland Islands. Immature and nonbreeding birds can travel widely, and vagrants have been found as far north as Australia and New Zealand. Ninety-five per cent of the world's king penguin population, however, occurs south of the Antarctic Convergence.

King penguins are very gregarious and can be found in the colonies year-round, since it takes fifteen months to rear a single chick. Within the colony, there are separate areas of breeding, moulting and roosting birds. Newly hatched chicks and twelve-month-old chicks can be seen side by side. Although it is possible for two chicks to be raised in three years, kings mostly breed biennially.

With their fluffy brown down, looking all the world like giant teddy bears, the chicks are so dissimilar to their parents that when they were first sighted, they were thought to be a separate species. In the bygone era of wooden ships, the chicks were called oakum boys because their feathers resembled the oakum used in caulking seams.

Kings choose to breed on raised beaches with easy access to the sea. Although they were extensively exploited for their oil in the nineteenth and early twentieth centuries, they have recovered substantially and the world population of king is now believed to exceed a million pairs. Many crested penguins also share this zone with the kings.

FACING PAGE:

King penguins, the second largest of the penguin species, breed only in the subantarctic. Volunteer Point in the Falklands has the most northerly colony.

ROCKHOPPERS

There are six members of the crested penguins genus, *Eudyptes* (good diver): the macaroni, royal, Fiordland, Snares, rockhoppers and erect-crested. Some taxonomists contest the status of the royal penguin, suggesting that it is not distinct enough from the macaroni penguin. Others contend that the Snares penguin and the Fiordland penguin are too similar to be separated. Three subspecies of rockhopper are also recognized, and in some camps, they are separated into two species, the northern and southern, based on differences in behaviour, bill length and song. All the *Eudyptes* are notable for the orange or yellow crest above their eyes, which is the easiest way to tell the species apart.

The rockhopper, *Eudyptes chrysocome* (golden haired), is a very noisy and quarrelsome bird, aptly named rockhopper from its habit of bounding up steep, rock-strewn slopes with both feet together. These tough penguins are dubbed rockies or jumping jacks in the Falkland Islands.

The smallest member of the crested penguins, the rockhopper is distinguished by its red eyes and the adults' drooping yellow crest. Immature birds have paler yellow eyebrows and lack the plumes. Rockhoppers can rocket 1 metre (3 feet) out of the water when they make an exit from the sea and leap 30 centimetres (1 foot) forward in a single bound— Superpenguin!

Male rockhoppers are generally larger than females. They nest in large colonies in caves on ledges and cliff tops, often high above the waves. On New Island, in the Falklands, a colony of some 3 million rockhoppers exists 60 metres (200 feet) above the sea. The rocky pathway to the colony bears scars from thousands of years of erosion by the sharp toenails of the rockies. These high nesting sites are believed to provide safety from seals.

Rockhopper penguins may share their colonies with king shags and black-browed albatrosses. They lay two large eggs on a nest of pebbles and grass, depending on what is available. Rockhopper penguins face two threats on land—marauding birds and bad weather, such as high winds and rain squalls.

MACARONI PENGUINS

The macaroni penguin, *Eudyptes chrysolophus* (gold crest), looks similar to the rockhopper but has bushier, more orange plumes that meet on the front of its crown. It is the largest of the genus, with a length of 71 centimetres (28 inches) and a weight of 5 to 6 kilograms (11 to 13 pounds). Macaronis inhabit the subantarctic and Antarctic waters north of the pack ice and are the most southerly of the crested penguins. The macaronis are also one of the most numerous penguin species on earth. An estimate in 1993 put their numbers in excess of 11 million breeding pairs south of the Antarctic Convergence.

The name macaroni comes from the species' long golden crests, which resemble the feathers that a group of flashy Englishmen wore in their caps in the eighteenth century. These same Englishmen had travelled to Italy and were responsible for introducing the Italian pasta macaroni to England. Their brotherhood consequently became known as the Macaroni Club. *Brewer's Dictionary of Phrase and Fable* has this to say about them: "The Macaronies were exquisite fops; vicious, insolent, fond of gambling, drinking and duelling . . ." These Englishmen were also the source for the line "put a feather in his cap and called him Macaroni" from "Yankee Doodle Dandy."

Macaroni penguins have prominent orange plumes that project backwards above their eyes.

ROYAL PENGUINS

An almost identical-looking species to the macaroni is the royal penguin. The royal, *Eudyptes schlegeli,* derives its species name from a nineteenth-century professor, H. Schlegel of the Leiden Museum. Slightly larger than the macaroni, the royals have an average length of 65 to 75 centimetres (25½ to 29½ inches) and weigh 5 to 6 kilograms (11 to 13 pounds). Royals breed only on Macquarie Island, and in 1984/85 there were estimated to be about 85,000 breeding pairs in some fifty-seven colonies. They were called royals because of their association with the kings. They differ from the macaroni by having white feathers on their face and throats.

SNARES PENGUINS

The Snares penguin, *Eudyptes robustus,* breeds only on Snares Island, south of New Zealand. Robustus refers to its large bill. The Snares penguin looks like the Fiordland penguin, but it has a white rim on the edges of its bulbous orange bill. The Snares weigh 2.8 to 3.4 kilograms (6 to 7½ pounds) and have an average length of 51 to 61 centimetres (20 to 24 inches). The Snares penguins are unusual in that they will roost in low trees where there is maximum shade. The remote Snares Island is a sanctuary, and no tourists are permitted to land, so the species is relatively protected from direct human interference.

Snares penguins breed only on the remote Snares Island south of New Zealand. RINIE VAN MEURS

FIORDLAND PENGUINS

The Fiordland penguin, *Eudyptes pachyrhynchus* (thick bill), is distinguished by three to six white stripes on its cheeks. It is the most timid of the eudyptids, breeding in loose colonies only on the west and southwest coasts of the South, Stewart and Solander Islands of New Zealand. The Fiordland penguin has an average length of 55 centimetres (21½ inches) and weighs 3.4 to 3.7 kilograms (7½ to 8 pounds). The population of Fiordland penguins is small, estimated at between 5000 and 10,000 pairs, but this figure is uncertain because some breeding areas in dense vegetation are inaccessible.

ERECT-CRESTED PENGUINS

The erect-crested penguin, *Eudyptes sclateri,* owes its species name to P. L. Sclateri, who was a fellow of the Royal Society of London in the early nineteenth century. Unlike the rest of the eudyptids, this species has a very stubby, brush-like erect crest, which gives it its name. The erect-crested penguin is unique because it is the only species that can raise and lower its crest, although the purpose of this act is unknown. Measuring some 67 centimetres (26½ inches) long and weighing 4 to 5 kilograms (9 to 11 pounds), these penguins have a medium build and breed only on the Antipodes, Bounty, Campbell and Auckland Islands, south of New Zealand. Erect-crested penguins are a highly gregarious species that nests in large colonies, sometimes on bare rock and at other times in tussocky vegetation. The population is estimated at 200,000 breeding pairs.

YELLOW-EYED PENGUINS

There is only one member of the genus *Megadyptes* (big diver), the yellow-eyed penguin, which is possibly the world's rarest. Its species name, *antipodes,* was used by Northern Hemisphere taxonomists to refer to islands on the opposite side of the world from Europe. With its light yellow crown and yellow band extending from around the eyes to the back of the head, it has the most unique and haunting markings of the smaller penguin species.

The very timid Fiordland penguins are endemic to islands off the south coast of New Zealand. PETER HARPER / HEDGEHOG HOUSE

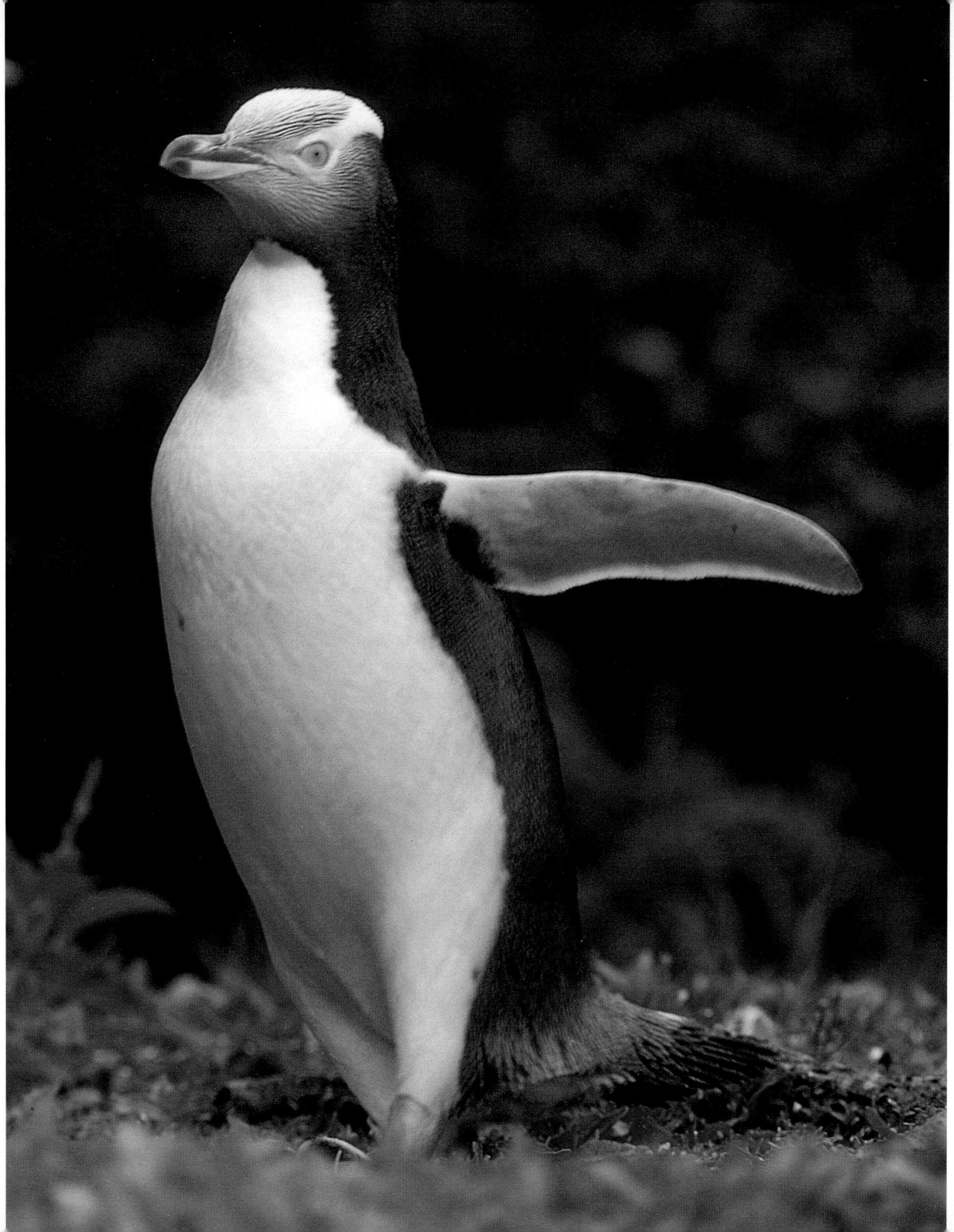

The yellow-eyed penguin breeds only on the temperate forested shores around the southeast coast of New Zealand and Stewart, Auckland and Campbell Islands. The yellow-eyed was originally called the *hoiho,* or "noise shouter," by the Maoris, because of its loud trumpet call. The yellow-eyed does not share its breeding grounds with any other penguin species. Ranging in length from 56 to 78 centimetres (22 to 31 inches) and weighing 4.5 to 6 kilograms (10 to 13 pounds), this medium-sized penguin is considered threatened; the population on the South Island of New Zealand has suffered greatly from human encroachment. Yellow-eyed penguins come ashore to their breeding ground every day throughout the year, and unlike most other species, they are very shy and will seldom land if people are visible.

LITTLE PENGUINS

Another timid penguin species, the little penguin, is perhaps the closest genetically to the order's fossil ancestors. The little penguin, or blue penguin, as it is known in New Zealand, *Eudyptula minor* (good little diver), occurs in the colder waters of southern Australia and New Zealand. In some parts of Australia, this species is still commonly referred to as the fairy penguin. Pauline Reilly, author and long-standing researcher of little penguins notes: "Anyone who has had close contact with the species finds its aggressive behaviour not at all 'fairy-like.'" A population on Phillip Island in Victoria, which she has been helping to monitor, has been observed continuously since 1967—the longest year-round study of any species.

The smallest of all the penguins, the little penguin is only 41 to 45 centimetres (16 to 17½ inches) long and weighs only 1 kilogram (2¼ pounds). It is also the most nocturnal of all penguins. It has a distinctive blue-black to blue-grey plumage on its back, is white underneath and has a dark bill. The little penguin is unique in not having any colours or crests on its head. It is also has a more stooped posture than any of the other species.

Australian populations are found mostly on offshore islands, where the risk of disturbance and predation is minimal. Little penguins feed mainly around inshore waters, such as bays, harbours and estuaries. They mostly choose to nest in sandy areas where they can dig shallow burrows, or they find shelter in caves and crevices on rocky shores.

Some New Zealand biologists consider the white-flippered penguin a separate species, *Eudyptula albosignata,* rather than a subspecies of the little penguin. The main differences between this form and the little penguin are that the white-flippered penguin has broad white margins on the leading and trailing edges of its flippers and that it has paler upper parts. It is also slightly heavier than the little penguin. Five or six subspecies of the little penguin are recognized across Australia and New Zealand.

The little penguin is aptly named, since it is the smallest penguin species. Little penguins are unique to the colder waters of southern Australia and New Zealand.

FACING PAGE: *The survival of the yellow-eyed penguin, found only in southern New Zealand and its offshore islands, is at risk because of loss of its traditonal breeding habitat and introduced predators.* RINIE VAN MEURS

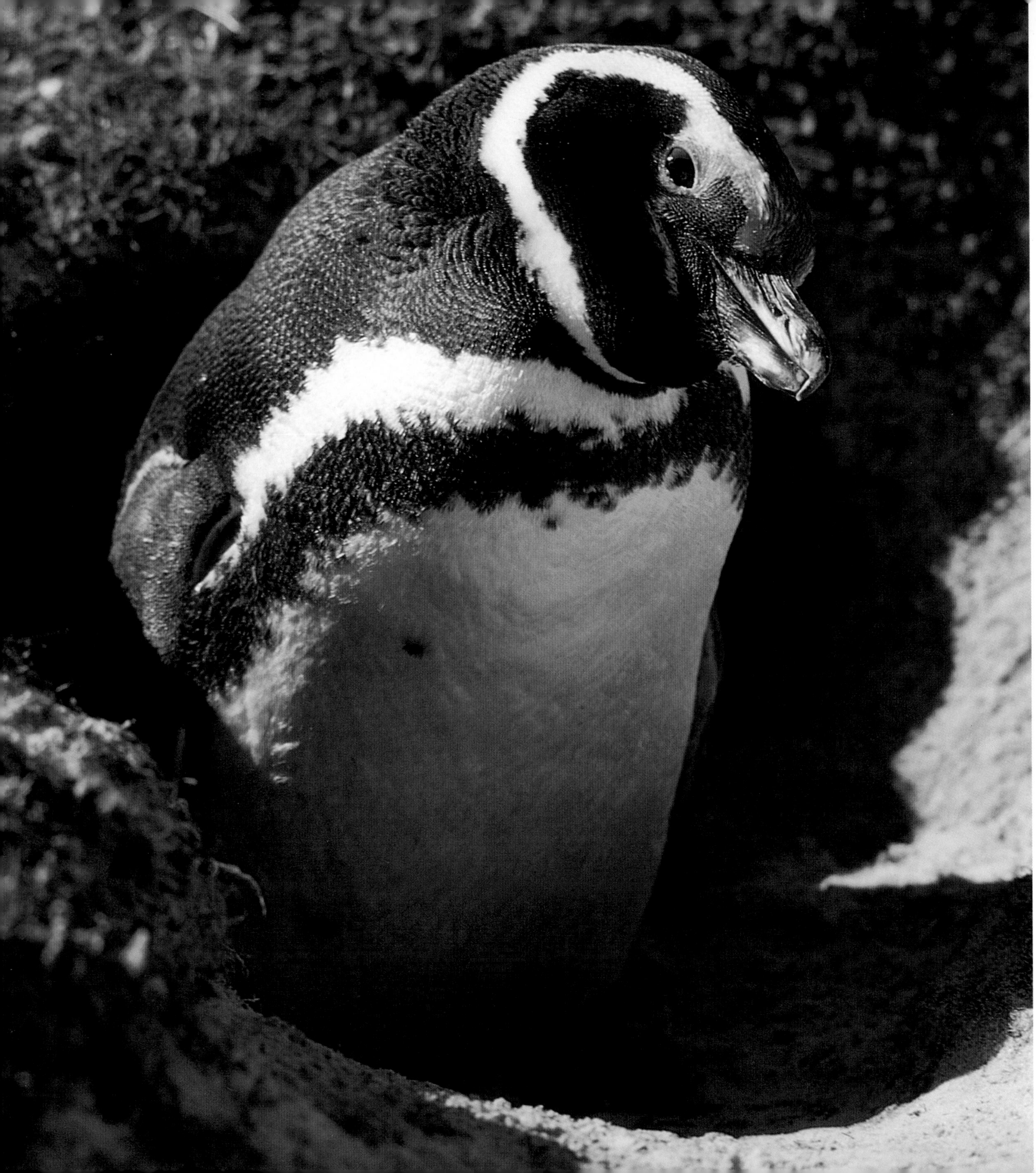

MAGELLANIC PENGUINS

The four ringed penguins, so named for the white ringlike markings on their chests and heads, share many attributes. Most are found in the more temperate regions, and to the untrained eye, they are very similar in size and markings. The one species that has a sub-temperate range is the magellanic penguin.

The magellanic penguin, *Spheniscus magellanicus,* was first identified by J. R. Forster, James Cook's naturalist, in 1781. The species name *magellanicus* was bestowed to honour Ferdinand Magellan, whose expedition in 1519 was the earliest to record this species. Magellanics are easily distinguished from the other ringed penguins by the double black band across their chests; the other ringed species have a single band. Measuring 70 centimetres (27½ inches) long and weighing 4 kilograms (9 pounds), this medium-sized penguin is the largest of the *Spheniscus* genus.

Magellanic penguins are found in the southern portion of South America and on the Falkland Islands. They breed in large and small colonies, which are less densely packed than those of other penguins because magellanic penguins burrow into soft soil or peat slopes on or near the shores. Most, if not all, colonies are on ground that once carried dense tussock grass. The burrows slope down about 2 metres (6 feet) and have a nest chamber slightly higher than the adjacent tunnel floor, which collects rainwater away from the eggs. Two white eggs, which rapidly become stained by the damp soil or peat, are laid between mid-October and mid-November on a nest of tussock grass. Fledglings leave the burrows in late January, and the adults vacate the colonies after they have moulted in March. Magellanics are very shy and will seldom come ashore or stay above ground if they detect humans nearby.

FACING PAGE: *Magellanic penguins, one of the four so-called ringed penguin species, nest in burrows to escape predators. They are found from the Falkland Islands to the southern coast of South America.*

The Temperate Species

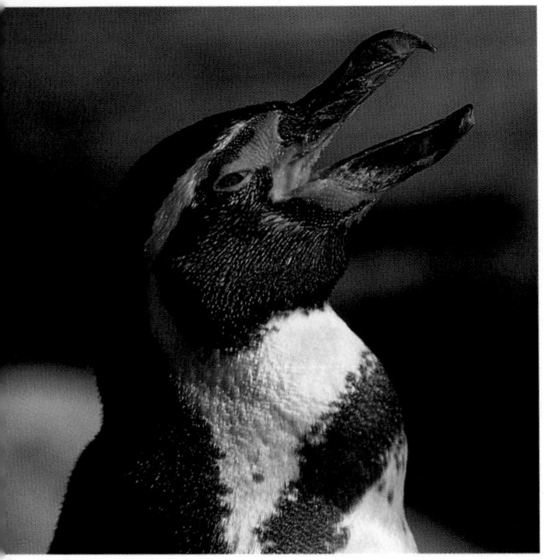

HUMBOLDT PENGUINS

One of the species that occurs in the temperate zone of South America is the Humboldt Penguin, *Spheniscus humboldti.* The species name is derived from the cool Humboldt Current, which in turn was named after the nineteenth-century German geographer Alexander von Humboldt. This nutrient-rich current supports the anchovy fishery on which the penguins rely for their food. Sometimes also called the Peruvian penguin, this species breeds in small colonies along the west coast of northern Chile and Peru. With an average length of 65 centimetres (25½ inches) and weighing 4 kilograms (9 pounds), the Humboldt is slightly smaller that the magellanic, with whom it is found in a stretch of about 300 kilometres (180 miles) in southern Chile. Ironically, despite the Humboldt penguin's proximity to human habitation, it is the species that is least understood by scientists. Because of its proximity to humans, it is also one of the most threatened species. Damage to its breeding areas caused by guano mining, the effects of El Niño, overfishing and predation have all been factors in the Humboldt penguin's decline.

AFRICAN PENGUINS

The African penguin, *Spheniscus demersus* (*demersus* means plunging or sinking), is often referred to as the black-footed penguin, in reference to its mottled feet, which are black and flesh coloured. Traditionally, this species was also known as the cape, the spectacled and, again, the jackass penguin. This is the only species commonly found in South Africa and was the first to be described by Europeans. Consequently, it is known as the "type" species. With an average length of 70 centimetres (27½ inches) and a weight of 3 to 3.6 kilograms (6½ to 8 pounds), it is similar in size to the magellanic penguin. The African penguin breeds only on the mainland and the islands of the south and southwest coasts of southern Africa, which are washed by the cool Benguela Current. Throughout this century the African penguin population has diminished considerably, first as a result of egg collecting and more recently because of oil spills and overfishing.

The Humboldt penguin is endangered because most of its traditional breeding ground has been mined for fertilizer and its prey species are overfished.

FACING PAGE: *African penguins, another of the ringed penguins, are found only on the south and southwest coast of southern Africa. The first species identified by Europeans, they are the "type" species.* RON AND VAL TAYLOR / HEDGEHOG HOUSE

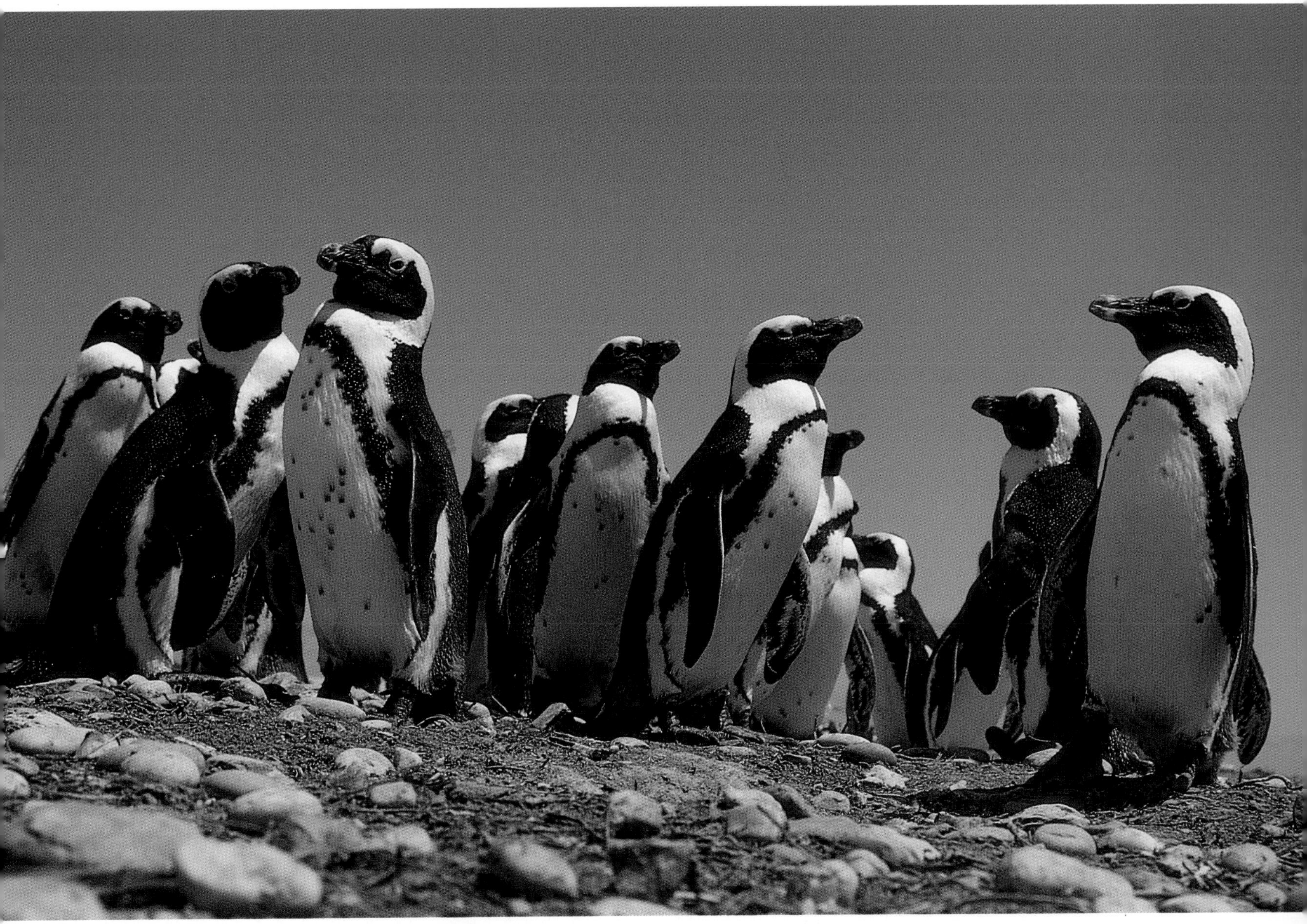

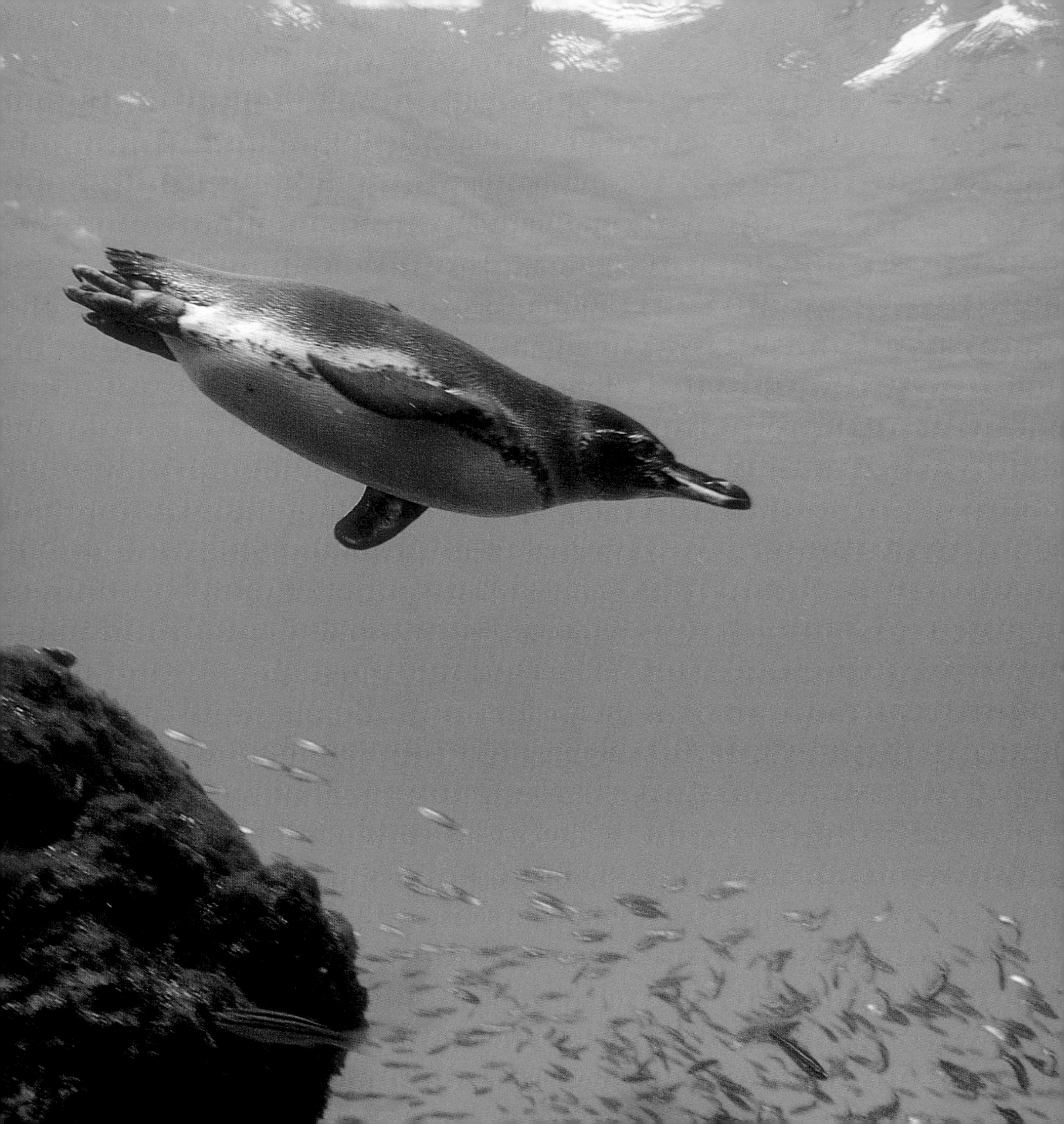

GALÁPAGOS PENGUINS

The Galápagos penguin, *Spheniscus mendiculus* (*mendiculus* means beggarly, in reference to the species' small size), is the most northerly of the penguin species, breeding on the equator. Measuring an average 53 centimetres (21 inches) long and weighing 2 to 2.5 kilograms (4½ to 5½ pounds), the Galápagos penguin is the smallest of the *Spheniscus* genus. It frequently breeds in the company of flightless cormorants, or boobies, and will reproduce only if there is a plentiful supply of small fish.

The population was estimated to be between six thousand and fifteen thousand individuals in the 1970s, but numbers have declined since then as a result of introduced predators, especially feral cats, dogs and rats. The Galápagos penguin is only able to breed on the west coast of Isabela and on most of Fernandina Island of the Galápagos astride the equator, because of the cool and fertile branch of the Humboldt Current, called the Cromwell Current. The failure of the cold current in 1982/83, as a result of the El Niño Southern Oscillation (ENSO), led to a 70 per cent decrease in the breeding population. Many birds were believed to have starved to death. Even with the cool current, the Galápagos penguins have to endure air temperatures that may exceed 40°C (104°F) and surface water temperatures as high as 29°C (84°F).

To escape the heat, they forage in the ocean during the day and spend the nights on land. To keep cool when swimming, they seldom porpoise and keep their flippers submerged when on the surface. On land they always shade their feet with their bodies to keep them cool and thus facilitate heat loss. In addition to keeping their wings at forty-five degrees to allow the maximum amount of air to pass over the less heavily feathered areas, they also pant when necessary and hide in shady places where they are available. If the bird is nesting, it will not have the same degree of freedom to escape the heat, but if it becomes seriously overheated, it will abandon the nest to cool off in the sea, regardless of the consequences. Under good conditions the Galápagos penguin can breed twice in a year, but in other years breeding may be skipped altogether. Because of the pressures on this penguin species, it is regarded in many circles as endangered.

FACING PAGE: *Galápagos penguins are the most northerly penguin species, breeding on the equatorial Galápagos islands, which are washed by cold currents.* MARK JONES/HEDGEHOG HOUSE

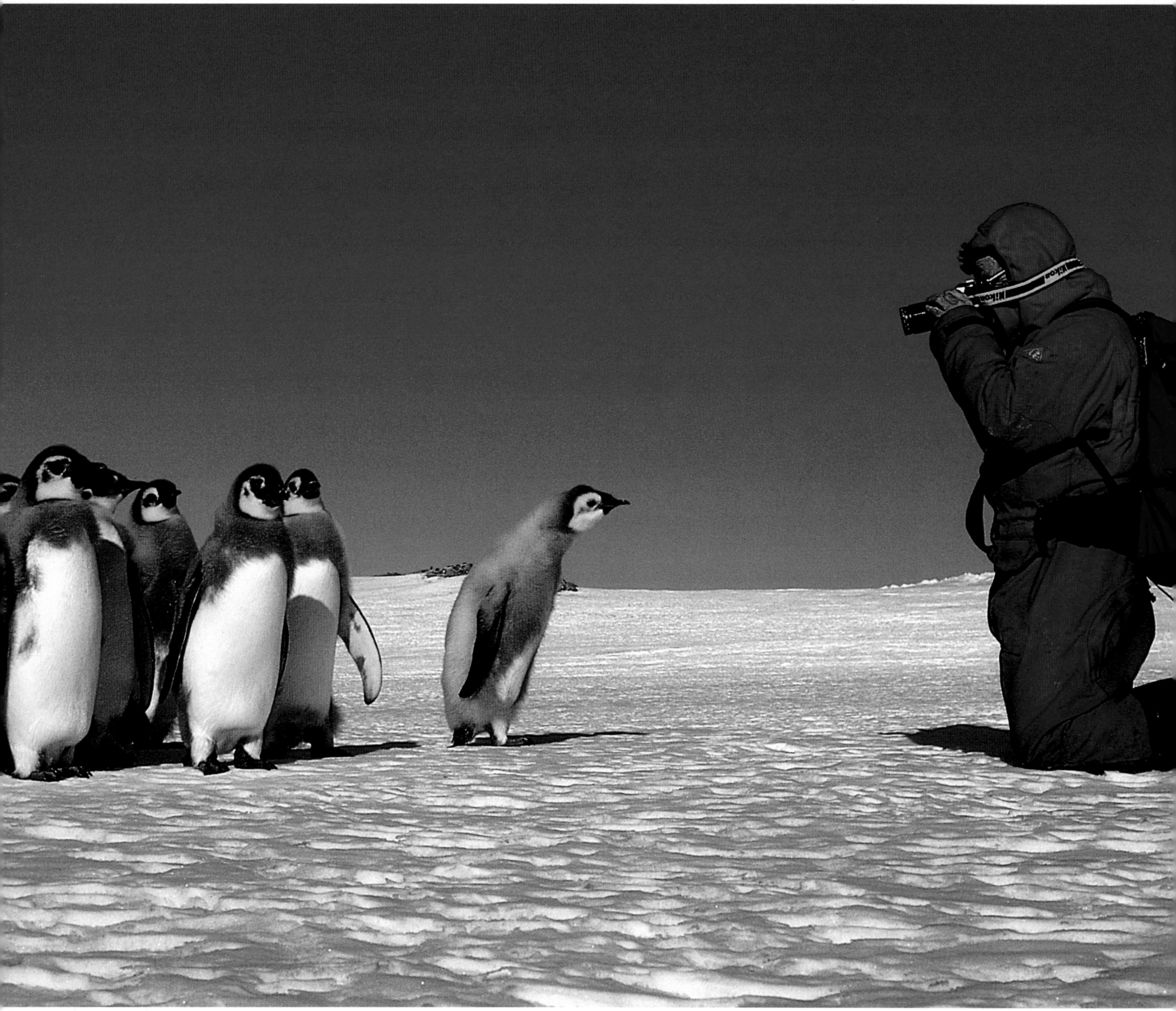

Part II

PENGUINS AND PEOPLE

Penguins are the most anthropomorphic of all animals. Everyone identifies with them … Why do we have such strong responses to penguins? First, they stand up straight and walk upright like humans, so we see them as little humanoids—a convention of head waiters, ten thousand nuns, plump babies wearing snow suits. On land they have a comical waddling walk which is very similar to a human toddler's. Free of terrestrial predators, they are very curious about humans and tend to walk right up to you.

—Diane Ackerman,
The Moon by Whale Light, 1992

FACING PAGE: *Having no land-based predators, Antarctic penguins are very inquisitive. A kneeling photographer—the size of an adult emperor, piqued the interest of these chicks.*

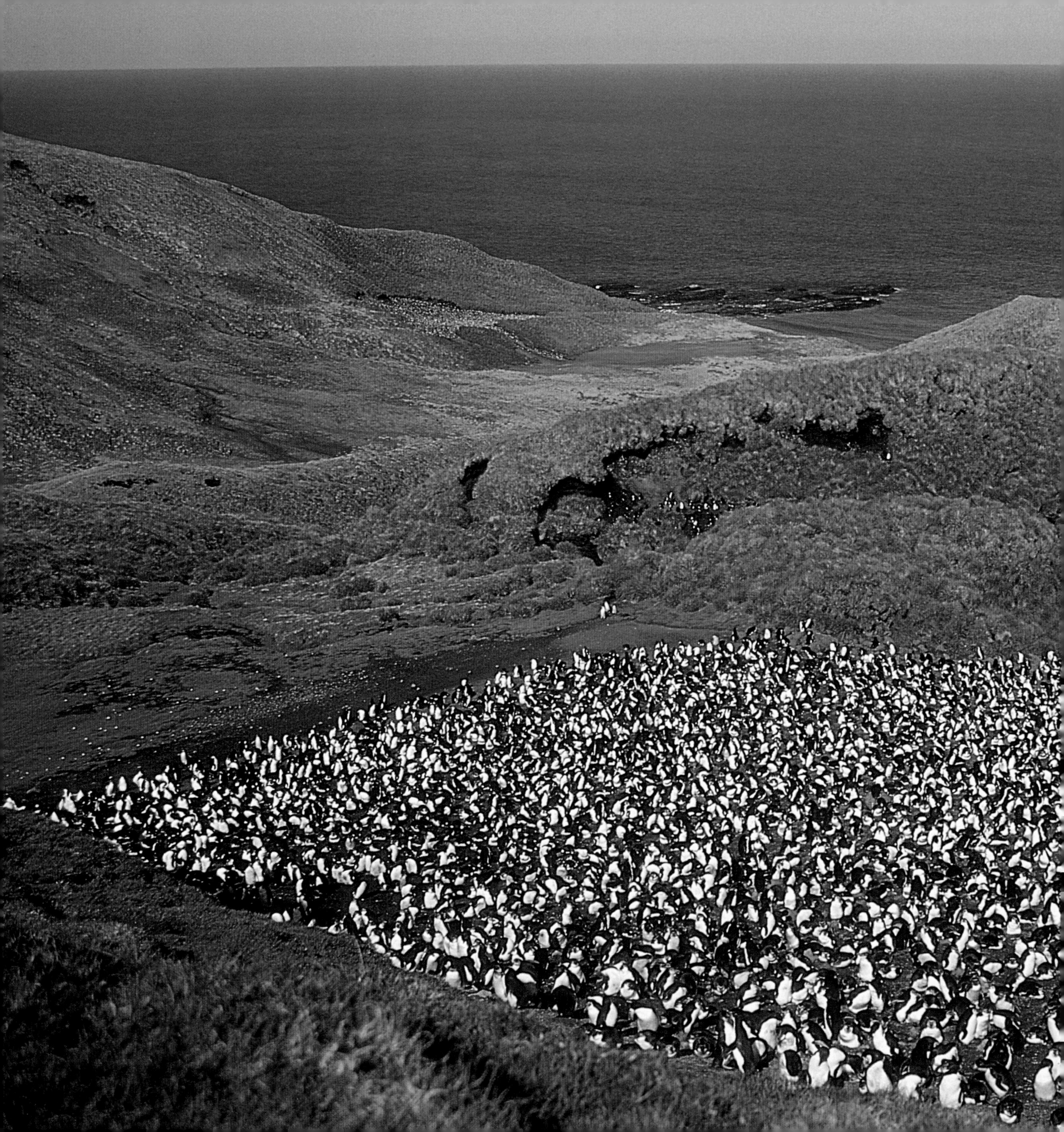

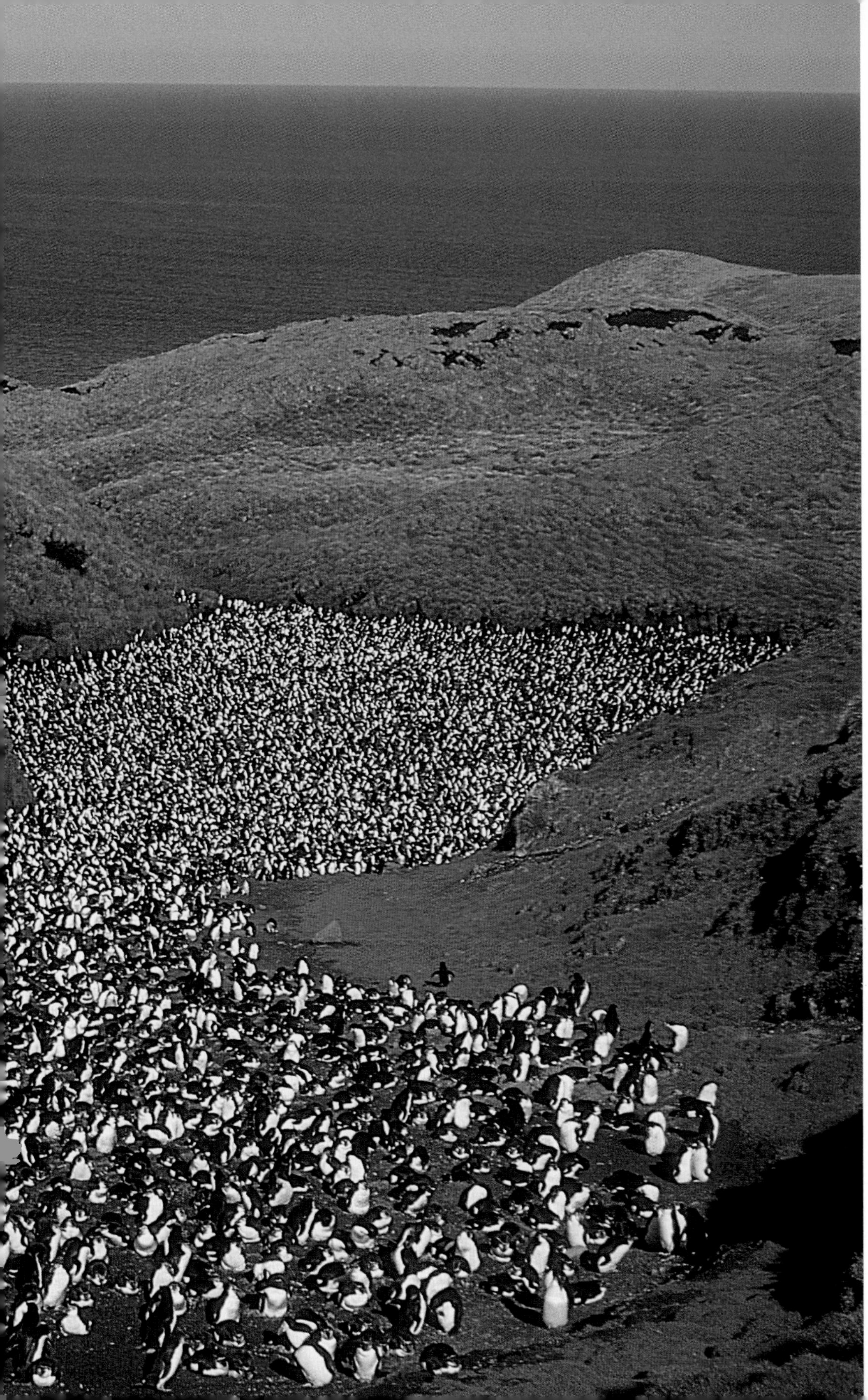

Though royal penguins on Macquarie Island were boiled down for their oil by the thousands in the 1920s, today they have completely recovered. ADAM DARAGH

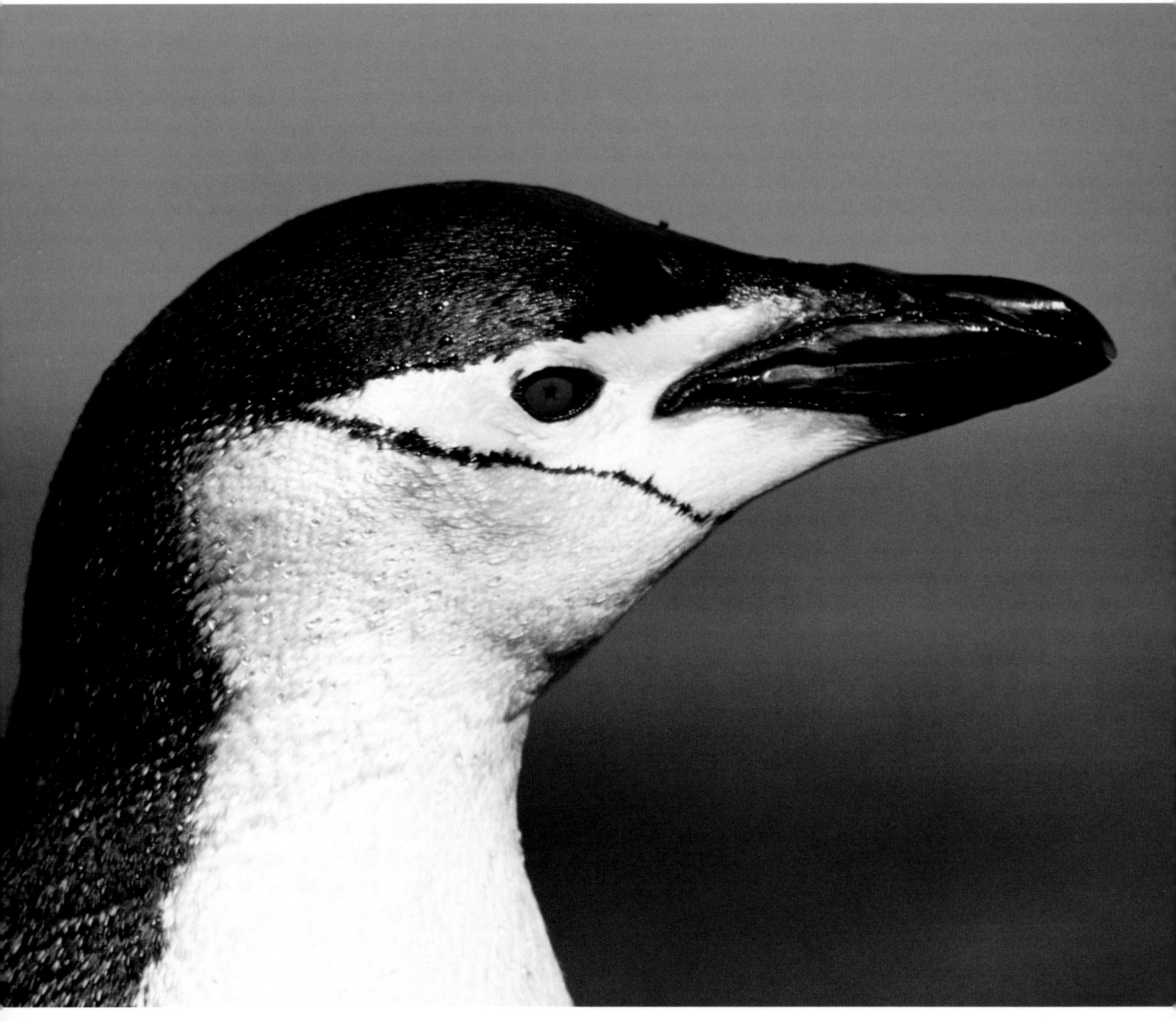

Chapter 4   **Past and Present**

....

I have often had the impression that to penguins, man is just another penguin—different, less predictable, occasionally violent, but tolerable company when he sits still and minds his own business.

—Bernard Stonehouse, *The Biology of Penguins,* 1975

Native Use of Penguins

For Native peoples of the southern lands, penguins were a source of food and clothing. It is known that the aboriginal people of Tierra del Fuego, the Alacaluf and Yahgan tribes, raided penguin colonies by canoe, eating the flesh and fashioning their densely feathered skins into cloaks and sometimes decorative purses. Penguins were also hunted by the Australian aborigines on the southeast coast of Australia. These Natives were undoubtedly the first to see the little penguin. Egg collecting was intense during the breeding season, but the adult birds were probably less favoured. In 1831 it was recorded that the penguins were usually soaked in water for many days before cooking to make them tender.

New Zealand's early Polynesian settlers, the Maoris, hunted and ate many birds, and it is believed that penguins were quite possibly part of their diet. There is also the suggestion that the Native people of southern Africa ate penguins or their eggs.

All of these penguin species in the southern waters were numerous when first encountered by European explorers, indicating that native hunting had little long-term effect.

FACING PAGE: *To natives, sailors and early explorers of the Southern Hemisphere, penguins represented a ready source of eggs and fresh meat. It was some time before penguins, including chinstraps like this one, were correctly identified as birds that swam rather than fish with feathers.*

The European Explorers

To early European explorers voyaging around the southern reaches of the globe, penguins were a vital and readily obtainable source of fresh meat. In 1578 Sir Francis Drake wrote of the "great store" of penguins near the eastern entrance to the Strait of Magellan in South America: "such was the infinite resorte of these birds to these lands that in the space of 1 day we killed no less than 3000."

This colony became a regular stopping place for vessels passing through the waterway. Here penguins were an important addition to their larder, according to Sir Richard Hawkins, who wrote in 1594:

> The Penguin is in all proportion like the Goose, and hath no feathers, but a certaine downe vpon all parts of his bodie; and therefore cannot flee, but auayleth himselfe in all occasions with his feet, running as fast as most men . . . The flesh of these Pengwins is much of the sauour of a certaine Fowle taken in the Llands of Lundey and Silley, which we call Puffins, by the taste it is easily discerned that they feed on fish. They are very fat, and in dressing must be flead as the Byter; they are reasonable meate roasted, baked or sodden; but best roasted. We salted some doozen or sixteene Hogsheads, which serued vs (whilest they lasted) insteed of powdred Beefe. The hunting of them (as wee may well terme it) was a great recreation to my company and well worth the sight ... In getting them within the Ring close together, few escaped . . . and ordinarily there was no Drove which yielded vs not a thosand, and more: the manner of killing them which the Hunters vsed beeing in a cluster together, was with their cudgels to knocke them on the head.

Penguin meat was not an epicure's delight, by all accounts, but to sailors living on poorly preserved beef, or no meat at all, it was a welcome change. In many cases penguins were salted down in barrels for the next leg of a long voyage.

Much later, south polar expeditions also supplemented their rations with penguin and seal meat, but storage in Antarctica was rather more simple. The slaughtered birds were simply left outside to freeze or buried in a snow cave for consumption later in the winter. Sometimes, in an emergency, penguin flesh was all a party had to live on.

In 1903 the crew of the Swedish Antarctic Expedition's vessel, the *Antarctic,* was marooned for a winter on Paulet Island when the ship was crushed and sank. Luckily this landing spot was home to a very large colony of Adélies penguins. The twenty men calculated that they would need three thousand to four thousand birds to survive the winter. They were only able to kill a third of that number, however, before the last of the birds

FACING PAGE: *Many populations, such as these king penguins in the Falkland Islands, were as much at risk from introduced predators, such as cats and dogs, as they were from the cooking pot.*

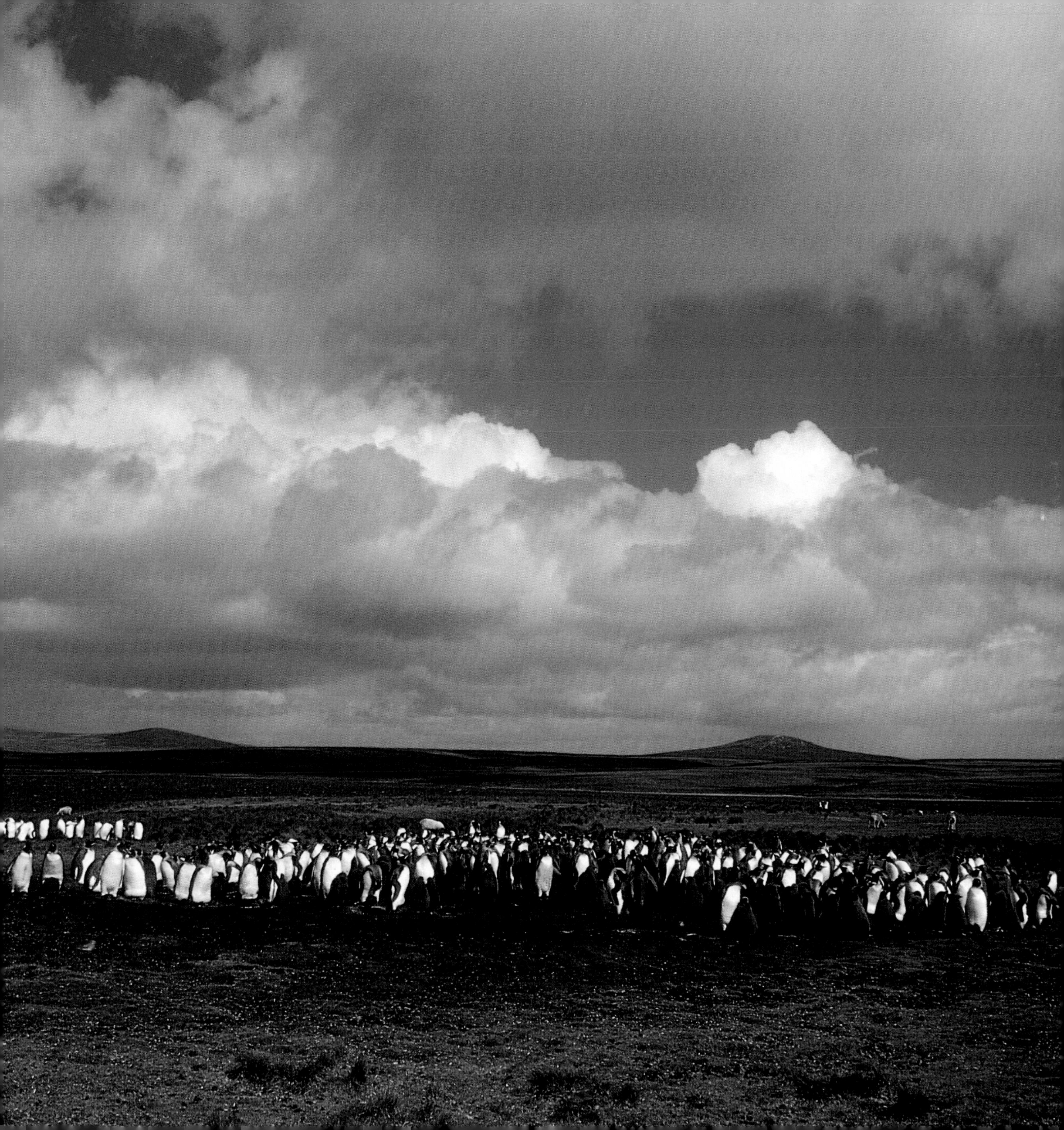

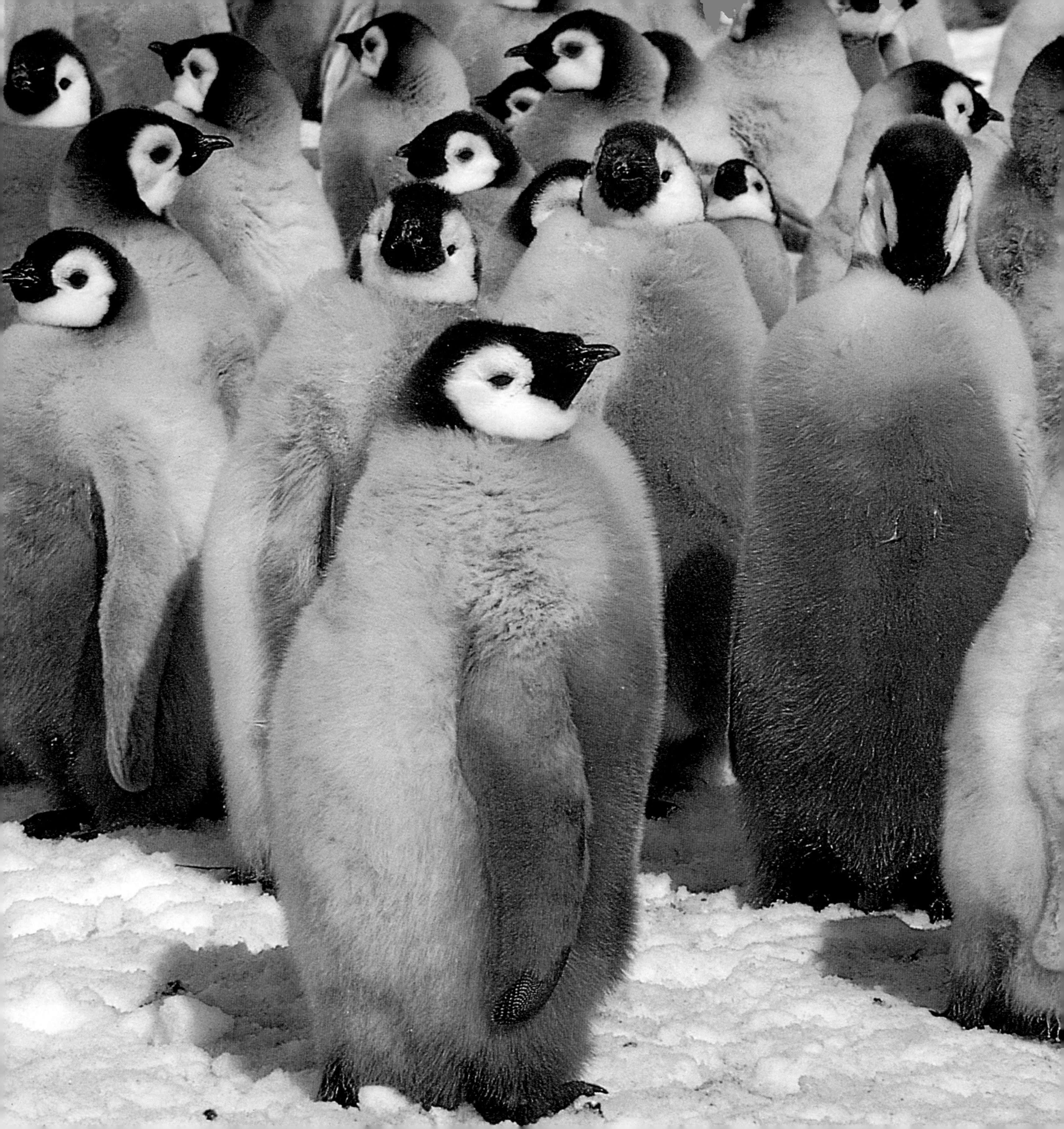

left, having completed their moult. Without the penguins, the men would have starved, but in all events, the eleven hundred carcasses proved to be sufficient.

Carstens Borchgrevink's British Antarctic Expedition (1898-1900) was the first to deliberately spend a winter on the Antarctic continent. Their camp on Ridley Beach at Cape Adare was in the midst of one of the largest Adélie rookeries on the continent. Here Borchgrevink observed and wrote about the penguins' breeding cycle in scientific detail. But for his party, as for many subsequent early expeditions, the arrival of the penguins heralded a much welcomed break in their diet of "seal beef":

> The flesh of the penguin was rather good, especially as we prepared it in the main camp, where we boiled it, whereby it lost a good of deal of the blubbery taste and afterwards roasted it. When served on our wooden table under the name of "ptarmigan" it was considerably improved as an edible.

All the subsequent early expeditions that spent the winter in the Antarctic, from Nordenskjöld, Scott and Shackleton to Mawson and Amundsen, supplemented their larder with penguins, but 1915 was a particularly bad year for wildlife in the Weddell Sea. After their ship, the *Endurance,* was crushed and sank, Shackleton and his men had to live on penguins and seals for much of the sixteen months they were marooned on the floating sea ice. Hurley was one of the main procurers, as he recounted in his book, *Shackleton's Argonauts:*

> Penguin-stalking is much the same as seal hunting. But, while neither seal nor penguins puts up any défence, the element of risk is supplied by the killer whales, which are apt to poke their ugly heads through the thin ice with a snort that immediately imparts to the hunter a marvellous speed and a keen desire to get back to a solid flow. I had many narrow escapes ... Occasionally I came upon large convoys of penguins too numerous to cope with single handed. Then I would heliograph to the camp with a small signalling mirror, and all hands would turn out, armed with clubs, to the slaughter. One day we added 300 penguins to our depleted larder. The birds were evidently migrating from the southern rookeries to the northern pack limits. The skins were reserved for fuel, the legs for hoosh [a thick soup, usually made from pemmican], the breasts for steaks and the livers and hearts for delicacies ... Twenty penguins, cooked by the fuel of their own skins was a fair daily average.

Later, when the crew spent the winter under the upturned boats on Elephant Island, they survived on chinstrap penguins and seals. By midwinter the penguins were more valuable for heating than eating, according to Hurley: "June opened with a threatened shortage of fuel. Six hundred and six penguins had been captured in the six weeks since we had

FACING PAGE:

Emperor penguin chicks were a part of the diet of Shackleton's ill-fated expedition that spent sixteen months trapped by the ice in the Weddell Sea.

landed; but while we had cold-storaged the carcasses, we had used up the skins for the stove."

By this stage the men were so desperate for tobacco that they even tried smoking penguin feathers—not very successfully, by all accounts.

Even in the 1980s penguins were still considered a source of emergency food by modern expeditioners, although today's field parties seem to lack rough-hewn experience in obtaining such a meal. The ANARE [Australian National Antarctic Research Expeditions] Field Manual suggests penguins as an emergency source of food, saying that "penguins may be killed by breaking and cutting the neck or by squashing the air out of their lungs by sitting on them for a fairly long period. Penguin stew is very palatable."

Despite the numerous expeditions through the decades, the taking of penguins for their meat had only a small effect on population numbers, especially in the Antarctic. It was the slaughter of penguins for their oil that devastated many colonies, particularly those on the subantarctic islands.

Early expeditions faced great hardships because of scurvy. Cook's expedition, like many of the era, took penguins by the thousands for fresh meat. MITCHELL LIBRARY

Oil

Before they breed and moult, penguins build up energy reserves in the form of thick layers of blubber, which also help insulate them from the cold. This blubber was rendered into fine oil that was prized as a lubricant, a base for paints and a fuel for lamps.

The first record of boiling penguins for their oil was in the 1820s. Whales and seals, especially elephant seals, were the main source of oil, but when the availability of these species began diminishing as a result of rapacious killing, the hunters turned to penguins to help fill their barrels.

Macquarie Island was particularly infamous for the activities of New Zealander Joseph Hatch, who for some twenty-five years harvested penguins for oil. He began his efforts on the larger elephant seals and king penguins but found the former too difficult to transport to his works; with the latter, it was difficult to extract the oil without contaminating it with blood. The smaller and more plentiful royal penguins became his main quarry. From January to March they were boiled down in the digesters—each bird yielding a pint of oil. There were many colonies of royal penguins on Macquarie Island. The largest, with an estimated half a million birds, was at the Nuggets, where he located his works. As Conan Fraser recounts:

> at the height of the season the men worked in two twelve hour shifts and were able to process more than 2700 birds a day. The penguins were clubbed to death as they filed up a narrow creek to the huge rookery inland and taken to the "Hall of Smells" where they were loaded into the top of large digesters. After 12 hours of cooking the oil would rise to the top and would then be run off and cooled …
>
> To counter public protest Hatch claimed, that after 25 years of operation, the rookery was in fact larger than when he had started. He was called a liar, but subsequent research has shown that he was almost certainly right.

The Australasian Antarctic Expedition, led by explorer Sir Douglas Mawson, landed a scientific party on the island in 1911 and occupied it for the next four years. In 1919, the very influential Mawson added his voice to the growing public concern about the slaughter of royal penguins. As a result of his influence, Macquarie Island was declared a sanctuary in 1920, bringing to a close a very sordid chapter of penguin exploitation.

A similar story can be told about most of the other subantarctic islands. After sealers on Heard Island and South Georgia had run out of seals to top up their barrels, they

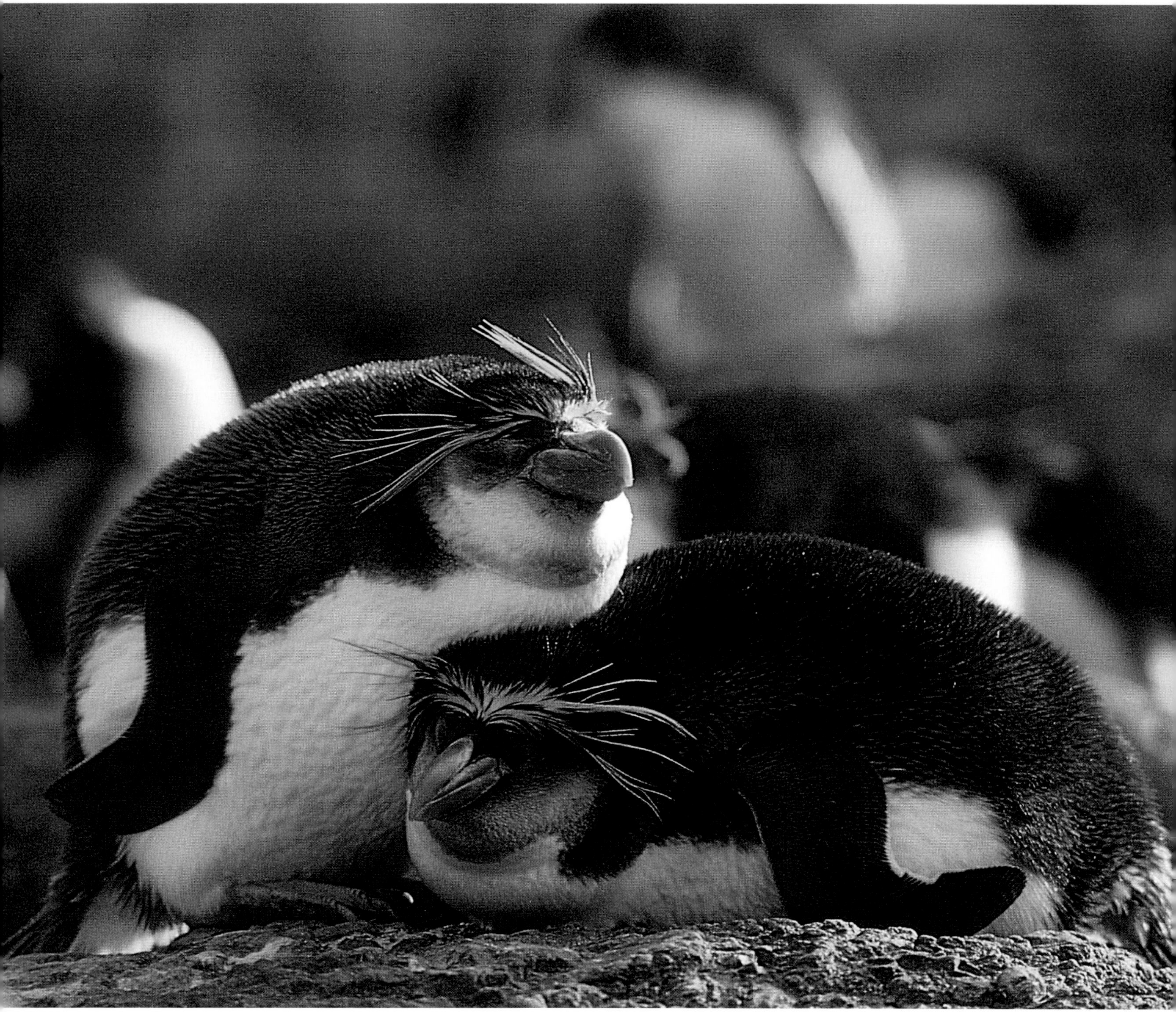

moved onto penguins, which were also boiled down in large quantities. Penguin skins were also used for firing the try-pots. At the height of the industry, 500,000 to 700,000 birds were taken annually from South Georgia alone. Sealers nearly exterminated king penguins from Heard Island.

The Falkland Islands were also a major site for the penguin oil business. One rockhopper was found to yield a pint of oil suitable for tanning and lighting. Thousands were driven into stone corrals to be clubbed and cooked. The industry peaked in the 1860s, when the potential profit was three pence per penguin. More than half a million birds were slaughtered in a three-year period. The market then slipped, but it enjoyed a brief revival in the 1870s before fizzling out.

Skins

Penguins were also exploited for their finely feathered skins, but the skin trade was never as extensive or as long lived as the penguin oil industry. Magellanic penguin skins were probably the first to be turned into clothing, at the hands of the aboriginal people of Tierra del Fuego in the 1880s and 1890s. There was a thriving market in penguin skins in Montevideo and Buenos Aires, where the white-feathered parts were used for trimming women's clothes.

After their moult, rockhoppers were killed on Tristan da Cunha to make highly prized tassel mats. During the moult, they were rounded up into pens and the loose feathers stripped off to be used in mattresses. Humboldt penguin skins were also used to make hats and purses, and penguin "fur" muffs were popular in the fashion markets of Europe.

There was even a brief trade in penguin skins from New Zealand's subantarctic islands in the 1880s, also to meet "a fashionable demand for ladies' muffs (open ended fur cylinders in which to warm the hands)." A number of ships returned to New Zealand, each with cargoes of around 3000 skins, and one of the merchants alone had accounts for purchases of some 15,000 skins before the trade collapsed.

FACING PAGE: *Royal penguins on Macquarie Island were harvested for their oil for some twenty-five years.*
ADAM DARAGH

Egging

Penguin eggs were another valued source of food for early sailors and explorers. They were variously regarded in journals as everything from "acceptable" to "delicious." Penguin eggs tend to have red yolks, apparently because of the carotenoid (a carrot-coloured pigment) in the krill, which is a major food source for many penguin species.

There were several techniques of keeping eggs fresh. One was to immerse them in seal oil and then store them in barrels between layers of sand. This method would preserve them for up to nine months. Another technique was to store them in flour, as Antarctic expeditions reported doing.

Commercial egg collecting was carried out on Dassen Island off the west coast of South Africa for many years. Teams of men went through the colony every day during laying season (15 February to 15 August) collecting all the eggs with a scoop on the end of a long stick. In the 1890s, some 300,000 African penguin eggs were sold annually. It is amazing that the colony was able to survive after such plunder.

The Falkland Islands were the other main site of large-scale egg collecting, which started as early as the late 1700s and developed into a tradition that continues up until today. Both black-browed albatross and rockhopper penguin eggs were collected from rookeries on New Island, and according to local naturalist Ian Strange, it became the practice for some whaling fleets to establish depots at places such as New Island for holding stores of eggs, which were sold to other vessels. Until the 1960s and early 1970s, collecting eggs was a part-time business for a number of islanders.

Not all eggs were as easy to obtain, however. Magellanic penguins nest in deep burrows, and so gathering their eggs was considerably more difficult, as a 1933 report describes:

> Egging for Jackass [magellanic] eggs is not very popular, for although the eggs when fresh are more like hens eggs than those of either of the other species [gentoo and rockhopper], and are very good for eating, they are difficult to collect in large numbers, and the collector runs the risk of being smothered in Jackass fleas, which will remind him unpleasantly for several nights of his otherwise enjoyable expedition.

Until recently there was a traditional egging week around November 9, and this day was a school holiday for children devoted to egg hunting. Penguin colonies near Port Stanley, the main centre in the Falkland Islands, were wiped out as a result of this practice. A colony of rockhoppers at Sparrow Point near Stanley yielded 25,000 eggs in 1871. Today none of this species can be found there.

FACING PAGE: *Egging—collecting penguin eggs for food—was an important industry and a popular pastime in the Falkland Islands for many years.* PETER GUILDING

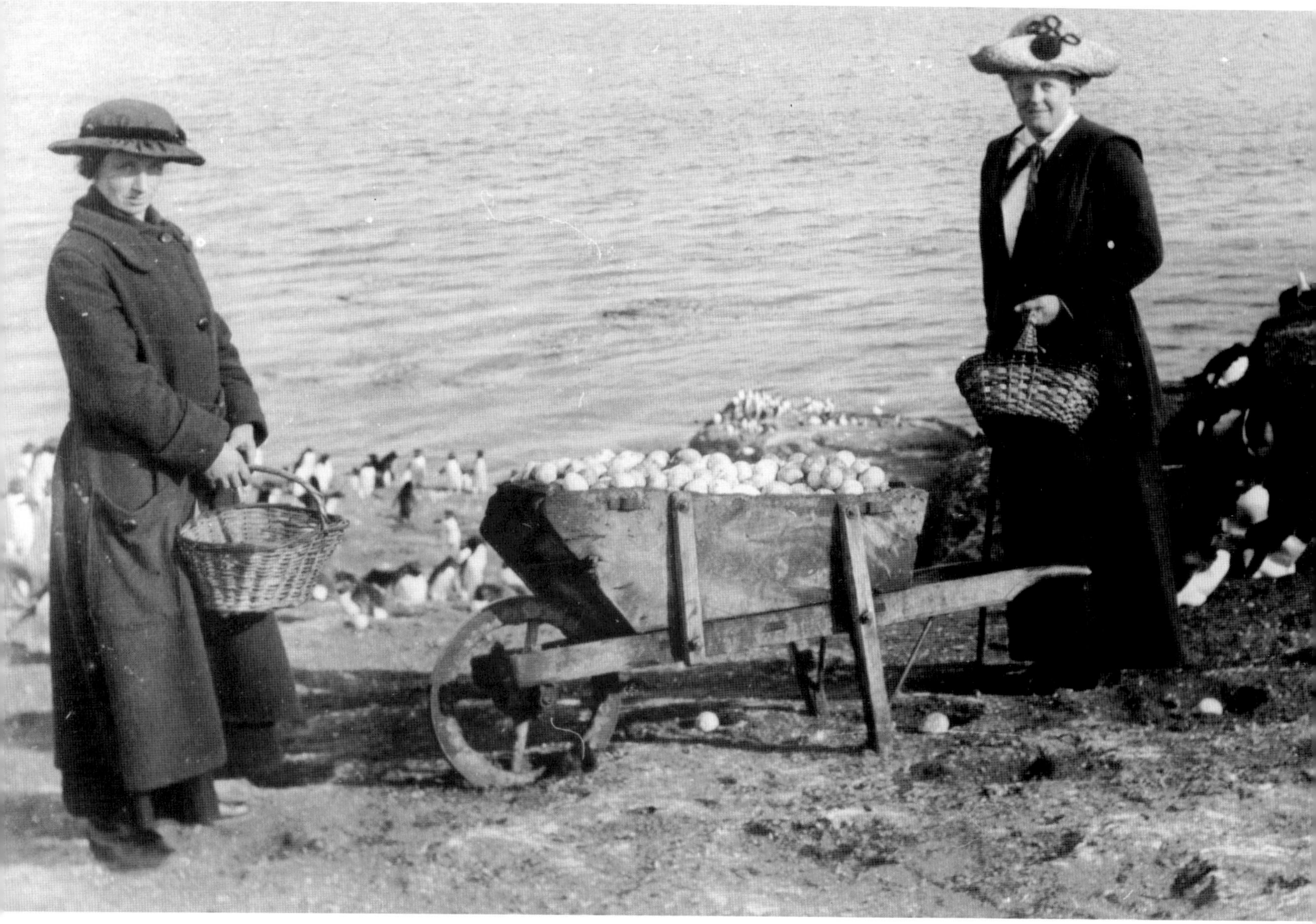

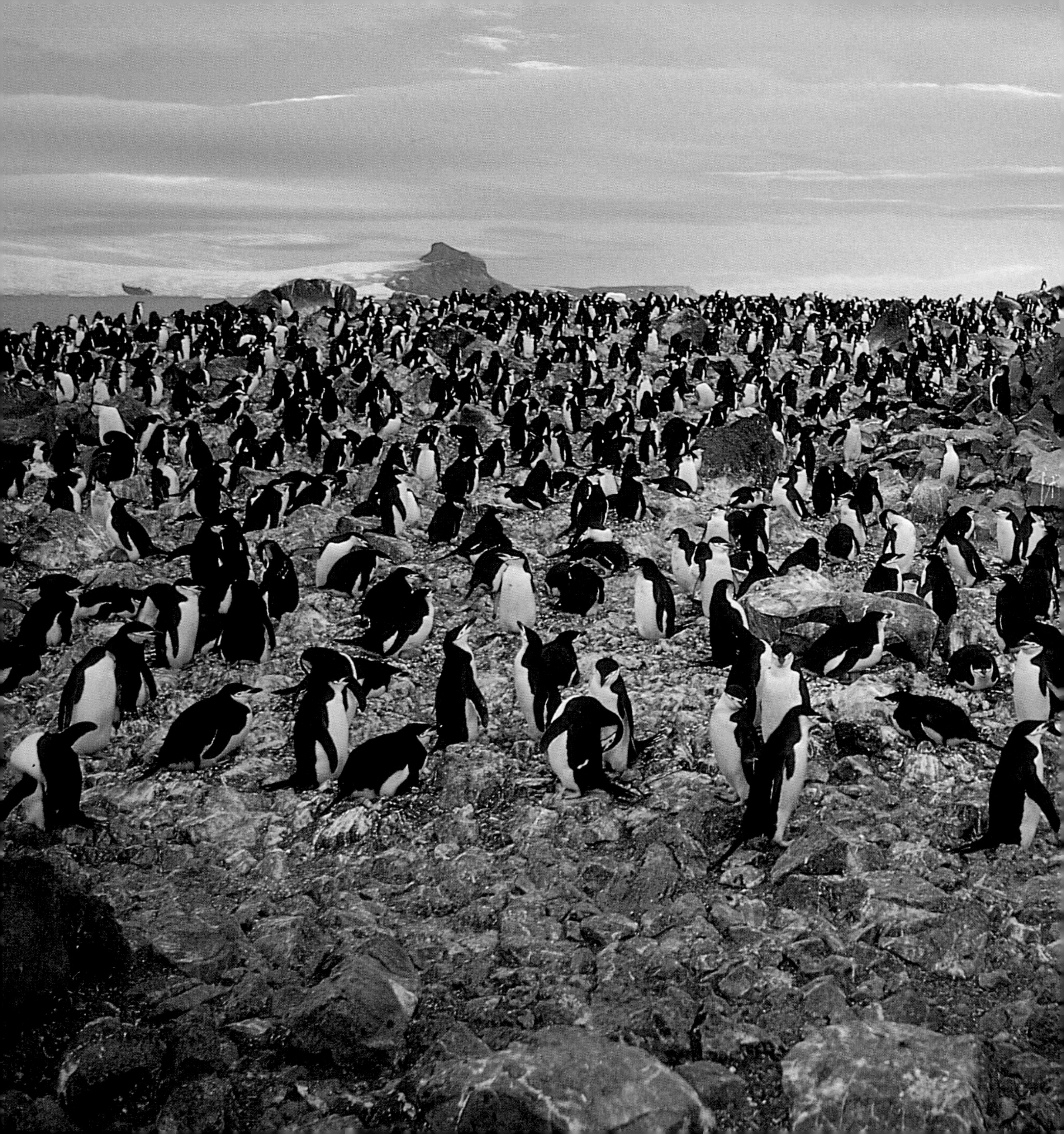

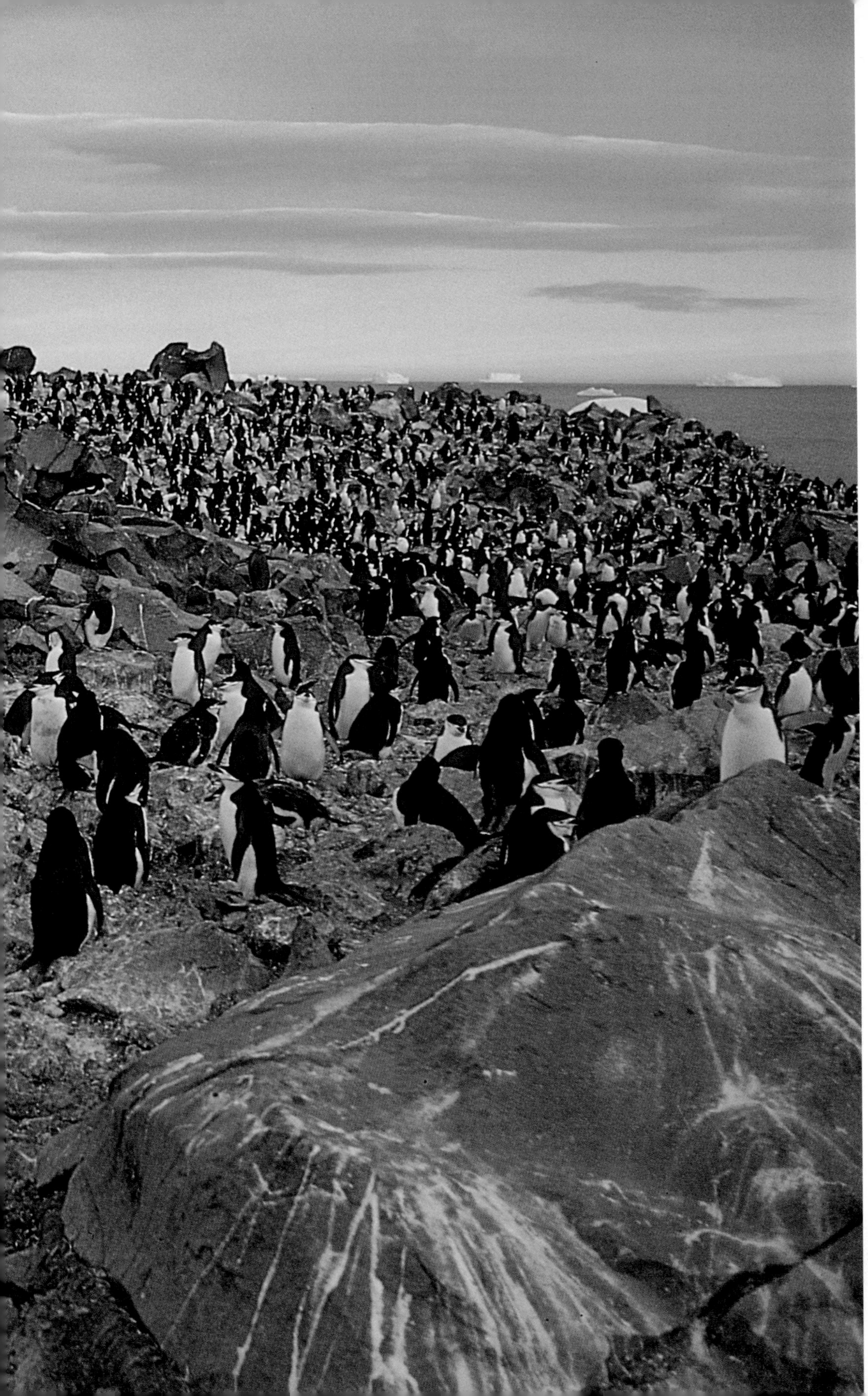

Over the centuries, vast colonies of penguins and other sea birds deposited guano to great depths. In places, guano has been mined for fertilizer, depriving some species of suitable places to nest in burrows.

Guano

On islands off Peru and Chile, over millions of years, thick deposits of sea bird droppings accumulated. Known as guano, the Inca word for this naturally dried fertilizer, these deposits were up to 50 metres (160 feet) deep in places. Humboldt penguins were able to burrow easily into the deposits to make their nests. When Europeans discovered how rich guano was as fertilizer, they began to mine it extensively—eventually resulting in a billion-dollar industry. Between 1848 and 1875, some twenty million tons were removed. The guano was eventually stripped back to bare rock, leaving no place for the penguins to nest, and so numbers of Humboldt penguins were significantly reduced.

The Plunder Continues

These multifarious ways of killing penguins or using them or their by-products for economic gain peaked in the late nineteenth and early twentieth centuries, but it is surprising how some heinous practices persist in isolated places.

As recently as the 1950s, live Galápagos penguins could be purchased at fishing docks in Ecuador for as little as $25. It is hard to imagine that they became popular as household pets; no doubt many ended up in the cooking pot.

For a long time fishermen on the west coast of South America have also caught Humboldt penguins in their fishing nets and even used them as bait in their lobster pots. A researcher recently counted four hundred Humboldt penguins accidentally killed in nets in one year alone—an alarming number for a species that is regarded as threatened. This same species is now supposedly protected in Chile and Peru, but wardens are being bribed and eggs and birds are regularly poached.

The magellanic penguin was the most recent to be threatened with commercial exploitation. In 1981 a Japanese company sought a concession from the Argentine government to harvest 40,000 penguins in the first year, and eventually 400,000 birds a year, to be used for food, for oil and in the production of high-fashion gloves. A public outcry thwarted this plan and led to a major conservation effort focussed on this population.

The Popularity of Penguins Today

Unknown to the European world until the 1500s, penguins escaped a role in traditional folklore. Early descriptions from the field portrayed them as good for eating and little more. Stuffed museum specimens and dried skins could hardly convey the natural wonder and comic attributes of these crowd pleasers.

It wasn't until live penguins found their way into northern zoos in the nineteenth century that they began to gain the privileged position they now enjoy. In a rating by zoologist Desmond Morris, penguins came in as one of the top ten animals that appeal to humans.

Penguins have become stars of the animal world by virtue of their inherent human-like traits and humour. As the different forms of media have evolved, so penguins have quickly been co-opted. Penguins were immortalized in print early on, and their silver screen debut as cartoon characters came not long after the genre was created.

Over the last thirty years, there has been a significant shift in the world's perception of penguins. They have won the hearts and minds of communities far from their traditional homes, a remarkable turnaround from their days as fresh meat and oil.

The erect-crested penguin has a very stubby, brush-like crest and is found on islands south of New Zealand. ADAM DARAGH

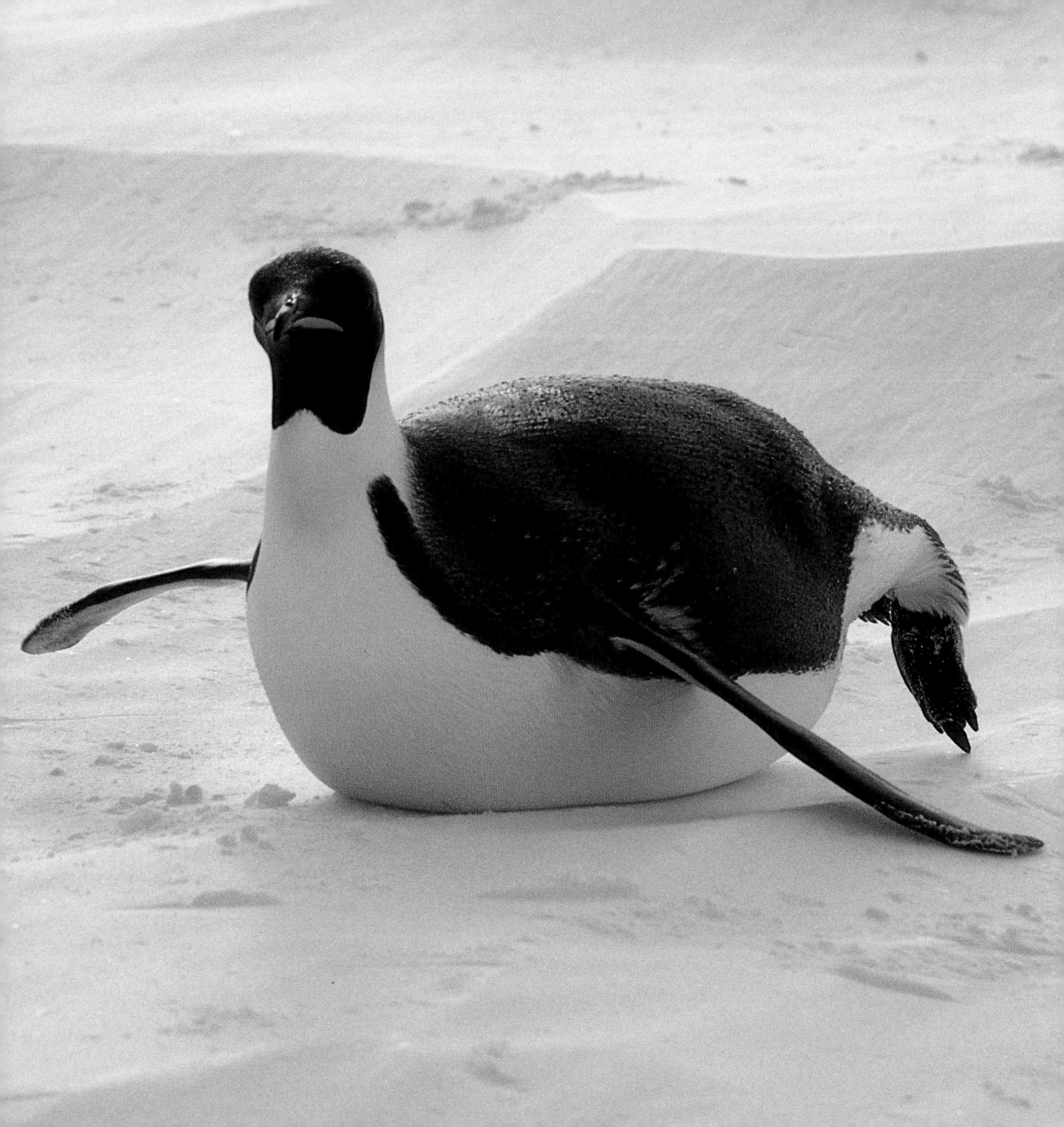

Chapter 5 # The Fragile Future

··

*Penguins acquainted with humans seem to accept
us as another quaint and somewhat clumsy kind
of penguin, just as we tend to think of penguins as
quaint and clumsy humans.*

—George Gaylord Simpson,
Penguins Past and Present Here and There, 1976

Penguins have not always been treated with the respect that they enjoy today. As you have seen, thousands were eaten by early sailors and explorers and millions were slaughtered for their oil during the nineteenth century. Today penguins are almost universally protected by national governments. All penguins south of 60° south are also legally protected under the provisions of the Antarctic Treaty.

Regardless of such protection, penguins are still vulnerable to climate change, habitat destruction, overfishing of their food sources, pollution, oil spills and human encroachment on nesting areas. Understanding these pressures on penguins and the nature and extent of human interference is vital to preventing the decline of individual populations and perhaps even the extinction of one or more species. Moreover, it is necessary to monitor penguin populations because they are indicators of the health of the planet.

Although the Antarctic penguins are not in immediate danger, some species in temperate regions are threatened. With an increase in tourism to the Antarctic and the popularity of penguin viewing sites in South America, New Zealand, Australia and Africa, it is important that tourists understand how best to observe these birds with a minimum of disruption. Biologists have devised guidelines, but it is also necessary to

FACING PAGE: *Emperor penguins
can survive the harshest Antarctic
winter, but they are threatened by
environmental change and other
effects of human activities.*

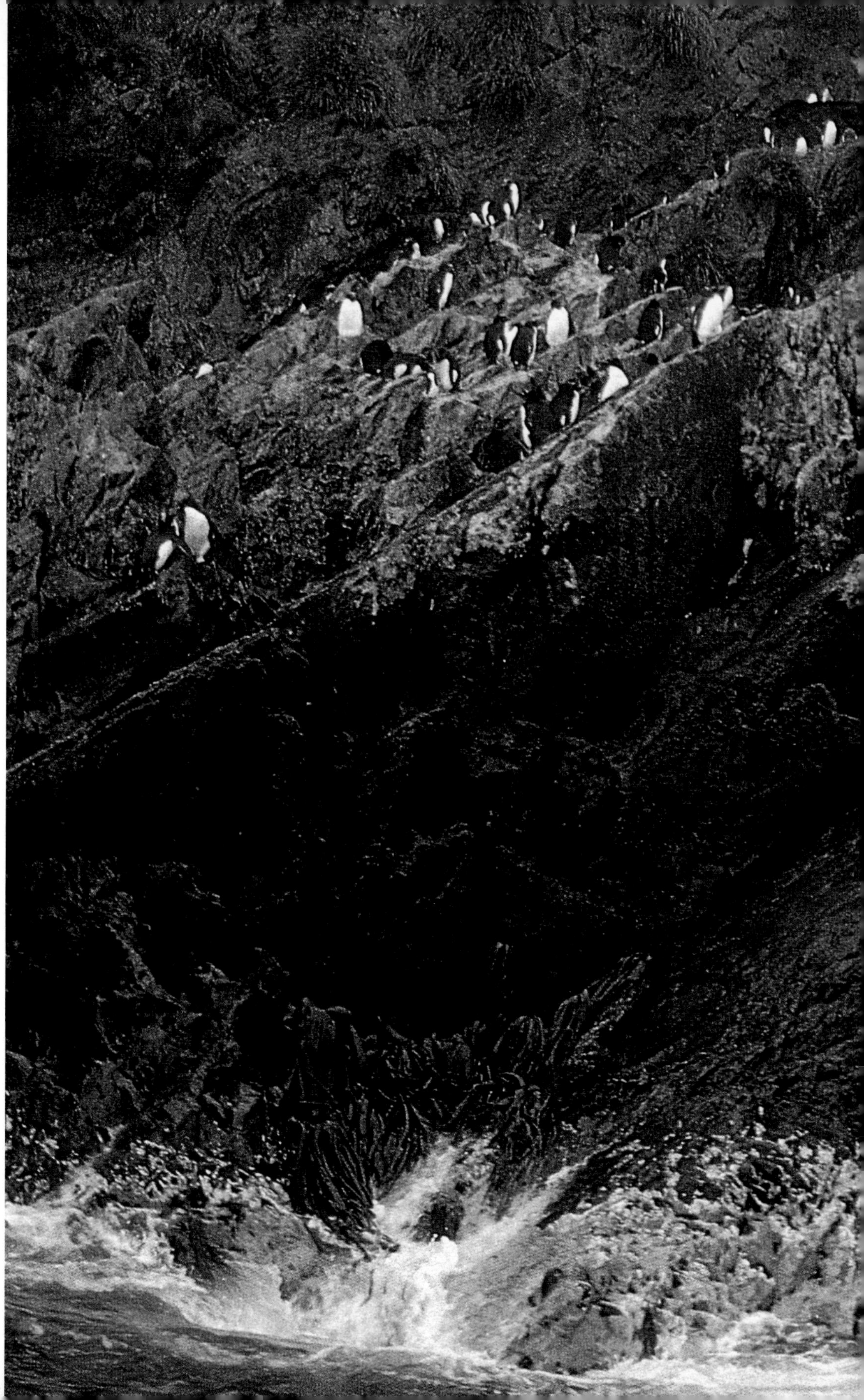

Macaroni penguins battle heavy seas to land on the shores of South Georgia. Life for these and many other species of the Southern Ocean depends on the viability of their food species, which is in turn dependent on sea temperature patterns..

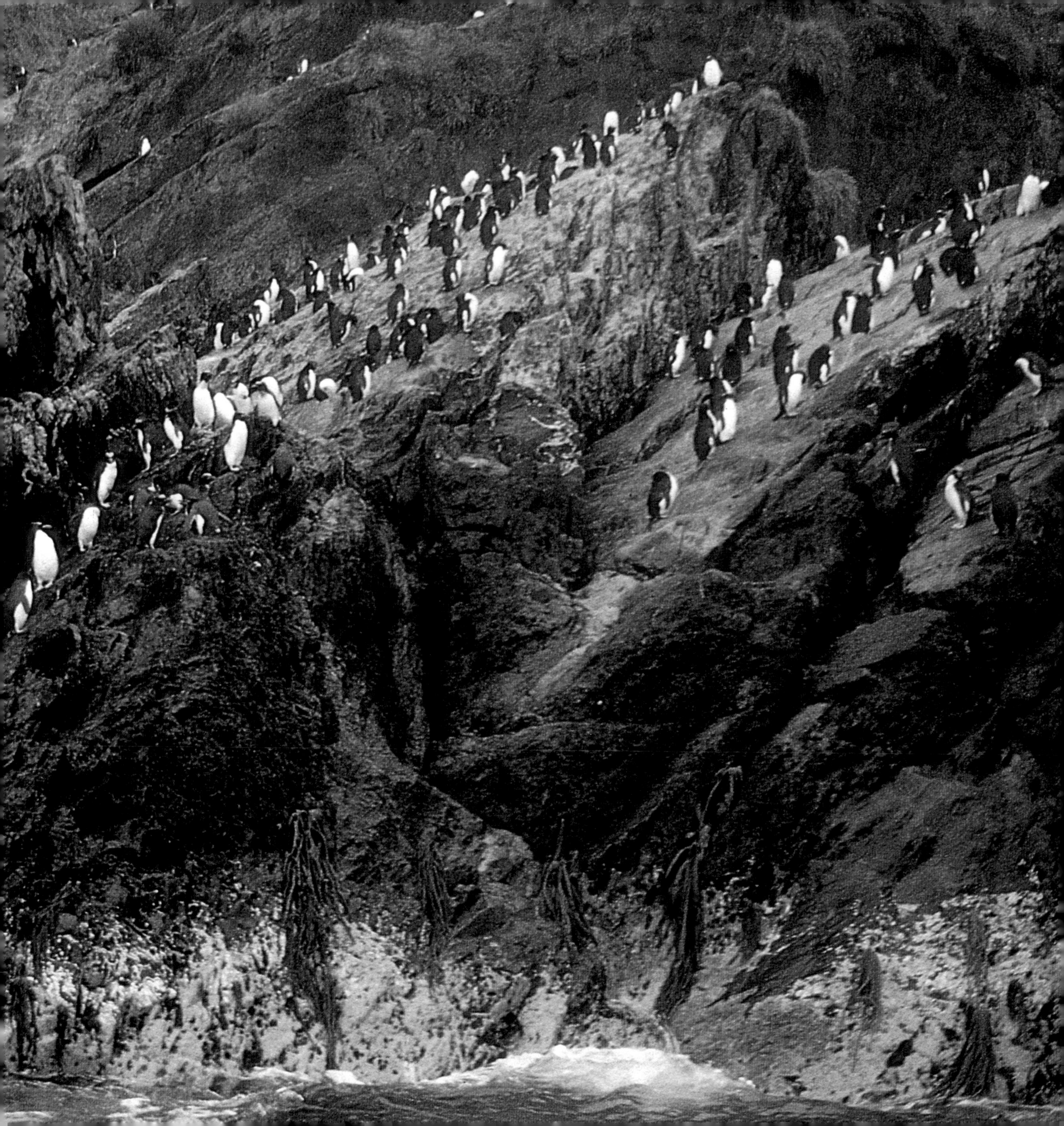

manage heavily trafficked sites to prevent disruption of breeding behaviour.

Penguins occupy a wide geographic range—from the tropics to the high southern latitudes. There are consequently many opportunities for human or natural phenomena to interfere with their ecology.

Climate Change

Penguins have endured short- and long-term natural variations in the earth's climate and oceanographic conditions for millions of years. Those species that we have evidence of only through fossils clearly did not survive variations in their environment, but the current level of speciation seems to have been stable for about 10 million years. There is now reason to suggest, however, that human-induced global warming over the next decades could result in large-scale climate changes.

Evidence suggests that penguin populations are highly sensitive to even small-scale changes in sea temperatures. Increases in the chinstrap population along the Antarctic Peninsula are thought to be tied to a gradual warming in the area, which has reduced the winter sea-ice cover. Conversely, the increase in numbers of Adélies in the Ross Sea region over the last ten to twenty years seems to be tied to increases in the extent of sea ice in the region. Local factors, such as variations in precipitation, weather and temperatures, have also been shown to be significant.

Climate change affects ocean currents, which in turn have consequences for fish stocks and prey species on which penguins feed. This sensitivity has been observed over the past 100 years through the effects of the El Niño Southern Oscillation (ENSO), which has caused variations in the amount of upwelling of cold, nutrient-rich waters along the Peruvian coast of South America. El Niño raises the sea surface temperatures and decreases the fish available to sea birds. Penguins are more sensitive to this variation than other sea birds because they are unable to forage over large distances and instead rely on specific marine areas rich in food. Galápagos penguins are among the most susceptible to loss of food sources because of their complete dependence on the cold current that washes the western shores of the Galápagos Islands, bringing lower temperatures and the necessary small schooling fish. When the upwelling and the resulting food are absent, these penguins do not moult and either skip breeding or fail to breed successfully. The little penguin in southern Australia appears to be similarly dependent on cool, nutrient-rich currents to breed successfully. The Humboldt and African penguins are also at risk from the effects of El Niño.

On occasion, other penguin populations also experience what is termed a crash. In these instances, countless birds are found washed up on beaches. In 1985/86 thousands of dead and dying rockhopper penguins were sighted around the Falkland Islands. Both adults and chicks seemed to have starved to death as a result of a natural shortage of krill. In 1993 rockhoppers on the Falklands again suffered a crash on top of an overall marked decline in numbers of this species over the last sixty years.

Even Antarctic species are not immune to these crashes. Adélie penguins in the vicinity of Australia's Mawson Station in 1994/95 failed to breed successfully, and this failure has been attributed to a lack of krill.

Although the actual cause of these crashes is usually difficult to determine, they are believed to be connected to shifts in the availability of food species. A crash at South Georgia in 1978/79, when king penguins failed to breed, a colony of 3000 pairs of gentoos fledged only one chick, and there was a very low birth rate among fur seals, was also attributed to the absence of krill that season. These anomalies are affected by, or are a function of, changes in water movements, water temperatures, turbulence and availability of nutrients. All these factors are influenced by climate and particularly climate changes.

PAGES 84–85: *The Antarctic is easily altered by factors such as global warming, which can affect the ice cover, and the thinning of the ozone, which results in much higher levels of ultraviolet light reaching the earth's surface.*

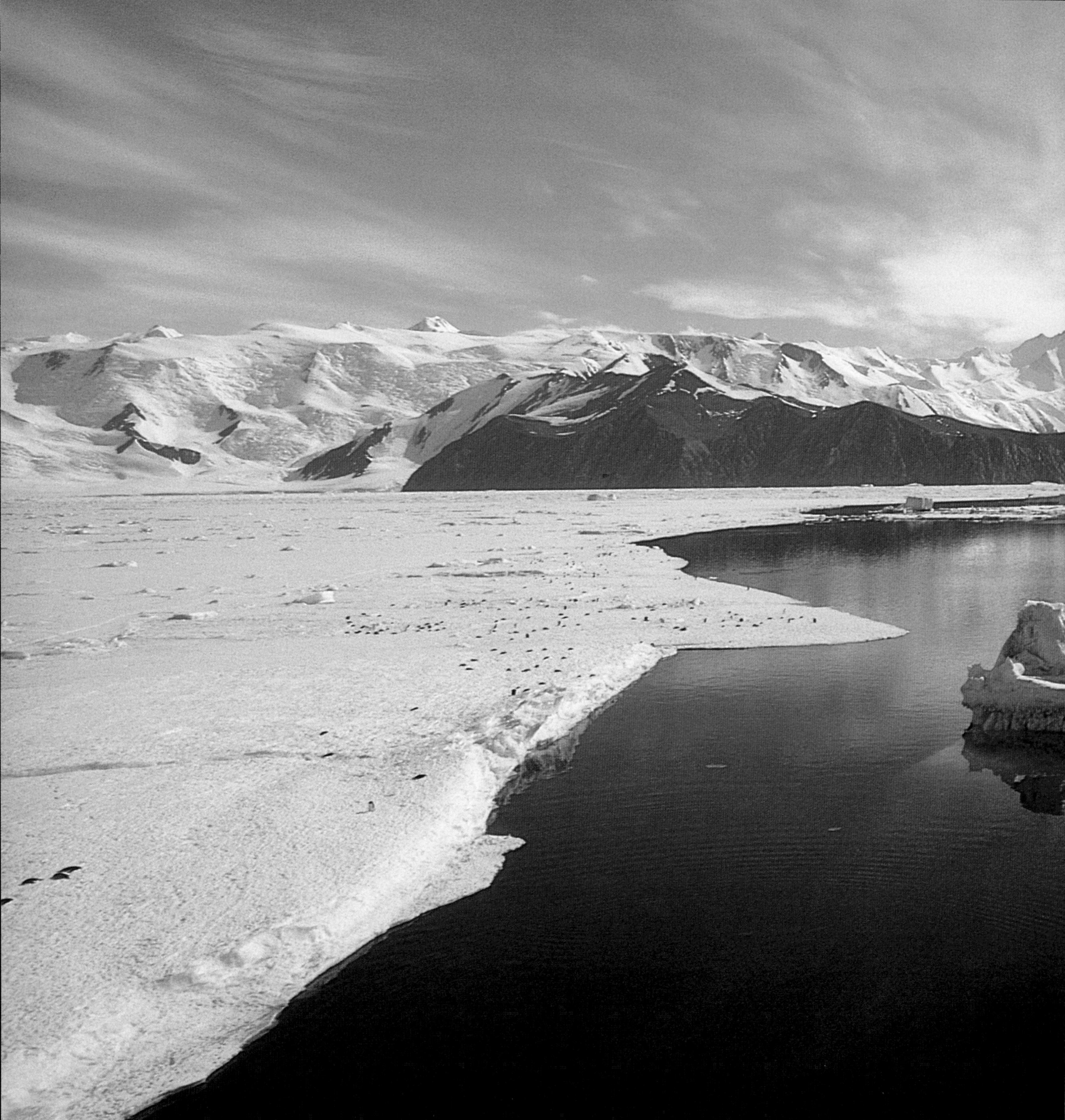

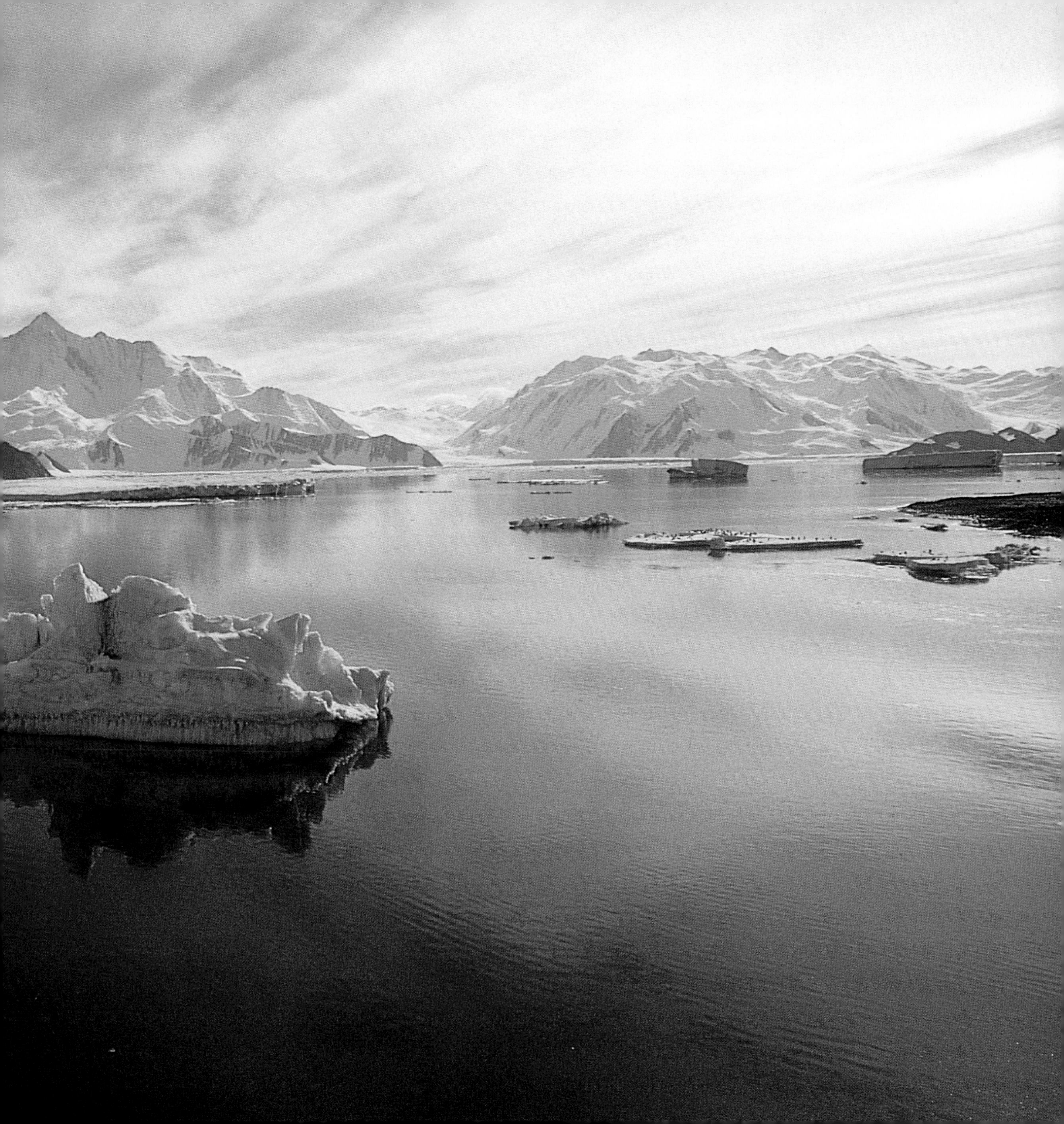

Pollution

Oil spills have a disastrous effect on most sea birds. Penguins are particularly at risk because they spend so much of their time in the water. Penguins cannot detect such pollution and can unwittingly swim into slicks while travelling on the surface or as they come up to breathe after a dive. Then, as they preen, affected penguins ingest the toxic oil. A coating of oil also tends to destroy the insulation and buoyancy of their feathers. When water enters the feathers, the birds can become hypothermic and die.

Oil slicks from tankers passing around the Cape of Good Hope, the southern tip of South Africa, have caused considerable problems for African penguins. These problems have become much worse over the last few decades as the supertanker traffic has increased. In 1968 a spill of 4000 tonnes of oil killed an estimated 15,000 penguins. In June 1994, a disastrous spill that resulted from the sinking of the bulk ore carrier *Apollo Sea,* near Dassen Island, affected countless thousands of birds. Some seven thousand were caught for rehabilitation in a major effort by the South African National Foundation for the Conservation of Coastal Birds (SANCCOB), Cape Conservation and other government agencies. The SANCCOB organization, which has been in existence since 1968, regularly rehabilitates hundreds of African penguins that are affected by the all-too-common oil spills. In this instance, it was able to return 65 per cent of the affected birds to sea, a lower rate than the organization's typical rehabilitation success rate of 80 per cent, but severe weather at the time of the spill hampered rescue efforts and prolonged the period the birds were under stress. As a result of this latest disaster, the South African government announced attempts to enforce stricter regulations to try to prevent pollution from tankers.

The magellanic penguins of South America are also at risk. An estimated 17,000 adult birds at Punta Tombo in the province of Chubut, the largest colony of this species in Argentina, were affected by a single spill in 1991 from an undetermined vessel. Large spills, however, are not the major source of oiled birds, according to P. Dee Boersma of the Magellanic Penguin Project. The regular dumping of ballast water from oil tankers and other ship traffic, she contends, results in the death of approximately 20,000 adults and 22,000 juveniles off the coast of Chubut each year. Oil-related mortality is thought to have contributed to the overall decline in the population at Punta Tombo since records began to be kept in 1987.

Over the next ten years a major oil-drilling industry is also likely to develop in the waters around the Falkland Islands. Some 15 million penguins live in the South Atlantic,

Oil spills, such as occurred on the coast of South Africa, are one of the main threats to penguin species that inhabit these temperate waters.
CAPE TIMES, CAPE TOWN

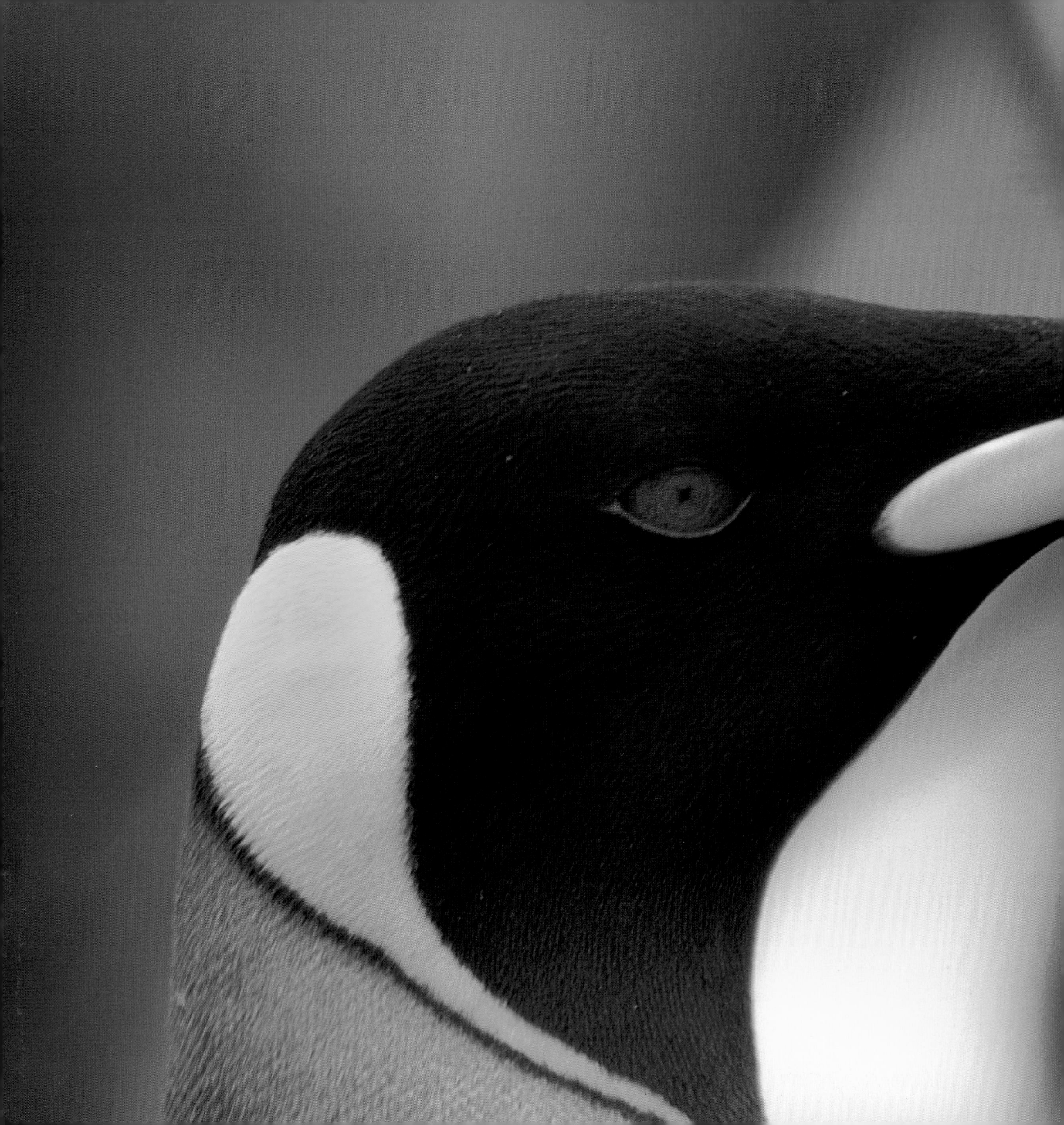

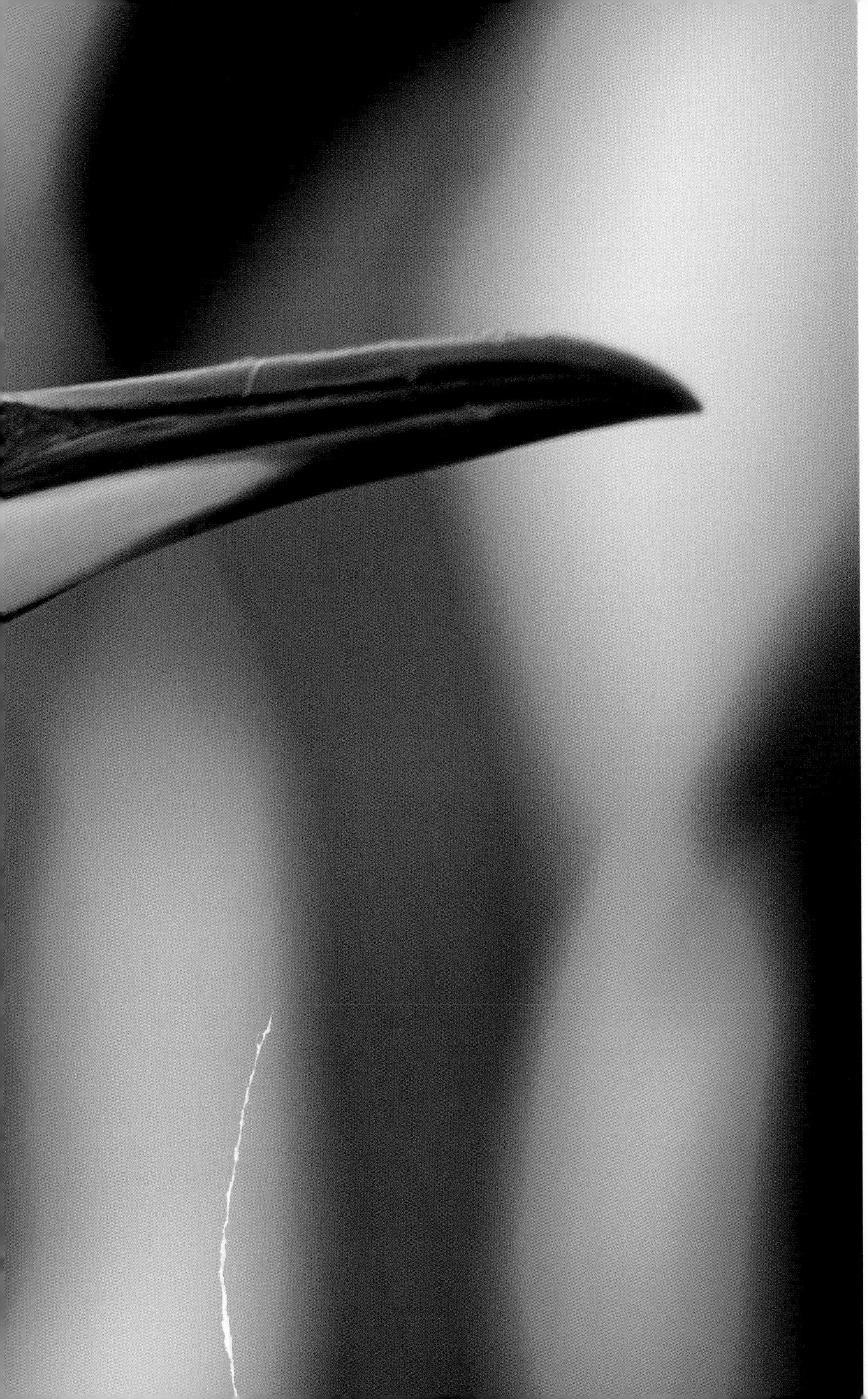

King penguins symbolize all that is beautiful and fragile about penguins. Like all penguins, they are highly susceptible to environmental variations. Scientists use their breeding success as an indicator of the health of food species such as small fish.

and should a major oil spill take place in the region, there could be frightening consequences for the local penguin populations.

The prospect of oil drilling farther south, in Antarctica, has been thankfully postponed for some fifty years, following the signing of the Madrid Protocol. Antarctic birds are not free from the threat of accidental oil spills, however, as was dramatically illustrated by the sinking of the Argentine supply vessel the *Bahía Paraiso* when it hit a submerged rock near U.S. Palmer Station in 1989. An estimated 1.14 million litres (300,000 gallons) of diesel fuel fouled the beaches and killed penguins, south polar skuas, comorants and krill. It took years to clean up the mess, and a long-term study of penguins was disrupted by this spill.

As more and more tourist ships enter Antarctic waters and increasingly large vessels are used, the potential for a major accident also increases. By the mid-1990s, sixteen vessels made multiple excursions across the Drake Passage to the Antarctic Peninsula. Although the largest of these cruise ships, the *Marco Polo,* only carries four hundred of its capacity of eight hundred passengers out of concern about the impact of large numbers of tourists, it is nevertheless a massive ship that carries a very large fuel supply.

Overfishing

On the coasts of South America and southern Africa, fishing for sprats and bait species has directly reduced the food available for penguins. In addition, many penguins get caught on long lines and in purse seine nets and die. And since the Falklands began selling squid fishing licences to other nations' fleets, there has been growing concern about the penguin species that breed in this region, since they also feed on squid.

Krill fishing in the Antarctic could have a major impact on the polar ecosystem. Following the whaling era, when there was a surplus of krill, the populations of some Antarctic penguin species increased, but this increase could easily be reversed by overfishing of the krill stocks. In the 1960s, Antarctic krill were considered the last large untapped source of protein, and a fishery developed through the 1970s. By the 1980s, commercial krill catches reached 500 000 tonnes per year, but lack of demand and problems in processing and marketing the catch have capped the industry. Nevertheless, this harvesting has occurred in very localized areas, and it could well be having an adverse effect on local predators.

The rapid growth of the fin-fishing industry in the subantarctic has also put severe pressure on a number of species of fish around South Georgia and the South Shetland Islands. It is very difficult to monitor the behaviour and population levels of these pelagic species, but it is proposed that by monitoring the top predator, which in many instances is the penguin, the health of the fishery and the ecosystem can be assessed.

Loss of Habitat

Penguins spend most of their lives at sea, but they must come ashore to breed and moult. It is here that they often compete with humans for space. In the temperate regions of the Southern Hemisphere, urban coastal development greatly impinges on penguin habitats, especially when forests are cleared and land is farmed.

This competition has been most pronounced for the yellow-eyed penguin on mainland New Zealand, and as a result this penguin population has declined by 75 per cent over the last 40 years. Attempts to halt this drop by returning areas of land to its former state and minimizing predation have been difficult to achieve. The yellow-eyed penguin typically breeds only in the cool coastal forests, but since these have been cleared the penguins have been forced to nest in scrubland and pasture, where they are vulnerable to the trampling of nests by cattle. With insufficient shade in open areas, the adults and downy chicks have also been shown to suffer heat stress on sunny days during the breeding season. Sheep and cattle also graze the ground so close that rabbits can thrive, and the introduced species that prey on rabbits (feral cats, stoats and ferrets) also take penguin chicks. Areas of coast are now being destocked and fenced through the efforts of the Yellow-eyed Penguin Trust. Flax plants are being reintroduced to cleared areas to help provide suitable nesting sites. Yellow-eyed penguins are also very shy and will seldom come ashore if approached by humans. Consequently, colonies in the vicinity of urban areas are always being disturbed.

The competition between humans and penguins for space has also been a factor in the far south. Since only 4 per cent of the Antarctic is snow free in the brief austral summer, the brush-tailed penguin species establish their rookeries on the coastal areas of exposed rock. Many of these sites are also the most convenient sites for scientific bases. In less enlightened times, bases were built in the middle of established penguin rookeries. The construction of the joint U.S./New Zealand base in 1957 at Cape Hallett, on the edge of the Ross Sea, meant that 8,218 penguins had to be relocated to another part of the colony. For years the base had to operate a penguin patrol during the nesting season. A team with a vehicle would roam the roads of the base collecting penguins that had come ashore to nest on their traditional sites. The patrol would then deposit them on the other side of a fence that had been built to cordon off the buildings from the rest of the colony. This base was completely closed in 1973, but a large tank of fuel stood for many more years—an environmental time bomb waiting to go off.

The Chilean base, Presidente Gabriel Gonzale Videla, at Waterboat Point on the peninsula, is also on the site of a penguin colony. Here there is continuing competition for nesting territory.

Many of the other forty-plus scientific stations around the continent are within striking distance of penguin colonies, which often get visited by off-duty expeditioners on recreational outings, official delegations and scientists conducting experiments. All these groups have the potential to disturb the breeding behaviour. An Adélie colony at Cape Crozier on Ross Island, the southernmost colony of this species, was the subject of considerable pressure as a result of helicopter flights carrying visitors from McMurdo Station and passing directly over the rookery. The numbers of Adélies have declined, and now helicopters operating in the vicinity of rookeries around the continent are tightly regulated.

FACING PAGE: *Penguins in Antarctica sometimes face competition with humans, since bases are mostly built on snow-free rock outcrops, where many species rest. Emperor penguins breed on the fast ice during the middle of winter, but they are still vulnerable to interference and depletion of their food species.*

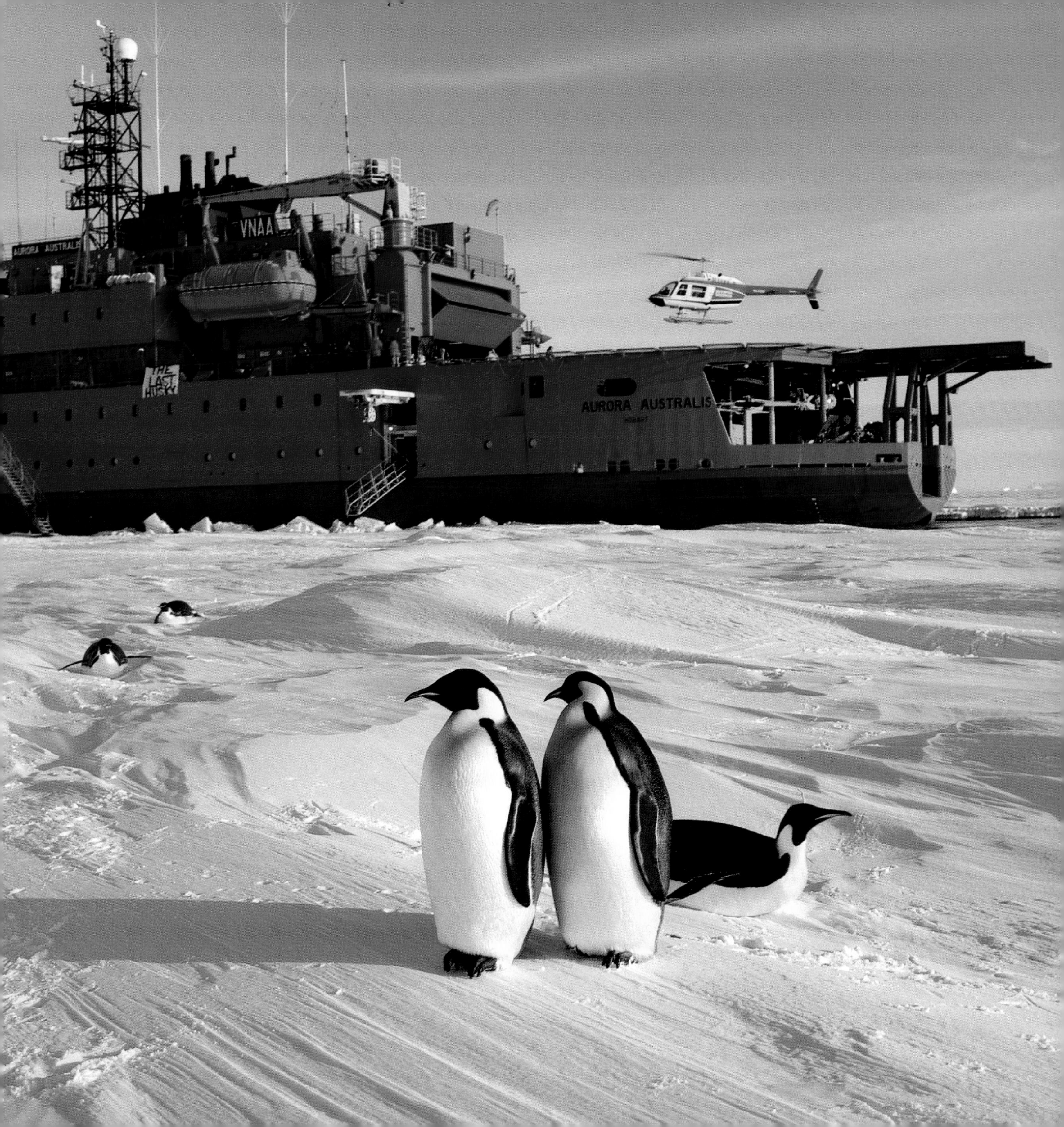
AURORA AUSTRALIS
VNAA
THE LAST HUSKY
AURORA AUSTRALIS

Introduced Animals

No introduced species except humans beings have had a major impact on penguin populations in the Antarctic, but in the early days of exploration renegade huskies were responsible for localized carnage. An Australian expeditioner, Bob Dovers, living with a small French party at Port Martin, Terra Adélie Land, recounted in his book *Huskies* in 1951 that one dog escaped and killed some 500 Adélie penguins in an afternoon. Little wonder that later most huskies were kept chained all the time, except when they were pulling sleds. Huskies are natural hunters, and curious penguins wandering into the dog lines were quickly dispatched.

Recently, under the terms of the Madrid Protocol, a broad agreement between the Antarctic Treaty nations designed to enhance environmental management in the region and minimize the impact of all activities there, all huskies in the Antarctic were removed. In future, no introduced species except human beings is technically allowed into the Antarctic. A dog was seen on a cruising yacht recently at Deception Island on the tip of the Antarctic Peninsula, illustrating how difficult it is to police such regulations. One or two dogs are hardly going to have substantial impact on Antarctic penguin species, but should some introduced species carry a disease that can be caught by penguins, the consequences could be serious.

The buildup of toxic pesticides in penguin eggs has been reported by Greenpeace, and the risk that poultry viruses such as Newcastle disease will get into Antarctic populations is a very real concern for managers of Antarctic operations. To this end, many countries have strict regulations for handling of all poultry products taken to the continent.

All these problems pale into insignificance compared with the devastation caused by introduced species in the more settled temperate areas. In New Zealand, dogs, feral cats, foxes, ferrets, stoats and weasels have all contributed to the decline in number of the yellow-eyed penguins. Little penguins that breed close to population centres in Australia have also been seriously affected by dogs, cats and foxes.

Tourism

Penguins in the wild are major tourist attractions in southern Australia, New Zealand, South America and, of course, Antarctica. Unrestricted access to penguin colonies adjacent to large human settlements usually results in serious disturbance of penguins' breeding behaviour and in a decline in their numbers.

This is dramatically born out by the example of the magellanic penguin colony at Seno Otway in Chile, 80 kilometres (50 miles) north of Punta Arenas, a city of 100,000 people. In the 1970s the colony had decreased to just a few thousand birds. A reserve was created in the 1980s, by which time numbers had fallen to several hundred pairs. Since the introduction of roped-off areas and walkways and a primitive hide at the back of the beach, the colony has risen to an estimated 5,000 pairs.

The Punta Tombo colony in Argentina has some 500,000 nesting birds in an area of 200 hectares (500 acres), one of the largest gatherings of magellanic penguins in South America. Although the reserve is isolated, the number of tourists has been growing since it was opened in the mid-1970s. Today around 50,000 visitors a year watch the birds.

Penguin Parade at Phillip Island, Victoria, on Australia's southern coast is perhaps the most popular penguin-viewing site in the world. Tourists with blankets and torches first began coming to watch the nocturnal little penguins land here in the 1920s after a bridge was built to the Island. It is estimated that at that time there were about 70,000 breeding pairs.

By the early 1980s, with unrestricted access, penguin numbers had plummeted to just 10,000 pairs. As a result of the encroachment of urban development on the colony and car traffic that killed several penguins a week, the Victorian government undertook a major management initiative. Over three hundred holiday homes were removed from the area, which was declared a nature reserve. Raised boardwalks and a large floodlit stadium at the back of the beach were built. Today the reserve caters to half a million visitors a year and generates over $30 million dollars for the local economy, which has financed a habitat restoration program, a feral animal eradication scheme, a research team and a visitors' centre. Numbers of little penguins at Phillip Island are now estimated to be back up to 25,000 birds.

The mini-boom in Antarctic tourism has been fuelled by glossy travel brochures that showcase the wildlife, particularly the penguin, as one of the main attractions. Expedition ships now take over eight thousand passengers to the Antarctic each austral summer aboard sixteen vessels that cruise the Antarctic Peninsula and the Ross Sea region. The

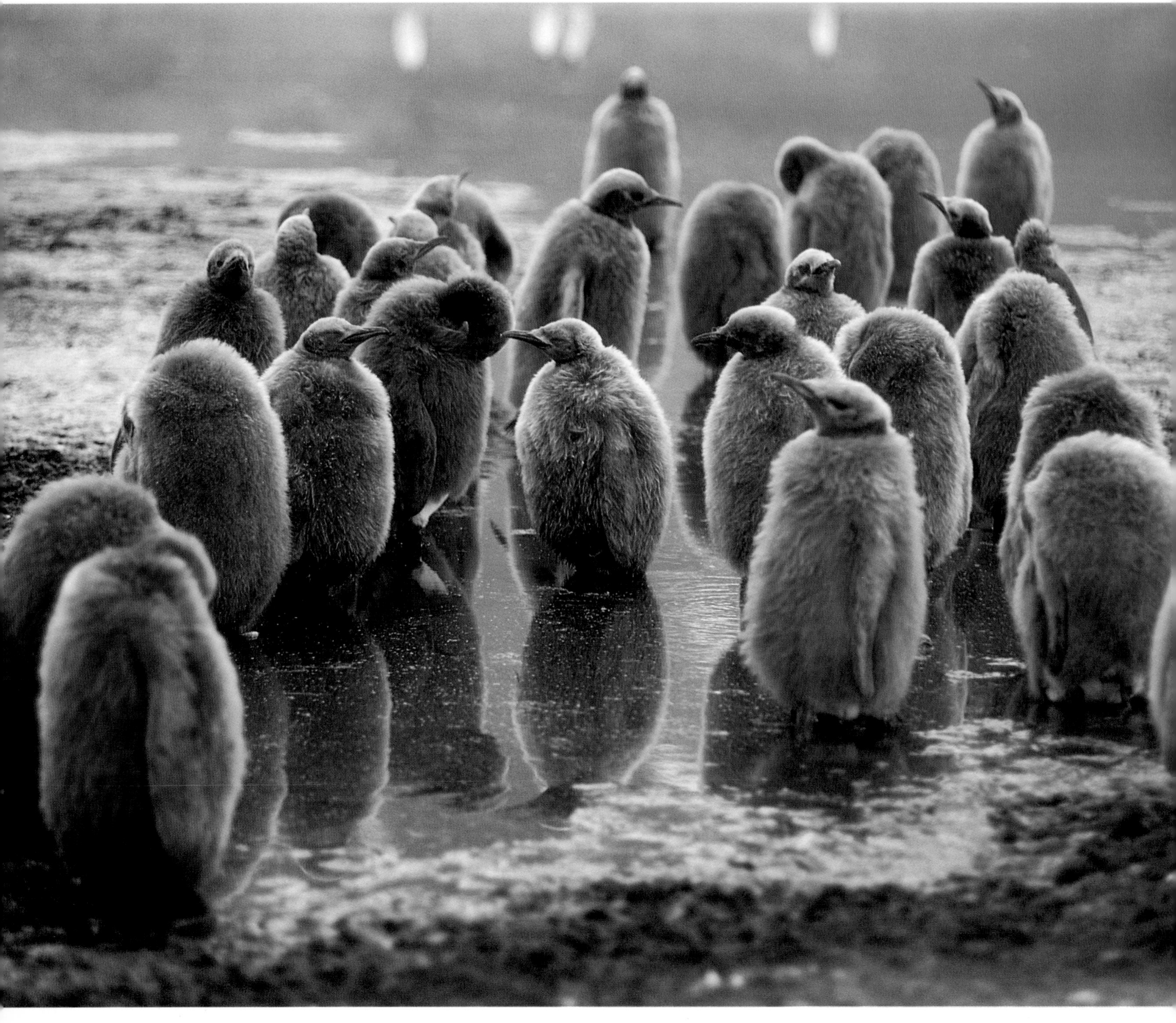

subantarctic islands are equally popular. Macquarie Island is visited by several ships each summer. The Campbell and Auckland Islands south of New Zealand are also growing in popularity. The Falkland Islands, South Georgia and South Sandwich Islands are the most popular of all the subantarctic destinations, often being visited as part of a cruise to the Antarctic Peninsula.

The combined staff of the many nations that operate scientific bases in the Antarctic number a further four thousand or more people who spend either all or part of the year in the far south. Hundreds more make a round trip to the continent as official observers, politicians, filmmakers, artists and journalists on the official government resupply ships and aircraft.

The Antarctic Treaty recognizes tourism as a valid activity and is now attempting to regulate tourist activities through legislation in member countries. To ensure high standards and the safe and responsible development of tourism in the Antarctic region in 1991, seven tour operators formed the International Association of Antarctic Tour Operators (IAATO) as a means of pooling resources and promoting thoughtful legislation that is compatible with responsible tourism. The association has published guidelines of how passengers should behave in the vicinity of penguin colonies, but as the number of shorter cruises increases, so the more accessible rookeries on the South Shetland Islands and the northern Antarctic Peninsula could suffer.

Although uncontrolled tourism could well create some of the environmental problems that the more temperate penguin species have experienced, the remoteness of the continent and the large penguin populations will act as a buffer to the growing band of tourists. Carefully managed tourism could well be one of the most lucrative activities in the Antarctic region. And virtually everyone who travels to Antarctica becomes part of a growing international lobby group that can speak out on behalf of the penguins.

King penguin chicks take some fourteen months to mature, meaning that the adults are successful in raising only two young every three years.

Threatened Species

As a result of all these factors—climate change, pollution, overfishing, loss of habitat, introduced animals, encroachment, and even tourism—certain species are considered at risk.

Threatened species are the Humboldt (Peruvian) penguin and possibly the Galápagos penguin. Species that are not threatened but are considered at risk are the yellow-eyed and the Fiordland penguins, and the future of the African penguin is not considered secure. These categories are arbitrary, and a species' situation can change (usually for the worse). Different organizations also have different criteria for what is considered threatened.

The main legal intergovernmental framework for trying to conserve endangered species is the Convention on International Trade in Endangered Species (CITES), which became effective in 1975. This established world-wide controls over trade in endangered and threatened species of plants and wildlife. There are a series of CITES appendices that list species that come under these regulations. The Galápagos penguin is the only species that is considered threatened by the U.S. Department of Fish and Game, which administers CITES matters in the United States. Even major international organizations have differences of opinion on these matters, however.

The International Union for the Conservation of Nature and Natural Resources (IUCN)/World Conservation Union divides the term "threatened species" into five categories; endangered, vulnerable, rare, indeterminate and insufficiently known. It also maintains the Red List of Threatened Animals. The only penguin on this list to date is the Humboldt, which is categorized as insufficiently known. This simply means that it probably belongs in one of the first three categories, but lack of information prohibits its listing.

A species survival plan has been established for the Humboldt penguin, based on the fact that in the 1960s the population was estimated at 50,000 and today it is believed to be down to just 5000 to 6000 breeding pairs in the wild and some 900 individuals in captivity. As discussed, there are many continuing threats to its viability and recovery.

Some biologists say the most vulnerable species, however, is the yellow-eyed penguin of southeast New Zealand. The yellow-eyed penguin population is estimated at less than five thousand individuals, and it has experienced a serious decline in numbers since 1990. Yellow-eyed penguins are unique among penguins because they are not colonial. Instead of crowding together in noisy colonies, they seek the privacy of secluded nests separated from other pairs, leaving the chicks vulnerable to ferrets and cats. They were also traditionally a bird of the forest, where they could enjoy a cool, shady habitat. Human encroachment on this habitat has contributed to their demise.

In 1992 the Conservation Assessment and Management Plan meeting for penguin species was held in New Zealand. This group produced its own recommendations suggesting that a broader selection of species needed to be treated as endangered (2) and vulnerable (5) as part of a total of 11 species that were considered. These findings were controversial among field biologists, and further meetings and assessment are proposed before any recommendations can be universally adopted.

With the global focus over the last two decades on environmental degradation and the need to maintain biodiversity, the world is increasingly conscious of the depredations of humankind. Threatened species, however, are a rallying point for community action on a local, national and international scale. Some threatened penguin populations have clearly defined problems, such as introduced predators, that respond to local solutions. In many instances, such as global warming, the problems are much more intractable. But because penguins are very sensitive to these changes, they have an important role to play in global monitoring.

PAGES 100–101: *Icebergs and penguins are the two main icons of the far south and are the reason that so many tourists are attracted to this austere place.*

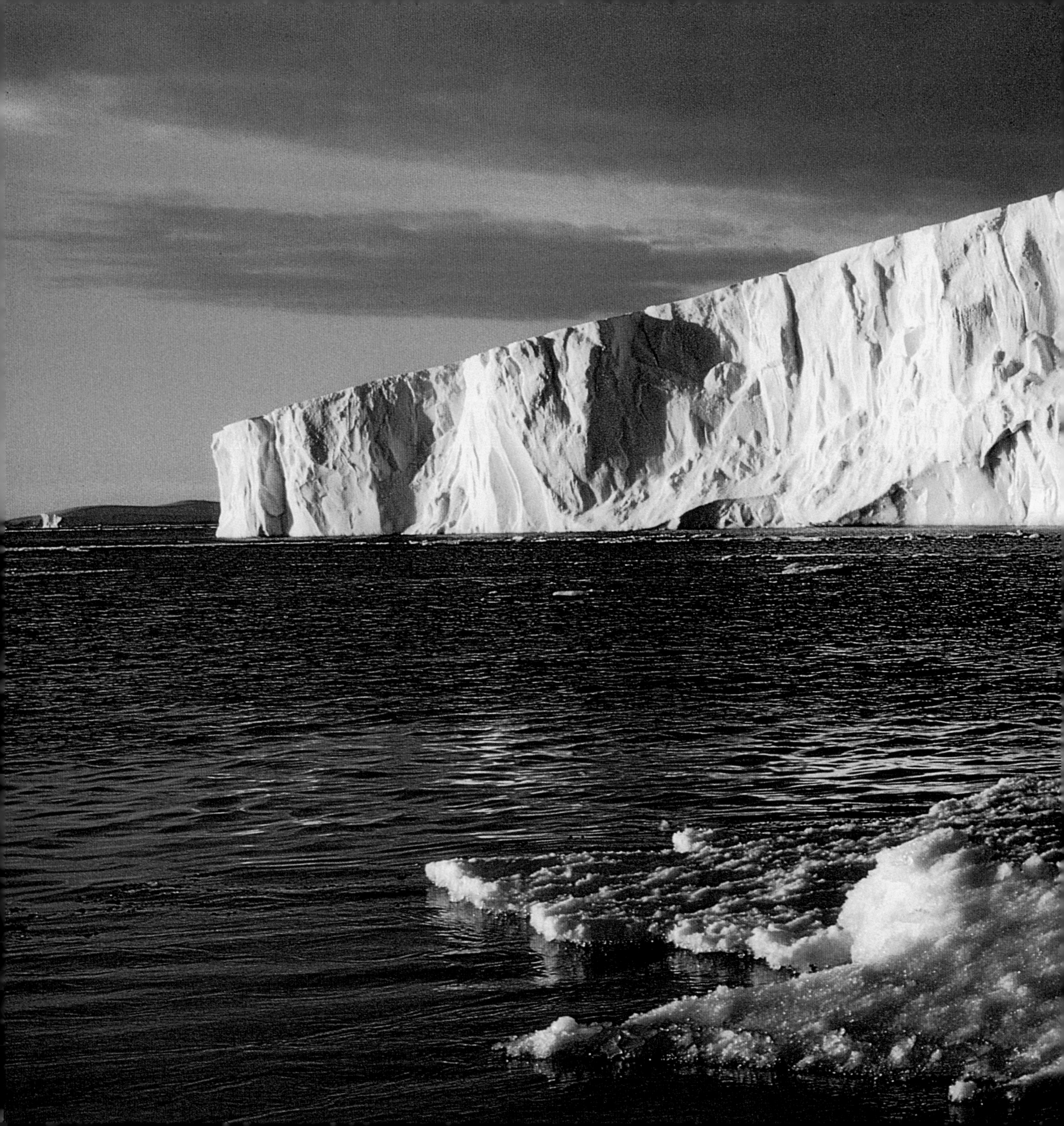

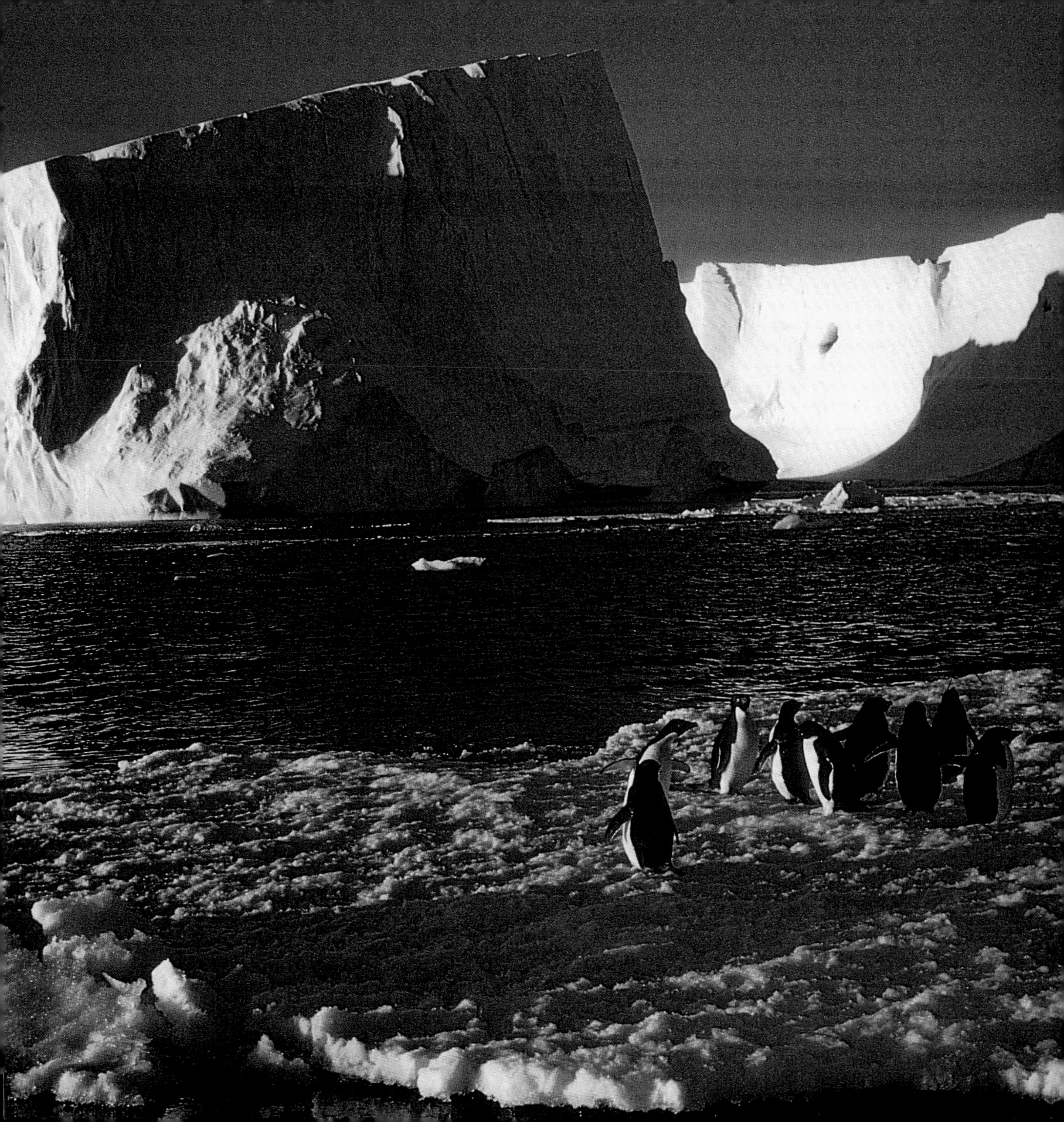

Monitoring the Ecosystem

Penguins comprise 80 to 90 per cent of the total bird biomass in the Southern Ocean. They are also among the main consumers of krill in the Antarctic and subantarctic regions. Changes in marine ecosystems, which krill are also very sensitive to, have a rapid and significant impact on the penguin populations. In particular, macaroni, Adélie, chinstrap and gentoo penguins are among the key indicator species that are now being monitored by international programs set up to safeguard the environment in the Southern Ocean. These include the Biological Investigations of Marine Antarctic Systems and Stocks (BIOMASS), and the Convention for the Conservation of Antarctic Marine Living Resources (CCAMLR). As part of these programs, each year data are obtained by biologists on a myriad of parameters, including the weights of birds at the beginning and the end of the breeding season, the size of the breeding colonies, the composition of diet, the nature of foraging trips, the number of chicks born and the number successfully fledged. All these factors help to create a picture of the viability of the region's penguin populations and consequently the health of the all-important krill and other food stocks.

Hope for the Future

Penguins have become increasingly popular as subjects for artists, illustrators and film-makers, and now academics are making their contribution to the popularity of penguins. Every four years scientists devote an entire international conference to presenting research findings on penguins. There is also a never-ending demand for penguin paraphernalia, especially among the steadily increasing community of travellers who have experienced these delightful and amusing birds first-hand on an Antarctic cruise.

This growing popularity is hardly surprising, given that, en masse, penguins are much more fascinating than even the best descriptions and depictions in photographs, books and films can prepare one for. Those that have been bitten by the penguin bug often seek any reminder that links them to their own intense experience of penguins. Seeing thousands of natural performers living out their busy lives, porpoising in schools, preening on the icy shores or being chased by hungry chicks deeply affects those fortunate enough to have this experience.

These ambassadors of the penguin nation, as well as their armchair admirers, have a mission ahead of them, however. For just as the popularity of penguins is spreading, so are the potential threats to numerous species and to local populations in remote locations. Many of these areas are without a constituency of concerned voters, or the problems are beyond the ability of any one country to solve.

For any penguin species to become extinct, as the great auk did, would be a tragedy. Penguins are now recognized as one of the species that can tell us about the health of the ecosystems in the Southern Ocean. It is crucial, therefore, that we become sensitive to the direct and indirect effects we are having on penguin populations in all regions of the Southern Hemisphere through pollution, global warming, tourism and the encroachment of human settlement. We need to speak out when populations are being threatened and lend support to the front-line organizations that are working to preserve habitats for penguins. As famous birder Roger Tory Peterson has observed: "Penguins may eventually prove to be the litmus paper of the sea, an indicator of the health of our watery planet."

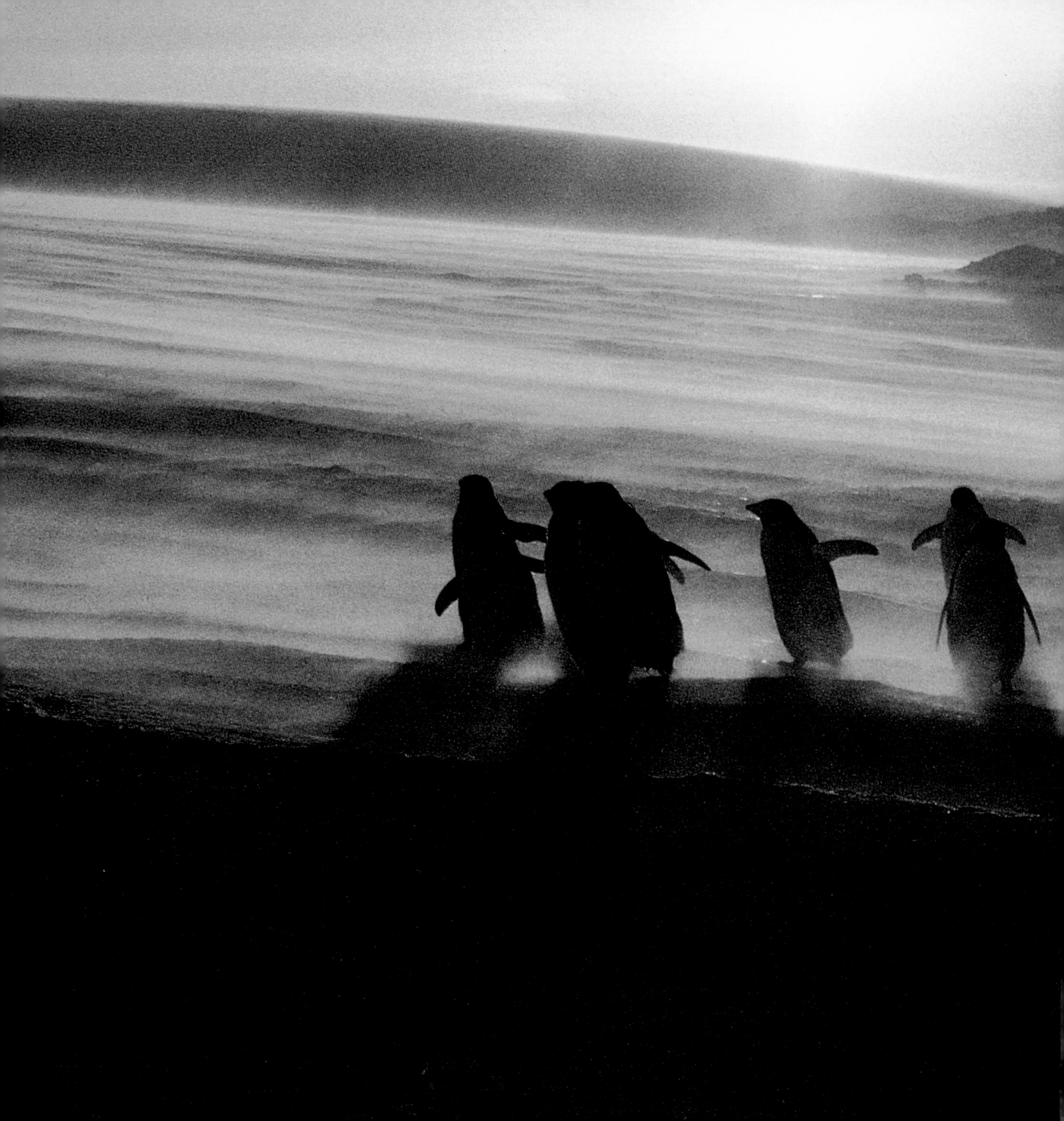

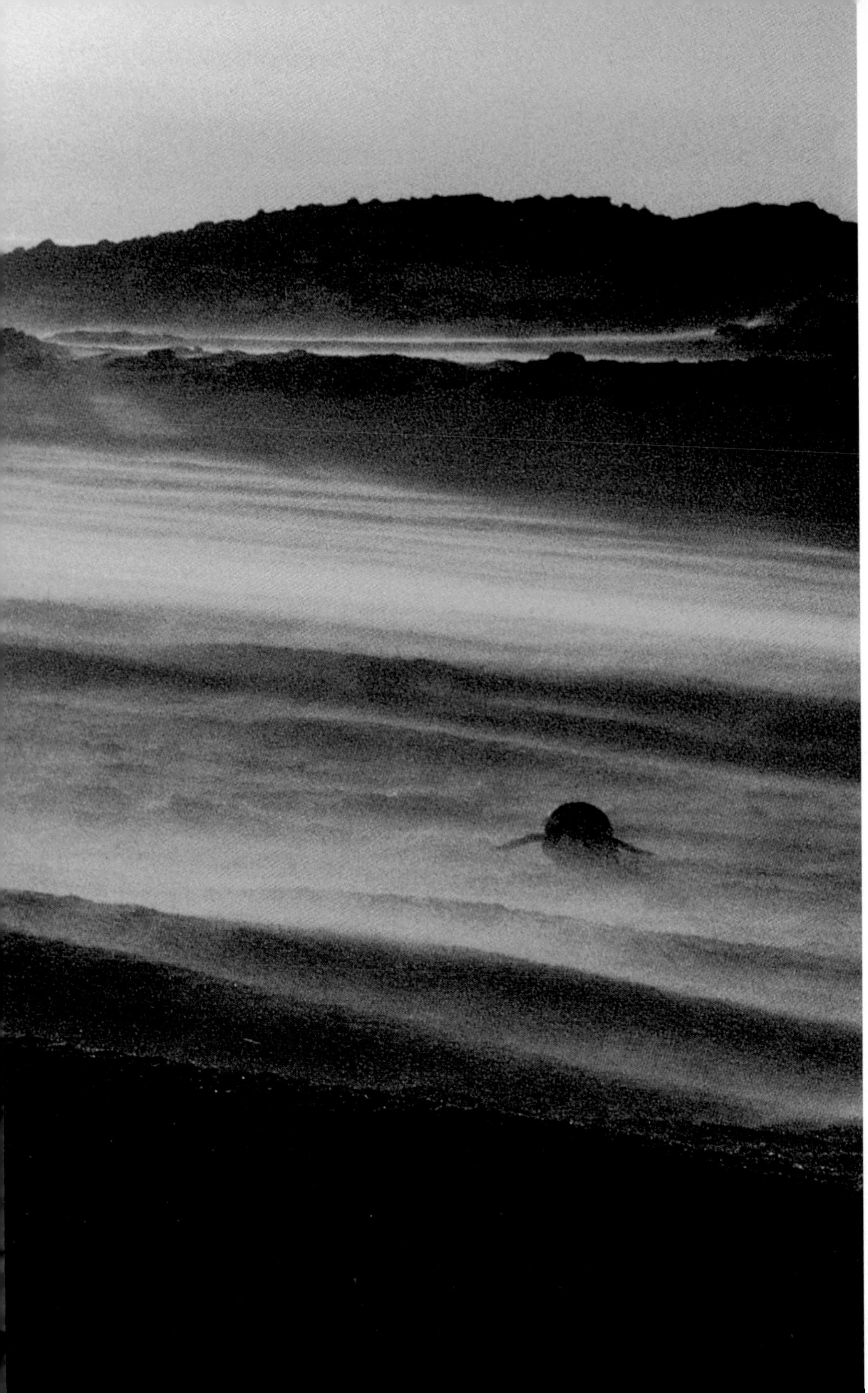

Adélie penguins are completely at home in the Antarctic, even in a ground blizzard at Commonwealth Bay, which has been decribed as the windiest place in the world.

For Further Reading

NATURAL HISTORY AND BIOLOGY

Cheney, Cynthia, ed. 1994. *Penguin Conservation.* Vol. 7, No 2. Portland: Metro
Washington Park Zoo.

Davis, Lloyd, and John T. Darby. 1990. *Penguin Biology.* San Diego: Academic Press.

Gaskin, Chris, and Neville Peat. 1991. *The World of Penguins.* Auckland: Hodder &
Stoughton.

Muller-Schwarze, Dietland. 1984. *The Behaviour of Penguins.* Albany: State University of
New York Press.

Reilly, Pauline. 1994. *Penguins of the World.* Melbourne: Oxford University Press.

Stahel, Colin, and Rosemary Gales. 1987. *Little Penguin.* Sydney: New South Wales
University Press.

Williams, Tony D. 1995. *The Penguins:* Spheniscidae. New York: Oxford University
Press.

HISTORY

Ackerman, Diane. 1992. *The Moon by Whale Light.* New York: Random House.

Atwater, Richard, and Florence Atwater. 1938. *Mr. Popper's Penguins.* Boston: Little,
Brown.

Cherry-Garrard, Apsley. 1922. *The Worst Journey in the World.* London: Penguin Books.

Gorman, James. 1990. *The Total Penguin.* New York: Prentice-Hall.

Kearton, Cherry. 1931. *Island of Penguins.* New York: National Travel Club.

Murphy, Robert Cushman. 1936. *Oceanic Birds of South America.* New York: Macmillan.

Peterson, Roger Tory. 1979. *Penguins.* Boston: Houghton Mifflin.

Simpson, George Gaylord. 1976. *Penguins Past and Present Here and There.* New Haven: Yale University Press.

Sparks, John, and Tony Soper. 1987. *Penguins.* New York: Facts on File.

Conservation Organizations

Over the past twenty years a number of organizations and conservation groups have arisen to preserve and protect one or more penguin species and their habitat. Most of these projects focus on those populations that are risk because of the expansion of some human activities.

The *Magellanic Penguin Project* was established in 1982 by the Wildlife Conservation Society, a division of the New York Conservation Society and the Argentine Province of Chubut's Office of Tourism to provide scientific information to manage magellanic penguins and tourism at Punta Tombo. *Magellanic Penguin Project*, c/o Wildlife Conservation Society, Bronx Zoo, Bronx, New York, 10460, USA.

The *Yellow-eyed Penguin Trust* of New Zealand has been conducting a program of buying back coastal farm land, fencing and de-stocking in the South Island in an attempt to restore breeding areas to their original condition. *Yellow-eyed Penguin Trust*, PO Box 5409, Dunedin, New Zealand.

Philip Island Penguin Reserve in Australia also conducts research and rehabilitates oiled, sick and injured little penguins in Victoria. *Philip Island Penguin Reserve*, PO Box 403, Cowes, Victoria, 3168, Australia.

The Falklands Conservation, the organization started by Sir Peter Scott, has mounted the *Penguin Appeal* in Great Britain—a program to attempt to raise funds (£750,000) to support wildlife research in the South Atlantic. The funds are for the Environmental Impact Survey proposed to assess the impact of surveying and drilling for hydrocarbons and for the continuation of a long-term sea bird monitoring program. This program will also involve basic research into the ecology of rockhoppers, gentoos and magellanic penguins and black-browed albatrosses. A study of the status and revegetation of tussock grass, the preferred habitat of several penguin species, is also under way. *Penguin Appeal*, Falklands Conservation, PO Box 2040, London, W12 0ZJ, UK.

The South African Foundation for the Conservation of Coastal Birds (SANCCOB), which has been in existence since 1968, regularly rehabilitates hundreds of African penguins that have been affected by the all-too-common oil spills in this part of the world. *SANCCOB*, PO Box 11116, Bioubergrant, 7443, South Africa.

Penguin Conservation, Metro Washington Park Zoo, 4001 SW Canyon Rd., Portland, Oregon 97221 USA. A journal for field workers and zoo and aquarium keepers that focusses on the study, care and rehabilitation of all species of penguins.

Index

Numbers in boldface refer to pages containing a full discussion of individual species of penguins.